50 DARK DESTINATIONS

"Succinct, contextualised and insightful. Reveals the complex reasons why so many of us enjoy 'grazing' on carefully curated spectacles of suffering, desolation and death. With this cutting-edge criminological analysis, we can actually learn something about ourselves."

Steve Hall, Teesside University

"Infused with interesting facts and sharp observations about famous and not so famous 'destinations' all over the world, this book is a page-turner. Simultaneously cool and serious, rich and approachable, *50 Dark Destinations* will provide you with a fresh way of viewing leisure, place and culture."

Georgios A. Antonopoulos, Northumbria University

"A fascinating collection of essays on dark tourist destinations. It digs beneath the commercialisation of harm, while bringing into focus the reasons for our obsessions with it."

Anthony Ellis, University of Lincoln

"A fascinating travelogue of trouble. The tourist gaze that animates the book is particularly chilling, revealing the global span of crime – and the insatiable global appetite for crime's ghostly residues."

Jeff Ferrell, author of *Drift: Illicit Mobility and Uncertain Knowledge*

50 DARK DESTINATIONS

Crime and Contemporary Tourism

Edited by
Adam Lynes, Craig Kelly and James Treadwell

First published in Great Britain in 2023 by

Policy Press, an imprint of
Bristol University Press
University of Bristol
1–9 Old Park Hill
Bristol
BS2 8BB
UK
t: +44 (0)117 374 6645
e: info@bristol.ac.uk

Details of international sales and distribution partners are available at policy.bristoluniversitypress.co.uk

British Library Cataloguing in Publication Data
A catalogue record for this book is available from the British Library

ISBN 978-1-4473-6219-7 paperback
ISBN 978-1-4473-6220-3 ePub
ISBN 978-1-4473-6221-0 ePdf

Cover design: Liam Roberts Design
Front cover image: Shutterstock/Grzegorz Janowicz

Contents

List of figures

About the editors

Adam Lynes is Senior Lecturer in Criminology at Birmingham City University, where he has taught since 2012, covering topics such as criminological theory, homicide, critical violence and deviant leisure. He is currently involved in a number of ongoing research projects including a monograph exploring new perspectives on crimes of the powerful, contemporary examinations into the role of public criminology and developing the concept of graze theory.

Craig Kelly is Lecturer in Criminology at Birmingham City University, where he has taught since 2018. In this time, he has taught topics such as crime, media, culture, research methods and deviant leisure. His previous work has centred upon violence, drug markets and theorisation of homicide. Alongside Adam Lynes, he edited a book in 2020 that sought to question how criminology analyses video games. He is currently involved in a number of projects including developing the concept of graze theory. He is also undertaking PhD research around violence within the homeless milieu in the United Kingdom.

James Treadwell has been Professor in Criminology at Staffordshire University since 2017, having started his career as Lecturer in Criminology in 2003 at the University of Central England. He has recently been researching prison and criminal drug markets, examining the cultivation of cannabis in economically deprived areas and prison-based drug supply as part of a larger project on bullying, violence and victimisation in prison. He is currently involved in a number of ongoing research projects including a monograph exploring new perspectives on crimes of the powerful with Adam Lynes. He is also a member of the executive of the British Society of Criminology and was academic advisor on the Howard League Commission into Ex-Military Personnel in Prison.

Acknowledgements

First, we would like to express our gratitude to our partners, Lore, Charlie and Abi, for their support while we put this collection together. A huge thanks is owed to Rebecca Tomlinson and Freya Trand for their support throughout the project – we know we were not always easy to deal with. Alongside Rebecca and Freya, we cannot forget Angela Gage for her enthusiasm and support as well as everyone else who made this possible from Policy Press! Perhaps most importantly, though, the main thank you for this book is owed to the contributors. We reached out to each one of them in the midst of a global pandemic with what must have seemed a rather random and unusual idea. Thank you for hearing us out and being a part of the project; we are forever grateful. Adam and Craig would like to extend a special thanks to Sarah Pemberton for enabling us to realise our vision and her unwavering support. John Bahadur Lamb and Max Hart for suffering endless book chats in the pub; we hope we didn't spoil the pints – cheers lads! A consistent source of inspiration and motivation within this process was, of course, Tim Gill. Finally, thank you to our colleagues at our respective universities, Birmingham City University and Staffordshire University, for giving us the time and space to work on the project.

Introduction

Adam Lynes, Craig Kelly and James Treadwell

> 'As a travel trend, dark tourism has gained significant momentum over the last few years. Even the Tourism Society has emphasised that the field of dark tourism has grown into becoming a thrilling and important topic for the tourism industry. With the broader rise in off-the-beaten-track tourism, dark tourism has also become widespread and diverse, as it goes beyond the territory of popular guidebooks and TripAdvisor rankings. In fact, the demand is rising among the more intrepid tourists who want to venture to the fallout zones of Chernobyl and Fukushima, as well as North Korea and Rwanda.'
>
> Akanksha Ghansiyal (2021)

To begin this book, we would like to take a moment to explain how and why it was written. At the time work began, the COVID-19 pandemic was sweeping the globe. We were locked in our homes and the only social interaction outside of our immediate 'bubbles' was via a multitude of social media and telecommunication platforms. The onset of the initial lockdown was declared as one of the authors was packing the final items into his suitcase for a family holiday. Over the coming weeks, as the anxiety of what laid ahead took a grip of the nation, we began to discuss more often about past holidays and adventures.

Around this same time, one of the authors, as they perused the immense Netflix library to pass time, stumbled upon a series titled *Dark Tourist* (2018). The series, hosted by New Zealand journalist and actor David Farrier, covered a wide range of locations and topics including Pablo Escobar, the Fukushima nuclear disaster, a tour based on serial killer Jeffrey Dahmer, voodoo rituals and last but not least a tour of the Manson family murders. The author, as is a well-known habit with most television shows on Netflix, binged the entire series in a matter of days. Excited and intrigued by what was displayed, he soon rang the other two authors with an idea: why don't we write a book that further explores some of the themes presented on the show? And what if we were to explore other, less discussed themes and topics within the context of dark tourism? These were two of the main aims of this collection, but first it is important to provide a bit of context regarding how academics have conventionally defined such a phenomenon.

Academic discussions tend to generally define dark tourism as those sites 'associated with death and tragedy around the world, where tourists visit with varying motivations' (Bathory, 2018), and 'those tourists who [are] interested in the memorialisation of the dead, who were concerned with historical atrocity and evil' (Hooper, 2016: 2). While there are discussions pertaining to when dark tourism, in its traditional sense, began, Sharpley (2009) notes that what is not up for debate is 'that visitors have long been attracted to places or events associated in one way or another with death, disaster and suffering' (p 5). Another key unifying theme in the field and examination of dark tourism is that such contexts were part of living memory and capable of generating increased levels of anxiety and doubt (Lennon and Foley, 2001). Sharpley (2009) also states how, as general tourism has proliferated over the past 50 years, dark tourism has also seen exponential growth in terms of both physical and digital contexts.

Early illustrations of death-related tourism included the Roman colosseums for gladiatorial games and the turnout crowds for public executions in medieval central London (Stone, 2006), making this type of tourism a phenomenon that has become both widespread and diverse over the last century (Ashworth and Isaac, 2015). Smith (1998), for instance, suggests sites or destinations associated with war constitute the 'largest single category of tourist attractions in the world' (p 205). However, war-related attractions, while diverse, remain one of numerous tourist destinations associated with death and suffering (Stone, 2006).

From graveyard tours (Raine, 2013), the Holocaust (Heřmanová and Abrhám, 2015), sites of devastation (Sharpley, 2005) and the macabre (Ibrahim, 2015), the dark tourism industry continues to thrive due to its ability to connect people to the past through objects, exhibits, spaces and dramatic recreation (McDaniel, 2018). Therefore, there has been a growing recognition that it is important to consider the social, cultural and geographical contexts in which people consume dark tourism and its theoretical underpinnings (Hohenhaus, 2013). General theorisations related to dark tourism generally focus on these aforementioned points and tend to fall within either the interpretivist or behavioural positions. For instance, the former relates to how various stakeholders may interpret such locations, and the importance of recognising differing understandings and connections such destinations have for diverse people and groups (Ashworth, 1996). The latter, on the other hand, is more concerned with the various motivations as to why people may visit such places (Seaton, 1996). Despite these theoretical and conceptual developments, though, most academic enquiry is generally descriptive in nature, and the definitions previously outlined have not been scrutinised or seriously challenged.

While this book aimed to provide further scholarly attention to destinations that fall within the orthodox definitions of dark tourism and subsequent theorisations, we were aware that there were discipline developments occurring that, if drawn upon, could reveal a far more contemporary, nuanced and critical interpretation that would not only begin to make us question why we are so interested in macabre forms of tourism, but also forms of tourism that we perhaps previously saw as non-problematic or harmful. In order to do this, two key theoretical frameworks need to be introduced and defined: graze theory and deviant leisure.

Graze theory is a new theoretical understanding of the public's consumption of violence and a critique of public criminology. Within this emerging concept, we propose that the public fascination with crime is not, as some would posit, a fascination with violence (Seltzer, 1997). Nor is it a vehicle for criminologists to bring attention to victims while engaging in the rather heinous juxtaposition of profiting from various forms of media glorifying the murderers. Graze theory, in essence, suggests that the very philosophy of what constitutes violence is often neglected in previous theorisations concerning the public's consumption of violence (see Seltzer, 1997; 1998). It adopts the Žižekian concept of objective violence in which, in his usual dialectic inversion, he draws our attention not to those forms of violence that disrupt what would otherwise be civilised normality, but to the actual constitution and reproduction of civilised normality as such. For Žižek (2008), objective violence is the form of violence that needs to take place to reproduce our sense of normality. Žižek's (2008) goal is for us to look away from spectacular forms of disruptive violence – including those places that become conventional dark tourist locations birthed from such incidents – and consider those forms of violence that shape our experience of everyday life. This Žižekian perspective on violence is one of the central underpinnings of this new theoretical paradigm.

Another theoretical underpinning of graze theory is Žižek's notion of the 'fetishistic disavowal', which Žižek summarises as, 'I know, but I don't want to know that I know, so I don't know' (2010). This, in essence, is a process of denial, the denial of one's position in the world relative to others. He argues that life functions on the basis of such denials. Taking this concept further, not only do we know that other people are treated badly, but that our entire system of life is founded upon such moral and ethical concessions. For instance, we buy clothing, electronics and arguably one of the most important symbols of status, iPhones, which are made in China despite knowing the horrendous conditions suffered by the workers that make them (Li et al, 2018). Young (2007) proposes the notion of social bulimia as an apt description of society's positionality within contemporary society. An increased alienation, alongside the perpetual fetishistic disavowal of the ontic violence increasingly impinging upon the populace, has sought to create a collective focus upon the physical and virtual representations of subjective, or physical, violence in an effort to negate the lived reality of an increasingly dystopian society. This tendency to 'brush up against familiar monsters' (Kelly et al, 2022) as a form of comfort and a channel in which to disavow objective forms of violence can be somewhat comforting but it also presents a barrier that we struggle to penetrate and move beyond. As such, graze theory is a contemporary critical framework that synethsises key Žižekian concepts in order to articulate how, as a collective, we generally struggle and fail 'to disentangle ourselves from the fascinating lure of this directly visible "subjective" violence' (Žižek, 2008: 1). To summarise, graze theory, in its most basic form, is the public consumption of extreme and spectacular violence as a way to disregard and disavow the wider spectrum of structural harms embedded in everyday life.

Another key theoretical framework that presents a contemporary and critical approach to potentially harmful practices, including dark tourism, is deviant leisure. Deviant leisure, the second element of the conceptual 'toolkit' vital in the framing for the subsequent arguments, follows suit in Žižek's proclivity to dialectic inversion, suggesting that more 'traditional' definitions of deviancy are rather narrow in scope and omit a range of potential harmful behaviours and activities (Atkinson, 2014). In defining this new perspective, Smith (2016) – aware of the inherent restraints of criminology – posits that '"[d]eviant leisure" began to orient itself toward a reconceptualisation of social deviance and an exploration of how individual, social, economic, and environmental harms are structurally and culturally embedded within many accepted and normalized forms of leisure' (Smith, 2016: 6). Deviant leisure also utilises zemiology, which was inspired by the notion that much of criminological research is produced and maintained by 'very powerful interests, not least the state, which produces definitions of crime through criminal law' (Hillyard and Tombs, 2017: 284). Such a perspective is crucial in transcending the proverbial cage in which many in academia and wider society unwittingly find themselves within, unable to perceive or inhibited from perceiving notions of harm outside of the traditional notion which is constrained via legal frameworks.

Raymen and Smith (2019) note that socially accepted and normalised forms of leisure such as the night-time economy, legalised gambling, tourism and lifestyle drugs cause a range of harms. First, there are subjective forms of harm that 'involve an easily identifiable perpetrator visiting harm upon a clearly identifiable victim in action related to a clearly defined leisure activity' (Smith, 2016: 7). Second, there are environmental harms that consist of those ecological damages caused in the pursuit of leisure activities including, for instance, the rising levels of waste on beaches. Third, socially corrosive harms fundamentally dissolve notions of community and actively promote exclusion as an important demarcation of the 'haves' and 'have nots'. An example of this, according to Smith (2016), is 'the creation of artificial scarcity, the privation of that which would otherwise be plentiful and free to the public' (p 9). Lastly, there are embedded harms which are 'embedded within legitimate consumer markets and while imbued with potential for the creation of malleable identities based on the notion of cool, are deserving of closer criminological scrutiny' (Smith, 2016: 9). For example, the gambling industry, now at the fingertips of everyone with a smartphone and routinely advertised online including in the form of YouTube advertisements, is at the heart of a myriad of individual and social harms. The inclusion of such a wide range of harms provides the means in which to adequately identify how even the most normalised and celebrated forms of leisure, including conventional tourism, sustain and perpetuate a range of harms omitted in orthodox dark tourism studies.

To summarise, via the lens of graze theory we can begin to transcend orthodox and myopic definitions of violence that fundamentally underpin current understandings of dark tourism, along with providing a critical framework in which to understand the multifaceted motivations behind the public's consumption of such content. So too, deviant leisure provides the contemporary criminological framework in which 'new frontiers' of identifying harm in the most culturally accepted forms of leisure can be explored. As such, it is important to see both theories as the theoretical 'Rosetta Stone' for this book, revealing previously ignored and misunderstood harms that for too long have been hidden by the fascinating allure of physical violence that disrupts our sense of 'normality'.

As we developed graze theory and incorporated deviant leisure into our approach, we simultaneously yearned for the chance to dig out the suitcase and escape the monotonous routine of home working, masked shopping and endless walks around the local area (dispersed by intermittent ends to lockdown). Our thoughts turned to life after lockdown. We hope(d) the world would open up again. We recognised evermore clearly the importance of connections with other cultures. Most importantly, we recognised the necessity of physicality and how much physical presence in a place matters. This was partially due to the need for a break from our own four walls but also informed by the rapidly advancing theoretical developments we kept coming across within our academic readings. We know from cultural criminology the importance of being, of space and how culture influences self and society. We see clearly from the deviant leisure perspective the multitude of harms our everyday social lives perpetuate. But more recently, we also saw the development of both sensory (Herrity et al, 2021) and emotional turns (Ronel and Segev, 2020) in criminology. So too, a greater recognition of how the past and present interact has come to the fore with the introduction of ghost criminology (Fiddler et al, 2022). Eventually the various conversations of travel, the future and of theory began to blend. At this stage we contacted over 50 academics, a mixture of criminologists, historians, psychologists and geographers. We asked them to write about a *dark destination*. A place people engage with in their leisure time but perhaps fail to pause and ponder the deeper, darker significance of the place or activity. The end result of it was this book, in which we have two subsequent objectives.

The first objective is the most important. As the world recovers from the COVID-19 pandemic and travel opens back up, we hope you have picked this book up. We hope that the book offers a clear call for change. Referring back to the opening quote from Akanksha Ghansiyal, it is actually quite apparent that destinations infused with traditional notions of crime, deviance and violence do not put off tourists, but instead only seem to attract them further and in ever greater quantity. If the world has to navigate a 'new normal', hopefully this book goes some way to raising the awareness of the need for a more ethical and sustainable approach to travel. It is time to question why we spend our days in museums filled with artefacts of violence. Why we engage in leisure pursuits that damage the natural environment. Why social media is filled with images of people smiling while stood at the sites of a past genocide.

The second objective is to offer a reframing of public criminology and to show that it can be done in a different and more contentious manner. A public criminology that does not offer a fetishism of gratuitous violence and the sublime. A public criminology of anti-graze in which academics offer important discussions to the public in an understandable and digestible manner. So, if we have been successful, within the proceeding chapters readers will be offered a range of contemporary issues in a considered manner from a diverse range of voices that seek to offer a deeper reflection on contemporary culture, place and space.

1

Cocaine Bear: Fun Mall, Lexington, Kentucky, USA

Travis Linnemann

Kansas State University

Introduction

On the east side of Lexington, Kentucky, USA, inside a nondescript industrial building turned gift shop sits an unlikely attraction, a medium-sized taxidermied North American black bear. Sometimes wearing a bright blue cowboy hat, other times a sideways baseball cap lampooning 1980s hip-hop style, around the bear's neck hangs a gold chain and plaque telling its story – this is that story.

Crooked cops, conspiracy and the sad death of 'Cocaine Bear'

In 1985, 'Cocaine Bear', aka 'Pablo EskoBear', was found dead in Tennessee's Chattahoochee National Forest, 'overdosed on 40 kilos of cocaine dropped by Andrew Thorton. You might remember Andrew from the Bluegrass Conspiracy. *Don't do drugs or you'll end up dead (and maybe stuffed) like poor "Cocaine Bear"*' (Smallwood, 2017, emphasis original). And that's pretty much it; no mention of how American hedonism and the drug war's ecological degradation is so powerfully captured in the Cocaine Bear's grim biography. The oddity of a wild animal that died horribly from accidental overdose is enough to lure thoughtless consumers eager to snap selfies and snap up all manner of overpriced 'Cocaine Bear' memorabilia.

It's unsurprising really. Americans veraciously consume drugs, using more of them, legal or otherwise, than arguably anywhere else on the planet (Gusovsky, 2016). The US also refuses to give up its now century-long drug war, refitting it to any number of particular panics – marijuana, crack, methamphetamine – as an excuse to harass the minority groups associated, while exporting it around the globe alongside its noxious twin, the 'war on terror' (Linnemann, 2016). While the policing of illegal drugs is no doubt big business, as the soon to be released big-budget *Cocaine Bear* (2022) film suggests, the allure of illegal drugs, drug dealers and all the grim violence and disrepute associated remain a useful instrument with which to capture the public's imagination and pocketbooks.

Consider, for instance, the tourist industry that sprung up around Albuquerque, New Mexico inspired by the two hit television series set there, *Breaking Bad* (2008) and *Better Call Saul* (2015). Each year thousands of tourists flock to any number of businesses that offer guided tours of on-camera locations and trade in drugs- and crime-related paraphernalia. In the US and elsewhere local economies have benefited similarly from their connection to the drug war, real or imagined. As uninspiring and crass as this sort of drug-adorned consumerism might be, there's something even more insidious about it sitting out in the open, the tale etched into the brass plaque dangling from that poor bear's neck. The final sentence stating 'don't do drugs or you'll end up dead (and maybe stuffed) like poor "Cocaine Bear"' . While the story of Andrew Thorton and the 'Bluegrass Conspiracy' remains part of local lore, like the US drug war generally, critical understanding of its implications evades the broad public, even upstart local entrepreneurs.

Andrew 'Drew' Thorton's biography characterises the worst of American privileged hubris and greed. Born to a wealthy Lexington family who made its fortune breeding racehorses, Thorton's formative years were spent in the elite private schools, golf and polo clubs that still serve the Southern aristocracy. After graduating from Sewanee Military Academy in 1962, Thorton became a paratrooper, joining the US Army's fearsome 82nd

Airborne Division, earning a Purple Heart on the bleeding edge of the Cold War as part of the forces that intervened in the Dominican Civil War in 1965 (Dorman, 2021).

Rotating out of military service, Thorton returned home and took a job with the Lexington Police Department (LPD), later earning a bachelor's degree in Police Science from Eastern Kentucky University in 1971 (my former academic home). It is here as a member of LPD's first 'narc squad' that the reputation for guns-blazing bravado to which Thorton aspired as a child and honed as a paratrooper came into full view. One Drug Enforcement Agency agent who worked closely with Thorton described him as a '007 paramilitary type … driven by adrenaline rushes' (Denton, 1985). And where better to feed such a habit than the front lines of the newly expanding 'war on drugs'? As his wife longingly opined, Andrew was 'a trained warrior—a very efficient killer trained by the US government. … He went onto the police force so he could do battle. He was happiest when he was on the cutting edge, when he tested himself' (Denton, 1985).

Publicly, Thorton nurtured his outlandish soldier of fortune image, sporting fatigues, body armour and swastikas, speaking of 'eyes for eyes, teeth for teeth' and quoting Sun Tzu. At 'Triad', his rural Kentucky estate, he built fortifications, stockpiled weapons and provisions and prepared for war. So brazen was Thorton that Triad even became a target of state police ground and aerial surveillance as a suspected 'guerilla warfare training camp for mercenaries'. After resigning from LPD in 1977, Thorton worked as a security contractor, or self-described 'free-lance military advisor' – likely as an agent of US intelligence, or at least with its blessing – returning to Cold War hot spots, advising anti-communist forces in El Salvador, Nicaragua and South Africa (North-Best, 2017).

All this continued until 1981 or so when Bradley Bryant, Thorton's oldest and dearest friend and another of Lexington's privileged sons who had set himself up as a 'private security contractor', was arrested in a Philadelphia hotel under highly suspicious circumstances. Alerted by maids who smelled marijuana smoke wafting from his room, police arrested Bryant and found him in possession of several semi-automatic weapons, disguises, more than ten fake Kentucky driver's licences and nearly $25,000 in cash. Stranger still, Bryant tried to explain away his predicament and the notebook that named Thorton, several other affiliates and their 'coded operations' by claiming he was on assignment for the Central Intelligence Agency (Guy-Ryan, 2016). Months later, the thread that began with Bryant's arrest unravelled to reveal the so-called 'Bluegrass Conspiracy', a sophisticated drugs and weapons trafficking operation stretching across North and South America. Thorton and two dozen other conspirators were soon arrested for trafficking tons of marijuana and for conspiring to steal automatic weapons from a California Navy base (Guy-Ryan, 2016). Eventually pleading guilty to reduced charges, Thorton received an unusually light sentence of six months in a minimum-security facility in Lexington. In the ensuing three years, various police agencies investigated Thorton's involvement in at least five 'vendetta deaths' or assassinations of prosecutors, witnesses and informants who were allied against Thorton and his crew (*Los Angeles Times*, 1985).

Thorton's charmed life of murky intrigue – drug running and drug policing, anti-communist counter-insurgency, underworld assassinations – ends abruptly in a suburban driveway in Knoxville, Tennessee, on 11 September 1985. Weighed down by a bulletproof vest, night-vision goggles, two handguns and ammo, survival gear, rations and vitamins, $4,500 in cash, six gold Krugerrands, two fake IDs, his membership card to the Miami Jockey Club and nearly 100 pounds of cocaine, Thorton leapt from a twin-engine Cessna in Gucci loafers to his death when his chute failed to open. Miles away and some days later in the Chattahoochee Forest, a medium-sized North American black bear too met its demise when it rooted through one of Thorton's errant packages.

After serving as a subject for forensic death investigators, the bear was preserved by a local taxidermist and then donated to a Chattahoochee River National Recreation visitors' centre where it sat unassumingly for years until somehow ending up in the personal collection of outlaw country artist and noted cocaine connoisseur, Waylon Jennings. The bear was mostly lost to history following Jennings' death, until again reappearing as a 'mascot' for a newly opened Kentucky business in 2015. 'Meet our new mascot: Cocaine Bear', announces a press release. 'The cocaine-eating bear from the Bluegrass Conspiracy is getting wild at the Kentucky for Kentucky Fun Mall!' (Larkin, 2015).

So here we are at last, full circle, back at an unassuming gift shop in the American South. The bloody history of the US war on drugs, so potently characterised in the biography of one man, Andrew Thorton, a 'little boy who never grew up' as one Federal Bureau of Investigation agent described him. A man who trotted the globe – playing spy and soldier, policing and trafficking drugs – operating outside the reach of most laws, other than gravity. A biography that should serve as a point of critique, if not outrage, but one that is nevertheless obscured and subsumed under the edifice of a poor dead bear and transformed into hats, socks and snow-globes (yes, snow-globes).

Conclusion

Hunter S. Thompson – another Kentuckian who made a fortune from self-indulgent tales of drug-addled excess – famously wrote 'buy the ticket, take the ride', imploring his readers to 'tune in, freak out, get beaten', to not only know the price of their darkest desires, but to pay them willingly, regardless of who else might also suffer.

This ride, it seems to me, is the darkest sort of tourism and perhaps the story of our age. Read through the sad sign of the Cocaine Bear – rather than the scummy, crooked cop Andrew Thorton – it may as well just be 'buy the t-shirt, take the selfie'.

2

Whitney Plantation: New Orleans, Louisiana, USA

Thomas Raymen

Northumbria University

Introduction

In 2016, I, along with other members of the Deviant Leisure Research Network, attended the American Society of Criminology Conference in New Orleans, Louisiana. During our time in New Orleans, there were certainly plenty of 'dark tourism' experiences and observations that were of interest to a band of critical criminologists interested in crime, harm and commodified leisure. There were the obvious seductions and temptations of Bourbon Street and the French Quarter, in which many of us enthusiastically immersed ourselves. We toured around the fascinating and eerie 'Museum of Death' and observed racial abuse and sexual harassment associated with the tradition of 'flashing' in exchange for Mardi Gras beads (Redmon, 2015). If you drifted just a few blocks outside of the traditional tourist locations, the scars of hurricane Katrina were still visible. Plots where properties destroyed by the hurricane once stood remained empty, while others that were damaged stood derelict and unrepaired. In many ways, it was the ideal location for a criminology conference interested in crime, deviance, inequality and harm.

However, the topic of this chapter stems from a more serene tourist experience during our time in New Orleans. A small number of us visited the Whitney Plantation, a former slave plantation that now offers guided tours of the plantation site. The tour presents an education and a history about the horrors of slavery, with a focus on the lived experience of enslavement and plantation life through both touring the buildings and grounds, but also the historically recorded narratives of former slaves themselves. The Whitney Plantation continues to shape the inequalities of New Orleans today, with banks, financial institutions and other prestigious buildings in New Orleans all bearing the Whitney family name.

The commodification of plantations

The harms of the homogenised and hedonistic night-time economy are plain to see and well rehearsed (see Hayward and Hobbs, 2007; Smith, 2014; Briggs and Ellis, 2017). However, the transformation of slave plantations – arguably *the* fundamental tool of the astounding growth of 19th-century American capitalism (Beckert, 2014) – into a form of commodified 'dark' tourism and leisure is arguably of greater interest because it cuts straight to the heart of deviant leisure's ethical boundaries and dilemmas. At front and centre of the deviant leisure project is a focus on the harms associated with intensifying socio-symbolic competition and individualism through leisure's relentless commodification. The ubiquity of this scope means that the question for deviant leisure scholars is often not 'what is deviant leisure?' but, more problematically, 'what *isn't* deviant leisure?' At what point does a form of ostensibly pro-social leisure become a harmful form of 'deviant leisure'? This is the fundamental question at the heart of issues around slave tourism. Is it an exploitative and voyeuristic form of 'dark tourism' in which capital continues to be accumulated and extracted historically from the bodies and free labour of slaves who have long since been in the grave? Or is it, more optimistically, a *pro-social* form of 'ethical consumption' that advocates racial tolerance and a remembrance of an important period of American history?

However, the typical issues of voyeurism and the continued exploitation and marketisation of 'slave tourism', important as they are, are not the topics of concern in this chapter. Rather, the deliberately controversial focus of this post is quite radically different. It questions how slave tourism's consignment of slavery to history, to another space-time and alternative political economy, in conjunction with tourists, and guides' collective grieving, shock and moral opprobrium, amounts to a collective form of *fetishistic disavowal* (Žižek, 2008) that, through the act of ostensibly 'pro-social' consumption, avoids an acknowledgement of how modern-day forms of 'slavery' and human rights abuses continue to be a fundamental component of contemporary political economy.

This question emerged out of a lingering sense of discomfort as we freely strolled around the grounds of the Whitney Plantation. At the time, I was incapable of articulating the source of my discomfort. I certainly had concerns prior to the tour. I had heard and read of tours which provided a disproportionate focus on the 'Big House' – the residence of the White slave masters and the items and rooms within. The White masters on these tours are often spoken of in depth, while the slaves' role in the very existence of the plantation is often 'symbolically annihilated' and whitewashed (there's a term for you) from history; an invisible afterthought which eerily replicates the realities of these grounds while they were in operation as active slave plantations (see Small and Eichstedt, 2002 for more on this). However, the Whitney tour is critically appraised for its reversal of this trend and indeed it prioritised first-hand accounts of enslaved lives which did not attempt to brush anything under the rug. This was an endeavour aided by the Federal Writers' Project in the 1930s, which attempted to capture the lived experiences of those who had survived slavery as an important set of voices and narratives of America's fabric.

The tour

The tour guide, an African American with indefatigable energy, provided incredibly nuanced knowledge and additional stories which provided a textured feel for the brutality of slave masters and the incomprehensible psychological and physical toil of slaves themselves. Most importantly, an unexpectedly 'pleasant' surprise (if that is the right term to use) was how the guide offered a detailed account regarding slavery's function within the wider political economy of the day and the role of political economy as the key driver underlying slavery. In his award-winning book *The Half Has Never Been Told*, historian Edward Baptist (2014) bemoans this element that is all-too-conveniently forgotten through the retelling of slavery's history. Within this field, the apparently dominant narrative is that slavery was an economically inefficient practice connected to the backwards ways of the 'Old South'. According to historians and economists, labour that was free and incentivised worked more efficiently than slave labour, contrasting slavery against the modernising and abolitionist industrial North of the time. This, as Baptist points out, is simply false at every empirical level. Slave-driven cotton picking and production was the most prominent driver in the making of the US into the global economic power it is today. The explosion of America's cotton exports so drastically exceeded that of any other nation that it ceased to have any competitors. Through processes of torture, higher levels of cotton-picking efficiency translated into investment in more efficient factory equipment in the so-called 'anti-slavery' North. This meant higher wages in the North, lower cotton prices and it set the stage for a burgeoning and democratised consumer economy in cotton cloth-based products all over the world. As Baptist (2014: 128) acknowledges through forensic analysis of empirical data, 'most of the world eventually acquired clothes made in the industrial West from cotton picked in the US South'.

Coming away from the tour, none of my prior concerns were realised. Nevertheless, my discomfort persisted. Upon reflection, it was not just what was present at the plantation, but what was *absent* that was the source of my discomfort. Overwhelmingly, it was the historicisation of slavery in every sense that bothered me. It was the lack of acknowledgement in how slavery remains to be a persistent and fundamental aspect of contemporary political economy, is more ethnically diverse in the make-up of both its victims and perpetrators, and how, through our ethical consumption and condemnation of these practices, we could purge the word and practice of slavery to an 'other-space' of barbaric history, disconnected from our contemporary present.

Let me be clear: I am not criticising the current people of the Whitney Plantation for their endeavours. They do so in good faith and provide a stirring history that urges for such relations between one group and another to never be enacted again. In times of such racial tension across the US and beyond, tours which explore barbarism of slavery – told through the words of those who survived dehumanising injustice – are a valid and useful project. I am merely questioning the subconscious role that such consumption plays in denying ourselves the acknowledgement of what we already know: that 'slavery' is alive and well in our current global political economy, albeit in mutated forms; and that we all play a complicit role through other practices of consumption which are underpinned and made possible by these mutated methods of indentured servitude. This is the Žižekian fetishistic disavowal: *I know, but I do not want to know, therefore I will act as if I do not know.*

If such a process is enacted through the collective consumption of slave tourism, how is such a process enacted? I argue it is through the spatio-temporal othering of slavery, discarding it to another space-time. We can see this clearly enough in Baptist's (2014) observation that the whitewashed and economically inaccurate account of slavery serves the purpose of detaching the political economy of slavery from that of the present day. However, through consigning slavery to the reserve of *history*, we see this play out further. It happened in this place, but it is not *here*. It belongs to a different America, a different economy that has long since condemned slavery to the dustbin of history. As Žižek (2002) argues, despite our abstract fear of terrorism and war, it is something that happens somewhere else, played out in the archaic and conflict-torn realms of the Middle East, disconnected from our reality. Irrespective of their prominence within Western nations, practices such as female genital mutilation or honour-based violence don't happen here in the progressive, civilised and multicultural West. They happen somewhere else, an othered space from which we are happy to divorce ourselves.

We *culturalise* these practices. Slavery is also something which not just happens *somewhere* else but belongs to another time and set of economic arrangements. *Their* economy, the American economy of the 19th century, used slavery. Nowadays, our enlightened liberal consumer economy that caters to our tastes and desires enables us to buy tickets and tour the plantations for the purpose of collectively denouncing such practices. Thus, it is an economic practice that is fundamentally different to our contemporary real economy that is predicated on consumption. These are the stories we tell ourselves. But are they necessarily true? A quick survey of the production of commodities, institutions and events that underpins our leisure, consumption and 'real economy' quickly begins to reveal some frayed holes in this logic.

The problematic nature of contemporary consumption

Reach into your pocket and take out your smartphone. Inside every smartphone is the rare earth element cobalt, an essential component of lithium-ion batteries found in most contemporary electronic devices. In 2020, the Democratic Republic of the Congo (DRC) were responsible for 67.8 per cent of global cobalt production and Amnesty International's (2016b) report showed that 20 per cent of this comes from artisanal mines in which approximately 40,000 children labour, extracting cobalt manually without industrial tools, protective equipment and in hazardous conditions. Adults and children working in these mines are subject to enslavement, rape, torture, forced and coerced drug abuse by local militia groups who run these illegal mines. Much of the cobalt extracted from these mines is ending up in the 'legitimate' supply chains of some of the most recognisable corporations in the world. In 2019, the human rights group International Rights Advocates filed a lawsuit against Apple, Microsoft, Dell and Tesla on behalf of 14 families of Congolese children who died in the mines, accusing these companies of indirectly – but knowingly – aiding, abetting and profiting from these forced labour practices in the DRC by allowing illicit sources of cobalt into their supply chains. The case was dismissed on the grounds that there was insufficient causality between the conduct of the firms named in the lawsuit and the deaths of these Congolese children. Neoliberalism's complex and diversified global supply chains are the mechanism that provides adequate protection against such accusations. It seems, therefore, that slavery has simply been outsourced rather than vanished from today's global supply chain. Less than two centuries earlier, White American profiteers used enslaved Black men as 'drivers' to enforce discipline and maintain high work rates on their plantations (Baptist, 2014). Today, it seems a similar practice persists albeit in mutated form and at a distance, with sufficient plausible deniability.

This is not to say that questionable practices do not persist closer to home. Not far up the road from Whitney is the Angola Louisiana State Penitentiary. In a strange twist of meaning and fate, Angola is a former slave plantation-turned-prison. While prisoners won't be taken to the stocks or receive the bullwhip, they can be legally forced to work without pay under threat of punishment as severe as solitary confinement (Benns, 2015). A short documentary shows African American prisoners peppering the prison's horizon, working out in the field harvesting sugar cane, still the crop of choice since Louisiana's heyday of slavery. How is this legal? America's Thirteenth Amendment, which allegedly outlawed slavery, states in section 1 (emphasis added): 'Neither slavery nor involuntary servitude, *except as punishment for crime whereof the party shall have been duly convicted*, shall exist within the United States, or any place subject to their jurisdiction.' If one is imprisoned, they can be forced to work as punishment for their crimes. This was one of the mechanisms through which slavery persisted past 1863, and states such as Texas and Arkansas, in addition to Angola in Louisiana, continue to have this tradition in their own prisons.

However, the commentary on the documentary is most revealing. Opening the documentary in bewilderment, the narrator says: 'Once you pass through Angola's front gates you can't help but feel you've gone back in time … to a different America, to another South.' Is this not the exact form of fetishistic disavowal mentioned earlier? The historicisation of slavery, the moving it to a different spatio-temporal order despite what one sees in front of one's own eyes?

None of this is to mention what is happening in Qatar, which is hosting one of the largest consumer events in the world, the 2022 World Cup. Much of the infrastructure and stadiums being built in preparation for 2022 is being done by migrant workers under the *kafala* system. This is a 'sponsorship system' which requires unskilled migrant workers to have an in-country sponsor (usually an employer) to be responsible for their visa and legal status. Human rights organisations have long called for the abolition of the *kafala* system, arguing that it amounts to an 'ownership' of migrant workers by binding them to employers and offering easy exploitation. Indeed, this is playing out in Qatar as we speak. While the mainstream media attention it has received has been scant, news outlets have reported that thousands of migrant workers are held in squalid and over-cramped conditions, have their passports confiscated by their employers so that they are unable to legally leave the country and are withheld the meagre pay they are due and forced to work with threat of further withheld pay and other sanctions. Deaths related to the construction of the 2022 World Cup are rising rapidly, while FIFA's response was that it was 'disappointed' and 'looking into the matter' (Amnesty International, 2016a). As Amnesty International have established, this amounts to forced labour under international law. All the while, broadcasters and advertisers will accrue enormous profits throughout the 2022 World Cup, while many of the same tourists who have taken the tour of the Whitney Plantation will drink beer, revel in the festival of football and cheer their team on blissfully, despite having shaken their heads, gasped in shock and furrowed their brows at the historicised exploitation that occurred at the Whitney Plantation.

For many of us, when we buy our sublime consumer objects, we do not want to think too hard about where they came from. Even if we are unaware of the specifics, deep down we know that the affordability of our latest purchase is likely predicated on the inhumane suffering of people at some point in that product's supply chain. Yet we disavow this knowledge, acting as if we were blissfully ignorant. Indeed, to think too hard about these realities would likely be paralysing. In today's digital technopoly, we arguably have little choice but to own such products, with access to all manner of services largely dependent on the ownership of a computer or smartphone (Postman, 1992). To provide another New Orleans reference, we can see this same fetishistic disavowal in an interviewee in David Redmon's documentary (Redmon, 2015) Redmon's documentary traces the journey of the infamous Mardi Gras beads from the factories of China, replete with various human rights abuses, to the hedonistic and conspicuous consumption of New Orleans' Mardi Gras festival. When he asks consumers in New Orleans where they think the beads came from, he receives various responses such as "I don't want to know", "I don't care; I'm on vacation" and, when he tells them about the Chinese workers' wages and working conditions, receives responses such as "Get away!" and "Don't tell me that!"

Conclusion

Through the collective act of consumption, through our implicit celebration that slavery is no longer with us, and that we live in a society enlightened enough to denounce its horrors, I suggest that such tours partake in a collective form of subconscious sublimation of what we already know: that our economy of enjoyment is predicated upon similar practices persisting today. Even the reactions – the sighing, the gasping, the crying and the whispers of 'Oh my God' to one another – reflect almost a cathartic purging of slavery from our reality. Some might contest that the forms of labour I have described here do not constitute slavery. After all, individuals are not being bought and sold or bred like cattle. But when the largest event for the largest sport in the world is built by migrant workers in Qatar who are forced to work for free, under the 'sponsorship' of employers, with passports confiscated to prevent them from leaving; when artisanal miners are terrorised and tortured by militias; when young women are trafficked across Asia and Europe into so-called 'legal' brothels (Lorenz, 2019), what other term is there to use? 'Forced labour' appears to be the preferable term. However, is there not something else suspicious about our reluctance to use the term 'slavery'? To return to Edward Baptist (2014), he recalls how White abolitionists in the US North were reluctant to use the term 'torture' during slavery to describe the methods of punishment, preferring 'discipline' instead. It was the relationship and the reliance, Baptist argues, of the industrial North and their cotton mills upon the US South that drove this semantic reluctance. He writes:

> Perhaps one unspoken reason why many have been so reluctant to apply the term 'torture' to slavery is that even though they denied slavery's economic dynamism, they knew that slavery on the cotton frontier made a lot of product. No one was willing,

> in other words, to admit they lived in an economy whose bottom gear was torture. (Baptist, 2014: 139)

Perhaps, similarly, none of us care to admit that our consumer economy and leisure – be it clothes from Primark, our enjoyment of an international sporting event or accumulating beads during a drunken stagger down Bourbon Street – is predicated on a global economy whose bottom gear is slavery. Those are the dark corners of leisure that we would rather not explore.

3

National Portrait Gallery, Smithsonian Institution: Washington, DC, USA

Alice Storey

Birmingham City University

Introduction

The Smithsonian in Washington, DC, USA is the 'world's largest museum, education, and research complex' (Smithsonian Institution, 2021). You may think of it as a must-see tourist attraction when in the US, rather than a 'dark destination'. Yet, the Smithsonian's National Portrait Gallery houses a collection about the 'Scottsboro Boys', who were involved in an infamous death penalty case marred with racial discrimination and multiple wrongful convictions. This chapter discusses the case of the Scottsboro Boys as exhibited by the National Portrait Gallery, and the concerning trend of history repeating itself through the modern-day death penalty in the US.

The National Portrait Gallery's Scottsboro Boys collection

The Scottsboro Boys case involved nine young, Black boys who were riding a freight train in Alabama in 1931 and got into a fight with a group of White boys (ACLU, 2020). They were subsequently wrongfully accused and convicted of raping two White women while riding the train (ACLU, 2020). The Scottsboro Boys case took place against the backdrop of the South's brutal treatment of

Black people, with the lynching of Black men (Kaufman-Osborn, 2006: 27) being the norm during the Jim Crow Era (Hunt, 2016). The Jim Crow Era refers to the racial segregation laws that were rampant across the South, from 1877 to 1964, although arguably the Jim Crow legacy still lives on in the US today.

After the two White women accused the boys of rape, all nine were arrested – Olen Montgomery, Clarence Norris, Haywood Patterson, Ozie Powell, Willie Roberson, Charley Weems, Eugene Williams, Andy Wright and Roy Wright. In fact, they were almost lynched as a group of 10,000 people congregated in Scottsboro for the trials (ACLU, 2020). Most of these people were 'poor white farmers' who shouted racist abuse and asked whether there was 'enough rope', referring to their plans to lynch the boys (Linder, 2000: 551). However, instead of being lynched by an angry mob of White men, they were 'legally lynched' (Hargrove, 2001: 35) by an 'all-male and all-white jury' with a short trial and conviction, which saw eight of the nine boys being sentenced to death. The outcome of the Scottsboro Boys case was based upon 'race and racial stereotypes rather than on evidence' (Duru, 2004: 1337), and as the boys were awaiting execution, a letter written by one of the two women came to light, in which she wrote that she had lied about the rape accusations (ACLU, 2020). Despite this, the Alabama Supreme Court upheld all but one of the convictions, ruling that Williams must have a retrial as he was tried as an adult when he had only been 13 at the time.

All nine cases were appealed as one to the US Supreme Court, which held in favour of the Scottsboro Boys in a landmark ruling in *Powell v. Alabama* (1932). The Court found that the boys had been denied their Fourteenth Amendment rights, as 'the failure of the trial court to give them reasonable time and opportunity to secure counsel was a clear denial of due process' (*Powell v. Alabama*, 1932). The decisions of the Alabama courts were reversed and were remanded back to the State. When the case returned to Alabama, the State tried the boys again, in trials that were also fuelled by racial injustice and controversy (Linder, 2000). For a second time, the US Supreme Court stepped in and reversed the convictions, due to a breach of due process, this time in relation to the systematic exclusion of Black jurors (*Norris v. Alabama*, 1935). For a third time, the State of Alabama sought convictions of the

Scottsboro Boys. Eventually in 1937, Montgomery, Roberson, Williams and Roy Wright were released from prison as the State dropped the charges of rape against them. Powell remained in prison due to a conviction for attacking a prison guard. Norris, Patterson, Weems and Andy Wright were all convicted of rape and completed prison sentences (Carter, 1979). The last Scottsboro Boy passed away in 1989, yet it was not until 2013, 'after the legislature passed a law permitting posthumous pardons, [that] they received full and unconditional pardons' (ACLU, 2020).

The National Portrait Gallery houses a portrait of Clarence Norris and Haywood Patterson, drawn by Aaron Douglas circa 1935. This 'provides the opportunity to pair a critical historical story with a powerful work of art' (Reaves, 2011). It also serves as both a reminder to the world of the US historic racism, and a demonstration of the link between historic and modern-day racial discrimination in the country.

National Portrait Gallery: looking to the past, present and future?

The legacy of the Jim Crow Era and the racial injustice the Scottsboro Boys experienced lives on in the US. The entirety of the US criminal justice system is marred with racial discrimination. From the killing of Black men by police, right through to the death penalty, it is clear that more value is placed on a White life than a minority life.

The modern-day death penalty is more nuanced in its racial discrimination than at the time of the Scottsboro Boys case. Detailed studies have been carried out regarding the link between race and capital punishment, which demonstrate 'a correlation between holding racially biased beliefs and support for the death penalty in the [US]' (Hood and Hoyle, 2015: 286). The leading study is the Baldus Study, which was a sophisticated analysis carried out on sentencing within cases in the 1970s and the racial disparities in the death penalty in the State of Georgia (Baldus et al, 1983; 1985). The Baldus Study found that there was a 4.3:1 chance of a defendant receiving the death penalty for killing a White person than a Black person. From the data collected, the authors concluded that the race of the victim is almost as influential as a defendant having previously been convicted of crimes such as robbery (Baldus et al, 1983; 1985). Furthermore, when the raw data was analysed, it showed that even in this category Black defendants were more likely to be executed than White defendants (Baldus et al, 1983; 1985; Mears, 2008: 81).

Despite the clear evidence of discrimination, courts in the US have not been receptive to the findings of the Baldus Study. In the 1987 case of *McCleskey v. Kemp*, the appellant used it to demonstrate that 'the Georgia capital sentencing process is administered in a racially discriminative manner in violation of the Eighth and Fourteenth Amendments' (*McCleskey v. Kemp*, 1987: 286). However, in a 5–4 decision, the US Supreme Court rejected this argument and, in delivering the opinion of the Court, Justice Powell found that for an Equal Protection claim to stand, an appellant must prove 'that the decision-makers in *his* case acted with discriminatory purpose' (*McCleskey v. Kemp*, 1987: 292, emphasis in original). The majority found McCleskey had not done this, as he had relied solely on the findings of the Baldus Study, rather than on the facts of his own case (*McCleskey v. Kemp*, 1987: 292–293).

This problem has not improved over time. The Death Penalty Information Center (2021) carried out a study of all capital cases from 1976 to July 2021, which provided statistical results showing that '[m]ore than 75% of the murder victims in cases resulting in an execution were white, even though nationally only 50% of total murder victims generally are white'. Furthermore, a 2007 study sponsored by the American Bar Association demonstrated that Black defendants 'received the death penalty at three times the rate of white defendants where the victims were white' (Advocates for Human Rights, 2010: para 5). Additionally, while the federal death penalty is often cited by the US government in terms of the rare numbers of capital sentences and executions, the Federal Death Penalty Resource Council has provided statistics 'illustrat[ing] that the death penalty is applied more than three times as often against non-whites as against whites and more than twice as often against blacks as against whites' (Inter-American Commission on Human Rights, 2010). In the capital case of Orlando Hall, the federal death penalty in Texas was specifically cited, wherein 'black defendants are 5.3 times more likely than white defendants to face the death penalty in Texas federal prosecutions; and 10.3 times more likely than Hispanic defendants' (Inter-American Commission on Human Rights, 2010). This suggests that while the federal death penalty is not used as often, it is more discriminatory based on race.

More positively, in 2018, in *State v. Gregory*, the Washington State Supreme Court struck down its capital punishment statute based on a study on race (Beckett, 2016; *State v. Gregory*, 2018). However, generally, even well-regarded studies that provide clear data demonstrating the extent of racial discrimination in the death penalty are not acted upon by the courts. While the example of Washington State is certainly a positive, no other US state has followed suit to date.

Linking this modern-day racially biased death penalty to the injustices faced by the Scottsboro Boys, former Supreme Court Justice Stevens stated that 'the murder of black victims is treated as less culpable than the murder of white victims provides a haunting reminder of once-prevalent Southern lynchings' (Equal Justice Initiative, 2010).

Conclusion

The Smithsonian's National Portrait Gallery allows visitors to remember the racially motivated wrongful convictions of the Scottsboro Boys, but also to reflect upon how the Jim Crow Era still lingers today. It is abundantly clear that racial injustice permeates the death penalty, demonstrated by the myriad studies conducted, one of which has led to a state's abolition of the punishment. Capital punishment is an archaic and barbaric punishment that has no penological rationale in today's society. Racial discrimination is just one of the many fundamental flaws of the capital system in the US and, if it wants to move away from its historical legacy of racism as demonstrated by the Scottsboro Boys case, then one step in the right direction would be to abolish the death penalty across the US. Until that time, visitors may continue to visit the National Portrait Gallery and frame such injustices as a relic of a time long since passed, unaware that contemporary examples may one day also be viewed by such tourists in similar museums. In doing so, the current disproportionate targeting of minority groups will continue, along with little hope for the future.

4

From Newgate Prison to Tyburn Tree: the Old Bailey, London, UK

Peter Joyce and Wendy Laverick

Glyndŵr University and University of Hull

Introduction

This chapter focuses on the 'Hanging Parade' – the route taken by prisoners in London who were found guilty of murder, treason and other serious crimes. They were conveyed from Newgate Prison to Tyburn where they were hung. We will first explore the contentious history of capital punishment in England with a particular focus on the era now often referred to as the 'Bloody Code'. Attention will then shift towards the actual process of execution during this historic period in which the implementation of the death penalty was both prolific and theatrical. Lastly, a detailed account of the very steps taken by the condemned will be provided, illustrating the various experiences one would have encountered on the way to the gallows.

The 'Bloody Code': capital punishment in 18th-century England

In the 18th century, a distinction was drawn between clergyable felonies (serious criminal offences which carried the death penalty), non-clergyable felonies (lesser criminal offences or petty larcenies which included the theft of goods valued at below one shilling and occurrences of assault/brawling to which the death penalty did not apply) and summary offences which especially embraced economic regulation.

The penalty for felonies was invariably death which extended to many crimes that would now be regarded as minor. The number of crimes for which people could be executed grew considerably during the 18th century, from around 50 in 1688 to 225 by 1815 (McLynn, 1989: ix), the great bulk of which were property crimes, including arson, burglary and housebreaking and theft. This widespread application of capital punishment gave rise to a description of the legal system as the 'Bloody Code': the 1723 Waltham Black Act formed an important part of this Code.

From Newgate Prison to Tyburn Tree: the ritual of execution

The chief purpose of the death penalty was that of deterrence: it has been argued that 'the theatre of the gallows in the eighteenth century was a means whereby ordinary men and women could be made vividly aware of the consequences of criminal behaviour by viewing the "aweful" consequences displayed before their eyes' (Taylor, 1998: 124). To reinforce the deterrent effect, public executions were accompanied by processions and in some instances, following execution, judges might order the body to be hung in chains on a gibbet near the scene of the crime (a penalty often inflicted on highwaymen) where it would be left to rot. The ability to pass the sentence of gibbeting was extended by the 1752 Murder Act.

Religious ceremony preceded Tyburn executions. A service was held on the Sunday before the execution in the chapel at Newgate Prison: an open black coffin bore witness to the context of the event. On the night before the execution, the prisoner would experience the slow ringing of a handbell taken from the Church of Saint Sepulchre-Without-Newgate, which was connected to Newgate by a tunnel. It would be rung by the church's clerk who would also offer what was known as 'wholesome advice':

> All you that in the condemned hold do lie,
> Prepare you, for to-morrow you shall die;
> Watch all, and pray, the hour is drawing near

That you before the Almighty must appear;
Examine well yourselves, in time repent,
That you may not to eternal flames be sent.
And when St Sepulchre's bell to-morrow tolls,
The Lord above have mercy on your souls.
Past twelve o'clock! (Cited in Thornbury, 1878)

On the morning of the execution, the condemned prisoner attended prayers and was able to receive the sacrament. It was common for some of the main bells of the church to be rung, announcing that an execution was imminent.

The route to Tyburn Tree: a dark destination

For much of the 18th century in London, most executions took place at Tyburn, although some took place at Smithfield and Tower Hill and also at Newgate Prison. Between 1571 and 1783 about 1,100 men and almost 100 women were hanged at Tyburn (The Proceedings of the Old Bailey, 2018a). The majority of these consisted of poor people, it being pointed out that 'workplace theft, begging and vagrancy, prostitution, petty theft, shoplifting, and receiving of stolen goods are all points on the continuum linking poverty and criminality' (Shore, 2003: 144). The 'Hanging Parade' reinforced the intention of executions to exercise a deterrent effect. It entailed a prisoner being publicly conveyed from Newgate Prison to Tyburn in an open cart. The procession was superintended by the City Marshall and the cart was surrounded by armed guards on horseback to ensure no attempt could be made to free the prisoner (The Proceedings of the Old Bailey, 2018a). The procession would customarily halt at public houses along the way where the prisoner would be given a last drink of alcohol. These included the Bowl Inn and the Mason's Arms. At Tyburn, the prisoner would usually make a last 'Dying Speech' to the crowd (ostensibly to confess their guilt) and a cleric (termed the 'Ordinary' [chaplain] of Newgate Prison) would be present to pray for the condemned prisoner's soul. A noose was then placed around the neck of the prisoner who would be blindfolded (and sometimes hooded). Finally, the cart was pulled away. This led to death by strangulation (until the sharp drop was introduced in 1783) (The Proceedings of the Old Bailey, 2018b), a procedure which could last for up to 45 minutes.

Subsequently, if not gibbeted, the body would be available for anatomising and dissection. On occasions, brawls would occur between the friends and relatives of the deceased (who wished for religious reasons for the body to be buried whole to enable resurrection) and the authorities, but the latter usually prevailed. Redevelopment means that the route taken by prisoners cannot be faithfully followed today. Now a visitor would start at the Old Bailey (which formerly housed Newgate Prison) and end in the area around Marble Arch (where Tyburn gallows were located). This is a journey of around three miles. The most authentic copy of the original route would start at St Paul's underground station from where the visitor would proceed along Newgate Street to the Old Bailey. From there they would travel to Snow Hill and thence to Farringdon Road and Holborn Viaduct. They would then proceed to High Holborn until reaching St Giles High Street. Passing Centre Point in New Oxford Street, they would cross Tottenham Court Road and enter Oxford Street. Marble Arch is located at the top of this thoroughfare, and Oxford Circus and Bond Street underground stations are crossed en route.

Many of the landmarks on the original route (such as Holborn Bridge, Holborn Hill and the Bowl Inn) no longer exist. The site of the gallows at Tyburn (which were of an unusual design, consisting of a horizontal wooden triangle supported by three legs) no longer stands but is commemorated by a plaque that informs visitors that this was 'the site of Tyburn Tree'. It is surrounded by three oak trees representing the three legs of the gallows and located at the junction of Edgware Road and Bayswater Road. However, some of the old landmarks remain for the modern visitor to view. Although the Old Bailey stands on the site once occupied by Newgate Prison, one wall remains in Amen Court which can be accessed from Warwick Lane at the rear of the Old Bailey. Other surviving landmarks include the Church Saint Sepulchre-Without-Newgate (now titled Holy Sepulchre, London and which serves as the National Musician's Church). This was made famous by the mid-18th-century nursery rhyme *Oranges and Lemons* ('when will you pay me, said the bells of Old Bailey?'). It is located on the north side of Holborn Viaduct, which was opposite the prison. The handbell (or execution bell) is preserved in the nave of this church.

Today's visitors can also view the Church of St Andrew Holborn (which was designed by Sir Christopher Wren and restored following bomb damage experienced during the Second World War), the Church of St Giles in the Field (sometimes referred to as the Poet's Church and located at Giles High Street) and the Mason's Arms which is located in Upper Berkeley Street. This once had a tunnel connecting the cellar of the establishment to Tyburn and contained a cell in which prisoners were held prior to their execution. Although public executions were designed to emphasise the deterrent purpose of executions, many of the crowd simply viewed them as a day out. After 1783 (following the 1780 Gordon Riots in London), fears that crowds could trigger public disorder and rioting led to executions taking place inside Newgate Prison (or Horsemonger Lane Gaol in Southwark), although they were still visible to members of the public until 1868.

Changing attitudes

Inspired by classicist criminology, reforms took place in the early 19th century that vastly reduced the number of capital offences. Under the Tory government in the 1820s, a relatively small number of offences ceased to be capital offences, but reforms of this nature accelerated under the Whig government elected in 1832. By 1839, the only offences that carried the death penalty were 'treason, riot, arson of naval ships and of naval and military stores, murder and other offences involving attempts on or risks to life, rape, buggery, sexual intercourse with girls under ten years of age, and robbery and burglary when accompanied by personal violence' (Glazebrook, 2019). In 1840, rape ceased to be a capital offence.

The movement away from the death penalty rested on concerns that included changing sensitivities and apprehensions regarding elite views of the reactions of spectators, the 'simple pragmatism' that derived from an awareness of the ineffectiveness of capital punishment as a deterrent and the limits to the number of people who could be hanged without undermining the legitimacy of the justice system (Taylor, 2010: 153). This latter argument was elaborated by the claim that a key reason for the reform of the penal code in this period was the fear of revolution that might be brought about by 'brutal and unequal punishment' (Emsley, 2018: 11). These concerns had led to considerable inconsistencies in the application of the death penalty through practices that included 'benefit of clergy', 'pious perjury' and the application of mercy by a sentencer. Magistrates before whom property offences were tried often attempted to resolve the matter without the need for a trial to take place (Emsley, 2018: 9–10). Thus, very few people (around one in 20 in 1810) eligible for execution actually suffered this fate (Glazebrook, 2019), although more people were hanged in early 19th-century England than at any time since the early modern era (Gattrell, 1994).

Conclusion

To classicist criminologists (such as Cesare Beccaria and Jeremy Bentham), whose views helped inspire reforms to the operations of the criminal justice system in the late 18th and early 19th centuries, inconsistency in applying the death penalty undermined the predictability of punishment since a person was unable to calculate the pros and cons of committing a criminal offence. What was needed, therefore, was graded sentences. If the punishment fitted the crime, consistency in its application was more likely to be achieved. Accordingly, new forms of punishment based on imprisonment were developed during the 19th century. One of the most significant developments was the sentence of penal servitude which was authorised by the 1853 and 1857 Penal Servitude Acts, and which aimed to break the spirit of offenders. A sentence of penal servitude initially lasted for a minimum of three years (increased to five following the enactment of the 1864 Penal Servitude Act and which could be extended to seven if the convicted person had previously been convicted of another felony).

5

Jack the Ripper tour: Whitechapel, London, UK

Kevin Hoffin

Birmingham City University

Introduction

On a nightly basis, the streets of Whitechapel, East London become a hive of tourist activity. Unlike the West End, where groups of eager visitors enjoy the performances in any number of theatres, the intention of those that venture into Whitechapel is decidedly more sinister. It was here that in the late 1880s, the serial killer, Jack the Ripper, stalked the back alleys and murdered five women (Rubenhold, 2020). The mythology that has manifested around the mystery of Jack the Ripper is a staple of the 'true crime' genre of entertainment and has proliferated through the media for over a century. Retellings of the murders with various dramatic twists (supernatural ephemera, attempts at uncovering his identity) are common and ensure the popularity of the unsolved cases perpetuate. The area of Whitechapel has capitalised upon the historical murder of five women to underpin much of the economy. Examples include an East End chip shop, 'Jack the Chipper', and various Jack the Ripper-inspired gift shops. Most prominent (and arguably most problematic), however, are the guided tours aimed at tourists with a taste for the macabre. Each evening, the streets of Whitechapel are flooded by the surfeit of eager tourists being metaphorically whisked back to the 1880s. The reason for the abundance of eager tourists pounding the pavement, even during the deepest of English winters, is to follow the Ripper's footsteps. For the purpose of writing this chapter, the author participated in the Jack the Ripper tour, billed as 'The Original Terror Tour'. The guide, who identified as a 'Ripperologist', drew heavily upon a text, *One Autumn Night in Whitechapel* (Priestley, 2016), which contains information he shares on the tour.

The canonical five

The constructed media image of Jack the Ripper, primarily from films and TV series such as *From Hell* (2001) and *Ripper Street* (2012–present), is that of a highly intelligent, organised and methodical killer who always seemed to be one step ahead of the police. In reality, Jack the Ripper bears all the hallmarks of what we consider in criminology as being a 'disorganised offender' – an individual who hunts in a small geographical area, likely holds low-skilled employment and often attacks their victims in a 'blitz' style, in which they tend to dehumanise their victim (Wilson et al, 2015). These characteristics can be seen in each of the Ripper's victims.

The canonical five Ripper victims are Mary Ann Nichols, Annie Chapman, Elizabeth Stride, Catherine Eddowes and Mary Jane Kelly – all sex workers. Nichols' body was discovered at about 3:40 am on Friday, 31 August 1888 in Whitechapel. The throat was severed by two cuts, and the lower part of the abdomen was partly ripped open by a deep, jagged wound. Just over a week later, Chapman's body was discovered at about 6 am on Saturday, 8 September 1888 near a doorway in the back yard of 29 Hanbury Street. Her throat was severed by two cuts and the abdomen was slashed entirely open. Stride and Eddowes were killed in the early morning of Sunday, 30 September 1888. Stride's body was discovered at about 1 am in Whitechapel. The cause of death was one clear-cut incision which severed the main artery on the left side of the neck. Eddowes' body was found in Mitre Square in the City of London, three quarters of an hour after Stride's. The throat was severed and the abdomen was ripped open by a long, deep, jagged wound. The left kidney and the major part of the uterus had been removed. Eddowes' and Stride's murders were later called the 'double event'. Kelly's mutilated and disembowelled body was discovered lying on the bed in the single room where she lived at 13 Miller's Court at 10:45 am on Friday, 9 November 1888. The throat had been severed down to the spine, and the abdomen almost emptied of its organs. The heart was also missing.

Despite a high-profile investigation, no one was officially charged with these murders and to this day the individual responsible has never been identified. The reality and tragedy behind the 'myth' that was Jack the Ripper has seemingly been eroded, and in its place are now numerous television documentaries and dramatisations, graphic novels, true crime books, films and, of course, 'Jack the Ripper' tours.

The contemporary tour

The various Jack the Ripper walking tours, of which this writer took one, are undoubtedly the most iconic examples of true crime walking tour (Fonseca et al, 2016: 5) where guests follow preordained routes around the Whitechapel district of London. Guides with individualised levels of melodrama lead tourists between streets and alleys to points of interest (or close approximations to) of significant stories of the Ripper's exploits and sites where his victims were found (Rubenhold, 2020). They will inevitably regale the crowd with the various theories as to his identity that have been aired with a particular focus on their personal favourite interpretations, delivering these anecdotes as if they were cold, hard facts (Robinson, 2015; Priestley, 2016; Gray and Wise, 2019). Each tour guide tries to be innovative; some, for example, utilise multimedia, such as projecting images onto nearby walls of documented material including photos of the unfortunate victims in a twisted remediation. The simplistic misrepresentations that emerge in many forms of mediated crime, as well as those on offer here, offer little beyond their ability to perversely illustrate the murders and the mythologised elements of killers like Jack, as opposed to proffering any theorisation on the causes of said crime. The charismatic tour guides endeavour to make their retellings the creepiest, the most gruesome, while speaking under the guise of forensic realism; more often than not, their commentary proffers stylised, sensationalist accounts, devoid of analytical elements, where truth and fiction are allowed to overlap in the name of infotainment (Seltzer, 2007). Here the victims become little more than objects on a grizzly milieu, and their suffering gets woven into the killer's narrative. They are effectively objectified and reduced to pseudo-fictional caricatures where the only aspect of their lives that matters is their untimely end (Rubenhold, 2020). The grotesque pantomime is played out multiple nights per week, as the victims' tragedies are reiterated repeatedly for the satisfaction of paying tourists with an ever-increasing disavowal of the real human suffering that took place.

Historical tours of zoos of human suffering

Walking tours of the cruel and violent within urban areas are nothing new. These activities are believed to have roots in Victorian London (Beaumont, 2016; Draven, 2020), where the local rich and various members of the aristocracy would visit the poorest areas of the city for various reasons including voyeurism and/or philanthropy. This was commonly known as 'slum tourism'. Regardless of their intentions for undertaking such tours, this very activity equated to visiting 'human zoos' (Draven, 2020) and to carry the metaphor forwards, the Jack the Ripper tour is akin to being party to 'zoos of human suffering' where the brutality of the killings is placed front and centre, against a milieu of excruciating examples of Victorian poverty. As customers walk the Ripper tours, often in urban areas, there is a liminality at play. These city streets, that only hours ago would have been teeming with people going about their day, have attained a radically different meaning to these dark tourists who navigate them now. This begins an exclusivity, as the same physical space takes on diverging contexts (Beaumont, 2016). The 'regular' and the 'horror' or 'outsider' London (Mighail, 1999), these spaces plicate over each other, intertwining, and one mislaid step can be the crossover from one to the other. Commuters look on or, in their ambulation, trace the exact same steps with little or no thought or (perhaps even) knowledge that they are occupying potential historic crime scenes, while the tour's participants revel in it. Seltzer (1998) tells us that the act of killing is one that would metaphorically remove the killer from society, ensuring they are stood apart, the will 'to do something alien' (Honeycombe, 1982: xvii). Thus it may be determined that these tours and the arcane, terrible knowledge that tourists imbibe are an attempt to follow in Jack's footsteps, to retread the killer's hunt (Lynes et al, 2018) and venture outside the relative safety of society and its normality, in order to become a familiar of the 'Outsider' city.

Conclusion

The first 'Ripper' tour, aptly named the 'original Jack the Ripper murders tour', began in 1982 – almost 100 years after the murders took place. If we focus exclusively on Jack the Ripper 'tours', there were 15 dedicated to Jack the Ripper, with the remaining tours including the murder sites in a wider tour of London and its other well-known attractions at the time I explored Whitechapel. All the Ripper tours seem to follow a similar design in that they offer tourists a walk through the Whitechapel area and, as with the original tour established in 1982, follow a chronological order of each of the Ripper's victims. On the tours the guides often refer to themselves as 'Ripperologists'. The term is clearly a corruption of 'criminologist' while perpetuating a false narrative of what all but a tiny minority of criminologists focus upon. After all, few tourists would attend a walking tour of littering sites or many of the other much more benign and less glamorous areas of deviancy and transgression that criminology focuses upon. Arguably, had Jack been apprehended, tried and executed for his crimes, the matter would likely have been closed and the name 'Jack the Ripper' would be lost to the sands of time (Fathers, 2020: 107). It is the mystery itself that has fuelled an entire industry on speculating on Jack's identity and remediating the crimes (Fathers, 2020: 107) and commodifying the victims' memory. While shivering away on a cold winter's night, it became clear that the tour allowed the paying crowds to 'play criminology', while simultaneously misunderstanding the discipline's nature. The group gained a vicarious thrill by briefly reinvestigating the historic scenes of depravity alongside modern technologies. Each of these tours, as they embark from each site of visceral events, constantly reignite interest in the killer, but one must question the reasoning, beyond morbid titillation and a fascination for mythologised, violent, true crime (Seltzer, 2007). While much of the group's focus was upon the details of young women brutally slain a century previous, nobody displaced their myopic gaze to notice the scenes of destitution so reminiscent of Victorian England before them. The homeless man huddled in the alleyway was ignored. So too were the newspaper headlines reporting the latest woman murdered in the nation's capital.

6

The Alcatraz East Crime Museum: Pigeon Forge, Tennessee, USA

Laura Hammond

Birmingham City University

> We are fascinated by the dark side and what makes a particular person act on impulses while most do not; curious to the motives that turn an ordinary person into a killer.
>
> Alcatraz East Crime Museum
> Official Souvenir Book (2019)

Introduction

The American National Museum of Crime and Punishment (Crime Museum) opened in 2008 in Washington, DC. As described in its advertising, it was the first museum in America to bring together the curiosity and passion for true crime, forensics and the history of law enforcement in an interactive environment. In 2016 the Crime Museum collection moved to a new home in Pigeon Forge, Tennessee.

Now to the Alcatraz East Crime Museum, its design is based on that of an old prison, although also draws inspiration from its namesake – the Alcatraz Penitentiary in California. It displays not only the original Crime Museum exhibits but continues to collect and share 'the story of America's favourite subject', through the presentation of original crime artefacts and interactive exhibits, with both a permanent collection, special collections and temporary exhibits.

No one needs a t-shirt with Ted Bundy on it: personal reflections

I have always been fascinated by crime; why people do what they do, what drives and motivates them. That was why I decided to train as a forensic psychologist – so that I could work to answer those kinds of questions. Serial killers, in particular, I always found very interesting, wondering what happens to make someone take such extreme actions. When I started out, I had visions of a career studying the dark depths of the criminal mind, like the Federal Bureau of Investigation (FBI) profilers I had read so much about and seen presented on both the big and small screen.

I'm clearly not the only one. Our Forensic Psychology and Criminology courses at Birmingham City University are consistently among the most popular choices for incoming students, and modules focusing on crime and criminology always have a high uptake. But more than that, a few simple Google searches quickly reveal the popularity of the true crime genre. Serial killers, in particular, prove a topic of great interest for many. Films and television series centred on the subject of serial killing constitute a multimillion-dollar entertainment industry (Kelly et al, 2022), and 'murderabilia' – ranging from serial killer writings and art or body parts to kitsch merchandising, including serial killer t-shirts, calendars, trading cards, board games and even action figures, has become big business (Jarvis, 2007). You can get serial killer activity books and colouring books, top trumps and pairs games. Even a cookbook themed around the last meal choices of those executed for the multiple murders that they committed (Lecker, 2020). To humour you: John Wayne Gacy requested crispy fried chicken and deep fried shrimp, Aileen Wuornos hamburgers and Timothy McVeigh mint chip ice cream.

If you're anything like me, then you are likely to be drawn to the Crime Museum – Alcatraz East, an oasis of interesting exhibits detailing the history of crime and law enforcement in America. The museum houses enough artefacts and specimens to satisfy the most morbid of curiosities. There's Ted Bundy's 1968 VW Beetle, which played an integral part in murders that he committed and was instrumental to his conviction because of the DNA evidence it yielded. There are clown outfits that John Wayne Gacy used to wear when attending charity events, earning him the moniker 'The Killer Clown', as well as a range of his personal belongings. There are the handcuffs used to restrain Jeffrey Dahmer upon his arrest, and equipment seized from the Unabomber Ted Kacsynski that were used in creating the explosive devices he sent. There are art works by Charles Manson, items of jewellery made by Albert DeSalvo while in prison and Charles Manson's guitar. There are some personal artefacts from Bonnie and Clyde, and there is even the Bronco from the O.J. Simpson chase.

There is also a gift shop. A gift shop that is a dream for the crime enthusiast, with everything you could want (and a lot of things you did not know you wanted!), including books, kitchenware, toys, games and clothing. I started to laden myself with items: gifts for colleagues (with similar interests and inclinations to myself), things to use in activities with students and – for myself – a t-shirt with Ted Bundy on it. When I saw it, I thought that it would be something a bit different, and an interesting talking point. It was only as I was making my way over to the counter that I questioned whether this was a purchase that I actually wanted to make. Because – looking past the novelty value – is it really appropriate to wear a t-shirt embellished with a person who confessed to 30 murders, and likely killed many more? And more to the point, why would I want to?

A society obsessed with the torn and open wound and psyche

> [T]he serial killer makes a particularly appropriate (even emblematic) celebrity because both figures inspire feelings of attraction and repulsion, admiration and condemnation.
>
> Schmid (2005: 5)

Why are we fascinated by the macabre deeds of those who break the law and cause pain and suffering? Why do we turn criminals into celebrities? Why do we love serial killers? These are just some of the questions I asked myself as I made my way through the museum and still ponder to this day. As Seltzer (1997) discusses, over time, a culture has developed in which we are fascinated by violence – by 'torn and open bodies', as well as 'torn and open psyches'. He uses the term 'Wound Culture', which he describes as 'the convening of the public around scenes of violence … a collective gathering around shock, trauma, and the wound' (Seltzer, 1997: 3). Roy Hazelwood, a former FBI profiler, notes that lots of people are excited by violence, referring to the fact that when there is an automobile accident involving fatalities, many people stop – some to help, but most because they want to see the carnage.

Humans have a morbid curiosity regarding violent or tragic events, those that exceed the kinds of things that most of us are likely to encounter in our everyday lives. The lack of familiarity, and thus the novelty value, can be used to explain this, but when we consider serial killers, it's hard to understand how that curiosity manifests to the extent that they become celebrated figures. Many cite the media as playing a key role in what might be referred to as the 'celebritisation' of serial killers. A celebrity, as Daniel Boorstin (1962) notes, is 'a person who is known for his well knownness. … He is the human pseudo-event. … He is made by all of us who willingly read about him' (p 11). So too, as Bonn (2014) discusses, the public's curiosity about serial killers leads the news media to focus a tremendous amount of time and attention on them relative to other offenders. He refers to an old adage used by reporters: that 'if it bleeds, it leads'. It is this intense media spotlight, he argues, that elevates them to the realm of criminal rock stars (Bonn, 2014). Sokolowska (2019) too argues that the process of producing and reproducing accounts of serial murder contributes to the ever-growing popularity of those who perpetrate these acts (Sokolowska, 2019), although he notes that the reasons for such widespread fascination with people whose often singular talent in life is for murder are unclear (Sokolowska, 2019). Schmidt succinctly summarises such considerations, noting that: 'The famous serial killer combines the roles of monster and celebrity in a particularly economical and charged way, and this is why famous serial killers are such a visible part of the contemporary American cultural landscape' (Schmidt, 2005: 8).

In one of the most extensive explorations of these issues, Bonn (2014) proposes that this fascination is based – at least in part – on a need to understand why anyone would do such horrible things to other people, particularly complete strangers. He suggests that identifying the motivations of an unknown serial killer provides an exciting crime puzzle to solve for professionals and non-professionals alike. Moreover, he suggests that experiencing horror in a safe, controlled environment or setting is appealing and serves an important purpose for many people, with a fascination with serial killers being akin to a love of horror movies – being scared, which can be cathartic, in a setting with little risk of actual harm. He says that he believes that items such as serial killer trading cards allow the public to exercise its fears by getting close to the fire, so to speak, without getting burned. Statistically, this seems to be supported, with your chances of falling prey to a serial killer being very low. So too, there are relatively few cases with interest in and coverage far exceeding the reality of such offending (Kelly et al, 2022).

Public opinion polls show that the general public believes that serial killers are responsible for about 25 per cent of all murders in the US (Bonn, 2014). In actuality, the FBI estimates that serial murder accounts for less than 1 per cent of homicides committed in the US. With the annual homicide rate being around 15,000, this equates to fewer than 150 people killed by serial killers in the US each year (Horridge, 2018). Moreover, rates appear to be declining, possibly because of advances in investigative methods and techniques, including improved data collection and crime linking, as well as advances in forensic science. It might also be that societal changes have reduced potential victim pools, with people being more alert to dangers and less likely to put themselves in vulnerable positions, for example, not hitchhiking, notifying others of their whereabouts and so on (Cottier, 2020) – perhaps the only tangible benefit of public interest in the phenomenon. In contrast, and for the purpose of comparison, around 2,250 people are killed by abusive partners each year in the US – more than ten times as many as are killed by serial killers, with rates increasing year on year.

I came to realise very early on in my career that it would not consist of interviewing serial killers or staking out crime scenes, that instead it would involve working with large volumes of crime data, working with more common and prevalent crimes, and working with those involved with or affected by crime in a range of different capacities. Much of my work focuses on understanding crime with the aim of prevention, reducing risk and vulnerability to both crime perpetration and victimisation. In essence, studying serial killers, given their scarcity and the varied and often unique nature of this kind of offending, does not offer much regarding such endeavours. My work has more frequently focused on crimes such as domestic violence, those that are sadly far more common, and which more of us are likely to be personally affected by.

As part of my work, I have been privileged enough to work with some amazing organisations who support those affected by crime, including a charity called Support After Murder and Manslaughter (SAMM), which offers peer support to those bereaved as a result of murder and manslaughter. I cannot help but wonder what kind of a message it would convey to them, how they would feel, were I to turn up to one of our meetings wearing a t-shirt with Ted Bundy on it. Such considerations echo the following quote: 'Take a moment to imagine what the families of the victims feel when they realize the callous "murderabilia" being offered for sale came at the price of their loved one's life' (Dimond, 2014: x).

As Kelly et al (2022) discuss, the public's consumption of serial murder-related media comes at the expense of confronting and understanding the realities of such acts of physical violence, along with more systemic or structural forms of violence including the harms, crises, injustices and inequality created within the era of late capitalism. Not only are the complexities of violence and harm disavowed in the consumption of serial murder, but another consequence of this 'celebritisation' of the killer is the lack of consideration towards the victims. This includes not just direct victims, such as those murdered by a serial killer. It also includes the people left behind – their families and friends, who themselves face extensive and long-lasting repercussions (including – but certainly not limited to – negative impacts on their mental and physical health and financial hardship). They – and the victims themselves – are often forgotten, and all the while others are profiting from peddling their stories.

This fascination with serial murder at the expense of the victims can be traced back over 100 years. The sad fact is that almost everyone in the world has heard of Jack the Ripper, but very few could name any one of his victims. As Sokolowska (2019) discusses, the figure of Jack the Ripper can easily be found in hundreds of forms from over the past century – in books, and in graphic novels, such as Alan Moore's *From Hell*; in TV shows such as *Whitechapel* and *Ripper Street*, as well as many films of various titles; in video games; in board games; in multiple podcast discussions; and even as a wax figure. Mary Ann Nichols, Annie Chapman, Elizabeth Stride, Catherine Eddowes and Mary Jane Kelly were the unfortunate women who had their lives cut short by the Ripper. Many of those outlets listed do not even refer to them by name. A news article in 2021 detailed how customers had been boycotting a fish and chip restaurant that had recently opened in Greenwich for glorifying a serial killer. 'Jack the Chipper' is the second restaurant with this name opened by owner Recep Turhan; he never received any negative feedback with regards to the first outlet in Whitechapel (near where Jack the Ripper committed his crimes), but since opening up on the new premises he has received lots of negative posts and reviews on social media, and even been subject to verbal abuse from those who find the name distasteful and disrespectful. In a news interview Turhan defended the name, saying 'they were historical events. I wasn't celebrating what he did. It's a play on words' (Corbishley, 2021). Turhan faces a difficult dilemma. From a business point of view, it is a catchy name and a good gimmick (I can imagine it is a popular final destination for those doing a Jack the Ripper tour!). But arguably, it does, like the merchandise, games and products discussed previously, perpetuate the 'celebritisation' of serial killers. To counter some of the negative criticism, Jack the Chipper offers a 50 per cent discount to women, 'to show we're not here to be disrespectful or damaging in any sense'. Would this have appeased Annie Chapman's sister or Mary Jane Kelly's mother? Such considerations are perhaps best put by Sokolowska (2019), who stated that: 'It is hard to say which is more disturbing, the status of celebrity achieved by some murderers for often unspeakably violent crimes, and with that a vicious circle of remembering, or forgetting the victims as individuals' (Sokolowska, 2019: 115).

In making celebrities of serial killers, through sensationalisation and extensive promotion of their stories – including through the sale of 'murderabilia' – we lose sight of the victims, of the reality of the abhorrent crimes that have propelled them into the public arena. We should focus instead on remembering the victims, on ensuring their legacy. We should be celebrating those who protect us from crime, the bravery and dedication of those who ensure that those responsible are brought to justice, and the achievements of those whose work, methods and technological advances ensure that justice is delivered for the victims, families and all those who are affected by crime every day. So, if you choose to visit the Alcatraz East Crime Museum – and I would recommend to anybody that they do – focus on all the other, so much more important exhibits. The museum maps out the history of crime and law enforcement in America throughout the ages, and – as such – provides rich insights into a key element of what has made America the place that it is today.

There are exhibits on the Salem Witch trials, displays on the Wild West, with memorabilia from Wyatt Earp and the shootout at the O.K. Corral, Billy the Kid, Al Capone, Butch Cassidy and the Sundance Kid and Jesse James. There's a particularly interesting section looking at the Prohibition and the impacts of this on crime. There are exhibits exploring how law enforcement has changed over the years, which provide rich insights into the challenges faced by those working in such fields. There are numerous exhibits providing details of high-profile cases, including the assassination of JFK, the murder of Tupac Shakur and the abduction of Amber Hagerman (including explanation of the Amber alert system and how it is used); these provide rich examples of how cases influence subsequent policy and practice. And there is a Crime Scene Investigation lab, which charts the development of forensics, and explains how different methods work and are used in solving crimes. You can experience elements of the criminal justice yourself: see what it is like taking part in an undercover surveillance operation; see inside prison cells and what life might be like 'inside'; stand in the docks and experience what it is like to be in a courtroom or take part in a trial. Opportunities are provided for you to learn how to protect yourself from crime and how to prevent crime. For example, there are detailed exhibits exploring different types of cyber-crime and online scams, with case examples to help understand them better; examples of counterfeit goods and how to spot them; and exhibits on how to be alert to the dangers of fraud. Crucially, there are memorials and tributes to those who have lost their lives to crime throughout.

Conclusion

If – like me – you are fascinated by crime and criminality, if you want to know the why and how of it all, you'll find that this mapping out of the history of crime and law enforcement provides a much more nourishing and enriching experience than looking at random paraphernalia associated with serial killers. In the gift shop, maybe buy some interesting books on the history of law enforcement or kits to learn about forensic science techniques, instead of a t-shirt with a serial killer on it. Or donate the money you might have spent to a charity supporting victims of crime instead.

I didn't buy the t-shirt. No one needs a t-shirt with Ted Bundy on it.

7

The Museum of Death: Hollywood, Los Angeles, USA

Loukas Ntanos

Birmingham City University

Introduction

The Museum of Death that is located on Hollywood Boulevard in Hollywood was founded by J.D. Healy and Catherine Shultz in 1995. It features a wide range of artefacts primarily related to the subject of death, such as crime and morgue scene photos, body bags, coffins, suicide devices, autopsy films, car accident photos and skull collections. The museum is open seven days a week and admission costs $17. The self-guided tour lasts approximately an hour and is promoted as a means through which the public can be educated about death in the US. Along similar lines, there are no age restrictions based on the premise that death is a subject that affects us all. The endeavour was successful enough to underpin the foundation of a second Museum of Death, this time in New Orleans.

Homicide artefacts and souvenirs constitute the main selling point of the Museum of Death, as visitors seem to hold a very genuine interest in exploring those items that relate to notorious criminals and their crimes. Some indicative comments on Tripadvisor are as follows:

> [H]eard about this place by chance whilst in LA. A must see if you are into serial killers, gore, death etc.

> Some really awesome and shocking things on display. Reasonably priced to enter with cool souvenirs to buy. (Tripadvisor reviewer, 2019)
>
> It's well worth spending some time here, and it covers what every one of us will be subject to. Many aspects of ritual and ceremony surrounding peoples' demise are shown. One of the most explicit segments concerns autopsies and their developments over time. Criminal deaths are a main feature and there are fascinating accounts of the most notorious mass-murders. The Charles Manson killings are given a whole room of videos and posters, outlining in detail the horrific events and their investigation. (Tripadvisor reviewer, 2019)

The enduring public fascination with multiple homicide cases is undeniable. Specifically, among the most popular exhibits of the museum are *murderabilia* collectibles related to the case of Charles Manson, such as t-shirts, postcards, posters, letters and family photos. Murderabilia is a considerably broad term that is used to describe those items that relate to violent crimes which are sold online and in physical stores. Thereby, items created, owned or used by multiple homicide offenders fall within this domain (Jarvis, 2007). This chapter takes as its main focus the murderabilia industry and the ethical controversies surrounding it. It therefore aims to outline some of the key arguments for and against it. In doing so, it will shed some light on the embedded harms of the industry; harms that visitors of such sites as the Museum of Death would not usually consider or be aware of.

A response to murderabilia

The term murderabilia was first coined by victim advocate Andy Kahan and has predominantly been considered in terms of legality and morality (Lynes et al, 2021). The first discussions of the term date back to the 1970s and the crimes of serial homicide offender David Berkowitz, who was found responsible for killing six people between 1976 and 1977 in New York City. The case of Berkowitz had received considerable media attention and had therefore been deeply embedded in public consciousness. This effectively elevated Berkowitz into some sort of celebrity status. Consequently, soon after his arrest, Berkowitz was approached by producers and publishers who offered him money for his personal story (Bonn, 2014). The thought that a serial homicide offender would essentially be profiting from his crimes appalled the public. As a direct response to the outcry, legal frameworks were established for the first time in order to regulate murderabilia. These frameworks were named 'Son of Sam' after the serial killer moniker of Berkowitz (Mauro, 2012). According to these laws a criminal could not profit from expressive or creative works relating to their crimes, and any proceeds would be given as compensation to victims and their families (Loss, 1987). This marked the beginning of a debate that still remains today.

The Son of Sam laws were eventually found unconstitutional by the Supreme Court on the grounds of violating the First Amendment principle of free speech (Hurley, 2009). They were specifically found to be content-based as they regulated speech based on its content. This effectively meant that convicted criminals should not be deprived of their right to freedom of speech. They should be able to communicate their stories with no restrictions, and to engage in producing expressive works, such as writing books that draw upon their crimes, or sell their stories to producers and publishers who approach them (Bonn, 2014). Further to this, Son of Sam laws were found over-inclusive as they targeted the proceeds of any criminal who had been convicted of a crime, not just homicide offenders (Hurley, 2009). As a result, several states had to amend their Son of Sam laws accordingly.

Apart from legalistic arguments, supporters of the murderabilia industry argue that the sale and distribution of these macabre commodities can contribute to the sense making of criminal behaviour, as they are thought to be providing valuable insights that law enforcement officials and criminologists can draw upon (Kelly, 2000; Nelson and Prendergast, 2009). The overarching idea is that the examination of these items, especially expressive works of criminals such as books and personal letters, can facilitate an understanding of their personalities and motivations.

Further to this, it has been argued that convicted criminals should have the right to produce, publicly display and eventually profit from their art, as this can result in positive psychological changes, such as higher levels of confidence and self-esteem (Chang, 2005).

An exploration of ethical controversies

The idea that items can gain commercial value due to their link with violent crimes, usually homicide events, has sparked considerable debate among academics, legislators and criminal justice system workers (Schmid, 2004). Opponents of murderabilia tend to place considerable attention on the impact of murderabilia upon those affected by the crime it commemorates. Indirect victims of homicide, for instance, such as close family members and friends of the primary victim, are thought to be reliving their victimisation (Hobbs, 2000). This is uniquely harmful, as these individuals suffer from the killing of their loved one, but also from the way in which their loss essentially turns into a commodity (Hobbs, 2000; Chang, 2005; Nelson and Prendergast, 2009; Mauro, 2012). What is a tragic event for them is a morbid fascination for others. The psychological harm is devastating. However, this is merely the symptom of an underlying disease. The murderabilia market raises further questions as to whether free trade policies, prevalent in neoliberal, capitalist societies, encourage individualism and profiting even at the expense of others (Hall, 2012; Hall and Winlow, 2015). We therefore need to consider whether the mere existence of such a macabre industry simply reflects our value system, a system that prioritises wealth above suffering, competition above empathy. We also need to consider whether we have essentially become a society that celebrates death and gore (Jarvis, 2007). Finally, it has been argued that the way in which society embraces the murderabilia industry has further implications for the public image of the criminal justice system that is thought to be failing victims by allowing the commercialisation of crimes (Kelly, 2000). Recent academic assessments reinforce this, as family members of homicide victims feel that the criminal justice system lacks in empathy and compassion (Englebrecht et al, 2014).

Conclusion

Tourists are welcomed with open arms in such sites as the Museum of Death, where they are given the opportunity to explore and buy merchandise relating to their favourite serial killers. They subsequently leave the museum satisfied with their newly acquired souvenirs that serve as reminders of their visit, as well as an authentic link to homicide cases that shocked the public (Denham, 2016). The implications of this type of commodification need to be considered, however. For one, turning serial homicide offenders into celebrities leaves very little room for considering the victims of their crimes. The sensationalism that surrounds those cases has resulted in society celebrating offenders such as Charles Manson, leader of the Manson Family cult, and mastermind behind a series of murders which took place in California during the summer of 1969 (Mercer, 2017). Indeed, Manson is still remembered today. His crimes have withstood the test of time. The same cannot be said about his victims. These remain in the shadows of the larger-than-life, media-constructed celebrity figure who instructed their killings. In cases like this it is the victim rather than the offender who becomes *the other*. For as long as we continue to *other* them, we will see more being preyed upon, as we have enabled a context in which serial homicide offenders achieve everlasting fame and status. Maybe a small step to address this is by remembering the victims. In the case of Manson, these were Gary Hinman, Sharon Tate, Voytek Frykowski, Stephen Parent, Jay Sebring, Abigail Folger, Leno LeBianca, Rosemary LeBianca and Donald Shea.

8

The Royal Armouries Museum: Leeds, UK

Sarah Jones

Birmingham City University

Introduction

A place of historical violence, the Royal Armouries Museum offers an insight into the evolution of human warfare, boasting a diverse collection of arms, armour and artillery from around the world, dating from antiquity to the present day. The museum's live action combat demonstrations and historical re-enactments bring historical warfare into the realm of reality and convey the archaic ways of warfare and violence. The museum holds over 8,500 objects on display and includes royal armours of the Tudor and Stuart kings; arms and armour of the English Civil Wars; British and foreign military weapons from the Board of Ordnance and Ministry of Defence Pattern Room collections; hunting and sporting weapons, as well as a collection of Oriental arms and armour.

A less violent world?

This menagerie of small arms, defensive material and artillery, represented by the collection, highlights how violence and warfare, in their historical sense, were arguably a way of life and human nature. Narrating the history of violence in warfare, as the Royal Armouries Museum does, draws attention to the degree of, and as such our understanding of, violence in the contemporary world. Concepts surrounding violence and its transitionary state imply that there has been a shift in violence over the course of human history. Pinker (2011) contends that violence is in decline and has been for thousands of years and therefore, we may now be living in the most peaceable era in existence. This optimistic consideration sees that violence, and the subsequent decline of violent behaviour in the contemporary era, is due to society becoming more civilised and therefore less violent. Furthermore, this decline, according to Pinker, has been paralleled by a decline in attitudes that tolerate such violence (Pinker, 2011), yet this neglects to see that violence comes in diverse forms, other than solely physical. This is where violence, and the explanation for its decline, can be questioned.

Hall (2012), although not disputing this decline, asserts the notion that the decline in fatal and serious violence within society was not accompanied by a general decline in crime or driven by an improvement in social harmony. The impetus to this decline was, however, the transition to capitalism and the drive to strengthen the nascent market economy (Hall et al, 2015). As such, 'the primary purpose behind reducing and sublimating physical violence was not to establish a peaceful, sociable existence for society but to maintain a safer environment for the intensification and democratic expansion of aggressive yet rule-bound socio-symbolic competition' (Hall, 2014: 14). For Hall, therefore, the drivers of the decline in rates of fatal and serious violence lie in the dual economic function of the pseudo-pacification process (Hall, 2014; Ellis, 2019). The changing nature of violence over time is all too apparent when looked at through this lens.

When considering the ways in which violence is showcased by the Royal Armouries Museum and, as such, consumed by the public, Žižek's (2008) suggestion of subjective violence can be considered to help in our understanding of how we perceive violence. In the many displays of historical warfare and weaponry at the Royal Armouries Museum, violence is portrayed as being subjective, in that the violence depicted is direct and physical. Žižek posits that this type of violence can be constituted as crime, terror or civil unrest (Žižek, 2008). This subjective violence, therefore, is encapsulated in the historical narratives of warfare seen at the Royal Armouries Museum. With this in mind, we can question why we, as consumers, are drawn to venues that exhibit and depict violence and warfare such as the Royal Armouries Museum. What is it about violence that we gravitate towards?

The morbid fascination

'The unusual or the unique is interesting to people and thus to tourists, whether it is a natural phenomenon, an artistic or historical structure, or a spectacular event, it is just out of the ordinary and thus attractive to experience the unique as a satisfaction of human curiosity' (Hartmann, 2005: 7). Hodgkinson and Urquhart (2016) express that people have always had a somewhat morbid and voyeuristic fascination with the macabre and a desire to witness and vicariously experience violence, suffering and death. When exploring our fascination with violence and why we are drawn to it as consumers, it has been suggested that the public, as an audience, seek to be exposed to elements of the darkest side of humanity, such as violence, which has been sanitised for wider public consumption through the union of educational and entertainment strategies (Huey, 2011). The 'sublime in crime' (Burke, 1958) is presented to museum visitors, for example, in ways that intentionally merge the macabre with the educational. The nature of the sublime encounter and the stories told through culturally specific narratives have historically played a significant role in reducing individual and collective anxieties. What these forms of storytelling permit is a means of transmuting unmoored, generalised fears of unknown and unknowable threats into the horror, shock and revulsion provoked by a specific misdeed or malefactor. These affects are then morphed into pleasure (Huey, 2011). We can see that there is an interesting relationship between consumption and violence, one that seems to be somewhat normalised and disavowed, as too is the violence that is portrayed at places such as the Royal Armouries Museum.

Conclusion

From walking around the Royal Armouries Museum on any given day, you can quickly be taken aback by the amount of families and children on school trips pacing the halls and exhibits of the museum. Gore and violence has long been proven as a way to infuse enthusiasm and hunger for knowledge in young people, perhaps best exhibited by the series 'Horrible Histories'. This raises some questions, though. Is the violent warfare of the past so far distanced from contemporary Western culture that horrific instances of visceral violence are now a palatable day trip? Alternatively, is the guise of education a way in which we unwittingly fetishistically disavow the realities of warfare, violence and harm? In taking young children for a trip to see the jousting, machine guns and assorted tools of destruction, do we not further socially embed (Smith, 2016) the normality of violence and violence denial alongside consumer culture?

9

The Black Dahlia tour: Los Angeles, California, USA

David Wilson

Birmingham City University

Introduction

The City of Angels – the epicentre of where dreams are made in the form of Hollywood – has a long history in making stars in front of the silver screen. Countless individuals, fuelled by a desire for fame and nourished by the dazzling lights that call to them, promising fame and fortune, have ventured to Los Angeles. For a small lucky few, their hopes and dreams are realised – they join their idols in the pantheon of Hollywood legends, and may even etch their names into the very fabric of the city in the Hollywood hall of fame. When the lights fade, however, and the limousines disappear over the horizon, the perils of the pursuit of fame occasionally emerge and the darker underbelly shows. The murder of Elizabeth Short is arguably one of the earliest and most famous cases related to the perils of the pursuit of stardom. Her murder, still unsolved to this day, has sparked numerous books, film adaptations, conspiracy theories and, naturally, guided tours. There are numerous tours in which the murder of Short is included, but it is also important to note that tours generally cover a range of other high-profile murders including the Manson murders and the murder of actor Sal Mineo.

The murder of Elizabeth Short

> The woman was lying on her back with her arms raised over shoulders, and her legs were spread in a twisted display of seductiveness. There were cuts and abrasions across her body, and her mouth had been sliced to extend her smile from ear to ear.
>
> TheBlackDahlia.com (2018)

Elizabeth Short was born on 29 July 1924, in Boston, Massachusetts, the third of five daughters born to Cleo and Phoebe Mae Short. At a young age, Short developed a strong affinity for cinema and by her teens she had set her sights on becoming an actress. By the mid-1940s, Elizabeth Short was living in Los Angeles, California, working as a waitress to support herself while dreaming of catching her big break into Hollywood's acting scene. Her chance at stardom, however, would never come.

The morning of 15 January 1947 was a cold, dreary one for Los Angeles. Betty Bersinger, a local housewife, left her home on Norton Avenue in the Leimert Park section of the city. She was headed for a shoe repair shop and took her 3-year-old daughter with her. As the two of them walked up the street and approached the corner of Norton and 39th, they passed many vacant lots bordering the sidewalks. Development had slowed in the City of Angels due to the outbreak of the Second World War and because the war had ended only a year and a half prior, the city was still struggling to pick up the pace of construction.

While Betty walked along the sidewalk, she noticed something white among the weeds. As she glanced at the strange object, she understandably thought someone had disposed of a store mannequin. For Betty, it seemed like an unusual object to throw away, and stranger still, it appeared as though the mannequin had been separated into halves. Upon closer inspection, she realised that the mannequin was not a mannequin at all – it was actually a woman who had been cut in half. Betty gave a panicked scream and quickly rushed her daughter away from the ghastly crime scene. She quickly hurried to a nearby house to call the police.

Officers Frank Perkins and Will Fitzgerald arrived at the scene within minutes. When they noticed the naked body of a woman who had been cut in half, they were able to confirm Betty Bersinger's story and immediately called for backup. The police noted that the woman's body seemed to have been posed. Investigators also believed she had been tied down and tortured for several days due to the rope marks on her wrists, ankles and neck. Her naked body had been cleanly sliced in half, just above her waist. There was no blood present on the woman's body, and there was none on the grass beneath her either. Investigators determined that she must have been killed elsewhere, cleaned of blood and then dumped in the vacant lot overnight. Detective Lieutenant Jesse Haskins described the condition of the body when he first arrived at the crime scene:

> The body was lying with the head towards the north, the feet towards the south, the left leg was five inches west of the sidewalk. … The body was lying face up and the severed part was jogged over about ten inches, the upper half of the body from the lower half … there was a tire track right up against the curbing and there was what appeared to be a possible bloody heel mark in this tire mark; and on the curbing which is very low there was one spot of blood; and there was an empty paper cement sack lying in the driveway and it also had a spot of blood on it. … It had been brought there from some other location. … The body was clean and appeared to have been washed. (The Murder Squad, 2020)

The police soon discovered that the mutilated woman was none other than Elizabeth Short, the aspiring actress who instead of fame and fortune found only pain and death in the city of the stars. In a twisted irony, Short quickly rose to fame through the extensive media coverage of the ongoing investigation. *The Examiner* and the *Los Angeles Herald-Express* sensationalised the case, with one article from *The Examiner* describing the black tailored suit Short was last seen wearing as 'a tight skirt and a sheer blouse'. The media nicknamed her as the 'Black Dahlia' and described her as an 'adventuress' who 'prowled Hollywood Boulevard'. Through her untimely demise, Short had risen to national and even international attention. Similar to other unsolved murders, the mystery behind Short's death has fuelled the imaginations of news reporters, authors and screen writers alike. Arguably one of the most returned to topics of this macabre murder is that of her facial injuries – often referred to as a 'Glasgow smile'.

The Glasgow smile: a criminological overview

Made famous by Heath Ledger's Oscar-winning performance as the Joker in 2008's *The Dark Knight*, the Glasgow smile (also often referred to as a Glasgow grin, Anna grin, Chelsea grin or Chelsea smile) is a moniker for the result of cutting a victim's face from the edges of the mouth to the ears. The cut – and the scars it leaves behind – create an extension of what resembles a smile. Sometimes, to further hurt or even kill the victim, he or she would then be stabbed or kicked, most notably in the stomach so that the face would be ripped apart when the victim screamed. The practice originated in the Scottish city of Glasgow, which gave it its name. It also became popular in Chelsea, London and other areas of Britain, for gangs hoping to leave a message for rival gang members.

The history of the Glasgow smile can be traced back to the 19th century, where the city witnessed a surge in street-level violence with the rise of the notorious Penny Mobs (Davies, 2013). By the 1930s, the unprecedented levels of violence and physical assaults between rival gangs caused the city to be dubbed the 'Scottish Chicago' (Davies, 2007), with stories of men's faces being mutilated with cut-throat razors gaining international attention. This less-than-flattering comparison with one of North America's most dangerous cities did little to quell the violence and, by the 1990s, the United Nations declared that Scotland had the sixth fastest-rising murder rate anywhere in the world (Seenan, 2005). Most of the 109 homicides recorded in 2006 took place in the west of Scotland, with Glasgow emerging as the most violent city in Western Europe with a murder rate of five deaths per 100,000, up from 4.49 the previous year (this is even more startling when we consider that the average homicide in England is approximately 0.6 per 100,000).

According to Strathclyde Police, doctors in Accident and Emergency departments across the Glasgow area deal with around

300 attempted murders a year and a serious facial injury, including the potentially life-threatening Glasgow smile, every six hours. Most of the assaults are gang-related, with alcohol and drugs being major factors (Briggs, 2011). Much of the violence takes place at the weekends in bleak housing projects and city parks, or even sometimes in the city centre, where gangs battle each other with knives, machetes, swords and iron bars.

Over time, the Scottish authorities introduced increasingly more punitive measures to control the chaos, but most initiatives only worked in the short term. Tougher sentences were introduced, but these only created vacuums for younger gang members to step into (Kirkhope, 2006). Issues surrounding austerity and a lack of legitimate opportunities that may see such members turn away from a life of crime were rarely, if ever, addressed. In recent years, Karyn McLuskey, head of Strathclyde's Violence Reduction Unit, spearheaded a Violence Reduction Scheme and nearly 500 gang members from eastern Glasgow engaged with it. Violent offending has fallen by 46 per cent, gang fighting is down by 73 per cent and weapon possession, including razors sometimes, has dropped by 85 per cent. Glasgow is no longer the murder capital of Western Europe but the 'booze and blades' epitaph has proven difficult to shift. Visitors should still be wary in certain parts of Glasgow, a place where there are more scarred faces than anywhere else in Britain.

While Glasgow may have witnessed a reduction in gang violence, the theme of mutilating rival gang members has since seen a surge in other parts of the world. For example, Central American gangs such as the 18th Streets and Maras, as well as Mexico's Los Zetas, are known for their extreme mutilation of rival gang members in order to intimidate and scare others and maintain their respect and dominance in the region. While it may not appear – at least on the surface – as being as severe, the central motivation of maintaining respect in the eyes of others and creating fear in the hearts of rivals can be traced back to the Glasgow smile. Hall (2002) argues that interpersonal violence is related to a crisis in the traditional capitalist order where the separation between criminality and legality are blurred, and where hyper-masculinity is deeply embedded and pointless hostility rages on the margins of neo-capitalism. In particular, the injuries of class, which consist of shaming and self-doubt, 'set the scene for contests for dignity' (cited in Ray, 2011: 95). With reference to this notion of dignity, the mutilation of others – including the Glasgow smile – is instrumental violence intended to steal another's perceived dignity in order to bolster and reconcile one's own.

Conclusion

As we have already witnessed with the murder and mutilation of Elizabeth Short, the use of the Glasgow smile has transcended its gang origins and has since been used by individuals with no gang affiliations. For instance, most recently, 30-year-old Andrew Clewes, who owned a barber shop, attacked and attempted to give a Glasgow smile to a woman he had never met before over an argument concerning money (Murphy, 2017). While the use of the Glasgow smile has been mainly associated with gangs, this recent case, along with the mutilation of Elizabeth Short, demonstrates that such facial trauma is designed to humiliate, dehumanise, strike fear and demonstrate power and control over others. With reference to the previously highlighted examples, it is evident that the Glasgow smile is worthy of further criminological examination.

10

The 'Execution Dock': Wapping, East London, UK

Wendy Laverick and Peter Joyce

University of Hull and Glyndŵr University

Introduction

This chapter focuses on the crime of piracy and how the state responded to this problem in the 18th century and early years of the 19th century. So too, it will be discussed how such a problem has been commodified and transformed into a dark tourist destination in the City of London, England.

The golden age of piracy

Piracy entails the theft of goods being transported on the water: robbery on the high seas. The ship carrying the goods might also be captured and subsequently used by the pirates. Piracy was not unique to the 18th century and had previously been directed at Greek and Roman shipping. It still exists today in some parts of the world. However, what has long been termed 'the golden age' of piracy (Fiske, 1897: 338) spanned the mid-17th and early 18th centuries, in the period approximately 1650–1720. In this period, several thousand pirates operated although their activity was not constant. Several waves of piracy occurred, the last of which was around 1700–1730, with a peak in the early 1720s.

The period 1713–1715 is an important one in the history of piracy since a series of peace treaties under the overall heading of the Peace of Utrecht ended the hostilities associated with the War of the Spanish Succession (1701–1714) in which the UK and France had used privateers in the naval war conducted against each other. Privateers were similar to pirates but were sponsored by the state to attack vessels belonging to other countries, the official authorisation being a certificate known as a 'Letter of Marque'.

In the post-Spanish Succession period after 1715, many of those involved in privateering had to become 'self-employed' in the form of pirates who were the enemies of all established governments. This development affected England more than other European countries, resulting in it being referred to as a 'nation of pirates' (Burgess, 2009: 894).

Some of the pirates who were active in the final wave of the golden age are well-known historical figures. They include William 'Captain' Kidd (1645–1701), John Rackham (usually known as 'Calico Jack') (1682–1820) and Edward Teach (otherwise known as Blackbeard) (1680–1718). The pirate regarded as the most successful was Bartholomew Roberts (known to history as 'Black Bart') (1682–1722) who looted more than 400 vessels. Piracy was not confined to men, and women pirates included Mary Read (1690–1721) and Anne Bonney (born 1698 and who disappeared from history around 1721).

Pirates in the 'golden age' were active throughout the world, but especially in the Caribbean, the Atlantic (East) Coast (where the UK colonies in America were located), the West Coast of Africa, the Indian Ocean (targeting the trade routes from India to the US via Africa) and the South China Seas. The targets of the pirates were ships conveying goods that included gold, silver, sugar and cocoa back to Europe. Pirates were frequently associated with smugglers who would sell the goods that had been plundered or sometimes they engaged in the smuggling trade themselves.

Execution Dock: location

There are few venues more iconic than the Tower of London which attracts Londoners and tourists alike who come to view this spectacle of the late Victorian age. Boat trips upriver are especially popular, passing under Tower Bridge and heading for places such as Woolwich, Greenwich and ultimately to the mouth of the river, the Thames/Essex Strait.

As visitors head upriver from Tower Bridge, they are passing through places steeped in crime and criminal justice history. The left shore of the River Thames (as the visitor proceeds upriver) houses the place which is the focus of this chapter.

Execution Dock: a dark destination

Since 1536, persons accused of piracy and other maritime crimes would be tried by the Admiralty Sessions, part of the High Court of Admiralty, which was convened at the Old Bailey. If found guilty, they would be condemned to death, the execution taking place at low tide on the Thames foreshore in the area of Wapping, East London, known as Execution Dock.

The method of execution was hanging and, in common with other executions of this nature (until 1783 when the 'new drop' was introduced), the condemned person with a noose around their necks would either climb a ladder which was then pulled away (or in some cases the prisoner was pushed off by the executioner) or be placed on a cart which was removed, having first made a final 'dying' speech.

In many cases involving pirates, a short rope was used which served to prolong the condemned person's misery. They would die of asphyxiation and in their death throes would provide onlookers with the gruesome spectacle of spasms that appeared to onlookers as a kind of airborne dance (which was referred to as the [Admiralty] marshall's dance). It has been described as 'the involuntary thrashing of limbs that occurs during hangings. … They swing, their tongues protruding and their eyes bulging – staring but unseeing' (Darby, 2014). However, there is some dispute regarding the intentional or consistent use of this means of death for pirates (Ruggeri, 2016).

The dock's precise location is not known. There are several contenders for this site's location, all in fairly close proximity, three of which are public houses – the Captain Kidd, the Town of Ramsgate (where a small passageway on the western side of the public house opens onto the Wapping Old Stairs which convey the visitor onto the bank of the River Thames) and the Prospect of Whitby, where a set of steps, Pelican Stairs, to the left of the establishment lead onto the Thames' foreshore. Another possible site of Execution Dock is the Sun Wharf Building on Narrow Street, Limehouse, which has a large E painted on its side. Alternatively, old maps suggest that the location is at King Henry's Stairs, a name that replaced Execution Dock Stairs in the early 19th century (A London Inheritance, 2020) and which is close to the Captain Kidd.

Following death, the body was either left on the noose or was cut down and chained to a post on the foreshore. In either case, it would remain until covered by three Thames' tides. In cases involving more infamous pirates, the body would subsequently be placed in an iron cage known as a gibbet (a harness made of iron hoops and chains designed to hold the head, body and legs in place) and hung somewhere along the Thames where it would remain on public display to deter seafarers from committing maritime crime. Bodies that had been gibbeted were usually covered with tar, to stop birds pecking at the flesh.

If not gibbeted, the 1752 Murder Act made provision for the corpse to be available for medical dissection either to the Royal College of Physicians or to the Company of Barber-Surgeons. The intention of the legislation was to intensify the terror associated with the death sentence (Linebaugh, 2011: 77).

The Royal College of Physicians ceased to use the corpses of executed felons by the 1730s, and the Barber-Surgeons were thus the main beneficiary of the 1752 legislation. Bodies were taken to the Barber-Surgeon's Hall, commonly accompanied by a large procession of people. Prior to the procedures of dissection and anatomisation (which limited numbers of people were allowed to view from the building's gallery), the body was placed on public display. The Barber-Surgeons were (and still remain) one of the City of London's Livery Companies and their building (which is not the original although it stands on the same site as the first building that was erected in the mid-15th century) is located at Monkwell Square, Wood Street, London.

The route to Execution Dock

The conveyance of a condemned pirate to Execution Dock evidenced the main purpose of punishment in the late 18th century as deterrence. This required the event to receive as much publicity as was possible and in an age without mass circulation newspapers or other forms of modern media, a procession was the chief way to achieve this penological purpose.

Prisoners who were to be hung at Execution Dock were generally held at Marshalsea Prison (although Newgate Prison was sometimes used). Marshalsea no longer exists, although remnants of it (and a plaque to commemorate it) can still be found in Borough Road in Southwark. The one remaining wall of the prison can be viewed on the north side of St George the Martyr's Church.

Prisoners were conveyed to Execution Dock in a horse-drawn carriage in a procession led by the Admiralty Marshall (or one of his deputies) who carried the Admiralty Court's ceremonial silver oar which was also on display during court hearings. The route would take them across London Bridge, past the Tower of London and thence to Execution Dock.

As it progressed, the procession would pass by a public house called the Turk's Head Inn which was located in Wapping High Street. This was the designated place where condemned persons would customarily receive their last drink of alcohol (a quart of ale) before their execution. This public house was destroyed in the London Blitz in 1940 and was relocated to Green Bank, Tower Hamlets, where it served as a community café and is now a French-Anglo bistro, La Tète de Turc. It can be accessed from Wapping overground station via Scandrett Street which stands between the Town of Ramsgate and Wapping Police Station.

This route was taken by many condemned pirates, one of the best known being Captain William Kidd who was executed there in 1701. In Kidd's case, the rope used to hang him snapped. Although custom and practice used in this period might view this as God stepping in to protect an innocent man who should therefore be allowed to go free, this did not happen in this instance. A new rope was fetched and Kidd was executed. His body was then gibbeted on the Thames foreshore at Tilbury Point where it remained for three years.

Today, the various sites competing for being the dark destination of Execution Dock can best be reached from Wapping overground station. As the visitor faces the River Thames, the

Captain Kidd and then the Town of Ramsgate are to the right in Wapping High Street and the Prospect of Whitby and Old Sun Wharf Building are to the left in Wapping Wall and Narrow Street, Limehouse respectively.

Conclusion

The 'golden age' of piracy ended in the decade 1720–1730, mainly because of the scale of crackdowns by states. This arose from international treaties which resulted in 'a systematic and adequate policing of the seas' (Barbour, 1911: 566) whereby governments used warships and executions to eliminate pirates. Many were killed in battle or were captured and executed at sea. Similarly, methods of punishment also underwent significant changes during the 19th century.

In an era in which policing was based on underpinnings constructed in medieval Britain (the parish constable system), it was hard to prevent crime. Thus, the main 18th-century response to crime was to deter its commission by scaring people through making the gruesome consequences of criminal acts as public as possible. But the 19th century witnessed a move away from capital punishment. The last executions for piracy at Execution Dock took place in 1830 when George James Davies and William Watts were executed for the part they had played in a mutiny (and related subsequent events) on the *Cyprus* in 1829, which was transporting criminals to Tasmania. In 1832, the procedure whereby the body of an executed person could be made available for medical dissection ended and in 1834 gibbeting ceased. In this year, the jurisdiction of the Admiralty Sessions (which had commenced in 1536) also ended.

11

Auschwitz: Oświęcim, Poland

Tammy Ayres and Sarah Hodgkinson

University of Leicester

Introduction

Tourism is central to contemporary society and our pursuit of leisure, pleasure and relaxation, which includes dark sites. Sites of human suffering and death as former atrocities have always been of great public interest as visitors seek to learn about and vicariously experience some of the darkest periods in history. The rising interest in dark tourism in recent years has led to a critical reanalysis of visits to sites associated with the Holocaust, or 'Holocaust tourism' (for example, Hodgkinson, 2013; Podoshen, 2017; Wright, 2020). Former National Socialist concentration camps and 'death camps' have been open to the public since the opening of the Auschwitz-Birkenau Memorial and Museum in 1947. Any form of Holocaust representation is subject to controversy, and the reconstruction and commodification of these sites have always been contentious (Cole, 2000; Benton, 2010). Despite moral concerns about the voyeuristic motivations of visitors, and the damage tourism can have on both the sites themselves and the reconstruction of the past (Ashworth and Hartmann, 2005), continued public access to these spaces is vital for the historical preservation of the sites, and educating future generations about the Holocaust (Reynolds, 2018).

A hauntological account of the Holocaust

Over 75 years after the liberation of these sites, we face a crisis in Holocaust remembrance as so few survivors now remain to bear direct witness to these atrocities (Marshman, 2005; Hodgkinson, 2015). The tourist can therefore represent a significant 'tertiary witness' (Seedman, 2006) to ensure we never forget. While tourism and the increasing commodification of sites for public consumption can potentially cause sanitisation, simplification and manipulation of historical discourse, it is also necessary if we are to remember and continue to be haunted by, and learn from, past atrocities. In the following chapter, we draw upon hauntology (Derrida, 1994; Gordon, 1997), specifically Fiddler's (2019) spatio-hauntology, to examine a range of Holocaust sites located across Germany, Austria and Poland, visited by the authors in their research on Holocaust tourism.

The concept of Holocaust tourism falls under the wider banner of 'dark tourism' which was first coined by Lennon and Foley (2001) to describe the growing interest in visiting sites of death and disaster. Therefore, dark tourism is broad in scope and research has covered a vast range of 'dark' destinations, but Stone (2006) considers visits to 'dark camps of genocide' as the most 'authentic' and 'darkest' form. 'Authentic' as they are in situ sites located at the actual places of mass death and suffering, and 'darkest' as they are most often oriented towards a serious and sombre educational representation of death on an unprecedented scale. As such, sites like Auschwitz-Birkenau and Mauthausen constitute spaces in distress. Whether it is the pile of shoes, glasses and suitcases of those murdered there or the bullet holes left in Auschwitz's Death Wall by the firing squads, to the gas chambers themselves, trauma and human suffering lingers and haunts these dark destinations. Spaces that are filled with a foreboding sense of death, suffering and human misery. Spatial crypts, which contain phantoms of the past (Fiddler, 2019). Of those who died. Horrific spaces haunted by the horrors of humanity. Yet such spaces represent the banality of evil (Arendt, 1963) as violence and cruelty are an integral component of contemporary capitalism and its civilised human existence (Žižek, 2008). As outlined by Bauman (1989: 8), the 'truth is that every "ingredient" of the

Holocaust – all those many things that rendered it possible – was normal'. It is in this context that Holocaust tourism must be viewed, as throughout history, capitalism, according to Arendt (1963: 134), has implemented these 'administrative massacres' as a standardised form of behaviour. Nonetheless, tourism centred on sites of genocide is inherently controversial, and the morality of reconstructing such spaces for tourist consumption has been frequently debated and berated.

Holocaust tourism is arguably the most contested form of dark tourism, despite the long history of visits to such sites. Auschwitz-Birkenau was opened to the public just two years after its liberation from Nazi forces, quickly becoming a destination for those with a personal connection to the sites (that is, survivors and their families) and those with more of a general interest. Although a niche tourist experience until the sites became more accessible, the opening of these former concentration camps and death camps of the National Socialist regime has always been a 'grey' moral area. As early as 1948, there were calls to close and demolish Auschwitz, as well as frequent debates about which victims were to be remembered and how the site was to be presented (Benton, 2010). Similar debates and controversies surround many other Holocaust sites. Dachau (located just outside Munich in Germany), established as the 'model' German concentration camp in 1933, has always tended to distance itself from the Holocaust, downplaying its Jewish victims and emphasising its role as a camp for political prisoners (see Marcuse, 2008; Hodgkinson, 2013).

As the sites of mass suffering and death, former Nazi concentration camps are undoubtedly one of the 'darkest destinations' which have become increasingly accessible and marketable to the general public. They have become an accepted part of the mainstream tourist itinerary due to growing supply and demand (Lennon, 2010). The scale and nature of the atrocities committed in such places, and in particular the orchestrated killing of millions of people within these camps during the Second World War, give these sites a dark and compelling fascination for visitors. It is important, however, to recognise that people visit such sites for a range of often complex and multifaceted motivations – not all of these motivations are 'dark' or superficial (Biran et al, 2011) – which to date has not been well researched.

Figure 11.1: Tourists entering Auschwitz-Birkenau

Source: Photo by Tammy Ayres

Tourists, whatever their initial motivations, are drawn to certain aspects of these sites, the 'darkest' and most 'authentic' spaces and 'dark artefacts' that resonate most strongly with the extent and nature of the suffering experienced in these camps. As illustrated in Figure 11.1, these places see much larger traffic of tourists with queues outside, the taking of photos and even 'selfies', and many visitors wanting to touch the surfaces or linger for longer to take in the in situ places of death. This may initially seem macabre and in some cases distasteful and disrespectful but is arguably important in terms of the need for visitors to bear witness and have an emotional reaction to our darkest historical events. Here, visitors come face to face with the ghosts of the past as the past lingers and haunts these dark sites (Gordon, 1997). Crypts built by violence (Derrida, 1994). A 'collective burial ground' that facilitates a 'collective mourning' and reparation as visitors experience a haunting transmission of trauma (Schwab, 2010: 22). In fact, the transgenerational transmission of trauma from one generation to the next is well documented in the Holocaust literature (Hirsch,

2004). Despite attempts to preserve the authenticity of these sites, however, their conservation, and in some cases, reconstruction, has been subject to much controversy.

The authenticity of these sites has been questioned as many sites have been extensively reconstructed. This 'staged authenticity' (MacCannell, 1973) may aid visitors in getting a more tangible sense of the functioning camps but ultimately implies an authenticity that is not there, often presenting a sanitised and unrealistic representation far removed from the horrific conditions of the wartime camps. This sanitisation can risk an anesthetisation to the historical realities, and often visitors are unaware of the extent of reconstruction, especially since the representation and memorialisation of the Holocaust varies globally, which has led to the Holocaust becoming 'dispersed and fractured through the different ways of memoralizing it' (Huyssen, 1995: 30). Instead, these sites produce 'the effect of truth independently of its own literal truth' (Žižek, 2002: 1), acting as 'theatres of memories', recollections that haunt the living and are articulated to create collective memories of the Holocaust (Huyssen, 1995: 256); a 'cobweb of semblances which constitutes our reality' (Žižek 2002: 12).

Dachau memorial site feels almost too pretty and 'clean' to resonate as a site of such suffering and persecution, with its sanitised and simplified representation of the Holocaust (Marcuse, 2005; 2008). Pretty tree-lined roads lead to reconstructed camp buildings and memorials. The gatehouse is spotless, the pathways tidy and pristine. There is a beautiful café at the entrance to the camp. This sanitised reconstruction of the site recalls the use of the camp in the early 1930s as Nazi propaganda, as visitors were taken around this 'model' camp as an example of the good conditions prisoners were kept in. But it somewhat distorts the reality of the later camp and the appalling conditions, suffering and deaths of those encamped there towards the end of the war. Such camp memorial sites can be quite heavily controlled and highly politicised, actively discouraging more complex and pluralistic interpretations (Morrison, 2010). Rather than evoking strong emotional responses to atrocity, overly sanitised and unidimensional representations can desensitise us to the level of human suffering (Cohen, 2001).

Subsequently, some critics argue that sites of the Holocaust should not be preserved, rebuilt and restored, but left to fall into disrepair (van Pelt, 2003). At Auschwitz-Birkenau memorial site, this balance is maintained by reconstructing Auschwitz I with its guided tours, and leaving Auschwitz II in a more unreconstructed state with the visitor left to navigate the site unguided (see Dalton, 2009). In Auschwitz II the residential barracks (sheds) that housed the millions of human bodies reduced to bare life (Agamben, 1995) are strewn around a desolate expanse. Inside what looks like cattle sheds, stacked on wooden shelves – called *buks*, designed to accommodate four people – over 700 people would have resided in each block, which had no toilets, no electricity and only two small iron stoves that provided inadequate heat. Visiting in the middle of winter, it is difficult to describe just how cold these buildings were or how suffocatingly small each *buk* actually was. What is evident is these are haunted spaces. Spatial crypts full of trauma and suffering that have shaped the collective imaginaries of the Holocaust.

While it is generally recognised that former concentration camps should be made available to the public – as both a site of learning and remembrance – site managers are faced with difficult choices in terms of balancing the need to preserve the site for educative and memorial use, while facing commercial pressures that often result from commodification and the demands made by the tourists themselves for their creature comforts. The main visitor entrance to Auschwitz-Birkenau could be the visitor centre for any tourist attraction, and Dachau can feel much like a public park. Mauthausen feels sparser, and more uncommercialised than some of the other sites. It feels bleak and somewhat desolate, and the buildings are left bare and in disrepair. While they charge admission and have a small educational gift shop, and basic café, it felt more utilitarian than those at Dachau, for example. We felt it struck a sensitive balance between remembrance, education and tourism. It has an extensive memorial park, and due to the international composition of those who were imprisoned and died within the camp, it is careful to represent all victim groups with individual monuments to different nationalities, ethnicities, religions and identities. Historically, controversy has always surrounded which victims are represented at such destinations – such as whether one victim group's story is foregrounded over a more complex and inclusive history (Benton, 2010).

In the past, camp memorial sites have been used for political leverage, or dealt with contested memories of the past, and it is no different in the present. Remembrance is inherently difficult in many of the countries affected by the Holocaust, and arguably most difficult in those countries that bear some of the burden of responsibility and where history may be most dissonant (Hodgkinson, 2013). The representations can reflect the national identities or political leanings of the country in which they are located. For example, even today, Sachsenhausen (located in former East Berlin) feels very different to other sites, as the remnants of the Soviet camp remain along with statues reminiscent of post-war Soviet propaganda. Auschwitz, originally as a camp dedicated to Polish victims of National Socialist atrocities, was later repackaged to become a universal symbol of the Nazi destruction of the Jews. While the educational and memorial functions of the sites can help in the forging of national identities, critics argue that the politicisation of sites can potentially create a heritage dissonance (Tunbridge and Ashworth, 1996; Wright, 2020).

Further to debates about the reconstruction of the sites themselves, opening them up as tourist destinations does have some inevitable unintended consequences. The enormous public interest in the Holocaust, and the accessibility of the sites as mainstream tourist attractions, can result in large numbers of visitors, which may hinder the sombre and emotional experience some visitors anticipate (Hodgkinson, 2013). Often there are many large school parties and we witnessed unsupervised teenagers at some sites dislodging memorial pebbles, climbing on memorials and behaving disrespectfully. Furthermore, some of the sites tend to be used as more general recreational spaces (for example, Dachau), which can create a strange juxtaposition between the 'dark' past of the site and its reuse in post-modernity. While this is relatively innocuous, visitors often witness disrespectful behaviour, littering, vandalism and the stealing of artefacts. Such behaviours illustrate the selfish hyper-individualisation and moral relativism characteristic of contemporary neoliberal society and human subjectivity, which overrides the collective good and which does not consider the experiences of others. At Mauthausen, the shower heads were stolen by tourists as 'mementos' of their visit; now none remain, and tourists are no longer allowed in the gas chambers or to touch any of the artefacts (such as the crematoria ovens). Auschwitz in 2009 saw the theft of its infamous gates (bearing the Nazi slogan *Arbeit Macht Frei*), illustrating that this ethical stance, as Smith (2019: 313) highlights, has led to 'increasingly extreme and destructive leisure-scapes in which the individual should be free from any authority trying to impose upon [their] individual needs and desires'. Many sites have also been the target of anti-Semitic damage, illustrating the highly contested and politicised nature of these dark spaces.

Conclusion

To conclude, Holocaust tourism sites as dark sites of death are also sites of consumerism and leisure acting as 'spatial crypts' (Fiddler, 2019: 474) haunted by the 'ghosts of past violence' (Linnemann, 2015: 517). Death, specifically the death of the 'Other', has been commodified, packaged up and sold back to us as entertainment, leisure and tourism under the guise of education and historical preservation where the tourist may have a vital role to play as a tertiary witness. People, however, visit these sites with complex and often ambivalent motivations, which is often reflected in their behaviour. Some exhibit emotional and somatic responses, while others take selfies and steal artefacts to fulfil their desire for a memento of the occasion, evidence of their authentic experience of the Holocaust, as authentic experience matters in contemporary consumer society (Žižek, 2014), although these experiences are anything but. Instead, the representation of these sites, which often involves a 'repackaging' of the Holocaust for mass tourist consumption, results in a 'staged authenticity' (MacCannell, 1973) characteristic of contemporary society, which is a society of the spectacle, dominated by hyperreality where imagery, aesthetics and symbolism dominate (Debord, 1994; Baudrillard, 2000). In this context, Holocaust tourism illustrates what Žižek (2002: 9) calls the 'passion for the Real'. Consequently, tourists experience these dark sites of death 'as a nightmarish apparition' while the reality is disavowed (Žižek, 2002: 19). There is no denying that the Holocaust was abhorrent and should never be repeated, but it is certainly not unique, nor is it an aberration of Western civilised values or unlikely to ever happen again. Such suppositions merely ignore the millions who have died and who will continue to die as part of capitalist globalisation and its inherent violence (Žižek, 2008). Something routinely disavowed in this era of capital realism (Fisher, 2009).

12

Jeju 4:3 memorial: Jeju Island, South Korea

Robin West

London Metropolitan University

Introduction

For many today, the mention of things 'Korean' invites attention to the global popularity of South Korean culture, from K-pop to kimchi, or the almost atavistic survival of Kim Jong Un's North Korean communist autarchy. However, the neat division in the public imagination of the bipolar political systems and distinct cultural values that coexist on the Korean peninsula perhaps eclipses the dark and complex reality of a divided nation and its people's attempts to come to terms with the past. This chapter addresses Korea's difficult past and how it has become the object of the dark tourist's gaze. Following an overview of dark tourism in South Korea, it centres on approaches to victims of state crime through the case of the memorialisation of the 1947 Jeju 4:3 massacre of insurgents and civilians, an atrocity that occurred in the run-up to the Korean War. Long suppressed by successive regimes, with its mention in public discourse criminalised until comparatively recently, accounts of the 4:3 'incident' shed light on the criminal excesses of South Korea's post-colonial authoritarian rule and the impact of ideological conflict on a civilian population. However, with memorials to the massacre's victims now included on tourist circuits, how can embracing the concept of dark tourism play a role in overcoming long-standing historical injustice and restoring honour to victims as visits to the dark past and victim advocacy are combined?

Dark tourism in South Korea

The 1950–1953 Korean War that transformed a de facto partition into enduring separation saw not only the destruction of the country's infrastructure and cities, but the decimation of a population already split along mounting ideological lines. Catastrophically, the war broke out five years after Korea's liberation from brutal Japanese colonial rule and was in part its consequence following the latter's Second World War defeat, but now global forces aligned to economic liberalism faced off those of the socialist 'People's Armies'. It has been suggested, then, that the Cold War struggle between capitalism and communism became fully visible on Korean territory on the back of a predetermined civil war (Cumings, 2011) and remains played out politically and symbolically along the 38th Parallel, the boundary intended to temporarily demarcate the two Koreas on the signing of an armistice halting the fighting but not formally ending the war. Nearly 70 years on, in the spring and summer months, coachloads of tourists join the numerous licensed tour operators (signing a waiver absolving South Korea, the UN and the US from responsibility in the event of unanticipated complications) heading for the Demilitarized Zone (DMZ) and Panmunjŏm's iconic Joint Security Area. Here, they supposedly experience the tension and suppressed aggression of one of the most volatile borders in Asia, if not the world. Besides buying souvenirs ranging from baseball caps to North Korean banknotes, tourists gaze through telescopes into the seemingly isolated world of the Democratic People's Republic of Korea, perhaps never fully aware of the impact of the past 70 years on all Koreans' lives in terms of familial separation and ruptured national identity. Even before the 2019 Panmunjŏm summit between Donald Trump and Kim Jong Un amid mounting threats of nuclear confrontation, the DMZ tour had long been one of the 'not-to-be-missed' attractions on Seoul's sightseeing itinerary with tour guides providing a not entirely objective commentary on the causes and consequences of national division.

The DMZ tour is probably the more conspicuous example of dark tourism in South Korea today with its spectacle of national catastrophe and connotations of shared grief (Frew and White, 2016), but one that nevertheless suggests a performance catering more to the voyeurism of the international tourist gaze, particularly as resident Korean citizens are not permitted on tours. Yet, as the opening paragraphs suggest, Korea has a traumatic history beyond civil war and national division stretching from its 35-year colonial subjection under the Japanese through to the authoritarian grip on the South's population by successive right-wing juntas between 1948 and 1987. The modern South Korean state has consequently been built largely on the twin pillars of anti-communist sentiment and economic miracle with the added measure of post-colonial identity reconstruction. But the process of modernisation and the eventual establishing of a viable democracy in the late 1980s had become inseparable from the unforgiving demands of rapid industrial development and security in the face of the threat from the North. These were frequently countered by student and labour protests that coalesced into a strong democratic movement challenging the draconian policies and repressions of military dictatorship. In turn, the state responded with violence. Under the often rogue operations of the Korean Central Intelligence Agency (KCIA), a 'trip to Namsan', the Agency's Seoul headquarters, inevitably implied torture if not disappearance (Cumings, 2005). The most notorious suppressing of South Korea's democratic movement was the state's response to the 1980 Kwangju Uprising, resulting in an estimated 2,000 of the city's population killed and some 3,000 wounded in a massacre by South Korean troops. Framed by the government as a 'communist-agitated incident' (Shin, 2003), Kwangju citizens protesting the imposing of martial law and calling for the recognition of their human rights armed themselves as elite forces were deployed to the city. The army's brutal repression of fellow citizens nevertheless contributed to the collapse of military rule and eventual democratic elections.

Since the 1990s, as democracy reshaped South Korean society, efforts were made to reaffirm national identity in part through the state-sanctioned memorialisation of victims of Japan's colonial oppression and by coming to terms with the legacies of the authoritarian persecutions and atrocities, to varying degrees and not without contestation. Sites such as Seoul's Seodaemun Prison, once the redbrick manifestation of Japanese formal control, were refashioned as places of national, yet difficult, heritage. Today, visitors view reconstructions of torture and, as in many contemporary memorials to oppression, walls bearing the faces of independence heroes executed by the Japanese. The extensive grounds of the May 18th National Cemetery at Kwangju opened in 1997 with emotionally charged exhibits uncompromisingly depicting the atrocities of 1980 while classing the perpetrators of the authoritarian regime as criminals. These sites of former atrocities now appear in the popular tourist guides to the country alongside suggestions for eating and entertainment. In 2017, Seoul Metropolitan Government announced a 'Human Rights Tour' that would guide visitors along a route taking in the architecture of colonial rule, but also the former buildings of the KCIA (the Namsan headquarters now house the city's youth hostel). As a *Korea Times* headline declared, 'The "Dark Tour" will take visitors to places where cruel tragedies occurred' (Lee, 2017).

Figure 12.1: Tourists entering the 'execution building' at Seodemun Prison History Hall

Source: Photo by Robin West

It would be tempting here to pursue an argument that addresses the social harm of dark tourism in relation to the degrees of moral ambiguity that surround the consumption of places that have embedded meanings for those that lived through 'dark' times. But, to peer into the small structure housing Seodaemun Prison's gallows (as illustrated in Figure 12.1) next to the tunnel where bodies of executed prisoners were hurried away at night, to view graphic footage of the May 1980 events at the Kwangju memorial or wander among the traditional graves where the city first buried its (predominantly student) dead, with mementos and fading portraits placed by families, can nevertheless engender an empathy in the observer that is hard to categorise at first. As Dalton (2015: 177) argues, dark tourism at spaces of past criminality can potentially fulfil a moral and civic duty by invoking ethical sensibilities via its educational function, one that may counter the moral criticisms of 'manufactured emotion' and 'trivialisation' in which trauma and victims are reduced 'to free-floating images cut loose from context and complexity' (Stone, 2009: 58). However, concealed narratives of victimisation endure below outward representations, often obscured by dominant symbolism that the sites discussed foreground. And it is these that may even escape recognition by the empathetic gaze.

Discussing the Korean case, Henderson (2002) describes tourism on the peninsula as a 'state tool' that capitalises on existing enmities economically and politically; therefore, we need to grasp the inherent political meanings and purposes to fully understand its implications. And, as Baker (2010: 194) elaborates, successive governments in South Korea, 'both authoritarian and democratic, have tried to make memories of … events compatible with their ideological orientations'. So, there are important points to consider here, first in establishing a distinction between the more disinterested tourist gaze and the role that such sites play for the general tourist in providing experiential learning and opportunities for empathetic identification with victims (Roberts, 2018). On the other hand, it is important to understand the ideological role of such sites, from being factors in national reconciliation through to the political staging of accounts of past events. The recent history of Seodaemun Prison History Hall as a monument to victims of the struggle for independence and a tourist destination is a good example of what we could refer to in terms of a hierarchy of victimisation through representation. Its 'commodified colonial memory' (Burge, 2017: 35) and connotations of independence amount to state-approved memorialisation of only some of the prison's victims. Beyond its colonial context, the prison operated under the juntas until 1987, yet only fragments referring to the victimisation of democracy activists are on show, post-colonial memories being 'summed up in a single panel' (Huang and Lee, 2020: 88). Similarly, as Martin Jay commented after visiting the Kwangju memorial, the makeshift traditional graves were emptied by a government keen to distance itself from the atrocities of its authoritarian predecessor and bodies reburied in monolithic rows (Jay, 2003). It is almost as if the state has laid claim to victims, nevertheless. Popular grassroots protest prevented the levelling of the now empty gravesite.

The memorialisation of victims of Jeju 4:3

The hidden dimensions of victimisation can be raised to the surface through dark tourism-related activity. Famed for its natural environment and tourist economy, South Korea's Jeju Island is also the site of historic atrocity committed against its civilian population by forces allied to South Korea's post-independence authoritarian government. What is known as the Jeju 4:3 Massacre took place from 3 April 1947 until 1954 during a counter-insurgency operation against suspected communist rebels and sympathisers. Although not insignificant numbers were killed by insurgents, the reality of 4:3 was the routine mass slaughter of civilians by government forces and right-wing youth militias, with an estimated 30,000 of the island's population killed. The scale of the killings was systematically suppressed by successive governments until 1987 when, under pressure from social movements, discussion of the massacre re-entered the public sphere. Prior to this, mention of 4:3 was regarded as a criminal act. Between 1998 and 2000, the government officially recognised the massacre, passed a bill promising recognition of victims and reparation, and established a Truth Commission, before finally issuing a presidential apology. South Korea has developed a culture of addressing historical injustices committed by authoritarian

Figure 12.2: Graves of known victims of the massacre and memorial sculpture at Jeju Island's 4:3 Peace Park

Source: Photo by Robin West

regimes with the 2007 Jeju Special Law providing a legal basis for memorial foundations, and in 2008 the Jeju 4:3 Peace Memorial Park and associated museums were established (illustrated in Figure 12.2), becoming popular with tourists.

While 'obligation' and sense of 'personal duty' are key motivations for visiting the 4:3 Peace Park (Kang et al, 2012), a small non-governmental organisation (NGO) on the island seeks to capitalise on the educational aspect of dark tourism in broader terms of social and legal justice, stressing the fact that atrocities such as 4:3 should not be understood purely in a historical context. There are still victims and honour to be restored. Furthermore, similar acts of state violence continue as events in Myanmar and elsewhere attest. 'Jeju Dark Tours' is dedicated to preserving the numerous sites overlooked or ignored for political purposes by the official memorialisation process. Fully embracing the concept of dark tourism, the NGO uses the touristic experience of sites to publicise their complex history and engage with ongoing arguments related to the production of truth surrounding 4:3. As we saw, there is often a hierarchical tension between those the state enshrines as victims and the lived reality of victimisation; and, therefore, how victimhood is represented at dark tourism sites. Although working closely with other Jeju institutions, the NGO is at times critical of aspects of the construction of collective memory it regards as conforming to purely symbolic or state-appropriated narratives. But what is particularly innovative in Jeju Dark Tours' operation is its parallel advocacy role as activists working to ensure that the historic injustices of the 4:3 period are overturned, locating itself in a network of human rights-focused NGOs typical of the institutionalised culture of social movements in South Korea. It works closely with a team of activist lawyers involved in legal cases brought against the government by surviving 4:3 victims and bereaved families, notably in a recent series of retrials of those imprisoned or subjected to preliminary hearings during the counter-insurgency period. Being convicted or merely associated with the rebellion triggered wide-ranging repercussions in the forms of stigma and social exclusion, not only for primary victims but also for subsequent generations. Since 2019, there have been ten retrospective acquittals framed as the restoration of honour.

Conclusion

Dalton (2015: 8) suggests that criminology has invested much of its energy in exploring the causation of crime and developing sub fields such as victimology and the critiquing of criminal justice administration, with little attention directed to the 'physical and cultural after-life of spaces and places where crime has occurred'. The case of the memorialisation of Jeju massacre victims and others discussed here proposes a perspective that goes beyond unconstructive perceptions of dark tourism by not only focusing on the cultural afterlife of spaces of state criminality, but by recognising that many of the state-induced injustices in South Korea remain alive and unresolved both legally and in collective consciousness. The underlying thread of this chapter therefore works towards an approach that recognises the potential of the study of dark tourism in relation to an in-depth victimology that explores the past's persistent role in present-day lives and the opportunities that arise to right historic injustice.

13

Museum Dr. Guislain: Ghent, Belgium

Sophie Gregory

Birmingham City University

Introduction

In 1986, one of Belgium's first asylums for the insane opened its doors as the Museum Dr. Guislain, a place where curiosityseekers can learn more about the often dark history of psychiatry. The museum houses a series of exhibitions, including a collection of late 18th-century instruments used to restrain patients at the old Ghent madhouse for men, and an extensive series of photos concerning psychiatry and 'madness'. At the time, there was a great deal of resistance against opening this piece of heritage to the public, due to the shame and taboo attached to the way psychiatric patients had been treated in the past. However, some of these difficult histories are somewhat softened by the museum's setting, reflecting a shift towards a more humane approach to mental health treatment. Hosted in the old buildings of a former psychiatric hospital built in 1857, it was the first institution in Belgium specifically designed for the treatment of the mentally ill. With its majestic buildings and serene gardens, Joseph Guislain aimed to facilitate the recovery process through architectural design. The hospital attracted travellers all over Europe at the time and was considered a model institution. Today, visitors can sit back and experience this tranquil setting in the museum's pub courtyard garden – once a former bathhouse that served

Guislain's patients, now a cosy meeting place just outside the city centre of Ghent.

Asylum tourism

Places of incarceration have long been magnets for dark tourism (Lennon, 2010). Venues considered significant heritage sites in the history of the incarceration of people diagnosed with mental illness commonly function as popular tourist sites. Such venues feed off public fears surrounding mental illness and the plight of the incarcerated patients. Historically, the asylum experience was curated and designed by officials to make visitors feel a certain way, much like museum spaces today. Similarly, Bennett (2005) argues that most modern public museums are major power centres created by elites determined to impose their view of history and behavioural norms on an unsuspecting public. Consequently, museums are more likely to perpetuate social norms than to bring about radical change.

As the understanding and treatment of mental illness has changed, so too has the phenomenon of asylum tourism: from viewing the insane to viewing the asylum grounds. Visitors once travelled to see the 'spectacle' of mental suffering at the asylum, eager to witness the bizarre and unfamiliar (Miron, 2011). Such institutional visits have been likened to a theatrical performance, designed to excite and entertain the audience (Goffman, 1961). Over time, as the asylum evolved, tourists came to admire expanses of green lawns and impressive buildings. Some even sampled the institution's food! Public tours were designed to foster closer ties between the community and the institution, shed light on the treatment process, secure donations and dispel the stigma associated with insanity. However, while some officials thought public visits served an essential role in legitimising asylums, others believed public tours were an outdated and harmful pastime that exploited the powerless patients (Miron, 2011). Subsequently, by the end of the 19th century, asylum tourism had virtually disappeared.

The closure of large psychiatric hospitals in the late 20th century led to a renewed interest in asylum tourism, now attracting urban explorers who seek out closed and abandoned buildings with a dark past, often hiding stunning architecture. These adventurers find locations that are generally considered to be off limits to the public, with the aim to explore and record their forgotten history (Garrett, 2010). Unlike preserved asylums and museum artefacts frozen in time, these derelict and decaying spaces are not smoothed over in spectacular ways, leaving room for the imagination (Pinder, cited in Garrett, 2010). Similarly, these settings have also become popular hotspots for ghost hunting tours, where ghostly legends provide visitors with an opportunity to engage with dark histories in ways that are exciting, experiential and educational (Ironside, 2018). However, such attractions have garnered criticism from disability rights advocates, who fear such attractions exploit misplaced fears about people with psychiatric disabilities, which contributed to their segregation from society in the first place (George, 2014).

From asylum to prison

Incarceration and confinement of various kinds have been used throughout human history (Peters, 1998). Notably, people with mental health problems have long been present in such spaces (Mills and Kendall, 2018). Despite the deinstitutionalisation of mental hospitals in the second half of the 20th century, asylums did not disappear. They returned in a new form: the modern prison (Parsons, 2018). Indeed, asylums and prisons both share a common history of systematic segregation and oppression (Scull, 1979). Both spaces held marginalised and vulnerable people – often referred to as 'inmates' – who had been involuntarily removed from society, considered an object of shame. Goffman's (1961) critique of the asylum and prison as total institutions also emphasises their shared characteristics; they stripped people of their individuality, infantilised them, and made them dependent on the very regime that was supposed to help them, consequently causing significant harm. Prison is widely considered an unsuitable environment for those with mental health problems (Seddon, 2007). However, despite substantial evidence that suggests places of incarceration and confinement produce and exacerbate mental distress, prisons continue to lock up large numbers of people experiencing mental health problems (Mills and Kendall, 2018).

Conclusion

When strolling freely through the gardens of an asylum for the insane, admiring the architectural design, or enjoying a pint in the museum's pub, it is perhaps all too easy to forget about the emotional distress of involuntary incarceration. This chapter has focused primarily upon the changing nature of voyeurism within the context of institutionalised mental health settings. Throughout its history, transitioning from asylums to prison estates, tours to urban exploration, consumption has often been at the fore.

People are naturally attracted to sites of suffering and tragedy. Asylum tourism continues to satisfy our human curiosity for *darkness* by offering a peek behind the closed gates. For those seeking a more immersive experience, the consumption of prison has never been more accessible, from a night behind iron bars in a boutique prison hotel, to an Alcatraz-themed bar where you have to smuggle your liqueur past the warden. Even so, when strolling freely through the garden of an asylum, admiring the Victorian architecture of a prison ceiling from your hotel bed or enjoying a pint in the former bathhouse used by patients, it is perhaps all too easy to forget about the emotional distress of involuntary incarceration. Such experiences could never adequately convey the real sounds, tastes and smells of actual confinement.

14

Karosta Prison Hotel: Liepāja, Latvia

Melindy Duffus

Birmingham City University

Introduction

Karosta Prison Hotel can be found in Karosta, which is the military port of Liepāja city. As one of Latvia's most unique and popular tourist destinations, it sees approximately 20,000 people visit each year, serving as a tourist attraction in the form of a museum and a hotel (Magnetic Latvia, 2016). Historically, the grounds of Karosta Prison Hotel housed an infirmary (Dragicevich et al, 2016). Ironically, the same establishment that was previously designed to save lives was transformed throughout the 20th century into a military prison (Dragicevich et al, 2016). Karosta Prison has a brutal history, such as when the Nazis executed most of the inmates by gunshot during the Second World War (Boyd, 2021). Under Nazi, Soviet and Latvian reign, Karosta Prison has had a continuum of rulers whose aim is to promote exclusivity and as such suppress free will. In today's form, Karosta Prison provides tourists with the opportunity to spend the night on a prison bunk or an iron bed, in a facility that is argued to be even harsher than Alcatraz and requires those who stay to sign a disclaimer (Karosta Prison, 2021a). The focus of this dark destination is on authenticity and treating tourists in the same way as those inmates who lived in

Karosta Prison for many years prior. Despite establishments of penal tourism being able to provide guests with entertainment and education, they can arguably come at the detriment of those who have experienced pain in the same locations. In turn, this can perpetuate generational trauma and it is therefore important to provide insight into the dark element of such tourist sites.

Penal tourism

The revival of pre-existing prisons into museums is one that has interested many people, ranging from academics researching the topic to tourists visiting the locations (Strange and Kempa, 2003; Ross, 2012; Wilson, 2017; Stone et al, 2018). Penal tourism in the form of prison museums is popular worldwide, with over one hundred in existence (Walby and Piché, 2011). Exactly why penal tourism is so popular with so many people is a topic of great discussion (Wilson, 2008). Unlike many tourist destinations, penal museums are based on pain, hurt and punishment, and as such they capitalise on presenting dark forms of entertainment (Williams, 2007). Some argue that people have found prisons to be places of particular interest due to the varied experiences that have occurred within them, from escape attempts to deaths and other forms of suffering and violence (Aslan, 2015). As such, visiting a former prison, whether that be a hotel or a museum, has become a common form of dark leisure. This form of tourism has been labelled 'penal tourism' (Strange and Kempa, 2003).

Penal tourism can take many formats, and although it will often involve former prisons, it does not commonly involve overnight stays, but rather day-long trips (Wilson, 2017). In turn, the hotel element of Karosta Prison Hotel distinguishes it from many of its peers in the sphere of penal tourism. This extra level of spending the night within the former prison provides customers with an extended experience of prison life, and leads to further questions as to what intrigues tourists to want to immerse themselves within the prison experience to this extent. Furthermore, it provides scope to discuss the harms that dark destinations, particularly in the form of penal museums, may present.

Penal museum experiences: fact or fiction?

Penal museums are sites of 'memorialisation' for past imprisonment and punishment (Bendix, 2002). As they often demonstrate acts of the past, it suggests that we now live in less punitive times. Taking this viewpoint, it could be suggested that a person's desire to attend former prisons for tourism purposes revolves around society's innate longing to reflect upon more retributive penal practices, that although may be desired, are no longer practised today (Stone, 2006). Furthermore, it provides tourists with access to environments that were not purposefully designed for tourism, through a combination of entertainment, education and a high degree of commercialism (Stone, 2006). Those who choose to visit penal museums, or destinations that are considered part of penal tourism, are often presented with the label of a penal spectator. In the words of Brown, the penal spectator:

> [L]ooks in on punishment and yet is also its author. In this looking, this subject acts as a bystander and outsider as opposed to an engaged participant or witness. She may stare curiously or reflectively, peer sideways from her peripheral vision, or gape and gawk directly, but the object of her gaze is inevitably other people's pain. (Brown, 2009: 21)

Penal museums can revoke less and more punitive reflections for the penal spectator (see Strange and Kempa, 2003; Wilson, 2008; Brown, 2009). Penal spectatorship can see some sympathise with the pain, suffering and trauma of the destination (Brown, 2009), and others come together with enthusiasm and energy (Pedersen, 2017). This is similar to the way that 'the execution of a Death Row prisoner can evoke cheers from one person and tears from his neighbour' (King and Maruna, 2009: 148).

Nevertheless, penal museums have gained popularity based on individuals' desire to enter a space that provides them with an insight into an activity that they have not been exposed to. The brutalities that have taken place within prisons add the deepest level of clarity to their place as dark destinations. Due to the pain that has occurred within these spaces, different techniques are used within these penal museums to try and regulate tourist perception (Brown, 2009). To do this, penal museums, in a similar way to traditional museums, are designed to centre on specific steps that support 'organised walking' with an aim of communicating a particular message to those who visit, rather than tourists simply wandering around (Bennett, 2005). This is a key issue of penal museums as it can misrepresent the experiences of prisoners, as only the desired message is presented. This adds a heightened level of harm, as it may diminish the historical truth presented to tourists. One way of doing this is through the varied activities designed for tourists within penal museums. For example, a tourist favourite and a common theme within penal museums is this focus on escapes (Aslan, 2015). Karosta Prison Hotel runs two successful escape rooms seemingly based on educational ideas yet absorbed into entertainment-focused exercises. Escape rooms have become widely popular around the world within recent years (Fotaris and Mastoras, 2019). However, escape rooms are often built within locations that would not be considered deviant, and although they may have deviant sub-themes within their storyline, such as solving a crime or saving a character, are not stereotypical of dark leisure (Fotaris and Mastoras, 2019). However, by engaging in an escape room within a location that many at one time would have liked to escape from, this is in line with tourists' interest in partaking in dark leisure experiences. It is ironic, and representative of the glamorisation present within aspects of penal tourism, that Karosta Prison Hotel has escape room activities, yet has referred to itself as '[t]he prison nobody has ever escaped from' (Karosta Prison, 2021b). This directly links to the issues raised earlier regarding a specific narrative being presented.

Commodification of human suffering

Penal museums in the 'darkest' form will take their tourist customers on real-time tours of the most punitive historical destinations, including death rows, detention camps and execution chambers (Miles, 2002). Even the less 'dark' penal museums use other entertainment means such as voice recordings, photographs and former prisoners as tour guides (Shackley, 2001). Karosta

Prison Hotel is not alone in placing a large focus on authenticity. In line with many dark destinations, video, audio and motion sensor technology is used to intensify the authenticity of the experience. To develop this further, Karosta Prison Hotel follows traditional prison protocol in the sense of punishment, whereby guests who fail to comply with the rules of the 'prison' are punished, albeit via physical exercise and cleaning.

People who visit prison museums with the desire to immerse themselves within the tourist experience are often noted as taking part in penal spectatorship. One issue with penal spectatorship has been noted by Pederson (2017) who condemns penal spectators as voyeuristic bystanders of the pain and suffering of others. Many of the activities at penal museums involve trying to authentically portray the experiences of those previous inmates. At Karosta Prison Hotel, one of the entertainment-based activities that shows elements of dark leisure is the opportunity for visitors to take part in 'Behind bars: the show'. This is a historical reality show that involves the audience (Karosta Prison, 2021c). This activity focuses on visitors experiencing the life of a prisoner, with a key focus on authenticity. Due to the nature of prisons, authenticity often comes in the format of portraying punishment. This feeds in to promoting tourists finding pleasure in the distress of others and therefore potentially fetishising punishment within penal tourism. This is harmful, as by putting a heightened focus on the brutality of the past, it can present a damaging image of current practice by implying that all current prison conditions are acceptable based on us having progressed from the levels of previous brutality. While we can acknowledge that prison practices have changed, including the abolishment of capital punishment within Latvia (Hood and Hoyle, 2009), it downplays the existing pains that are present in current operating prisons.

Undoubtedly, prison tourism may permit the public some insight into the injustices of the past, and the therefore potential progressive measures of the present. Furthermore, like many other 'dark' tourist sites, prisons can encourage a sense of personal, if not collective, shame and regret among the viewing public. However, with the aforementioned heightened focus on the brutality of the past, it can present a damaging image of current practice, implying that all current conditions are acceptable based on the severe levels of the past. Findings of tourists visiting Alcatraz found that few attended educational-based activities, such as guided tours, and more were drawn towards entertainment activities that centred around prior suffering, such as the cell blocks (Gould, 2014). This has implications for the lives of current prisoners and how their experiences are presented to the public. If the public's knowledge is based primarily on entertainment-based activities from penal museums, with a lack of focus on education, it can reduce the public's concern regarding legitimacy, visibility and current practice within prisons. The commodified experience of sites such as Karosta can never truly reflect the smells, sound and fear experienced by those incarcerated (Warr, 2021), and as such, prison hotels and other assorted penal complexes that have been turned into tourist destinations aide in the fetishistic disavowal (Žižek, 2010) of the real harms that imprisonment encapsulates.

Conclusion

Penal museums are popular worldwide and continue to bring in large numbers of people. Despite a desire to educate visitors, there is greater pressure to place a focus on the entertainment side of the attractions. As such, penal museums thrive on societal desires to reflect upon retributive penal practices and as a result adapt their activities to cater for the audiences that they attract. This, however, can bring out hidden harms within these penal museums. Evidently, Karosta Prison Hotel is extremely successful as a tourist destination; however, it has not avoided attracting these hidden harms. One of Karosta Prison Hotel's most popular attractions is the escape rooms, despite the prison in its operating time having not had any prisoners escape. This focus on emphasising or adapting the truth to enhance the entertainment factor of the penal museum can be harmful in providing a false truth of the past. Additionally, with a lack of focus on education, it prevents tourists from gaining a true understanding of the pains of punishment. It places the focus on the commodification and trivialisation of human suffering, and a lack of a desire to understand the impact of punishment. This not only impacts those who served a sentence at Karosta Prison, but also those who are currently imprisoned across the world.

15

The Clink prison-based restaurant: Brixton, London, UK

Dan Rusu

Birmingham City University

Introduction

The Clink Charity works alongside Her Majesty's Prison and Probation Service (HMPPS) to reduce prison recidivism by 'changing attitudes, transforming lives, and creating second chances' for those who are in prison or in the process of re-entering society. The charity and HMPPS run four prison-based restaurants together, which are open to the public. These are: The Clink Restaurant at HMP High Down, which was the first to open in May 2009; The Clink at HMP Cardiff, 2012; The Clink at HMP Brixton, 2014; and The Clink HMP Styal, 2020. Each of these are registered catering colleges and help serving prisoners to gain their City and Guilds National Vocational Qualifications in hospitality and horticulture; the idea behind it is that this will help them with employment post-release. Considering that the hospitality sector as of 2019 dealt with a major skills deficit (Harkinson and Moore, 2019), the Clink went some way in alleviating the pressure. Nevertheless, consumer spending as of May 2021 is at less than 70 per cent of the pre-pandemic levels, remaining one quarter lower than in 2019 (Office for National Statistics, 2021).

While 'prison fine dining' may come across as oxymoronic to some readers, a short study of Tripadvisor customer reviews of the

Clink restaurants will show that customers rate these as some of the best restaurants in their cities of residence (Gebbels et al, 2021). For example, Brixton ranked 20th out of 16,740 restaurants in London; Cardiff ninth of 118; Styal first of 71 restaurants in Wilmslow; and High Down ranked first of 126 restaurants in Sutton. The mission statement of the Clink Charity is to 'change public perceptions of prisoners, create second chances, and transform lives'. The following sections will provide a criminological analysis starting from each one of these statements, while inviting readers to a critical reflection around the benefits as well as the potential hidden harms which prison tourism may obscure.

'Positive criminological' implications: 'transforming lives'

Penal theorists have argued that imprisonment represents a form of civil death; once new prisoners walk through the prison gates, a series of degradation ceremonies (Garfinkle, 1956) serve to strip them of previous identities in a process called the 'mortification of the self' (see Goffman, 1961). In this context, the Clink experience may provide prisoners with the necessary resources to reconstruct their identity, provide a 'replacement self' (Giordano et al, 2002) in prison and assist them to perform these new identities upon release and in the community. In other words, working at the Clink may lead to 'transformation from prisoner to hospitality worker' (Giousmpasoglou et al, 2019: 2). To say that desistance from crime is conditioned by a fundamental change in how offenders perceive themselves has become mere truism in criminological thought (see Maruna, 2001). The potential for using this experience as a turning point that 'knifes off' past controversies and offers a reason for conforming to conventional life should not be understated (see Laub and Sampson, 2003; Maruna and Roy, 2007). Altogether, having a place to work is seen as fundamental to a successful re-entry (see Uggen, 2000; Berg and Huebner, 2011; Visher et al, 2011; Andersen et al, 2020).

The Clink have reported outstanding outcomes of the programme, with prisoners being a staggering 49.6 per cent less likely to reoffend by entering the programme. The identity change discussed in the previous paragraph is critical to this process. Beyond obvious individual benefits to those undergoing such 'interventions', the Clink is committed to transform public perceptions to criminality. I will turn to this important point in the next section.

Going the second mile: 'changing public perceptions'

The Clink Charity takes pride in the fact that their impact extends well beyond the individual undertaking the training – they are changing public perception of prisons and prisoners more broadly. Research supports that prison visits/tours can indeed change public perceptions of prisoners. For example, research that used carceral tours as a pedagogical tool found that students' expectations about the 'prison environment and security … prisoners, and staff' and 'perceptions of, and attitudes toward, the prison system' (Wilson et al, 2011: 5; see also Rockell, 2009) were challenged. In fact, much of students' prior knowledge on prisons had simply stemmed from the media, which 'have much to answer for in representing prisoners as inarticulate, unreflective, and aggressive' (Wilson and O'Sullivan, 2004 in Wilson et al, 2011: 350–351; see Piché and Walby, 2010, for a response). In this sense, prison tours can challenge media stereotypes about prisoners (see Boag and Wilson, 2013; Wilson, 2017) and debunk a series of myths (see Rockell, 2009) which leads to diminished prejudice and an increased level of empathy towards prisoners (Boag and Wilson, 2013).

By interacting with prisoners, customers challenge their own stereotypes around prison life and prisoners, which, in turn, assists with prisoners' reintegration through socially accepting them as returning citizens (see McNeil, 2012). Thus, customers feel that they are actively contributing to prisoners' rehabilitation.

Two birds, one stone?

Clients come to the Clink restaurants to enjoy an excellent meal while paying their tribute and contribution to the great cause of rehabilitation. Fine dining, in this sense, is reconceptualised as a great opportunity for charity work – a place where customers can fulfil some of their moral duties (cf Žižek, 2009). For example, a reviewer on Tripadvisor made the point: 'They [prisoners] do not receive a penny in wages or tips. All monies go to the charity to rehabilitate those from prison into a job. Their success stories are amazing' (Cardiff reviewer, in Gebbels et al, 2021: 8). One may add that 'their success stories are also our success stories', which ultimately make guests feel good about themselves as they consume the right type of products (see Žižek, 2013). Interestingly, recent doctoral research revealed that very few prisoners working at the Clink at HMP Cardiff believe that clients' ultimate motivation to visit was to support rehabilitation. In fact, it was suggested that for customers 'the Clink was a spectacle, providing insight into an unknown world' (Graham, 2020: 115).

Is this the whole story?

Against the abundance of research indicating the positive effects of such interactions between the public and prisoners, there are several critics who draw attention to the potential harms that prison visits and 'prison tourism' may obscure from view at a superficial glance. In their view, 'prison tourism' does little more than simply objectify and dehumanise prisoners while putting them on display to entertain guests (see Arford, 2017). For example, Graham (2020) found that the prisoners working at the Clink at HMP Cardiff felt that customers were drawn by the idea of being served by prisoners which created a divide between them and the public. Some of the men felt that they were 'othered' and compared the Clink to a fishbowl and a zoo.

Viewed this way, if not organised ethically (see Minogue, 2009), prison tours can represent a form of symbolic violence that dehumanises individuals and elicits feelings of shame in prisoners (see Adams, 2001; Arford, 2017; Huckelbury, 2009; Piché and Walby, 2010). Žižek made the point that 'charity is the humanitarian mask hiding the face of economic exploitation' (Žižek, 2008: 19). While this definition may be provocative, research has found that some prisoners experience their working conditions as exploitative (see Peled-Laskov and Timor, 2018). Then, in the Žižekian sense, the prisoner is not the receiver of benefits and advantages but is in and of itself exploited through seemingly benign means.

Preparations for what?

The Clink's mission statement is firmly based on improving the re-entry experiences and reducing the recidivism rates of prisoners by cultivating a set of skills that support them in their career prospects once released. That our current service-based economy seems prepared to absorb as many new employees as possible in jobs commonly described as 'McJobs' is merely a Pyrrhic victory. Some would argue that these individuals, once released, are thrown into the vortex of precarious, flexible and ephemeral (cf Winlow and Hall, 2006; 2013; also see Lloyd, 2018; 2019) 'post-modern jobs' of the leisure service economy (see also Bauman, 2005). This 'new' service economy, with its competitive individualist ethos, and increasingly used zero-hour contracts and part-time work, may offer a sense of false security and optimism to these returning citizens as they enter unstable waters upon release. Added to such fluid and ephemeral work are a set of 'pains of freedom' (Shammas, 2014) well consecrated in penological literature (see Crewe, 2011; Durnescu, 2011; Liem and Kunst, 2013; McNeil, 2019). Such pains refer to experiences of stigma, lack of work and being on probation (especially referring to deprivation of autonomy and time; see Durnescu, 2011).

Nevertheless, the overall message should be one of optimism. Depending on their sentence length, usually, prisoners restart their life from scratch after they are released. The Clink Charity offers a smooth transition into jobs which can provide some sense of stability and assist ex-prisoners to 'swim [with] the tide' (Crewe et al, 2016).

Conclusion

To enjoy the Clink restaurant's exceptionally well-received gastronomic delights, guests enter the dining room in a way comparable to a rite of passage (see Van Gennep, 1960). After the neophyte is thoroughly checked and vetted, she is funnelled through the imposing prison gates, which are symbolically imbued with the abundant suffering experienced by many prisoners and their families throughout the years. This creates the 'thanatopic' (Carrabine, 2017) dialectic of 'pleasure and tragedy', which spices up an extraordinary culinary experience. The Clink is committed to changing public perceptions of prisoners, create second chances and transform the lives of prisoners. This chapter provided a criminological analysis of these desiderates and has pointed to potential harms which prison touring may obscure from a superficial glance. The Clink's humanist ethos fosters an environment where prisoners are treated as individuals with skills and aspirations who can 'do good' both in prison and after their release. This strengths-based approach (Maruna and LeBel, 2015) ensures that Clink graduates can unlock their potential and become important contributors to our society and ultimately desist from crime.

16

The 9/11 memorial and museum: New York, New York, USA

John Bahadur Lamb

Staffordshire University

Introduction

As was famously written, '[t]errorists want a lot of people watching and a lot of people listening, not a lot of people dead' (Jenkins, 1975: 158) and nothing invokes the theatrical nature of extreme violence as remembering the 9/11 attacks, carried out by Al Qaeda against the US in 2001. The sheer horror of 3,000-plus individuals being murdered created a spectacle the likes of which we can only hope not to see again. Like a theatrical event, the attacks attracted an audience of millions of people around the globe (*The Guardian*, 2001) who sat and watched the horror unfold on their television sets and millions more will have seen the footage replayed on the news, over the internet and, even, as part of university courses studying a range of topics as varied as international relations, military history, terrorism studies and law enforcement. Such a huge audience was inevitable as the attacks are indelibly stamped on the course of history and rank alongside events such as the fall of the Berlin Wall and the death of Princess Diana. Even 20 years later, many people report being able to recall exactly where they were when either they saw the attacks unfold or heard about them (Hartig and Doherty, 2021).

Such a traumatic event has clearly changed people's lives and not just those who lost loved ones in the attacks themselves.

First responders, who risked everything to save people on the day, have died in large numbers (Freedman, 2004). Military families from across the US and allied countries have experienced the death or serious injury of members of their armed forces (Watson Institute, 2022) and numerous civilians in Iraq and Afghanistan have died as a result of the Global War on Terror which the attacks spawned (Watson Institute, 2022). As such, it is unsurprising that there is a collective desire to memorialise the attacks and have a location which can be visited that can serve as a focal point for the grief, sadness and remembrance of all who have been affected.

The juxtaposition of terror and consumption

However, the 9/11 memorial and the associated museum have become an oddly juxtaposed pair. One, the memorial pools, serve as the official memorial to those killed in the attacks and are in essence sacred ground (Baptist, 2015). The other, the museum, is a quasi-voyeuristic experience which enables those that have no direct connection to the events of 9/11, the rescue attempts or the wars that day spawned to consume collective grief (Kennicott, 2014). While the waterfall pools are a sombre, austere place which encourages quiet reflection on the sheer scale of loss generated by the attacks and is a fitting and respectful memorial, the museum is a jumbled confusion of competing influences, which has been noted by many authors since it opened (Hess and Herbig, 2013; Kennicott, 2014; Wainwright, 2014; Baptist, 2015).

First, the museum is explicitly a paid-for environment with tickets costing from $26 through to $75 depending on the level of access needed (9/11 Memorial). While it is arguable that this helps limit visitor numbers and provides money for the management of the site, it also creates a layer of consumption. Visitors have to choose to part with their money here, rather than at the many competing sites and attractions that New York offers. Thus, visitors are choosing to consume the experience the museum offers, and this immediately places the 9/11 museum in the realms of 'infotainment' as visitors are clearly seeking an experience worthy of the cost. When viewed through this lens, it becomes unsurprising that there are numerous accounts of visitors taking 'selfies' with exhibits (Cherelus, 2016) and that a gift shop exists on the site.

Second, the museum is set seven stories underground and there is a distinctly religious feel to the way that visitors descend into darkness to witness the horror of that day. As has been pointed out previously (Doss, 2011), such theatrical elements are part of the process through which cultural memory is built within a society. The quasi-religious experience of descending into the metaphorical hell displayed within the 9/11 museum is an attempt to create memorial mania (Doss, 2011), which seeks not collective reflection but, rather, a collective expression of grief, rage and a siege mentality whereby the very ideals of America are under attack.

Conclusion

If we accept that 9/11 was perceived as an attack on the very idea of what it is to be American, then it becomes unsurprising that the memorialisation has been commodified. Rather than being disrespectful, this commodification is arguably a direct expression of the collective desire of Americans to reaffirm their culture and shows how culture, grief and history are intertwined. This intertwining of consumption with memorialisation does not detract from the importance of sites of collective grief, nor does it derogate from the cultural significance of remembering those who were lost in the tragedy. In many ways, consumption enables such remembering, as I personally experience every time I see the fridge magnet I bought during my own trip to the memorial and the museum. As the magnet says, 'honour the brave' who died or sacrificed themselves to protect others that day and in the days that followed.

17

The Tuol Sleng Museum of Genocidal Crimes: Phnom Penh, Cambodia

Eamonn Carrabine

University of Essex

Introduction

In the 40 years since Tuol Sleng prison (also known as S-21) was established as a museum to document, archive and educate visitors about the Khmer Rouge genocide, it has become a troubling symbol of atrocity tourism and the uneasy politics of memory, mourning and witnessing encountered at such sites. There, in what had once been a school, those who were alleged to have committed crimes against the state were interrogated, tortured, starved and killed. Of the estimated 14,000 prisoners it detained from 1975 to 1979, only seven are known to have survived (Linfield, 2010: 54). When the Vietnamese liberated the barricaded compound of Tuol Sleng in 1979, they found dead bodies in shackles, bloodstained walls, human bones, stacks of corpses in shallow graves, torture instruments, photographic archives, 'confession' files and bureaucratic memos left by the fleeing Khmer Rouge. The army preserved everything and within two weeks a group of journalists from socialist countries were invited to the prison, while the museum was officially opened in July 1980. Inside, the display of physical horrors, objects and pictures are so vivid and shocking that the visitors find it a deeply disturbing experience.

Today, it is mostly international tourists who visit and arrive with some knowledge of the site's sinister role during the Khmer Rouge period, while for Cambodian people, these memorials occupy an uncertain political role in the post-genocide landscape. It is because of the scale of the atrocities committed by the Khmer Rouge in the 1970s that a complex politics of memory has arisen in the country and that these sites of official commemoration are often experienced as theatres of macabre spectacle, prompting important ethical questions on the display of crime at them and in the global circulation of a horrific past. Nevertheless, it is important to situate 'dark tourism' in a much larger critical discussion of leisure and death more generally (see Kaul and Skinner, 2018, for a collection of essays that achieves this) while recognising that the trope of 'dark' itself needs to be subjected to more nuanced interrogation (Bowman and Pezzullo, 2010). To that end, this chapter takes a cue from studies that have enlivened the concept of 'moral geographies' in relation to travel and citizenship. Here, it is important to note that understandings of Cambodia's darkness and intrigue draw heavily on the 'Phantasmatic Indochina' of French colonial rule in mainland Southeast Asia, an imaginative geography 'whose luminous aura sustains … erotic fantasies and perpetuates exotic adventures of a bygone era' (Norindr, 1996: 1). More recent associations of Cambodia with violence, danger and dependency are themselves also 'amplified by representations and practices generated from within Cambodia's burgeoning tourist industry' (Hughes, 2008: 321).

The turning of death into public play often results from mediatisation, here defined as the 'simultaneous reporting and witnessing around the world of global suffering', where tourists are increasingly significant, collective witnesses to it (Urry, 2004: 210). But as John Urry goes on to point out, such sites of death, although now characterised by play, are not necessarily Disneyfied or McDonaldised, but rather involve complex performances of place, grief, respect and emotion. Here, items, objects and the location itself become collectively significant through a process of 'sacralisation' (Urry, 1990: 9–10) and frequently invite comparison with pilgrimage (Keil, 2005: 480). Indeed, Rainer Schulze (2014: 124) distinguishes between 'pilgrims' and 'tourists' in his discussion of those who visit Holocaust memorial sites, where the former 'come to mourn the people who died and suffered at the camps, honour their memory and learn more about the context and practice of their incarceration', while the latter are those who visit 'because the site exists and often is on a tourist trail or who are fascinated by the deaths that occurred there'. Consequently, it is important to begin with the mass political violence that Cambodia experienced, and that will enable us to understand why there is a complex politics of memory at work in the country.

Genocide

The genocide was perpetrated in Cambodia by the Khmer Rouge between 1975 and 1979, under the dictatorship of Pol Pot. The Khmer Rouge attained power after five years of civil war (1970–1975), which itself was a destructive 'sideshow' of the Vietnam War (Shawcross, 2002). Although it was largely an indigenous revolution, the US economic and military destabilisation of Cambodia was a major factor shaping Pol Pot's rise and formation of a 'prison camp state' in the name of 'Democratic Kampuchea' (Kiernan, 1996: 9). The regime hermetically sealed the country from the outside world and immediately embarked on a horrifying rule of terror that would cause the death of two million people, almost a third of the country's population (Chandler, 2008). The atrocities committed against civilians were carried out in a Maoist-inspired 'total revolution', to forge an 'entirely new, productive communal society' (Tyner et al, 2012: 858). Within hours of marching into Phnom Penh on 17 April 1975, which for the Khmer Rouge constituted the beginning of 'Year Zero', there began the forced removal of all inhabitants from the Cambodian capital city into agricultural collectives and labour camps. It was a brutal campaign of social and spatial cleansing that sought to rid the country of its urban, educated and professional classes so as to construct a pure, homogenous and self-sufficient peasant society.

Driven by an agrarian, anti-materialist ideology, the new regime sought to completely dismantle everyday life and the many social institutions surrounding it. As David Chandler puts it: 'Almost at once, and without explaining their rationale, the Khmer Rouge forcibly emptied Cambodia's towns and cities, abolished money, schools, private property, law courts, and markets, forbade religious practices, and set almost everybody to work in the countryside growing food' (Chandler, 2000: v).

By the time a Vietnamese invasion, on 7 January 1979, forced the Khmer Rouge from power (though remnants retreated into the jungle and waged a guerrilla war that lasted a further two decades), it gradually became clear that in such a brief period, so many had perished from starvation, untreated disease, exhaustion as well as torture and execution in orchestrated, state-administered violence. Most of the deaths, and all of the executions (estimated at nearly a million), resulted from a security apparatus dedicated to overseeing the rapid transformation of Cambodia's 'economic development' (Tyner and Devadoss, 2014: 4). At the centre of the system was S-21, a former high school in Phnom Penh that had been converted into a secret prison in October 1975, where 14,000 prisoners were killed. Hundreds of thousands of victims were executed in the countryside, and the mass graves in which they were buried are the infamous 'killing fields' of Cambodia. The agricultural character of the regime 'saw many of these victims bludgeoned to death with crude instruments including axes, bamboo poles, and ox-cart axels' while others 'had their throats cut or were hacked to death with machetes' (Dalton, 2015: 59).

No doubt it is because of the sheer scale of these atrocities that a complex politics of memory has arisen in post-genocide Cambodia. The Tuol Sleng Museum of Genocidal Crimes in Phnom Penh opened in 1980, just months after the end of Khmer Rouge rule, at the S-21 interrogation and torture facility and continues to operate today. As do the killing fields of Choeung Ek, ten miles east of the capital, where prisoners from S-21 were taken to be murdered (see also Chapter 18 by Luke Telford in this volume). When the site was discovered in the early 1980s, the remains of 9,000 bodies were found in mass graves, 'many were headless, naked, their hands tied; the separated heads were blindfolded' (Sion, 2014: 104) and it is but one of more than 500 sites of mass murder that have been unearthed (Williams, 2004: 240). The Cambodian government and their Vietnamese advisors immediately set about defining the Khmer Rouge as 'genocidal' and 'fascist' to prompt comparisons with Hitler's Germany and downplay the regime's distorted socialist ideology (Chandler, 2008: 360). To facilitate this tactic, these two sites were quickly established as internationally visible places exposing the violent horrors perpetrated under Pol Pot to the wider world and to ensure the 'continued production of a coherent memory of the past' (Hughes, 2003: 26). They have since become major tourist destinations, attracting thousands of visitors every year, and while there are other memorial sites, these are mostly in the provinces, inaccessible and not easily identifiable to foreign visitors.

Images

The reason why scholarship has largely focused on Tuol Sleng and Choeung Ek lies in the political agenda surrounding these memorials and what it means to display the crimes of the Khmer Rouge in this way. For instance, it has been argued that 'these highly visible and officially commemorated sites serve to obfuscate other, more mundane sites (and practices) of violence' in everyday 'landscapes and legacies of violence that are "hidden in plain sight"' (Tyner et al, 2012: 854). It is here that the question of how to memorialise this past is posed most acutely and can be seen in the controversies generated by atrocity photography. There are two predominant types: the action shot, depicting and preserving some moment of horror, and the identification picture, often in the form of a headshot and used to identify victims who were later killed or disappeared (Williams, 2007: 56). As part of its permanent exhibition, the Tuol Sleng museum displays thousands of photographic portraits of prisoners produced between 1975 and 1979. Initially passport-sized prints, stapled to the detainees' case files, they deliberately employ Bertillon's famous mugshot perspective (Dalton, 2015: 79). The images were not incidental to S-21, rather the entire 'photographic documentation process was indicative of a larger bureaucratic effort to establish political legitimacy' (Tyner and Devadoss, 2014: 366). The mugshots, selected and enlarged by East German photographers in 1981, have been posted on numerous boards ever since the museum opened (Chandler, 2000: 27). Furthermore, it has been argued that the portraits 'have become "undisciplined envoys" of Cambodia's past, circulating on a global scale and through various media' (Hughes, 2003: 24).

Crucial was the discovery in 1993 of some 6,000 photographic negatives in a rusting filing cabinet in the museum's archive by two North American photojournalists, Douglas Niven and Christoper Riley, who embarked on a project of cleaning, cataloguing and printing the S-21 images. It is clear that their aims were not simply to recover and place the photographs in the Tuol Sleng museum setting, but 'to go global with exhibitions and a publication (which involved holding copyright on the photographs) – necessarily involved the photographs in the circulations of international news and visual arts media' (Hughes, 2003: 30). There is no doubt that the global exposure of the photographs generated considerable interest, but important questions remain over the ongoing circulation of the images. Paul Williams addresses some of these issues in his discussion of one of the most reproduced headshot pictures, of a mother and child, in the following way:

> The combination of the woman's youthful beauty, her resigned expression, and the infant in her arms is visually poignant and speaks eloquently of innocence. Beyond its callous overtones, the dilemma that arises from 'preferring' some headshots over others is partly due to a modern paradigm that holds that the dual powers of photography – generating documentary records and creating works of art – should be kept separate. The conventional separation of headshots and portraiture in both style and intent is conventionally maintained due to their allied connotations of government identification versus artistic expression, or state subject versus creative personhood. While the technical conventions of the portrait and headshot are similar, they are assumed to show only *either* intimate character *or* bureaucratic supervision and reform. (Williams, 2007: 66–67, emphasis in original)

As he goes on to argue, it is when these categories become blurred that ethical questions come to the fore, as the controversies surrounding their display in a fine art context make clear.

From May to September 1997, a selection of 22 prisoner portraits from Tuol Sleng went on public display at the Museum of Modern Art (MoMA) in New York in an exhibition titled *Photographs from S-21: 1975–1979*. Rachel Hughes (2003) has described the heated debates that ensued over their display, where Niven and Riley were criticised for selling art-quality prints from the Tuol Sleng archive, and for holding copyright over the pictures, while the exhibition itself failed to acknowledge the connections between Cambodia's modern history and the United States. Others argued that through 'selecting those images that were most aesthetically satisfying and emotionally powerful, the curators performed their own kind of culling' and by radically divorcing them from 'the conditions of their creation, and by exhibiting only a digestible number, the images at MoMA were granted autonomy from the location and magnitude of what occurred' and consequently lose much of their 'evidential status' (Williams, 2007: 67). By presenting them in such a museum context, they become 'colonial spoils', 'exotic' displays that reinforce an 'enduring power imbalance within and against which the contact work of travel, exhibition and interpretation occurs' (Hughes, 2003: 36).

It is important to finish this discussion by recognising that for Cambodians, memory and memorialisation are not performed at either the main sites of Tuol Slong or Choeung Ek, or for that matter on official holidays, which serve other purposes and are directed to international tourists. Rather, as Brigitte Sion suggests, 'remembrance of the genocide does take place, but quietly, traditionally and locally – in each village, in each stupa, next to the pagoda, on religious holidays. There, human dignity is respected, mourning rituals have meaning and the spirits of the murdered can eventually find rest' (Sion, 2014: 116).

Anyone who has visited Tuol Sleng and Choeung Ek will have been struck by just how unsettling and disturbing an experience it is, which is partly to do with their raw proximity to death and trauma. Their 'untouched appearance' has been described in the following way:

> Tourists to other sites of genocide have become accustomed to artifacts and buildings *presented* 'as is' that are, in fact, heavily mediated. Roped sections,

> glassed walls, guides and docents, restricted areas: all are parts of a typical, and passive, encounter with the 'real thing.' By contrast, at Tuol Sleng and Choeung Ek the general absence of guards or other visitors provides the opportunity to explore—to one's nervous limits. Inside the cells are wire torture beds to touch, hastily laid and bloodstained brick walls to lean against, and rusted ammunition boxes and barbed wire to handle. The unhindered intrusion produces a heightened sensitivity about how far to enter and how long to stay. (Williams, 2004: 242, emphasis in original)

Today, the sites operate as major tourist attractions that rely on the display of gruesome horrors to generate considerable revenue. It is the utter ordinariness of the place that makes it even more shocking: 'the suburban setting, the plain school buildings and the grassy playing area where children kick around balls, juxtaposed with rusted beds, instruments of torture and wall after wall of disturbing portraits' and as *Lonely Planet* goes on to advise, 'Tuol Sleng is not for the squeamish' (Lonely Planet, nd; a).

Conclusion

These places of death and leisure are complex, entailing performances of respect, grief and emotion. Visitors to Tuol Sleng are 'returning to a moral terrain in which mass political violence and its ongoing social and (geo)political effects are approached through dutiful exposure' (Hughes, 2008: 328). Yet, it is hard not to disagree with Derek Dalton's (2015: 69) impression that one is left 'not so much with a wealth of knowledge of the "how" and "why" of genocide, but rather a repository of sensations, impressions and feelings about the horrors I had been given a vicarious insight into' from visits to both sites. But they are far from unique in the genocide and their contribution to the political uses of memory mobilised by the government is significant. Not least since they divert attention away from the need for justice. Former Khmer Rouge officials who participated in or witnessed genocidal crimes are still active in government and still enjoy impunity (Sion, 2014: 102) to the extent that an 'officially enforced amnesia' (Chandler, 2008: 356) sits uncomfortably alongside ongoing efforts by activists and scholars to register the broader context of the genocide. The selective memorialisation of the past is bound up with a lack of reconciliation that continues to haunt the country, such that in a 'context of unattained justice the memorials' will 'remain disconnected from any historical narrative' (Williams, 2004: 235).

18

Choeung Ek killing field: Phnom Penh, Cambodia

Luke Telford

University of York

Introduction

Under the leadership of King Norodom Sihanouk, Cambodia obtained national independence from the French Empire in 1953. The nation enjoyed relative political stability and security until a bitter civil war besieged Cambodian society from 1967 to 1975 between the Cambodian government and the Khmer Rouge. The latter were totalitarians who believed the state was corrupt and ineffective in dealing with social problems brought by a capitalist society, including uneven geographical development between rural and urban localities and myriad economic inequalities (Becker, 1998; Kiernan, 2008). They were also dissatisfied with the global economy and believed that only national autonomy would liberate Cambodia (Tyner et al, 2012). Indeed, up to half a million Cambodians died in this civil war, engendering profound human suffering and harm (Becker, 1998).

Waged by the US against neighbouring communist-ruled Vietnam to try and stem the spread of support for communism in Southeast Asia, the Vietnam War also detrimentally impacted upon Cambodia and generated further political instability. Bombing by the US resulted in thousands of civilian deaths and destroyed infrastructure, particularly in rural areas where the Khmer Rouge attracted most of its support (Kiernan, 2008).

With the arrival of 300,000 American soldiers in Vietnam in the late 1960s, a large amount of Cambodia's rice production was smuggled across the border to feed both armies (Kiernan, 2008). This meant tax revenue from rice exports fell by up to two thirds, plunging the nation into economic ruin. While US troops withdrew from the region in 1973, the civil war ended in 1975 with the victory of the Khmer Rouge.

Pol Pot, the Khmer Rouge and the killing fields

Led by Pol Pot, the Khmer Rouge sought to construct an agrarian, homogeneous society in Cambodia, which they rebranded as Democratic Kampuchea. Pol Pot immediately ordered the evacuation of the capital city, Phnom Penh, as two million people were led to the countryside to be labourers on farms (Atkinson, 2013). The soldiers, who were largely from impoverished peasant groups, probed the evacuees about their social class and thus occupation; those who possessed any modernised skills such as teachers as well as students were viewed as threats to the state and were 'never to be seen again' (Atkinson, 2013: 4). All forms of money, religion, education, libraries and infrastructure such as hospitals were destroyed as the Khmer Rouge sought to return the citizenry to 'Year Zero' (Mey, 2012), erasing 'both time and space to create (in their minds) a pure utopian society' (Tyner et al, 2012: 858).

New forms of education emerged that sought to equip people with the technical skills required to work in the agricultural society, which included 14-hour workdays, with illiterate peasants often being appointed as teachers in the rural villages. People were forced to live in barracks and labour in working groups rather than with their families, as the regime viewed the family unit as regressive (Pilger, 1979). Children were indoctrinated in brainwashing classes, often culminating in them murdering their parents for talking about their previous life as all historic forms of knowledge were illegal (Atkinson, 2013). Ethnic minorities such as Vietnamese and Chinese Cambodians, in particular, were targeted by the Khmer Rouge, as well as those who previously possessed skilled jobs (Mey, 2012). This resulted in one of the worst state-driven genocides in history, involving between one and three million fatalities from starvation, disease and murder (Heuveline, 1998). The latter largely occurred across the Khmer Rouge's 300 killing fields. However, only one – Choeung Ek – has received official commemoration and been commercialised (Tyner et al, 2012).

The Choeung Ek stupa

Choeung Ek was the largest killing field and lies nine miles southwest of Phnom Penh. It is estimated that around 9,000 people were killed and buried here (Tyner et al, 2012). In 1989, it was transformed into a 'dark destination', eventually attracting visitors from capitalist countries such as the United Kingdom, France, Germany and the US (Sion, 2011). Indeed, I visited the destination in 2016 as part of a trip with my partner to Southeast Asia. The site is relatively small and contains a large Buddhist stupa and fenced excavated pits, often containing wooden signs with minimal description in poorly translated English on how the victims were murdered (Sion, 2011). In retrospect, though, there were forms of harm that were relatively hidden from view of the international traveller. This includes the disregard for historic Khmer Buddhist religious practice, the omission of important historical details and the socio-economic insecurity of the tuk-tuk drivers who often stand outside Choeung Ek.

The destination contains a commemorative monument in the form of a large Buddhist stupa, encouraging remembrance of those that died at Choeung Ek at the hands of the Khmer Rouge. Historically, stupas were constructed under Buddhism for sacred objects to be enclosed such as the cremated remains of a senior monk, since Buddhism emphasises the importance of cremation as part of its belief in reincarnation (Hughes, 2006). However, the stupa at Choeung Ek deviates from this historical trend as it contains a 62-metre-high rectangular glass display case containing over 5,000 uncremated skulls of those murdered at Choeung Ek (Sion, 2011), forming a *shock and awe* tactic for international tourists. Death brought by violence in Khmer Buddhism is regarded as particularly unfavourable, as the tradition believes that the spirit of the dead in the form of a ghost remains at the site of death, negating the process of rising again in a different physical body (Hughes, 2006). Therefore, many Cambodians refuse to visit the Choeung Ek stupa, regarding it is a dangerous site, while others believe that it is tantamount to inflicting more violence on those that were brutally executed (Hughes, 2006; Sion, 2011).

While the stupa exposes the horrors of the regime, it was constructed in 1989 during a transient moment of religious freedom after the fall of the Khmer Rouge, with the recognition that it will likely attract international tourists in the future (Hughes, 2006). Although there was little outrage from locals about this (Hughes, 2006), it tells us something deeper about how the profit motive and commodification engender a process – to use Karl Marx's phraseology – whereby 'all that is solid melts into air, all that is *sacred is profaned*' (Marx and Engels, nd, emphasis added). Globalised capitalism displays little regard for religion, culture and tradition; it is concerned solely with opening new markets to maximise profitability. A historic religious practice of Khmer Buddhism could be abandoned to transform a site of atrocity into a tourist attraction, laying the foundations for globalisation's long-running commodification of death (Johnston and Mandelartz, 2016). Essentially, capital continues to be accrued from those that were executed by the Khmer Rouge over 40 years ago, with profits going to the Japanese corporation that since 2005 has managed the site – JC Royal Company – rather than the family members or local communities of the victims (Sion, 2011).

As Tyner et al (2012) outline, the stupa is set up to cater for international consumers and, as a result, there is a relative *absence* of historical detail about the social, economic, political and cultural conditions that engendered the Khmer Rouge's rise to power, how they managed to engage in 'social cleansing' (Mey, 2012: 5) for around four years whereby around a quarter of the Cambodian population were erased (Kiernan, 2008) and how the Khmer Rouge were eventually defeated. This dark destination provides an opportunity to inform international travellers about the Cold War era and the historic ideological battle between communism and capitalism, as well as the historic prevalence of utopian ideological worldviews on how to organise society, particularly in the aftermath of the First World War, even if those utopian ideals often ended in barbarity and mass death. The site's lack of historical details is also elucidated by its failure to report how the Khmer Rouge brokered trade links with Thailand to import knives and axes, while they received over $12,000 worth of anti-malaria drugs by the American Friends Service Committee, which received approval from the US government (Tyner et al, 2012).

Western capitalist states were also complicit in Cambodia's impoverishment and famine after the Khmer Rouge were defeated by the Vietnamese in 1979. As Pilger (1979) documented, while US bombing destabilised the region and emboldened the Khmer Rouge, two million people needed international aid after the genocide, including many family members of those that died at Choeung Ek. However, the United Nations did not recognise the new government – the People's Republic of Kampuchea – after they helped defeat the Khmer Rouge (Pilger, 1979) because they were a communist party formed by the Vietnamese who ideologically supported the communist-ruled Soviet Union. This meant thousands of people continued to die long after executions stopped at Choeung Ek; yet the absence of these historical contextual details means tourists develop a short-sighted understanding of this era in favour of a historically simplified commercial adventure (Sion, 2011).

Lastly, as Sion (2011) noted, over 90 per cent of visitors to Choeung Ek arrive from outside of Cambodia and this was clear when I visited the site as I heard accents from the US, UK, Germany and China, as well as many other countries. Such tourist growth is often cast by many liberal commentators as important in the development of new jobs for domestic citizens. However, this has not necessarily manifested itself in increased living standards and economic stability and security for Cambodians. This is elucidated in the case of tuk-tuk drivers, who often stand outside Choeung Ek waiting for paying tourists to exit to transport them back to Phnom Penh. Tuk-tuks are three-wheeled motorcycles with a cart hooked to the back to transport passengers; they have been the most popular form of public transport for tourists since the 2000s, with over 10,000 tuk-tuk drivers labouring in the capital (Jack, 2020).

However, Jack (2020) highlighted how this labour market is saturated, meaning that while on good working days Cambodian tuk-tuk drivers can earn up to $20, they occasionally go several days without any demand for their services and thus income. Moreover, many drivers cannot afford to purchase their tuk-tuk and are charged high rental costs, heightening their economic precariousness. This insecurity was clear to me by the small fee we paid for the tuk-tuk driver's services to transport us to the killing fields and back to our hotel in Phnom Penh. Yet, I engaged in the psychosocial act of *fetishistic disavowal*. I could see that, despite the huge growth of tourism to Choeung Ek, poverty was still widespread outside of the main tourist areas, and I could see, and was told, that tuk-tuk drivers worked long and unsociable hours for relatively poor pay. However, I suppressed this knowledge from the conscious to the unconscious mind to continue onwards with my individualised pursuit of a commercialised, dark tourist experience.

Conclusion

In short, a visit to Cambodia's killing fields in 2016 revealed the barbarity of Pol Pot's Khmer Rouge regime. However, in retrospect, there were relatively hidden forms of harm from the international tourist. While the construction of the Buddhist stupa negated a historic Khmer Buddhist practice to engage in shock and awe and attract international tourists, money generated from Choeung Ek continued to be siphoned out of the country and into the profit margins of the Japanese corporation JC Royal Company. This dark destination's absence of important historical details meant that tourists to Choeung Ek obtained a rather myopic view of this period in Cambodian history, while the tuk-tuk drivers that provide the core means for tourists to get to Choeung Ek endure myriad economic and social insecurity. Ultimately, it is incumbent upon us to *look beyond the obvious* at dark tourist destinations and identify those forms of harm that are often hidden but socially injurious.

19

Blue lights in the Red Light District: Amsterdam, the Netherlands

Ben Colliver

Birmingham City University

Introduction

It is estimated that approximately 20 million tourists visit the Netherlands annually (Statista, 2021). Amsterdam, the country's capital, remains a popular tourist destination and millions descend upon the capital each year, many seeking a release from more conservative homelands. Amsterdam has become renowned for its liberal attitudes towards marijuana, pornography and sex work (Aalbers and Sabat, 2012). In the heart of Amsterdam lies De Wallen, home to the 'Red Light District'. Despite having three 'red light districts', it is the one in the centre of the old town that is the most popular. The 'Red Light District' gets its name from the illuminous red lights that hang in every window which houses a female sex worker, on display for passers-by to view. The Red Light District is a popular place for those seeking to engage in live sex shows, peep shows, pornography theatres and to pay for sex. RedLightDistrictAmsterdamTours.com (2020) claim that there are approximately 400 sex workers operating within the area on a daily basis, many occupying one of the nearly 300 individual windows located within an area of 17 different streets and alleys. Furthermore, it is estimated that around 15 per cent of sex workers within the 'Red Light District' are transgender. While transgender sex workers are able to work anywhere, most can be found within Bloedstraat, which is well known for its availability of transgender sex workers. Despite being considered a place of liberal values, arguably, such a place does not come without an accompanying dark side.

Liberal values, dark destination?

The Netherlands legalised sex work in 2000 in an attempt to 'counter human trafficking in the sex industry' (Verhoeven and van Gestel, 2017: 112). Sex workers in the Netherlands are therefore recognised as independent workers who are required to register with the Chamber of Commerce and pay income tax. Additionally, brothel owners must be licensed before they offer workspaces to sex workers (Verhoeven and van Gestel, 2017). There exist a multitude of debates around the benefits of decriminalisation[1] and legalisation[2] of sex work (Lutnick and Cohan, 2009). Despite the Netherlands' best intentions, Verhoeven and van Gestel (2017) argue that exploitation and trafficking still occur within the sex industry, with a number of criminal cases taking place in which suspected traffickers have been prosecuted and sentenced (Verhoeven et al, 2013).

While it is beyond the scope of this chapter to engage in all of the various debates surrounding sex work, one of the core contentions when assessing sex work relates to the level of autonomy sex workers have in entering sex work (Sanders et al, 2009). Some have conceptualised sex work as a forced activity characterised by exploitation (Marshall, 2016), while others have acknowledged it as a career choice, and therefore in need of a rights-based approach. Stoops (2016) has argued that sex work is not in and of itself dangerous, rather, that some sections of sex work can be. Others have also noted high rates of violence against sex workers and the impact criminalisation has on their engagement with the criminal justice system after such events (Corteen and Stoops, 2016). However, scholars have argued that this dichotomous approach to understanding sex work is too

1 Decriminalisation refers to the removal of all sex work-specific legislation.

2 Legalisation refers to the regulation and control of sex work by the government.

simplistic, and does not appreciate the complexity associated with navigating sex work (Sanders et al, 2009).

Despite many academic debates around the harms of sex work, this is beyond the scope of this chapter. Rather, this chapter seeks to address a concern outside of the practicalities of sex work, and considers the symbolic othering and fetishisation of transgender sex workers within the 'Red Light District'.

Blue lights and the fetishisation of transgender women

Research has investigated the fear of fetishisation that transgender people may experience and the consequent impact this may have on transgender people's confidence in pursuing sexual and/or romantic relationships (Bartholomaeus and Riggs, 2017). The fetishisation of transgender women has been noted across mainstream media (Tsai, 2010; Fink and Miller, 2013), gaming (Colliver, 2020) and social media (Colliver et al, 2019). While this fear may not be as present for transgender women working within the 'Red Light District', due to the nature of the space, the marking of transgender sex workers as the 'other', through the use of a blue light, contributes to the fetishisation of transgender women. While many transgender people are involved in sex work, in some spaces, sex work is the only profession available to them as a result of the many prejudices that transgender women may face (Ditmore, 2006).

While the argument can be made that the public display of sex workers is fetishising for all those involved, in this chapter, I focus on the implications of fetishising transgender women. Tompkins (2014) has argued that measuring desirability solely on the basis of an individual's transgender identity is fetishising, while simultaneously, suggesting a transgender person's identity is irrelevant does not appreciate transgender embodiment. However, in the context of sex work, and the very public display of transgender sex workers, 'transness' in the 'Red Light District' contributes to the fetishisation of transgender women. This is also reinforced through the online advertisement of the 'Red Light District', and *Amsterdam Guide* (2018a) provides tips on 'how to find ladyboys, shemales and transvestites in the Red Light District'. While acknowledging that these are terms often used by sex workers, the inclusion of these terms in the headline, which are commonly used to describe pornography involving transgender women, reinforces the fetishisation and sexualisation of transgender women.

Marking transgender women as transgender in this way heightens the visibility of transgender people within the sex industry. This heightened visibility may be harmful, as transgender people do not receive such visibility in mainstream media (Billard, 2016; Capuzza and Spencer, 2018). Consequently, a significant amount of transgender representation and visibility is centred on sex which reduces transgender identities down to sexual desirability and does not reflect the wider realities of being transgender. This is important, as it contributes to the delegitimisation and dehumanisation of transgender people, which arguably contributes to a culture of 'transmisogyny' (Serano, 2007).

This has implications for the everyday lives of transgender people and the positioning of transgender women as seductive and hypersexual constructs them purely in terms of their sexual value (Serano, 2007; 2009). Transitioning may also be eroticised, in which transgender women who have not undergone gender reassignment surgery are frequently objectified. While transgender women working within the 'Red Light District' who have undergone gender reassignment surgery may work within a 'red window', the demarcation of transgender women who have not undergone gender reassignment surgery with a blue light exacerbates this fetishisation. Findings by Ellis et al (2016) suggest that nearly half of transgender people experienced fear of being fetishised and objectified. The use of a blue light not only contributes to the fetishisation of transgender women, rather, it is dualistic, in that it also contributes to the 'othering' of transgender women, signifying to the wider population that they are 'different'.

Blue lights, red lights, othering and 'deception'

Not only may the use of a blue light to indicate that a sex worker is transgender contribute to the fetishisation of transgender women, but it is also a strong, public indication that these individuals are 'different'. It has been argued that transgender people are often either fetishised, or alternatively, constructed as undesirable (Mortimer et al, 2019). The use of a blue light symbolically positions transgender women as 'not real women', and in need of additional symbolic descriptors. Research has indicated that transgender people who experience sexual violence recognise their experiences as being explicitly as a result of their gender identity, because they were visible as a transgender person and because of transphobic verbal abuse that often accompanied sexual violence (Motmans et al, 2015).

This narrative is also reinforced through online tourist guides for the 'Red Light District'. *Amsterdam Guide* (2018b) provides information for visitors on 'how to avoid accidently sleeping with a man in Amsterdam's Red Light District'. The online guide draws upon a number of harmful stereotypes and narratives about transgender women that contribute to the 'othering' they may experience. The guide suggests that anyone who is drunk or stoned may not realise and may find themselves sleeping with a man. This not only delegitimises transgender women as inauthentic, it also constructs transgender women as undesirable, only to be sexually engaged with by mistake or under the influence of drugs and/or alcohol.

On the other hand, as there is no legal requirement for transgender sex workers to work with a blue light, some transgender women may work with a red light. *Amsterdam Guide* (2018b) notes that some transgender sex workers may utilise a red light, and rely upon obscuring the presence of a smaller blue light with a curtain, or may simply try to disguise the fact that they are transgender. The choice of a blue light or red light are both problematic. Working with a blue light may result in a transgender sex worker being 'othered', or seen as undesirable. Whereas, working with a red light may lead to accusations of deception. It has been argued that the stereotype of deception 'has been perhaps the most historically consistent and successful idiom through which transgender rights are abrogated and transgender lives are pathologised, demeaned, or cut short' (Fischel, 2019: 99).

It is here within the 'Red Light District' that we see the material, physical manifestation of this dichotomy in which transgender people are constructed as either hypersexualised or undesirable. This creates a culture in which it is easy to blame transgender people for their own victimisation. For example, the use of a blue light to distinguish transgender sex workers as the 'other' contributes to the delegitimisation of transgender women, positioning them as 'less-than' cisgender women. This creates a culture of hostility where transgender women become legitimate targets for violence. On the other hand, if a transgender worker works under a red light, they may be considered to be deceptive, which provides a 'justification' for those who enact violence against them. This has real-life implications for transgender women's experiences of violence and transphobic narratives influence international protective legislation. For example, the 'trans panic' defence is still a legal defence which perpetrators can draw upon to justify the murder of transgender women in the United States (Jamel, 2018).

Conclusion

In this chapter, I have explored the dualistic nature of blue and red lights within the 'Red Light District'. The use of blue lights simultaneously fetishise transgender women, while symbolically marking them as the 'other'. On the other hand, if transgender women operate under a red light, they can be held accountable for their own victimisation. Utilising Amsterdam as a case study is vital, due to the international nature of Amsterdam and the high level of tourist visitors. The symbolism of the lights in Amsterdam may therefore have global influence on the positioning and conceptualisation of transgender people.

While increasing visibility of transgender people is positive, such sexualised visibility may lead to a sensationalist conception and understanding of what it means to be transgender and marginalises transgender people as sexual objects. In a time when violence against transgender people, particularly transgender women, is rising globally (Turner et al, 2009), it is important to challenge such reductive representations. While this may not necessarily be the responsibility of Amsterdam, it does highlight the need for better access and inclusion of transgender people within the workforce outside of sex work. Additionally, it also highlights the need for wider non-erotic representation of transgender people within mainstream media, to address issues of the hypersexualisation and fetishisation of transgender bodies and people.

20

Trophy hunting: sub-Saharan Africa

Patrick Berry and Gary R. Potter

Alumni, Lancaster University and Lancaster University

Introduction

This chapter seeks to critically analyse trophy hunting as a form of dark tourism. Trophy hunting involves the killing of animals to keep and display body parts as trophies. Hunting is legal in many countries around the world, but big game hunting is at its biggest in sub-Saharan Africa, which accounts for seven of the top ten countries that export trophy items (Born Free, 2019). Tourists, predominantly from the US and Europe, pay substantial fees to shoot indigenous wildlife. Often portrayed somewhat romantically as a battle of wits between man (and participants are predominantly, although by no means exclusively, men) and beast, hunting is seen as an exciting and dangerous wilderness adventure. In reality, while hunting can involve tracking animals on foot and sleeping in tents, hunters are well equipped, well protected and well looked after. Costing hundreds to thousands of dollars per day, hunting safaris are a high-end luxury form of tourism. 'Canned' hunting, where animals are bred in captivity and released into enclosed areas to be shot, takes hunting even further away from any pretence of a fair chase or a reversion to some natural state of predator versus prey.

Trophy hunting is undoubtedly highly controversial in an age of species decline and endangerment (WWF, 2020), and of increased scientific and legal recognition of animal sentience. Debate is polarised: supporters of trophy hunting point to ecological and economic benefits that hunting tourism brings (Di Minin et al, 2016); opponents argue that conservation benefits are overstated, that hunting exacerbates economic and social divisions in local communities and, more fundamentally, that trophy hunting involves inflicting inexcusable levels of suffering on animals.

The dark ethical transgressions of trophy hunting

The most obvious 'dark' element of trophy hunting is that it involves the killing of animals for no justification other than human pleasure. While other forms of hunting – for food, or to protect livestock, crops or livelihoods – also involve killing animals, these are often seen as less unacceptable because the benefits associated with them are linked to tangible human needs. Trophy hunting serves no obvious purpose of necessity – hunters do not kill animals out of either a need to survive or to thrive economically. Motivation to hunt is purely embedded in the personal satisfactions of excitement and egotism. The trophies acquired are to signal prowess and personality to others – to seek admiration and approval from fellow hunters, and to advertise wealth and status to other social peers (Thompson, 1975; Gunn, 2001; Bryant, 2004; Courchamp et al, 2006; Bell, 2009).

The premature, violent and unjustifiable deaths associated with hunting raise many ethical questions. From an animal rights or species justice perspective, animals have the right not to suffer; death from hunting is often preceded by stress and injury, by hours or days of pain and suffering. For animals raised in captivity for canned hunting, suffering may be a feature of their entire lives. Ethical concerns around trophy hunting are passionately expressed both in literature and public discourse. All hunting forms can appear ethically dubious, requiring moral tolerance (von Essen and Nurse, 2017). Environmental ethics writers see trophy hunting as 'plastic hunting', where hunters receive unfair advantages and show a lack of respect for the animal when posing with the carcass (Loftin, 1988; Taylor, 1996). Hunting tolerance generally decreases when endangered or young animals are killed (Curcione, 1992), attracting public attention and backlash (Blevins and Edwards, 2009).

There are a plethora of ethical issues relating to how hunting takes place, from trapping and baiting, hunting with dogs, shooting from vehicles and more (Lindsey et al, 2006). However, the most unethical element is arguably canned hunting, where animals are raised in captivity and kept in abhorrent conditions and small enclosures so they cannot escape, guaranteeing a kill for the hunter (Di Minin et al, 2016). Between 80 and 90 per cent of lions hunted in South Africa are canned (Di Minin et al, 2016), highlighting serious ethical problems within the industry. Hunting for sport is fundamentally rejected by animal welfarists for reasons beyond the immediate concern of harms to the animals hunted. One issue here is the devaluation of wildlife, degrading the worth of animals by putting a price on their lives according to how much a hunter is willing to pay to kill them, rather than appreciating their value as living beings (Sheikh, 2019).

In line with this argument, many believe that humans should engage respectfully with animals. They scorn the international conservation community and anyone who accepts trophy hunting for aiding and abetting a highly immoral practice. At heart, being 'inescapably tethered to a system that involves killing and debasing individual nonhuman animals, as the only way to save their populations or species' is undoubtedly tragic (Batavia et al, 2018: 4).

The dichotomies of trophy hunting: a tool of conservation or economics?

From a broader ecological or conservation perspective, hunting wild populations may clearly have some impact on population levels – a particularly important consideration for endangered species. Intervening with the lives of wild animals can also have serious ramifications for wider ecosystems and biodiversity (White, 2011). However, trophy hunting is often defended as having a role to play in ecology and conservation efforts (Di Minin et al, 2016). Supposedly, it is sustainable through low off-takes and high fees, where a few animals are sacrificed to trophy hunters at high prices in order to reinvest the money into the conservation of species and habitats with minimal risks for species decline and ecological degradation (Bond et al, 2004; Leader-Williams et al, 2005). However, there are many questions – and a need for more research – over hunting's legitimacy as a conservation tool (Lindsey et al, 2006).

The Convention on International Trade in Endangered Species (CITES) and national laws regulate trophy hunting to ensure that the numbers of hunted animals are not excessive or unsustainable. Host countries are responsible for issuing quotas which designate the number of animals legally permitted to be trophy hunted (Sheikh, 2019). It is argued that, where quotas are carefully adhered to, 'revenues from tightly regulated trophy hunting can provide important incentives for careful management, protection and reintroductions' of especially endangered species (Lindsey et al, 2006: 461). Trophy hunting revenues have been seen to aid the reintroduction of some endangered species (Flack, 2003) and have stimulated the development of some wildlife conservancies (Weaver and Skyer, 2003). Revenues have been used to employ rangers to combat illegal poaching (Lewis and Alpert, 1997; Di Minin et al, 2015). However, many critically challenge trophy hunting's conservational value and express concern over quotas. Governments have been found to mismanage wildlife numbers (Caro et al, 1998; Taylor, 2001) and set unscientific quotas based upon guesswork, sometimes without specifications or age restrictions on the animals hunted (Packer et al, 2011). Further, some African states ineffectively monitor and enforce quotas, so weak governance allows trophy hunting regulations to be easily bypassed (Leader-Williams et al, 2009). The wealth of hunters can bribe outfitters to facilitate illegal hunts (Eliason, 2012) and there are many documented instances of high hunting rates causing species decline (Adams, 2004; Packer et al, 2009). Ultimately, there is no guarantee that quotas are accurate, being abided by or that trophy hunting is not endangering species, particularly when there is increasing pressure for large quotas (Lindsey et al, 2006) and animals being sold too cheaply to provide any benefit (Wilkie and Carpenter, 1999; Dickinson, 2021). The conservation objective of trophy hunting is clearly limited when it is hard to police.

It is argued that trophy hunting is a profitable use of land as many game ranches have been established over the years (Krug, 2001) and that trophy hunting land uses are twice as financially beneficial to conservation than protecting animals in national parks and can generate income where other land uses are not viable (Lindsey et al, 2006). Others stress that trophy hunting is imperative, and land would be converted for uses detrimental to biodiversity without it (Di Minin et al, 2013). The idea appears counterintuitive, capturing and raising animals in ranches to protect them by killing them, and many point out the ecological implications of this. Fenced game ranches in Africa are often small and overpopulated (Patterson and Khosa, 2005), and ranchers are known to hybridise species to create exotic trophies, disrupting genetics for the purpose of saleability (Hamman et al, 2003). Natural functions such as roaming and migration are obstructed (Estes et al, 2011; Woodroffe et al, 2014) and predatory animals are often persecuted to save large herbivores for trophy hunters (Ripple et al, 2016). The adverse effects of trophy hunting are well documented, underpinned by trophy hunting's unnatural and artificial impact on nature. From inbreeding (Milner et al, 2007) to disrupting social species (Packer et al, 2009), trophy hunting damages wildlife (Ripple et al, 2016). Evolutionary consequences from trophy hunting are hard to reverse (Coltman et al, 2003), and trophy hunting is an intrusive practice affecting mammals globally (Milner-Gulland et al, 2003). Further, local communities can find trophy hunting destructive (Sachedina, 2008). So, while supporters emphasise the importance of hunting revenue for conservation, their attention is misguided by failing to address many key issues regarding species welfare which seriously trouble the sustainability of trophy hunting (Coltman et al, 2003).

There is certainly a lack of consensus surrounding the legitimacy, acceptability and effectiveness of trophy hunting as a conservational tool (Lindsey et al, 2006). Proponents highlight the cruciality of trophy hunting as conservation efforts are already underfunded and would suffer dramatically without the revenues (Di Minin et al, 2016). Countries may ban trophy hunting on their own turf, or may ban trophy imports to curtail hunting elsewhere (Sheikh, 2019). Trophies are not required for conservation, and neither are the thrills and remorselessness intertwined with trophy hunting, which may lead us to question the sincerity of 'conservation' as a justification for hunting (Batavia et al, 2018).

Past literature has emphasised that trophy hunting is economically superior to alternative options, such as ecotourism

(Leader-Williams and Hutton, 2005; Lindsey et al, 2006). Even where tourism thrives, trophy hunting revenues are still argued as vital (Baldus, 2005). Since trophy hunters pay more than conventional tourists, more income is generated from fewer people (Chardonnet, 1995), thus reducing the carbon footprint and environmental impacts (Gössling, 2000; Di Minin et al, 2016). From an animal welfare perspective, emissions are not relevant to the trophy hunting debate (Ripple et al, 2016), but they may be from a broader ecological perspective. On the other hand, ecotourism may have greater benefits than hunting, with the potential of generating income over a sustained period greater than a one-time kill by a trophy hunter (Myers, 1981). There is also evidence that nature-based tourism is more significant in national development than trophy hunting, which accounts for just 1.8 per cent of total tourism revenues. Since the majority of African tourism is nature-based, the value of animals is obvious, and the majority would rather see wildlife alive than dead (Campbell, 2013).

Trophy hunting is also lauded by supporters for the benefits it provides to local communities, including employment opportunities, income and food, although most trophy animals are not typically edible (Fischer et al, 2015). The industry is reported to be lucrative, generating hundreds of millions of US dollars per year in Africa (Lindsey et al, 2006), which is vital to some countries. However, even proponents are not blind to the fact that trophy hunting is fraught with corruption and mismanagement (Lewis and Jackson, 2005; Lindsey et al, 2006). Revenues are distributed unfairly, contrary to agreements, to the point where local communities do not receive adequate funds (Child, 2005). Research suggests that less than a quarter of total revenues have been reinvested into wildlife management (Di Minin et al, 2016), and local communities have seen as little as a 3–5 per cent share of the revenue (Lindsey et al, 2006). This is a key driver behind negative attitudes towards trophy hunting (Mayaka, 2002), contributing to distrust between local communities and governments (Nshala, 1999). Unrest stems from the difficulty in recognising how trophy hunting fees are utilised, by whom and who they truly benefit. If local communities are not benefiting, it is extremely hard to identify the positives of trophy hunting. The crux of the matter is that trophy hunting is justified by the money that it generates, yet the genuine benefits are few and far between.

Conclusion

Arguments about the ecological and economic benefits of trophy hunting may be irrelevant to those who see this primarily as an animal rights or animal welfare issue, but it is clear that the ecological and economic benefits that are claimed may not be as strongly supported by the evidence as they are by hunting supporters. Even if such benefits could be better harnessed, and if hunting could be practised to both sustainable and humanitarian standards, there are other problems associated with the 'sport'. The financial value placed on many hunting trophies, particularly those coming from more endangered species, helps drive the illegal wildlife trade. Legal hunting can fuel and become illegal poaching (von Essen and Nurse, 2017) and support serious and organised crime.

Hunting, arguably, sustains and perpetuates more fundamental social divisions. Hunting can be understood as a primarily male practice which demonstrates patriarchal domination over nature (Gunn, 2001) and exhibits hegemonic masculinity (Sollund, 2020). Not only have trophies long symbolised power, success and status (Krier and Swart, 2016), they have also been associated with male supremacy (Mullin, 1999). The boasts of trophy hunters and their arguably disrespectful trophy collections demonstrate a 'victory' over nature, adding a new dimension to their 'manhood' on top of their power ascribed by wealth and a sense of camaraderie with other men (Kheel, 2008). Ultimately, killing animals larger than mankind 'may represent one of the last bastions of men to exercise "traditional, hegemonic masculinity" (Sollund, 2020: 12). Trophy hunting in Africa is also a colonial hangover (Born Free, 2019), perpetuating and reinforcing global power imbalances and ethnic and racial divisions, and feeding into the 'culture wars' of North America and Western Europe. It is perhaps not surprising that public support for trophy hunting is limited, and that more and more countries are more tightly restricting trophy hunting – or banning it completely.

21

'The ugly side to the beautiful game': Qatar

Grace Gallacher

Staffordshire University

Introduction

On 2 December 2010, the announcement that Qatar would host the 2022 World Cup sent shock waves through the sporting community, given that Qatar is a relatively small state with little in the way of footballing history (Brannigan and Giulianotti, 2015). The 2022 World Cup marks the first time the tournament has been held in an Arab country and over one million tourists to the state were projected (FIFA, 2022). It is not uncommon for countries to use mega sporting events such as the World Cup to enhance their global presence and alter their international image (Brannigan and Giulianotti, 2015; Millward, 2017). However, as this chapter will demonstrate, Qatar has failed to 'rebut Orientalist images of the nation, the Persian Gulf and Arab peoples more generally' (Millward, 2017). Indeed, the spotlight on Qatar and its treatment of migrant workers under the *kafala* system, its questionable LGBT+ laws and the way in which the bid was obtained have not only failed to rebut negative images of Qatar, but have attracted further criticism. This chapter will outline the controversies surrounding the bid, as well as examining some of the harshest human rights violations in modern history before highlighting why Qatar wanted to host the 2022 World

Cup, showing how Qatar is one of the most modern dark tourist destinations.

The bid: fraud and deception

There have been several 'extensive' reports on the bribery and corruption surrounding the 2022 World Cup bid (Brannigan and Giulianotti, 2015). Often coming from media sources and investigative journalists, it has been shown that many senior FIFA officials raised questions around the legitimacy of Qatar winning the bid to host the sporting tournament. As Brannigan and Giulianotti (2015) reported, there have been claims that, in 2011, over $1 million was paid to the African FIFA committee in order to buy votes for which the FIFA executive committee member at the time, Mohammed bin Hammam, has received a lifetime ban from football. The idea that these votes had been bought was further cemented when the United States federal prosecutors disclosed cases of profiteering, vote rigging and corruption by FIFA officials (Millward, 2017), exacerbated by the charges brought against the then FIFA president Sepp Blatter (of which he was later acquitted). Moreover, there are claims around then vice-president Jack Warner accepting over two million in Swiss francs from a film company that produced the Qatar bid's promotional videos (Watt, 2014). There is little doubt around the fraud and deception around Qatar winning the votes to host the 2022 World Cup; however, the decision was never rebuked.

Modern slavery in focus

In 2013, Pete Pattisson published a report for *The Guardian* highlighting the abuse and exploitation of the migrant workers preparing Qatar for the 2022 World Cup in a series of articles titled Modern Slavery in Focus. In the report, Pattisson brought to light some of the most appalling treatment of migrant workers we have seen in modern history. He reported the deaths of workers, violations of rights, forced labour, passport confiscation and wage theft, all which he claims amounts to the International Labour Organization's (ILO) definition of modern-day slavery (Engle, 2014). Since this report, there have been numerous investigations by international non-governmental organisations (INGOs) confirming such treatment, such as Amnesty International, Human Rights Watch and Fair Square, and a coalition of migrant rights groups and labour unions have petitioned for the conditions for workers to be improved and for compensation for loss of life, earnings and ill treatment (Human Rights Watch, 2022). These organisations have shown that migrant workers under the *kafala* system are being exploited into forced labour with very little in the way of rights. The *kafala* system means that the migrant employees are effectively sponsored by a *kafeel*, who assumes responsibility for the worker. These contracts are usually for a minimum of two years and are a result of recruitment agencies in host nations sourcing *kafeels* (Millward, 2017).

It is in this *kafala* system that loopholes in laws are being exploited and UN human rights violated (Engle, 2014). As Millward (2017) pointed out, the *kafeel* effectively controls the worker, which takes away all individual autonomy. The workers must apply to leave or move employment and in many cases the INGOs have found that the *kafeels* are withholding wages, keeping passports, removing work visas and refusing to allow workers to switch employment or leave (Amnesty International, 2022a). This is then compounded by inhumane working conditions and cramped and poor living conditions, such as 12 workers living in one room, violating the state's laws (Engle, 2014), little or no access to food and water (Amnesty International, 2022a) and the theft of wages (Pattisson, 2013; Millward, 2017; Amnesty International, 2022b). All of these elements not only reduce the workers to modern-day slaves but moreover, we can confidently assume that the almost 1.7 million migrant workers (Amnesty International, 2022a) are indeed *homo sacer*. *Homo sacer* is the idea that migrants are cast out of the political system (Rajaram and Grundy-Warr, 2004); indeed, they are seen as non-people, non-citizens.

However, more disturbing than the intervention of the rights of the migrants is the death toll linked to the construction of the infrastructure of the 2022 World Cup. Ganji (2016) reported that since the announcements in 2010 and 2013, more than 1,200 labour migrants have died, and predicts over 4,000 more deaths before the World Cup commences in December 2022. The workers are literally dying to construct the eight stadiums, airports and other infrastructure needed to host such a competition. This contravenes FIFA's ethos around the World Cup, meaning that Qatar's approach is 'not consistent with FIFA's objectives for the World Cup, namely, that it should "fulfil FIFA objectives to touch the world, develop the game, and build a better future through a variety of ways"' (Engle, 2014: 179).

What we can see from the treatment of migrants is that FIFA are not fulfilling this responsibility but moreover, by awarding the bid to Qatar, they legitimised the *kafala* system and the working practices within it (Millward, 2017). In this sense, FIFA epitomise what Tombs and Whyte (2015) stated as corporate irresponsibility whereby they claim that transnational corporations are set up to shift responsibility. In this case, FIFA have claimed that the 'treatment of migrant workers in Qatar belong elsewhere' (Millward, 2017: 767), indicating a responsibility of the state and subcontractors.

The importance of the World Cup: socio-symbolic status

Brannigan and Giulianotti (2015) have commented on Qatar's motivations in hosting the 2022 World Cup, outlining that countries often use sporting mega events to globally lift the profile of the country. Qatar is no exception, using the World Cup as a part of a wider strategy to improve tourism and as a symbol of modernity and change (Brannigan and Giulianotti, 2015). The World Cup then becomes symbolic in its role. It symbolises Qatar's status in the international community. It represents a competition which is purely socially constructed to gain international acknowledgement of winning. Another form of global platform in which countries can assert their sporting dominance. Asserting one's place in the social hierarchy using goods and status is not uncommon, as we have seen from researchers such as Hall et al (2009) who have highlighted such arguments. Qatar is doing this on an international level, using the World Cup as the status marker with disastrous consequences. This then can raise wider questions around the harm associated with football and symbolic tournaments and how much we as a public are willing to accept these harms as normalised. With an estimated one million people expected to visit Qatar in December 2022 (FIFA, 2022) we can see this in action.

Conclusion

This chapter has outlined the controversies surrounding the awarding of the 2022 World Cup to Qatar, a small state with limited football history. It has looked at the mistreatment of the millions of migrant workers who are literally giving their lives to produce a whole new infrastructure to support this symbolic status from Qatar. Moreover, it has brought to light some of the violations of basic human rights that the workers are facing under the *kafala* system. However, as we have also seen, this could have been avoided if FIFA had re-voted once the rigging came to light, or if they had taken any responsibility in the treatment of the workers rather than legitimising it (Millward, 2017). Ultimately, in a bid to create and prove to the global community that Qatar has changed and deserves an international symbolic seat at the table, what we have seen instead is the mistreatment of migrants and discrimination against women and the gay community. As Ganji (2016: 227) notes, 'Qatar's World Cup will be remembered as a human rights tragedy'. Yet, football fans in their millions will still visit Qatar to take part in the competitive tournament and see who will be hailed world leader of football for the next four years, thus making Qatar one of the darkest tourist destinations in modern history.

22

Burning Man festival: Black Rock Desert, Nevada, USA

Keith Hayward

University of Copenhagen

Introduction

Head northeast out of Reno, Nevada, and after a hundred miles or so of mostly single-lane highway, you'll reach Gerlach, a dusty old railroad town situated at the southerly outskirts of the Black Rock Desert. For 50 weeks of the year, the 300,000 acres of beautiful but inhospitable alkali flats, or playa, that make up Black Rock Desert are eerily quiet, empty save a few intrepid visitors and the Bureau of Land Management officers tasked with the area's protection and preservation. However, for nine days every August, this all changes, as the desert playa is dramatically transformed into a temporary city-like encampment – 'Black Rock City' – that, since 1991, has played host to the notorious Burning Man festival. Superficially viewed by the uninitiated as an off-grid hedonists' free-for-all, Burning Man is in fact a multifaceted event that brings together sculptural artists, fire and pyrotechnic imagineers, musicians and performers, futurists, counterculture community builders, and, yes, hedonistic and bohemian attendees (or 'Burners') from across the world. Although Burning Man is synonymous with dusty sandstorms and dry desert heat, the event's roots lie in Northern California,

Figure 22.1: The Man (2014)

Source: Photo by Keith Hayward

and a series of small summer solstice gatherings that took place at Baker Beach, San Francisco, in the 1980s (it's estimated that fewer than 50 people attended the inaugural Baker Beach event). A key feature of these parties were bonfire rituals, including the burning of small wooden effigies, and it is from this practice that the Burning Man festival got its name. Each year, a large human-shaped wooden sculpture (called *the man* – see Figure 22.1) is razed to the ground on the penultimate night of the event. The sculptural form of *the man* changes every year (as does that of 'The Temple', a secondary, more contemplative wooden installation burned on the event's closing day), while the festival itself also adopts a different annual theme.

Carnival, creativity and community

In many ways, Burning Man represents almost the exact opposite of a 'dark destination'. During daylight hours, the mega gathering – in 2019, over 78,000 people attended – takes place under an unremitting desert sun; while at night, the ink-black Nevada sky is lit up by breathtaking fire displays, laser art shows and the twinkling nightlights of a thousand campsites, all of which combine to give Black Rock City a magical, almost other-worldly feel. This surreal sense is further enhanced by the unique, carnivalesque atmosphere of the camp. Mutant art cars traverse the playa, stopping periodically to create temporary nightclubs; rollercoasters and fairground rides shoot fire into the night sky; new music echoes around the camp as hybrid pick-up bands form in shaded chill-out tents; and swarms of neon-clad bicyclists wearing angel wings or post-apocalyptic costumes weave in and out of the camp's backstreets and main Esplanade. Some years, there is even a replica of the Thunderdome from *Mad Max III*, where Burners can let off steam or settle scores using foam-padded bats. But, while artworks, architectural installations and performative celebrations are defining features of the festival (see Figure 22.2), Burning Man is no gallery or staid exhibition space. Rather, attendees are responsible for 'creating', rather than passively consuming, the festival. Consequently, no two days at Burning Man are ever the same as the event constantly evolves as a site of creativity and artistic self-expression (see Harvey, 2017; Guy, 2018).

But as the philosopher Mikhail Bakhtin (1984) reminds us, the ideal of 'carnival' is not limited to festive excess and the sense of 'a world turned upside down'. Carnivalesque expression also brings with it the notion of transgression, where the pleasures of the body are 'foregrounded in opposition to the dominant and accepted values of restraint and sobriety' (Presdee, 2000: 38). No surprise, then, that, over the years, Burning Man has also garnered a well-deserved reputation for hedonistic pursuits, including drug use, nudity and a relaxed attitude to sexual encounters. However, while it is certainly true that Burning Man's countercultural roots make for a relaxed, free-wheeling festival experience, it's wrong to assume the event is an unregulated space. Far from it. As well as federal Bureau of Land Management Rangers, the festival is patrolled by various local police agencies, and each year a small number of arrests – 58 in 2019, mostly for drug offences – are made. Entrance and egress from the camp is also monitored by law enforcement, with sporadic vehicle searches taking place. No 'city' of this size can function effectively without other important public services, and Burning Man is no different (on the festival's behind-the-scenes organisational operations, see Chen, 2009). The encampment is thus equipped with its own (volunteer) emergency medical stations, a fire department and a radio station for public service announcements. A volunteer group of 'Black Rock Rangers' also provide a rudimentary policing service, although this mostly involves dispute resolution. (On one of my visits, I witnessed the collapse of a raised geodesic performance stage and was impressed by the professionalism and efficiency of the camp's first responders.) The city's crescent-shaped layout is also carefully planned and managed.

But it is for an altogether different set of behavioural codes that Burning Man is rightly famous. Initially written by one of the event's founders, Larry Harvey, the festival, its attendees and all its affiliated communities and projects are guided by the following ten fundamental principles: radical inclusion, gifting, decommodification, radical self-reliance, radical self-expression, communal effort, civic responsibility, leaving no trace, participation and immediacy. Described by one commentator as not simply a camp guide, but skills to live by (Magister, 2019), 'The Principles' are a recent 'codification' of the festival's long-standing commitment to community inclusion, environmentalism and anti-corporatism. For example, a key aspect of the festival is the avoidance of any currency exchange. Instead, Burners engage in bartering, borrowing, sharing and gift giving practices that enhance communality and challenge consumer-driven market logics (Kozinets, 2002). Likewise, attendees are required to leave the desert playa as they found it, free of litter (or MOOP – matter out of place), 'burn scares' or vehicle drip spills. In sum, whether it's the values espoused in 'The Principles', or the thousands of acts of kindness that occur each day across the camp, Burning Man stands as a (albeit temporary) testament to what can be achieved when radical creativity, civic responsibility and self-reliance are placed at the heart of community life.

Figure 22.2: One of the many art installations that are created each year at Burning Man

Source: Photo by Keith Hayward

Controversy and commercialisation

In recent times, however, cracks have started to appear in Burning Man's famed sense of community, as the counterculture party in the desert has been rocked by a series of controversies. To start with, as the event has grown in popularity, it has attracted a rising number of super-rich attendees, including celebrities and high-profile figures from Silicon Valley and the wider tech industry. In stark contrast to the ethos of radical self-reliance, many of these high-wealth individuals construct lavish designer compounds – so-called 'turnkey' camps – that can include state-of-the-art kitchens, luxury toilets (most Burners hold their nose and use Portaloos) and even air-conditioned yurt bedrooms. In a further show of elitism, wealthy attendees – many of whom have paid thousands of dollars for their spot at these rich man camps – fly directly to the desert in private planes, circumventing the need to negotiate the traffic problems that often build up around Gerlach. On touching down at the makeshift desert airstrip, high rollers then hop on golf carts that waft them directly to their camp, while paid staff, or 'Sherpas', as they are sometimes sarcastically referred to, haul designer luggage behind them.

For many veteran Burners, such developments symbolise the death of Burning Man's original countercultural ethos. Indeed, in 2019, the event's CEO, Marian Goodell, called for 'cultural course correcting' to turn back the tide of luxury camps and Instagram commercialisation (Boucher, 2019). Others are more sanguine about this new breed of dude ranch Burners. Veteran festival goer, Kristen Berman, for example, argues that by funding Burning Man artists, turnkey camps are benefiting everyone; what's more, '[H]aving the most powerful men and women in the world experience the beautiful and loving social norms of Burning Man COULD ONLY BE A GOOD THING for our default world as it will infuse new ideas and ways of living' (Berman, 2014, emphasis in original). Recent events, however, suggest certain factions at Burning Man have little interest in infusing the minds of the rich and famous, choosing instead to register their discontent via the less spiritual method of direct action. In 2016, the White Ocean zone, a luxury camp co-founded by the son of a Russian oil magnate, was raided by a militant group of festival goers who cut power lines (to kitchen refrigerators), glued trailer doors shut and flooded parts of the camp with potable water.

The pushback against the festival's so-called 'parasite class' is not the only controversy swirling around Burning Man. Since the event's rapid expansion in the 2000s, concern has been raised by various groups, including the historic environmental society the Sierra Club, about the huge carbon footprint produced by transporting construction materials, people, provisions and water to the remote desert location. Even the festival's trademark fire art has been criticised for its supposedly 'wasteful' use of propane gas and other fossil fuels. Rising ticket prices have also been a source of criticism – in 2000, advance tickets could be purchased for $165; by 2018, that price was closer to $1,000 – with long-time festival goers suggesting that some in the organisation were prioritising profit over people (in 2013, Black Rock City LLC was replaced by a non-profit organisation).

Conclusion

In the future, Burning Man will no doubt continue to be criticised for some of its practices while being feted all over the world for its creativity and anarcho-hippie spirit of co-creation. In this sense, the end-of-the-summer, convention-breaking, fire ritual in the desert that is Burning Man ironically reflects a truth about the wider American society it purports to reject: that is, that while extreme opinions abound, the truth lies somewhere in between and can only really be grasped through first-hand experience.

23

Magaluf: Majorca

Simon Winlow

Northumbria University

Introduction

How can Magaluf, a resort in Majorca – a beautiful island off the coast of Spain, to which millions of tourists flock each year – even remotely be considered a 'dark destination'? Magaluf is particularly attractive to young people from Britain, Ireland, Germany and Scandinavia. They are drawn to the island because of the beautiful beaches and the almost guaranteed summer sun, but most come because of Magaluf's famed nightlife. They are young and they want to have a good time. They want to get drunk with friends, and of course they want to hook up with good-looking strangers. What could be wrong with that? Isn't it absurdly moralistic to find fault with the attitudes and behaviours of these young people? Aren't those behaviours reasonably universal, inasmuch as young people have throughout history carried similar attitudes and engaged in similar behaviours? And mightn't there be a regrettable element of class bigotry in problematising the behaviours of this group of young tourists? Shouldn't we instead critique the entitled hedonists of the Bullingdon Club or the middle-class liberals who every year head off to Thailand, Bali or Barbados to get drunk and seek out one-night stands?

These are interesting questions in and of themselves, but they tend to negate the traditional imperative of social science, which of course is to objectively appraise social life free from the interference of advocacy groups and vested interests. To understand the world in which we live, we must dispense with common-sense interpretations and dig beneath the surface of social life. This is why the intellectual agenda opened up here – 'dark destinations' – holds considerable promise for the social sciences. On the surface, we have obvious forms of dark tourism. These might involve the commercialisation of a murder site, or indeed any specific environment associated with dark deeds. However, it also involves an attempt to understand the motives of those drawn to such places.

The study of dark destinations also necessitates a perspectival shift, and in this brief chapter I will attempt to move away from the common-sense interpretation of Magaluf as a site of bawdy and youthful, but not particularly problematic, fun in the sun. If we shift our perspective, a range of parallax views are opened up. Put simply, a parallax view alters the way that we engage with the object in question. As we alter our perspective, the object itself, or our interpretation of it, changes. What seemed, from one perspective, to be one thing, turns out to be, from another perspective, something else entirely.

What is dark about Magaluf?

How might we develop an understanding of Magaluf as a dark destination? First, we might note that the sheer scale of tourism to the island has altered the lives of its residents enormously. Magaluf developed quickly as the era of commercial tourism began to get up and running in the late 1970s. Property was bought cheaply and commercialised. Large hotels began to spring up to cater for tourists attracted to the beautiful, wide beach and the picturesque coastline. Then, of course, a range of ancillary commercial services were needed to ensure that those tourists had what they needed. First, restaurants and small bars. Boat tours, car hire, mini-golf parks and supermarkets to service those who had opted for self-catering accommodation, rather than the traditional hotels. As the resort grew, more and more money spilled in. Some local families were able to capitalise on the huge opportunities opened up by rapid commercialisation, but larger corporations from the Spanish mainland – and, later, much further afield – were also keen to grab a piece of the action. Families that had for generations been involved in the local fishing industry quickly found themselves engulfed by foreigners who tended to speak English rather than Spanish. The small, contained and familiar world they had known was at an end.

The sudden influx of tourists and tourist money put a huge strain upon local institutions and infrastructure. The island needed new motorways, hospitals and sewer systems, and enough gas, water and electricity to cater for its rapidly growing population. It also needed to grow its local population of police officers, and this was especially the case as the families that had come to the island during the initial boom in package holidays were slowly replaced by single sex parties of young people (see Briggs and Ellis, 2017).

There are suggestions that these local institutions couldn't cope with the stresses and strains of rapid commercialisation. Tales of institutionalised corruption on the island abound. Oceans of money had washed over the island and its previously sedate and old-fashioned forms of governance were engulfed. Even today, in an era of supposed transparency, there is good reason to suspect that graft, backroom deals and corruption of all kinds constitute a regrettable norm on the island.

In the absence of reasonably robust forms of governance, organised crime grows. From the 1980s onwards, both legal and illegal commercial opportunities attracted organised crime groups from across Europe and further afield. As Magaluf continued to grow, opportunities existed to launder criminal proceeds. Local officials could be corrupted. Building contracts worth millions were on offer. But that is not all. Magaluf was built as a cash economy. Even now, in an era of chip and pin, many businesses prefer to deal only in cash. This presented opportunities not just for local store owners to under-report business takings, it also presented opportunities for organised crime groups to wash their ill-gotten gains.

Slowly, the overall tone of tourism to Magaluf began to change. As younger tourists replaced older tourists, the town's commercial base shifted appreciably. Legal businesses that catered for younger tourists replaced businesses that catered for older tourists and family groups. Of course, the influx of younger tourists also opened up illegal business opportunities. The sale of illegal drugs is now quite openly practised, and prostitution is hard to ignore.

Suggestions of police corruption have existed for some time. Certainly, during my time on the island, no police attention whatsoever was given to the open sale of illegal drugs or other commercially driven illegality. The police are, however, incredibly heavy-handed when it comes to dealing with ubiquitous youth drunkenness. I heard innumerable tales of police violence, mostly from young men. These were often accompanied by tales of the police issuing demands for cash. Failing to pay up would mean arrest and a missed flight home. In some cases, the police confiscated passports until money was handed over.

There is a good deal of violence in Magaluf. The main drinking strip is packed with tens of thousands of young men and women during the height of the tourist season. An established ethic of extreme intoxication pervades the island. Inevitably, there are flashpoints. Occasionally, the police respond, but it is difficult to get a car through the densely packed streets to the site of the incident. Tourists are pushed and pulled and occasionally struck with nightsticks as the police attempt to work their way through the crowd. There are also tensions between Spanish tourists, mostly from the mainland, and tourists from elsewhere in Europe. British tourists are in the majority, but they face considerable dangers when trying to make their way back to their hotels in the early hours of the morning after a night of heavy drinking. Tour operators advise young British tourists to stick together. Lone British tourists have been targeted for assault by Spanish tourists, apparently aggrieved at the British occupation of an island they consider to be theirs by right.

It is strangely illuminating to see the main drinking strip in the early morning, after the drinkers have dragged themselves back to their hotels. The scale of the devastation is quite instructive. An army of street cleaners tackle the main drinking strip. Vomit, urine and faeces are washed away by hosepipes and slow-moving street-cleaning vehicles. Another vehicle collects tens of thousands of empty beer bottles and discarded plastic beer containers. A highly efficient refuse collection system ensures the drinking strip is quickly ready for the nightly influx. Still comatose young men are also scattered about the place: in doorways, on benches and so on. Others sit on the kerb, trying to summon up a memory of where their hotel is located, and the energy needed to make it back there.

There are no young women out on the street at this hour. During peak hours, the main drinking strip is predominantly a male space. Along with my colleagues, Tony Ellis and Dan Briggs (see Ellis et al, 2018), I spoke to many young women who approached each night out with a measure of apprehension. Like the men, they were excited to discover what the night would bring, but they were also perfectly aware that sexual assault had become routinised to the extent that it is scarcely remarked upon. Our female contacts knew to stick together, and most felt more imperilled in Magaluf than they did on a night out back at home.

An Accident and Emergency (A&E) doctor at the island's hospital adds further detail on the dark side of mass tourism. Young tourists are often so dedicated to the pursuit of pleasure that they find themselves in great pain. Alcohol poisoning is incredibly common, as are broken limbs, which mostly result from moped crashes and drunken dives into shallow swimming pools or off cliffs into the sea. Women working in the sex trade, some of whom are recently arrived immigrants from Africa, also find their way into the A&E department. The main assailants tend to be men attempting to organise sex traffic rather than drunken tourists. The doctor feels engulfed. From his perspective, the problems grow worse with every passing year.

Some of our contacts reported feeling short-changed and rather disappointed by their short visit to Magaluf. Many expected to have sex, but the vast majority were disappointed. Some had been tempted by the huge number of prostitutes working on the island, and here again we heard stories of frustration and disappointment. Tales of small-scale theft were common. Most of our contacts had spent a huge amount of money. Many had spent so much money they feared returning home to face the music. They had run up debts – mostly bank overdrafts and credit card advances – because they believed that a holiday in Magaluf would allow them to experience the very things that seemed absent from their humdrum lives in the UK. The mundanity of the working week would be replaced by the extreme experiences they believed constituted 'the good life'. For a moment, they would be transcendent. They would deal with the debts when they returned to reality (see Briggs, 2013).

However, their experiences often weren't that great. There was drunkenness, certainly, but many felt exploited and hemmed in by mass commercialisation. They were aggrieved by being forced to overpay for everything on organised tourist excursions, which they had been led to believe would be sex-filled extravaganzas but turned out to be little more than a brief boat cruise around the bay, accompanied by watered-down ouzo and exorbitantly priced beer. Many had grown bored of the main drinking strip after a night or two. There were hardly any women there, and the main bars were prohibitively expensive. There were a few laughs the morning after as they sobered up on the beach and swapped tales of their various drunken mishaps and adventures, but their nights out in Magaluf were really quite similar to their nights out with friends in their home town. Pleasure seeking, many felt, could become quite mundane.

Conclusion

Magaluf can be a wonderful place to visit, but it also has a dark side. To catch sight of it, all one has to do is alter one's perspective. I have briefly mentioned how one might begin to address this dark side, but there is certainly more to be said. To know the world better, all social scientists really need to do is avoid trite, taken-for-granted assumptions and commit to the process of digging through the various sedimentary layers of reality. The more we dig, the better able we will be to understand and explain events on the surface, and the closer we will get to the fundamental forces that underpin our present way of life.

24

'Holiday Hooters': Hong Kong

Katie Lowe

University of Hong Kong

Introduction

> 'I am as good as gold at home but when I come to Hong Kong I know I am going to have a big blow out with the boys. Get a few bags in and that. The missus and kids are at home and I can.' (John)

Hong Kong is one of the world's busiest financial centres, colloquially referred to as the 'gateway' to China, with its ever-expanding Chinese roots and historical colonial connections to the United Kingdom. Its towering skyscrapers, dense population and 24/7 culture make it feel like a city that never sleeps. Among Hong Kong's iconic skyline lie law firms, international banks and multinational companies. Strategically positioned behind are two of Hong Kong's nightlife areas, SOHO and Lan Kwai Fong (LKF), heavily populated with bars, restaurants and nightclubs. For a certain type of drug user, these two worlds collide to create an opportunity to use cocaine recreationally on their frequent business trips to Hong Kong. These are the 'holiday hooters'. This short chapter draws upon ethnographic research of privileged expatriate cocaine users in Hong Kong (Lowe, 2020).[1] First, it introduces 'holiday hooters' and positions them as 'tourists', discussing how they access the closed cocaine market. Second, it reflects on how their global occupation and lifestyle create opportunities for them to use cocaine, making Hong Kong, for some, a destination for debauchery.

Who are the 'holiday hooters' and are they 'tourists'?

What does it mean to be a tourist given that people's migratory patterns are now fluid and global? 'Holiday hooters' (users) have previously lived and used cocaine in Hong Kong, before relocating for personal, employment reasons or, ironically, as a geographical cure to curb their use and 'partying'. Demographically, the users were over 30, White, male and female, in long-term relationships, married or married with children, heterosexual and largely originating from the Global North. They held full-time positions in finance, human resources and legal professions. The users displayed social and cultural capital from occupations, education and their ability to tap into the privileged social network of the 'expat bubble', with its pre-scripted and tightly woven social network, largely isolated from the local community and culture. More pointedly, they possessed economic capital, as their average monthly salary was 409 per cent higher than the average of Hong Kong (Census and Statistics Survey, 2017).

These users frequently travelled to Hong Kong for work. While they had ceased, or significantly decreased, using cocaine in their country of residence, they binge-used cocaine (both in frequency and amount) while in Hong Kong. These users were not 'tourists' in the traditional sense, given they had previously lived in Hong Kong. For some, visas were still required for entry and, although they were familiar with Hong Kong, they resided in a different country and their business trips, however frequent, were often short. Framing such a group as 'tourists' draws upon the fluid, mobile and transnational nature of their occupation and lifestyles. These users prided themselves on their ability to

1 Data for this chapter were taken from Lowe (2020) before the Hong Kong Protest (2019) and global COVID-19 pandemic (2020).

"have it all" (Daisy), to hold down a profession, travel the world, have a family and a robust global social life. Or, in their words, they "played hard and worked hard" and "the world [was their] oyster" (Tom).

'Dial-a-line': accessing the cocaine scene and navigating risks

> 'Within ten minutes of hitting LKF (party district), after jumping off the plane, I had some (cocaine) in my hand with the other hand holding a pint. It's that easy.' (Dave)

The cocaine market in Hong Kong is largely a closed one, so, how did these users access it? All had previously lived and used cocaine in Hong Kong. This familiarity with the cocaine market and risks of using cocaine provided the knowledge and contacts to reaccess it. Most users noted how efficiently cocaine was supplied compared to their home countries. Cocaine was used freely in a range of private and semi-private settings with minimal legal sanctions from the police and limited moral sanctions from the wider privileged expatriate community. Arguably, cocaine use was normalised in part of the privileged expatriate community (Parker et al, 1998), and was perceived to be freely used and easy to obtain (Lowe, 2020).

Cocaine was sold in one-gram clear plastic bags or vials and the market rate for one gram was HK$800–1,000. There were several ways in which it could be supplied in Hong Kong, ranging from delivery, purchased in a private location, a small amount from street dealers, and social supply. Users favoured delivery services and social supply, and there were two major forms of delivery services in Hong Kong, both easily accessible. First, WhatsApp dealers: users would message the order and arrange a delivery location and time. Deliveries were made to nearby streets or outside bars and clubs where users were, and typically took 10–60 minutes. Second, cocaine was also obtained through Hong Kong's iconic red taxi service. Commonly referred to as 'Dial-a-line', buyers would text the dealer with the order for cocaine and their current location, and dealers would send the registration of the taxi and estimated time of arrival. Users would then get into the taxi and take a short journey and cocaine would be purchased from the driver under the guise of paying for the taxi (Lowe, 2020).

The frequency of business trips meant users typically had access to 'working' dealers' numbers. If not, one would be acquired through fellow users and introduction made through a vouching system. Dealers also used WhatsApp to inform buyers of business hours, changes in phone numbers, discounts on purchases and, when a new shipment of cocaine was ready, this constant flow of information meant the user kept in contact with the cocaine market while out of Hong Kong. As Sam discusses: "You will be at work and it will be Friday morning and you will start getting texts from HK dealers telling you what they have in, what their hours are and deals and stuff … number changes. All that" (Sam). Yet more often than not, their cocaine use was not planned but seemed to be "simply part 'n' parcel of a night out" (Daisy). Cocaine was supplied through social supply; drugs were supplied 'not for profit', to 'non-strangers' (Potter, 2009) or by 'sorting friends out' with cocaine (Coomber et al, 2016: 20). Given the communal nature of cocaine use, it was freely shared between users. Users 'chipped in' for bags of cocaine (financially contributing and sharing); 'lines' and 'bumps' were given away for free, or in exchange for drinks, other drugs or cigarettes in user groups. Simply put by Dave: "Nine times out of ten you don't even have to order. It's just there or offered by other people. Mates and that" (Dave).

The users' previous life in Hong Kong as expatriates and the normalisation of cocaine use within the expatriate bubble enabled them to re-enter the closed cocaine market and use with relative ease and little risk. Yet their position as global citizens did present new risks, which users learnt to navigate when coming into contact with authorities at immigration. Learning from fellow users, they took extra precautions, such as: emptying pockets and purses before packing bags, so as "not to leave cheeky half a bag in there" (Joanne); wiping down credit cards used for cutting or iPhones for taking lines from; and deleting conversations and numbers with dealers from phones.

Work hard: alienation, anchors and opportunity

Users' jobs played a paradoxical role in their cocaine use in Hong Kong. First, occupations acted as one of the primary motivations for their cocaine use, with their desire to escape the pressure and alienation from the mundane, routinised long working hours both at home and abroad (Lyng, 1990). Second, it acted as a source of money, enabling them to afford such a costly drug. Third, their global roles provided the opportunity to frequently travel 'for free'. Fourth, it acted as an anchor (Decorte, 2001), shaping when, where, with whom and how much participants would use cocaine. These anchors were at their strongest in their home countries, as they were rooted in the conventional world with obligations and commitments to their occupations and families. Users described themselves as occasional users and their use was highly tailored around their ties to said anchors. Using in another country enabled them to compartmentalise their use, allowing them to "blow off some steam" (Sue) before returning to their law-abiding occupations and lives (Allaste and Lagerspetz, 2002; Chatterton and Hollands, 2003). By using in Hong Kong, they were able to create not only a physical distance from their anchors but also a mental distance – "It's OK if I do a few lines here. It does not count" (Ross). Through this compartmentalisation, Hong Kong became associated with cocaine use and partying, a place where normal rules, obligations and commitments could be manipulated or temporarily suspended – a destination for debauchery.

Play hard: the carnival setting of Hong Kong nightlife

Carnivals create spaces which allow periods of celebration, indulgence, release and transgression (Presdee, 2000; Langman, 2003). Carnival spaces are sanctioned by society, offering a place and time to release and escape without changing or challenging the status quo. Such spaces allow a period of sanctioned deviance while still maintaining social and moral codes. For these users, carnival presented itself through the temporary spaces in which users found themselves using cocaine – Hong Kong's 24/7 night-time economy. The clubs and bars offered users an opportunity to temporarily enter a 24/7 carnivalesque reality during their business trips, filled with fun and freedom and an abundance of opportunity, legitimating behaviours that would otherwise be considered deviant in their home country (Perrone, 2009). These carnival spaces offered users a way to 'temporarily obliterate the concerns of life' (Malbon, 1999: 102). The use of cocaine in such spaces added to users' escapism and pleasure received and craved, but also provided an outlet 'in which workers psychically renew their capacity for work' (Seiler, 2000: 203). Hong Kong nightlife offered users a place in which they could 'escape from the daily responsibilities, identities and insecurities' (Perrone, 2009: 96). It created a space to escape from reality, release anxieties and their commercialised lives (Presdee, 2000) through cocaine use. For these users, cocaine use within such settings provided the opportunity for hedonistic experiences without threatening the status quo of their position in mainstream society back home. The carnival sensations were intensified by the short duration of their stay and their previous hedonistic, and sometimes romanticised, experience of using cocaine in Hong Kong. For others, recreational cocaine use was simply part of the experience of Hong Kong. "I associate lines of Charlie with Hong Kong as much as I do Dim Sum, the skyline and neon lights" (Ross).

Conclusion

'Holiday hooters' drew upon their position as global citizens to carve out opportunities to use cocaine in Hong Kong's night-time economy. By doing so, 'holiday hooters' were able to physically and mentally distance themselves from the anchors which restrained them from using in their home country, enabling them to compartmentalise their drug use. Interestingly, the use of cocaine in Hong Kong was part of a wider trend where they leveraged their privilege, global citizenship and migrant lifestyles to facilitate their drug use and supply as users spoke of travelling to Thailand, Bali and India to use psychedelics, certain states in the US for marijuana and Thailand for purchasing prescribed drugs. For some, Hong Kong was simply one of many destinations of debauchery in which these privileged users worked hard and played hard.

25

Scilla: Calabria, Italy

Anna Sergi

University of Essex

Introduction

When you first set foot in the little town of Scilla, your eyes marvel at the beauty. That distinctive rock, with the castle on top; the beach underneath, and the blue-too-blue sea. A bunch of houses, their colourful roofs, pasted onto the rock like precipitating knots of bricks and concrete. When you pass through the tunnel that connects one part of the village to another, it's not just your eyes, but also your heart that will burst for beauty. This chapter will explore such a picturesque location and reveal that perhaps not all is what it seems in Scilla.

Heaven on Earth?

The small district of Chianalea, Scilla's best kept secret, will fill you with a feeling of having stepped onto an enchanted land. In your own personalised Narnia, you will walk a very long and twirling road – that's Chianalea essentially – and on every side you'll see small inlets, narrow cobblestoned roads, fishing boats parked on one side and balconies of another epoch, in houses of another epoch – right above the sea. On one side and the other, you'll have picture-perfect corners of heaven, with the sea possessing every corner, with the smell of the sea filtering through the air.

If you keep walking in Chianalea, you'll reach a couple of shops, local artisans and the bar with the best swordfish sandwich you'll ever eat. At the end of the road, you can relax by one of the little bars, or the couple of delicious seafood restaurants. With an Aperol spritz or a pint of beer, you'll sit on the cliffs overlooking the big distinctive rock, with the castle on top, the blue-too-blue sea. And you'll see the sun detonate in the sky, painting it red and pink like you've never seen before. The waves will crash on the cliffs, the white bubbly water will make you laugh. And you'll think that Calabria is stunning and appreciate that beauty is the real meaning of life. You cannot fail to fall in love with Scilla and its Chianalea district. You'd want to buy a house there, and sit everyday with the wind blowing from the Strait of Messina and Reggio Calabria, caught in between Sicily and Calabria, and your slice of pink sky. You promise yourself you'll come back over and over again; you'll write a book here one day. And eventually you might.

Not quite heaven on Earth?

But you won't buy a house. And the more you visit, the more you start wondering why Scilla is not more touristy, crowded and popular. You'll wonder how can Chianalea still be so untouched and such untapped potential go to waste? You'll wonder why, on the way there, you'd seen piles and piles of garbage by the sides of the road. And you'll wonder how it can be so difficult to reach the village in the first place, with very few local trains and no real reliable connections from airports and major train stations, leaving the car as the only realistic option. You'll learn that slow growth and low-level development – never fully planned – is for Scilla, the lesser of two evils. The first of these two evils would be the progressive de-pauperisation of the natural beauty that the place is blessed with. It's difficult, around here, to trust investments; it's difficult, around here, to trust institutions, public or private; it's difficult, around here, to trust intentions. Scilla is only 30 km from the capital city of Calabria, Reggio Calabria. The city of Reggio is an elegant yet messy place, with one of the longest waterfronts in Italy. A statue of the Goddess Athena overlooks the city of Messina, in Sicily, from the waterfront; the city of Reggio is the pulsating heart of the Calabrian economy and the economy of the South of Italy.

'Ndrangheta

In the city of Reggio Calabria, the Calabrian mafia, the 'Ndrangheta, is at home (Sergi and Lavorgna, 2016). In the town hall and in the main streets; in the social clubs and in the investments; in the masonic lodges and in the political elections; in lawyers' offices and in the banks. In Reggio Calabria, the 'Ndrangheta is not just home, it was born. The clans that today dominate in the city have formed a criminal enterprise run through a quadrumvirate, made of the heads of the families De Stefano, Tegano, Condello and Libri. These four families are first class 'Ndrangheta dynasties (Sergi, 2020): they made and sustained mafia rituals; they forged historical alliances with other 'Ndrangheta families in the province and the region; they have held the highest rankings in the criminal organisation for at least the last 50 years. The De Stefano family, especially, has had a role in shaping the 'Ndrangheta as it is today. Their reputation, their surnames, their activities, money, friendships and intentions have been scrutinised in numerous trials and sentences, some of which still ongoing at the time of writing. Judges have confirmed how the system of power in Reggio Calabria has not only been influenced and shaped by these 'Ndrangheta families, but also how they have been the protagonists of some of the most important political, economic and administrative events of the city. They were not alone, of course: politicians willing to compromise elections to strengthen their power; greedy entrepreneurs looking for more opportunities; masons for whom brotherhood has taken a different, dark meaning; corrupted public servants with varying motivations; and professionals – lawyers, accountants, financial advisors – for whom *pecunia non olet*.[1] In Reggio, it is not uncommon to wear more than one hat, to be mason and 'Ndranghetista; to be politician and mason; to be 'Ndranghetista and entrepreneur. A triangle of power, mafia and money so perfect that it has gone unpunished for a very long time.

The strength of the mafia families in Reggio does not stop in the city. The reverberation of their reputation, their power and their capabilities reaches out to the entire province, through

[1] Money doesn't smell.

alliances, continuous investments and the echo of their criminal history that intimidates and discourages. Other clans of the province, like the Alvaro and the Italiano clans from the towns of Delianuova and Sinopoli, are all in the extensive spider's web with the quadrumvirate of Reggio. One of the witnesses in the Gotha trial in 2020[2] explained: "They told me that everyone needs to get it in their heads that from Scilla, from Villa to Melito, they rule, the De Stefano must rule." This is why Scilla has often been playground of the De Stefano clan and its allies, when it came to local elections, when votes were 'guaranteed' to one clan or the other in an attempt to bring consensus and to drive public funds and administration in the pockets of few friends and associates. The little piece of heaven that is Scilla, with only 5,000 inhabitants, is also an ideal place to meet, eat together and discuss strategies, as it has been observed throughout the last decades. Having a hand in village politics and friends in Scilla ensures just enough consensus to dominate the local economy there too.

Of course, the village has its own local mafia clan too, which at different times supports or opposes the city clans in their expansion into Scilla. The 'ndrina Nasone has been one of those clans that became rich through extortion and involvement in the construction of the infamous A2 highway in the 1980s–1990s. On and off, in the past years, affiliates of this clan have been arrested for extortion, money laundering and membership of a mafia-type group. When in March 2018[3] the town council of Scilla was 'dissolved' because of mafia infiltration – an Italian administrative measure to counter the political influence of mafia groups – the situation appeared difficult to understand. On the one hand, the population seemed to back the work of the Town Council, swearing that there was no mafia in Scilla (Minniti, 2018). On the other hand, the Prefect who wrote the report detailing the status of the town to the Ministry of the Interior, preceding the dissolution, found that various members of the Council had 'inappropriate' friendships with mafia associates, and had favoured businesses

[2] Tribunale di Reggio Calabria, Sezione GIP-GUP, Araniti Antonino +37 (Processo Gotha, rito abbreviato); Sentenza 1.03.2018; p 1498.

[3] https://www.gazzettaufficiale.it/eli/id/2018/04/13/18A02610/sg (accessed 1 June 2022).

linked to mafia activities in the area for public works and funding. In a reality this small and this complex, it can indeed become very difficult to draw lines of direct and indirect culpability.

The problem, in mafia-dense territories like the one that from Reggio goes out to the province, in towns like Scilla, is not necessarily in the proactivity of mafia groups to 'control' or even dominate the *res publica*. The harm of mafia presence is palpable also in the abandonment, in the widespread belief that things are never going to change, that the status quo is not only unchangeable but somewhat also normal (Di Blasi et al, 2015). Where mafias exist and govern, and wherever their echo arrives, the territory suffers. Mafias cannot really *allow* beauty to blossom, because beauty is respect of nature; it is balance and not greediness; it requires acceptance of diversity and it is driven mostly by emotions and techniques, rather than opportunity and profit. Crucially, beauty – in urban or rural inhabited settings – could also entail disobedience to the rules, collaboration of the locals and unpredictability, which would all clash with mafias' need of control over the territory (Manoiu et al, 2015). Indeed, beauty is also in progress and mafias cannot really allow development, as development brings variety and variety would/could put mafias under scrutiny. As conservative drives, mafias push towards oppression and exploitation of the lands, rather than development and progress. In a town like Scilla, beauty is home, but this would require a strong yet gentle hand, to not only maintain that beauty but also not to exploit it and to actually nourish it. It is precisely that beauty that attracts mafia appetites and corrupt exchanges. Thus, the balance is very thin – Scilla needs to remain beautiful enough to attract some tourism, some investment, some funds; but it cannot be too beautiful because that would make it attractive to too many eyes, interests, investments, and ultimately mean the loss of control of the territory. Here, mafias, local and from the city, act as inhibitors, as obstructers of beauty and also as its guardians, without the possibility for progress.

Conclusion

According to Greek legends, Scilla and Cariddi were two sea monsters who lived in the Strait of Messina, in between Calabria and Sicily. Scilla used to be a beautiful nymph who refused to get married; she was transformed into a monster by Circe, the enchantress, who got jealous of Scilla when a Greek God fell in love with her. As an immortal monster, Scilla lived in the waters, in between Calabria and Sicily, devouring those who tried to cross the sea. Next to her lived Cariddi (also a locality near Messina, in Sicily), another monster who, three times a day, was said to create vortexes in the water to sink boats and ships crossing the Strait. After all, therefore, one might say that we are still living in the legend. The beautiful nymph transformed in an insatiable sea monster struggles to remember the beauty she once was because she is stuck in her current hideous form.

26

The Kray twins tours: London, UK

Craig Ancrum

Teesside University

Introduction

London's East End has a long historical association with poverty, deprivation and crime (Hobbs, 1995). A place where French Huguenots escaping persecution at home once rubbed shoulders with weavers from Ireland fleeing impoverishment and hunger, it has long been a cosmopolitan yet idiomatic cityscape. A dark, smoky and overcrowded mélange of both legitimate and nefarious opportunity so vividly captured by the pen of Dickens. Even after the demolition of the infamous 'rookeries' (Rook, 1899) and improvements in standards of living, the East End continued to be a place heavy with the cultural 'miasma' of crime and criminality, into the 20th century. It was into this run-down yet proud maze of terraced streets, pubs and corner shops that the infamous Kray twins, Ronald and Reginald, made their entrance into the world on 24 October 1933. There is a wealth of literature both academic and journalistic (Monk, 1999; Pearson, 2015) on the infamous brothers and their rise to fame and the twins have cemented a place in popular culture (Wattis, 2021).

The world the infamous twins were born into no longer exists. The bomb-blighted and run-down East End terraces where 'lively characters' could ply their trades are long gone (Hobbs, 1997). Many residents of the East End, including those from

Bethnal Green, joined in the exodus to new, more spacious residences in the burgeoning new towns of Essex and Kent (Wilmot and Young, 2011). The twins themselves, now both deceased, are products of a lost era yet still hold a fascination and air of mythos for much of the general public. Why? How is it that two small-time gangsters, certainly small in comparison to their US counterparts and later criminal elites, have come to hold such an entrenched place in UK cultural history? As Jenks (2003: 114) notes, the Kray twins' story and legacy is one of class and place as much as it is about crime; it 'is and always will be inextricably bound to the signs, symbols, rituals and folklore of London's East End'. Perhaps this explains the reverential view that exists to this day, that the twins 'kept the streets safe' and 'always asked after your mum'. These quotes are, of course, made up but are typical of the tone of the reminiscences often conveyed in TV 'true crime' documentaries. This chapter, by examining the phenomena of 'Kray tours', will argue that the attraction, for some, lies in the late capitalist fetishisation of violence in conjunction with a symbolic resonance for young men in particular (Hall et al, 2008) and is used, in part, to construct an identity laden with the masculine ideals of strength, power and bravery in a time when many men find themselves adrift in a post-modernity that has little room or value for the traditional working-class male habitus (Bourdieu, 1986).

All aboard the crime bus

The unique entrepreneurial culture of the area certainly plays a role in the formation of the Kray legend and the practices and culture of those 'ducking and diving' to make a living on East End streets have been well documented (Hobbs, 1997; 1998). Hobbs' notion of living the 'lush life' (Hobbs, 2013) is acutely evident in the Kray twins' biography.

In urban landscapes that have been particularly badly affected by the series of economic reconfigurations associated with the evolution of Western neoliberalism (see Harvey, 2005; Winlow et al, 2017), the 'success' and glamour of the twins is an attractive yet largely unobtainable symbol of achievement and status. Amid a growing attraction of instrumentalism, violence and criminality in socially excluded micro-communities in post-industrial Britain (Winlow, 2001; Hall et al, 2008), the notion of young men living in a time of uncertainty and 'crisis' (Beynon, 2002) adopting the stylish criminality and powerful machismo of the twins is not unfeasible.

There are currently several companies offering Kray-related tourist trips around the East End and, in the tradition of 'dark tourism' (Stone, 2006), the focus is on the murder of both Cornell and McVitie. Although not solely concentrated on killing, there is still a heavy reliance on the area's 'hauntology' and the murders feature prominently in the advertising: 'Join this tour and go in search of London's most notorious gangsters, Ronnie and Reggie Kray. This unique walking tour delves deep into the murky world of 1960's London to uncover gangsters, shoot outs, night clubs and murder.'

One of the most well advertised is a company called 'Into the Blue', who offer a range of experiences including 'adrenaline' activities such as flying and high-powered race car driving. Their 'Kray and London Gangster' tour includes the usual spots, The Blind Beggar pub where George Cornell was shot and killed by Ron Kray and the Repton Boys club in Bethnal Green. The tour is conducted by actor Vaz Blackwood who played gangster 'Rory Breaker' in Guy Ritchie's movie *Lock Stock and Two Smoking Barrels* (1998). The inclusion of these cultural references makes the marketing intentions clear. The company are advertising attractive cultural symbols (Hall et al, 2008) to a working-class, male-dominated demographic and simultaneously furthering the blurring between crime fact and crime fiction (Carrabine, 2008). The tour also trades heavily on the names of other London underworld figures including 'Mad' Frankie Fraser and Freddy Foreman and this is further evidence of the lionisation of the criminal and the disavowal of the victims of these celebrities. As noted by Farmaki (2013), dark tourism is demand-driven and there seems to be no end to the appetite for some sections of the public to be regaled by tales of a long-gone criminal past. Other criminal 'celebrities' are still profiting from their past life in crime and regularly host 'an audience with' nights across the country. Carlton Leach of the *Rise of the Footsoldier* film franchise, and Dave 'the yellow pages of crime' Courtney are just two examples and their audience is predominately male and predominately working class. Wattis (2021), Monk (1999) and others have written on the attraction of stylised ideals of masculinity and their attraction for disenfranchised males. Movie depictions which again the tours play on not only blur fact with fiction (Reiner, 2002; Carrabine, 2008) but also provide, for those involved in criminality, however small, the opportunity to reinforce their identity as 'lads' or 'hard men' (Wattis, 2021). This, and the desire to visit the area where the twins held sway, is in part pilgrimage (Digance, 2003) and also has within it an element of the *self-definition* and reaffirmation of the criminal 'self' as outlined by Wilson (2005).

Criminal identities and celebrity criminals

Late capitalist society and its inherit focus on consumerism has led to a situation in which material success is paramount. Reiner (2002: 24) argues further that in a materialistic culture, there is no end to the generation of aspirations, and consequently no end to their pursuit. Hall et al (2008) develop this idea with the addition of the importance, not just of material artefacts, but of their *symbolic* significance:

> [B]ut if we add to this the sociological fact that in a post-needs, desire-driven economy these 'material' goals are first and foremost symbolic goals, we see immediately that the first move in any strategy to reduce criminogenic consumer pressure would be to change interpretations of and attenuate emotional attachments to the symbolism that is now attached to material goods. (Hall et al, 2008: 1–3)

These dual-purpose acquisitions were acutely evident in the Kray twins' personas and envied and copied by both siblings. Freeman comments on how the twins themselves were avid fans of 'gangster' movies and adopted the smart style, confidence and machismo of their on-screen role models. Smart cars, expensive watches and jewellery as displayed by the twins are still very much desirable objects and their cultural value is enormous among those living on 'sink estates' and deprived areas across the UK. Participation in these tours or spending an evening being regaled by tales of crime from often violent 'ex offenders' such as Carlton Leach is just one more aspect of attempting to somehow help construct a status-rich identity and be able to cling to the, albeit less pleasant, aspects of working-class masculinity. The fact that in doing so they disavow (Hall et al, 2015) both the victims and the morals of those they hold in esteem is inconsequential.

Žižek (in Hall et al, 2015) contends that this disavowal goes further than just blanking out the direct violence done by these criminal icons but also denies one's place in society in relation to others, thus further allowing for the attempted construction of an identity that is unbound by status or social position. Winlow (2001) and Hall et al (2008) discussed how the breakdown of the traditionally strong links between work, local community and identity makes exploring the increasing consumerist basis for identity more important than ever (Beck, 1992). The contention here is that these iconic images of crime and criminals and the promotion of dark tourism enterprises play a role often overlooked in this process.

Conclusion

While for some, the notion of the Kray twins tour may be as just a harmless day out, if we apply the perspectives of deviant leisure (Smith and Raymen, 2018) and ultra-realism (Hall et al, 2015), it becomes apparent that there is a deeper cultural meaning and affect behind these types of dark tourist activities. While there may be no physical or systemic harm, there is evidence of what Žižek termed 'symbolic harm' (2008); by promoting and thus perpetuating the glamourisation of crime and the fetishisation of violence, the tour operators both exploit the disenfranchised and continue to provide a source of deviant identity to some working-class males. The main area of concern, however, is the promotion of an individualised, masculine ideal that for most is almost impossible to obtain. The Krays were perfect examples of the concept of 'special liberty' (Hall, 2012), using violence and intimidation to take what they desired, with no regard as to the consequences of their actions. This portrayal then becomes culturally diffused and there is evidence of special liberty in working-class criminality. The process of 'taxing', taking money or drugs with the threat or use of violence, is just one example (Treadwell et al, 2020). The belief by 'taxers' that they have the right to whatever fulfils their instrumental desires, viewing the victims as inferior and inconsequentially disavowing them, is special liberty personified. The area of motivation for dark tourism has been explored in detail elsewhere (Seaton, 1996; Lennon and Foley, 2001) but at least in relation to the Kray tours, the motivation for some is to draw on the experience and hauntology (Wattis, 2021) of the twins' era and utilise the experience to help to reaffirm an imaginary self-constructed identity in a period of male ontological insecurity (Hall, 2015). Linnemann (2015) and Wattis (2021) discuss the concept of 'haunting' and view this as a social phenomenon, contending that the violence and acts of victimisation that take place in an area then produce some kind of 'spectral force' that stays in the locale. The force is then helped to survive by the number of texts which relate to it in a form of spectral cultural reproduction. It is clear then that if we take this to be the case that the East End of London should be one of the most 'haunted' areas in the UK, given the plethora of cultural and symbolic references to the Krays and the East End. It is this sense of 'haunting' and the process of cultural mass promotion of deviant ideals combined with a contemporary crisis in masculinity that drives the demand for dark tourism attractions such as the Kray tours. As long as the rapacious culture industry (Adorno, 2002) continues to market and commercialise icons and symbols of criminality, meeting the demands and imperatives of the late capitalist neoliberal market, and as long as there continues to be areas of exclusion and deprivation, then there will always be an attraction in the 'glamour' of a criminal identity and Kray tours will continue.

27

Backpacking in the outback: Uluru, Northern Territory, Australia

Eveleigh Buck-Matthews and Craig Kelly

Birmingham City University

Introduction

> He saw hitchhikers as a form of wildlife who migrated through his territory who he could kill … for thrills.
>
> Colin Powis, survivor of serial murderer Ivan Milat, in Graham (2021)

Few travellers are unaware of the spate of backpacker murders that occurred in the Australian outback in the early 1990s. Between 1989 and 1993, Australian serial killer Ivan Milat murdered two men and five women. All of the victims were in their late teens and early 20s. In 1996, Milat was finally convicted and sentenced to life in prison for his crimes that spanned the breadth of New South Wales. The murders captured the public's imagination, inspiring various films including *Wolf Creek* and *Wolf Creek 2*, which told the fictional story of serial killer and outback local Mick Taylor, who stalked, killed and tortured unsuspecting tourists from Europe and the US. Botterill and Jones argue that the crimes of Milat 'occurred in remote areas where the likelihood of the killer being disturbed was minimal, coinciding with backpackers being outside of the routine policing arrangements' (2010: 41). The causes of such homicide will not be unpacked in this short chapter; the multitude and complex psychological, biological and social elements have been explored by more knowledgeable agents. Nonetheless, the case of the backpacker murderer serves as the ideal starting point for this piece that will highlight the impact of liminality that affects and constructs the 'backpacker', informing new vulnerabilities. This chapter will look at the vulnerabilities of those backpacking across Australia as well as the harms they themselves often perpetuate.

Backpacking

There is a well-established backpacker path in Australia. The expansive nature of the country means that there is a high reliance on private transport to cross and traverse the country. Large-scale research conducted by Loker-Murphy (1997) interviewed almost 700 backpackers in Australia, to explore the motivations. However, vulnerability, crime and victims did not emerge in the narrative. The research found, after performing cluster analysis, the most popular travel motivations among backpackers were to 'seek exciting/active/adventurous things to do' (p 31). In regards to what this ultimately does to someone's perception of risk taking highlights the vulnerability of people, especially young people, who may indulge in riskier activities than they would in other places. Israel (1999) identified key examples of the ways in which backpackers' vulnerabilities to crime increase: backpackers' positions as strangers in the places that they visit, their preference for independence which removes them from the protection of package travel, their desire to travel within a limited budget, their vulnerable strategies for transporting and storing possessions and the development of myths about backpackers among host populations. There has been an increase in the warnings against hitchhiking, in Australia and other countries; however, the real danger versus the moral panic that instances like Ivan Milat and the backpacker murders promoted is an interesting one. It can be argued that the small, but highly publicised, instances of homicide in relation to tourists in Australia skew the public perception. This was evident during the investigation and subsequent conviction of Ivan Milat in the Australian media: 'Nearly three quarters (74.70%) of the articles in 1993 and almost half (47.13%) of the articles in 1996 were identified under the sub-category,

"Backpackers as Victims of Crime"' (Peel and Steen, 2007: 1063). With the public imagination of backpackers being fed through the media lens, it is hard to unpack what is truly increasing harm in the Australian outback.

Backpacking and liminality

As identified by Israel (1999), travelling on a budget is a key aspect of backpackers, therefore hitchhiking has the potential to offer a free, sociable and convenient way of travelling for many. By choosing cheaper travel options, backpackers may hitchhike, travel at unsociable hours, or through the night, and sleep in insecure locations. Backpacking increases the necessity to travel cheap, therefore putting backpackers at risk of unregulated forms of transport and reliant on unfamiliar people. Also, according to Clarke (2005), getting to know the local population and making social connections is a key component of backpacking, and again hitchhiking offers the opportunity to 'meet the locals' and provides a purposeful interaction with the local community. There are, however, risks associated with hitchhiking for both the driver and passenger (Chesters and Smith, 2001). The practical and emotional elements that co-construct the backpacker lifestyle also have the potential to increase the vulnerability of the traveller. The main motivations and practicalities highlight the ways in which living a liminal, or transient, lifestyle while travelling puts backpackers more at risk of traditional forms of exploitation and violence (homicide, assault, theft) but also raise them as a target due to their embodied uncertainties in space. This is owing to their unknowledgeable progression through the landscape without social bonds, contacts or routine responsibility.

Many backpackers experience a level of *communitas* (Turner, 2017) derived from the liminal and temporal nature of their landscape. *Communitas* is a state that is created once a person steps outside of their normal routine, life and social structures (Skarpe, 2005), and this then enables alternative ways of operating to emerge. This section argues that this newly emerged way of being can increase backpacker vulnerability. As Buck-Matthews (2018) explored in relation to music festivals, young people's sociality and solidarity is accelerated in temporal spaces. With this increased sociality also emerges the possibility for this trust and connection to be exploited by predatory individuals. Backpacking therefore offers both a pull factor of adventure combined with the temporality. The result is the acceleration of trust between backpackers and also those whom they come into contact with. Backpackers seek out liminality, which is often lacking in other parts of their lives (Buck-Matthews, 2018); however, it also changes the criminological picture. *Communitas* can increase interpersonal risk by making people more trusting. Traversing, movement through space, increases the removal of routine controls, social structures (family), policing and spatial knowledge. The practical reliance on cheap forms of transportation, coupled with an increased level of trust for those travelling, combine to increase the interpersonal risks that backpackers can face.

We have so far explored the various ways in which the backpacker lifestyle can generate several susceptibilities and harms both to themselves and to others. In particular, while one is incredibly unlikely to encounter such a violent individual as Ivan Milat, this does not negate the fact that the increased sense of freedom and adventure regularly promoted via travel agencies and more recently social media comes with a myriad of potential risks and harms often underacknowledged and reported. The potential harms pertaining to such activities do not necessarily end here, though, and the following section will traverse further into more normalised and embedded harms of the backpacker way of life.

The hidden harms

While the overt gaze within the context of risk and backpacking is often drawn to the news-grabbing instances of extreme violence such as the offences perpetrated by Ivan Milat, a much more routine, normalised and widespread form of harm underlies such discussions. Australia as a nation was born as a result of colonialism and British penal colonies. As such, the violence that the nation was born from continues to cast a dark shadow, with First Nations people still disproportionally harmed. Within the context of backpackers, the engagement with liminal spaces, *communitas* and the representation of self often perpetuates such harms in the present day.

Inarguably, visiting national landmarks such as Uluru (commonly known as Ayres Rock) is firmly situated on the bucket list of many aspiring young backpackers. Often though, scant regard is paid to Uluru being sacred ground for the First Nations peoples of Australia. In recent years, as recognition of sacred land has become more commonplace, park rangers around Uluru have been inundated with 'sorry rocks'. *Sorry rocks* are rocks that tourists have taken from the site and later returned (Foxlee, 2015). Indeed, such engagement in the collective pillaging of the literal sacred ground, alongside further transgressions that signify a disregard for the Australian culture, has been prominent within the national conscience in recent years, resulting in changes in legislation. Increases in social media and the need for a 'once in a lifetime' picture to post on websites such as Instagram has led to frequent reports of photos of tourists naked on Uluru (Oakley, 2016). So too, visitors frequently scale Uluru resulting in the rock face being degraded. Away from the obvious ecological damage this entails, this is tantamount to scaling a religious building (Marks, 2016). The significance and regularity of issues have eventually culminated in a ban on climbing Uluru being imposed (Heaney and Jonscher, 2019).

Conclusion

Backpacking restores the concept of rite of passage to modern society (Bigger, 2009). Backpackers will traverse space feeling emboldened, seeking *communitas*, adventure and risk. Despite the moral panic around rare and spectacular instances of violence, young people continue to adventure along well-walked paths. This chapter has highlighted how unpacking the motivations of backpackers reveals their greatest weakness. A desire to trust, make connections and seek thrills beyond the 'everyday'. More explicit research needs to be done to explore the unique experiences and vulnerabilities of backpackers, who are driven by alternative motivations, often countercultural practices (hitchhiking), in temporal landscapes with little to no routine securities. So too, this piece highlights how *communitas*, liminality and social media's influence on the presentation of self culminates in a fashion which emboldens the disregard for culturally significant monuments and perpetuates historical harms. So, if you ever find yourself backpacking in the far reaches of the Australian outback, it is not necessarily the Ivan Milats of the world you should concern yourself with, but instead a careful consideration to the environment, path and cultures you are currently traversing.

28

The hippie trail: Nepal, South Asia

Emiline Smith

University of Glasgow

Introduction

Landlocked between Tibet and India, Nepal is a South Asian multiethnic, multilingual and multicultural country famous for its Himalayan range and its rich cultural heritage. Hinduism and Buddhism are Nepal's primary religions, which has resulted in centuries of sacred objects and architecture, including statues of deities, shrines, temples, monasteries and other monuments (Bangdel, 1989). So abundant is Nepal's sacred art and architecture that celebrated art historian Lain Singh Bangdel (1989) likened it to an enormous open-air museum. Legislation to protect this cultural heritage has been in place since 1956 (Yates and Mackenzie, 2018). Yet Nepal's sacred cultural objects have proven irresistible to foreign buyers: consequently, they have been looted continuously since the 1950s.

Flying into Nepal's capital is a special experience: on approach, clouds hug the Himalayas, the 'rooftop of the world', and when they clear, a city dotted with pointed temple roofs appears, nestled amid the mountains. This impressive panorama drew in the elderly North American elite when Nepal opened up to tourism in the 1950s: wealthy, retired travellers on post-war round-the-world tours who wanted to experience the many heritage sites of the Kathmandu Valley (Liechty, 2005). It also attracted young people from Europe and North America in search of enlightenment and spiritual authenticity along the pan-Asian overland 'hippie trail' from the 1950s to the 1970s (Gemie and Ireland, 2017). Nepal's capital Kathmandu became known as the perfect escapist hideout, as captured in Bob Seger's 1975 song 'Katmandu': 'I'm tired of looking at the TV news / I'm tired of driving hard and paying dues / I figure, baby, I've got nothing to lose / I'm tired of being blue / That's why I'm going to Kathmandu.' Through songs and other pop culture references, Kathmandu became the focus of Western projections of otherness, orientalism and counterculturalism (Liechty, 2017).

Looting heritage along the hippie trail

During this time, Kathmandu also became a hideout for Tibetan refugees fleeing Chinese persecution during the Cultural Revolution. They brought with them family heirlooms and sacred objects, which were ultimately sold for sustenance. The city consequently became a regional hotspot for all kinds of cultural objects, including textiles, statues, jewellery, manuscripts, furniture and costumes (Gluckman, 2009). As one of the participants of my doctoral research stated, Kathmandu then was 'the place to be' for suppliers to the London and American art markets based on the 'flood of material coming in from Nepal and Tibet' (Smith, 2019). As a result, Nepal's cultural objects, perhaps mementos of a countercultural pilgrimage or the start of a 'gentleman's collection', started disappearing from temples and pedestals in large numbers.

The outpour of cultural objects to satisfy European and North American demand became so severe that two foreigners independently started recording statues of deities, and evidence of their theft, across the country during the 1970s and 1980s (Bangdel, 1989; Schick, 1989). So dire was the rapid disappearance of Nepal's cultural heritage during this time that Rana (1985) wrote that 'the gods are being torn from Nepal to adorn Western homes and museums, leaving behind weeping devotees and depriving the Himalayan kingdom of some of its most precious art objects'. The scale of the looting is evidenced by the sheer quantity and quality of private collections established during the latter part of the 20th century. Interestingly, academics played a significant role in creating and stimulating a wider market for Nepali objects. Art historians like Dr Pratapaditya Pal and Professor Denman Ross would work closely with American museums and private collectors to build their collections, authenticating and validating potentially looted cultural objects in the process. As Pal (2014) notes, when he purchased a stunning set of four Chola bronzes for the Los Angeles County Museum of Art from his dear friend, art dealer Robert H. Ellsworth, 'they had the usual accretions from being buried in the ground'. As a result of this large-scale looting and foreign collecting during the 1970s and 1980s, Schick (2006: 66) warned that 'the land of the gods' would quickly be 'emptied to the point where nothing remains', urging collectors to reflect on the looted nature of their purchases (Dixit, 1999). But demand for Nepal's cultural heritage from art collectors and museums in North America and Europe steadily continued as tourism in the country exploded.

Most of the temples and sacred sites from which cultural objects were removed were and still are in use. They are an integral part of Nepal's rich cultural and spiritual life, which is difficult to miss when walking around any Nepali street. Shrines, pedestals, altars and religious iconography are visible on every street corner. These objects are an integral part of Nepal's living heritage, and no museum or gallery space could ever do justice to their original context.

One of the country's most iconic areas, Kathmandu Valley, has attracted tourists for decades because of its unique blend of traditional and modern architecture. This even led to the inscription of seven United Nations Educational, Scientific and Cultural Organization (UNESCO) World Heritage Sites across the Valley's main districts in 1979 (Tiwari et al, 2017). However, this area was one of the worst hit areas of the devastating 2015 Ghorka earthquake, which caused widespread loss of human life and damaged many monuments (Tiwari et al, 2017). Concerns arose that looting would increase after the earthquake; however, these proved largely unfounded (Yates and Mackenzie, 2018). Community crime prevention measures would have played a part in this, but the art market is also increasingly aware of the problematic narratives that can accompany cultural objects, particularly in light of widely publicised recent prosecutions of renowned dealers and collectors of looted Asian art (see Mashberg, 2015; 2021) and Nepal's increasing efforts to repatriate its stolen heritage (see Adhikari, 2021).

The complexity of glocal grey markets

The global illicit trade in cultural objects includes a variety of practices and narratives that often make it difficult to identify the legal and moral basis for an object's ownership, trade and movement across borders; hence, the term 'illicit' or 'grey' is used for this trade (Yates et al, 2017). Differences in legal frameworks, enforcement strategies and moral attitudes towards cultural objects facilitate this global trading network. Along the way, cultural objects are provided with paperwork and narratives offering an air of legitimacy, for example, through publication in art volumes and shipping documentation that mask their true origin, in order to 'launder' the objects' appearance on the market (Yates et al, 2017). Once on the market, the due diligence performed by stakeholders is insufficient to ensure the legal and genuine provenance of cultural objects (Mackenzie, 2011). The global illicit trade in cultural objects therefore thrives on this general lack of transparency and accountability.

Like many archaeologically rich countries, Nepal has a strict regulatory framework in place to protect its cultural heritage (Yates and Mackenzie, 2018). Still, Nepali cultural objects regularly continue to appear on the international market. Many cultural objects illegally excavated, traded and/or exported from their country of origin are not officially recorded, because they originate from a remote structure or archaeological site. Consequently, it is extremely difficult for archaeologically rich countries to protect their cultural heritage against the relentless demand of collectors, dealers, auction houses and museums. Once out of their country of origin, there are limited opportunities to repatriate (return) cultural objects, particularly without documentary evidence, unless the owner chooses to do so voluntarily. There are some international agreements that provide guidance for State Parties on how to protect their own heritage and how to cooperate with other State Parties to stem illegal trade and repatriate looted cultural objects, such as the 1970 UNESCO Convention on the

Means of Prohibiting and Preventing the Illicit Import, Export and Transfer of Ownership of Cultural Property. In practice, however, stricter market regulations and increased public awareness have effectuated increased repatriations in recent years.

The Government of Nepal recently prioritised the reclaiming of some of its looted foreign-held cultural heritage: for example, in early 2021, they requested the Dallas Museum of Art to return a statue of the deities Lakshmi-Narayana (Thompson and Smith, 2021). The statue was identified as part of the Bangdel (1989) publication, held to be stolen in 1984. It had become part of the museum's collection through donation from a renowned collector of Asian art. It took the combined efforts of various governmental departments, local and foreign activists, law enforcement and others to seize the statue and repatriate the statue to Nepal.

Conclusion

Tourism clearly played – and continues to play – an essential role in the loss of Nepal's living heritage, and of the looting, destruction and loss of cultural heritage around the world. The 'dark tourism' link here is the harmful effects that tourism can have on a living culture: in effect, the desire to own part of the culture being admired means the violent destruction of that culture, whether material or intangible. Numerous studies have discussed the potential negative and positive aspects of tourism on cultural and natural heritage, including looting and vandalism in and around World Heritage Sites (see, for example, Vella et al, 2015; Al-Ansi et al, 2021). In the case of Nepal, tourists' desire to commodify and collect deities and other parts of Nepal's cultural heritage have led to their continuous looting and destruction. Today's tourism industry uniformly exploits the aesthetic beauty of Nepal's cultural heritage with minimal contextualisation or deterrence of such looting. Yet, should Nepalis be grateful with such a thriving tourism industry and their cultural heritage 'properly taken care of' in private and public museums abroad?

29

The Museum of Confiscated Art: Brest, Belarus

Donna Yates and Hannah London

Maastricht University and College of William & Mary

Introduction

Located in the city of Brest on Belarus' border with Poland, the Museum of Confiscated Art[1] was opened in 1989 to display 'works of art and antiquities seized by customs officers during attempts to illegally export them abroad' (museum.by, nd), Housed in a historic cottage and expanded in 2016, the museum now consists of ten halls filled with over 400 cultural objects, many of which are Russian icon paintings from the 16th to early 20th centuries. The artworks are displayed alongside examples of the technology used by Belarussian customs officials to detect contraband (museum.by, 2016). While the museum serves a local audience, with special tours for school-aged children, families and availability as a function space, it also draws an international audience. At the time of writing, the museum boasts 4.6 out of 5 stars from over 400 reviews on Google, and 4.5 out of 5 stars from over 50 reviews on Tripadvisor. The museum is featured in such English-language travel sites as Atlas Obscura (nd) and Lonely Planet (nd; b).

[1] Muzey Spasennykh Khudozhestvennykh Tsennostey; Музей Спасенных Художественных Ценностей.

While a 'Museum of Art' is a relatively mundane title for a familiar and common type of institution, a 'Museum of *Confiscated* Art' is immediately marked as something different. 'Confiscated' as a descriptor, alongside other Russian to English translations such as 'Saved' or 'Rescued', immediately mark the art in the museum as being illicit in some way. Potential visitors assume, and are likely attracted to, the fact that what is truly on display is not the art, but rather the circumstances that brought the art to the museum. The museum, then, is a museum of crime, with crime narratives told through artworks.

The romance of criminality and the appeal of art crime

Within the museum, many of the objects are exhibited alongside demonstrations and illustrations of how they had been concealed for smuggling (Ajlouny, 2018). The pairing of a set of antique furniture with an explanation of its concealment in a cargo hold of milk powder, for example, makes the display a composite of object and crime. This fundamentally changes the museum experience for visitors, who are asked not to contemplate art, but rather experience deviance. One blogger who visited the museum, for example, noted that while religious icons are normally of little interest to them, the paintings held in the Museum of Confiscated Art intrigued them due to the 'romance of criminality'; imagining scenarios of theft and smuggling enriched his experience of the art (The Velvet Rocket, 2010). Another blogger writes that while they do not necessarily recommend the museum, they suggest it can provide a 'dose of quirk' (Saxena, 2020). From these remarks, we might gather that the word 'confiscated' in the museum's title bears greater weight than 'art'. It is this signifier that one Minsk-based reviewer on Tripadvisor credits as 'very tempting' and which 'seduced' them to visit.

The mass appeal of art crime stories is evident in decades of books, TV shows and film plots encompassing everything from the cute romance of *How to Steal a Million*, the comedy of the Marx Brothers' *Animal Crackers*, the action of *Dr. No* or *Oceans Twelve*, to the classic noir *The Maltese Falcon*. The 'seductive' and intangible power of art, paired with ideas of the monetary extremes of the art market, create a 'tempting' package for public consumption.

Crime mars the sanctity, grace and restricted nature of artworks. Art crime, particularly art theft and smuggling, trespasses on the exclusive space of the museum, where artworks are meant to be observed and not touched, protected and not moved, publicly shared and not privately hoarded. As such, a Museum of Confiscated Art is a museum of art that has been violated in a titillating way and is a showcase of museum failure.

The Museum of Confiscated Art may be the largest and most permanent museum of its kind, but art crime displays are not uncommon, which is a testament to their appeal. Recent examples include a showcase of artworks recovered by Italian police at the Museo Storico dell'Arma (ANSA, 2016), an exhibition devoted to an expensive watch heist at Jerusalem's Islamic Museum (Prusher, 2015), a collection of artworks stolen by Napoleon's armies at the Scuderie del Quirinale in Rome (AFP, 2016), an exhibition of artworks stolen from Czech Jews in Prague (Prague Daily Monitor, 2017), a gallery of stolen sacred antiquities returned to India from Australian museums (visited by one of the authors in 2017; IANS, 2017) and a semi-permanent collection of police-recovered archaeological objects at the famous site of Pompeii (visited by one of the authors in 2017). One of the most popular genres of art crime exhibition concerns the display of forgeries. Museums such as the Museum of False Art in Vledder, the Netherlands (Museum Valse Kunst, 2021) and the Forger Museum/Museum of Art Fakes in Vienna (Fälschermuseum, 2021), as well as many temporary exhibitions at museums around the world, use words such as 'fake', 'false' and 'forgery' to signal the deviance inherent in the displayed works, and expose visitors to acts and methods of art fraud. Although filled with paintings of immaculate craftsmanship, the 'fake' before 'art' of these museums emphasises that something is wrong – as if artifice is unnatural to the world of art. Rather than a pure encounter between visitor and production, some sort of deviant social situation mediates the space for the viewer and is perceived before the art itself. Again, the social, ethical or actual crimes that went into the creation of the artworks are on display more so than the artworks, and viewers are invited to engage in scepticism about the origins and merits of the works they are visiting. Criticising the gullibility of those who were fooled by the fake art is a strong component of the appeal of these museums and exhibitions; viewers with all of the supplemental information presented in the displays are easily convinced that they would never have fallen for the deception.

Returning to the Confiscated Art Museum, the explicit focus of this institution on acts that are publicly described as crimes masks the unstated reality of many museums in the world. Museums regularly present artworks to audiences without information as to their source or provenance, and the audiences regularly assume that the objects in these museums are there for ethical, moral and legal reasons. Yet our cultural institutions that have no qualifiers before 'art museum' are home to vast amounts of stolen art that has not been, and may never be, returned to its rightful owners. In many cases, these artworks were stolen during times of colonialism, imperialism and domination, or more recently, from illegal acts of looting and trafficking. Perhaps, then, what distinguishes the Museum of Confiscated Art from a Museum of Art is that the works housed there were halted by authorities before they could be successfully exported or laundered into other museum collections. Even in situations where artworks are repatriated, 'normal' and national museums in former colonised countries who received this returned art themselves become museums of confiscated art, and not by choice. In that sense, there are countless museums of confiscated art.

Acknowledgement of the true and illicit nature of many objects on display worldwide is part of a wider movement to identify and rectify the illicit acts behind museum collections. This movement itself can be a tourist experience that is both dark and meaningful. Alice Procter's 'Uncomfortable Art' project and tours are a notable effort in this vein. In somewhat of a parallel to the Belarussian museum's exhibition of art alongside methods of smuggling, she calls on museums to 'display it like you stole it' (Procter, nd), Procter seeks what the Museum of Confiscated Art intrinsically accomplishes: to present clearly to the public the dark situations that resulted in objects being held in a museum. If more museums 'displayed it like they stole it', and openly discussed the troubling truths about their collections, the Museum of Confiscated Art would hardly be of note.

The cultivated rarity of the Museum of Confiscated Art gives us a false sense of security, signifying with its qualifier words (confiscated, rescued, saved) that major museums are not filled with stolen art, fakes or cultural objects that are divorced from their true cultural context. Rather than any kind of uniquely dark object, these museums house our darkest fears about museums. By creating special museums to tell certain dark stories of art, we almost get a pass for not telling the dark stories of the 'uncomfortable art' in mainstream and familiar museum spaces.

Conclusion

To end on a note of redemption, it is worth considering the Salvage Art Institute (SAI), a travelling exhibition curated by artist Elka Krajewska. Under the aegis of the qualifier 'salvage', SAI displays artworks that have been damaged to the point of being written off as a 'total loss' by insurers. Deemed worthless by the art market and having been 'removed from art market circulation', SAI considers the objects in their collection to have been 'liberated from the obligation of perpetual valuation and exchangeability' (Salvage Art Institute, nd), While visitors may initially be drawn to the dark and titillating appeal of destruction, once artworks are freed from the constraints of monetary value, viewers are invited to simply enjoy them: to consider how and why they were made, and what, through the act of destruction, they have become. Indeed, the SAI considers these pieces to have undergone a transformation, stating that the objects are not art, but rather are 'No Longer Art But …', allowing viewers to fill in the blank (Salvage Art Institute, nd). Perhaps it is best to approach the works in the Museum of Confiscated Art in the same way, as 'No Longer Art', but rather an alluring hybrid of art and crime, liberated by the honesty of their display.

30

Steroid holidays: Sharm El Sheikh, Sinai Peninsula, Egypt

Nick Gibbs

Leeds Trinity University

Introduction

In this chapter, we will be jetting off to sunny Sharm El Sheikh, scuba diving in the glistening Red Sea, taking advantage of the cheap alcoholic drinks in the Naama Bay area and … legally purchasing some anabolic steroids. The following, which draws upon the author's PhD research and a small-scale digital ethnographic study of surface web travel and bodybuilding forums, will first examine the context of steroid use and supply in the UK, before addressing the legal loophole that facilitates what are termed 'steroid holidays'. Using Sharm El Sheikh as a case study, the modus operandi of steroid tourists will be illuminated before the attractions and dangers of this practice of dark leisure will be made clear.

The use and supply of anabolic steroids

The use of anabolic androgenic steroids (AAS), defined as a class of drugs that include the male hormone testosterone (or a synthetic derivative of it), has increased alarmingly over the last decade or so in the UK (Mullen et al, 2020). Clinically, AAS are used to treat male reproductive dysfunction, some forms of anaemia and breast cancer (Sagoe et al, 2014), yet, due to their muscle-building and masculinising properties, they are predominantly associated with strength sports and appearance enhancement. Steroids are commonly used as part of a 'cycle', whereby a course is taken in a set period before the user is 'off-cycle', where they assume a period of abstinence (Evans-Brown et al, 2012) and consume post-cycle therapy (PCT) drugs to stabilise their hormone levels and mitigate any ill effects of their AAS use (Christiansen et al, 2017).

However, despite the growing user base and relative normalisation of AAS consumption in numerous fitness settings (Hall and Antonopoulos, 2016; Turnock, 2021), recreational users must generally engage in the illicit market in order to procure steroids. Indeed, most AAS on the domestic market are produced in underground laboratories (UGLs) (Turnock, 2020) or illegally siphoned off licit pharmaceutical supply chains (Fink et al, 2019). Furthermore, UGL-produced AAS also carry a reputation, perhaps unfairly, as being poor quality or incorrectly dosed (Coomber et al, 2014) and therefore carry additional health risks for consumers (Graham et al, 2009).

The law and the loophole

Legally, AAS came under the Misuse of Drugs Act (1971) in 1996 in the UK (ACMD, 2010). Thus, without a prescription, AAS are a class C drug and possessing or importing with intent to supply is punishable by up to 14 years in prison (Home Office, 2021). Most recently, in reaction to the burgeoning online enhancement drugs market, it became illegal to import AAS into the UK via freight services (for example, post or courier) (Hanley et al, 2017). However, within UK law there exists one caveat which provides users with a means of bypassing the illicit AAS market and consuming pharmaceutical-grade products, and it is this discretion which forms the primary concern of this chapter.

The ACMD state that '[i]t is legal to possess or import/export anabolic steroids as long as they are intended for personal use and in the form of a medicinal product' (ACMD, 2010: 12). Thus, providing that they purchase licensed medicines in small enough quantities to be considered 'personal use', customers can legally travel to countries where AAS are available over the counter and return home with their products (NHS, 2018). This loophole has spawned the now common practice of 'steroid holidays' (Dunn et al, 2020), wherein certain sites of lax pharmaceutical regulation have become destinations for committed AAS users to soak up the sun, enjoy the beach and purchase their cycle. Dunn et al (2020: 3), in the first scholarly investigation into this phenomenon, describe these trips as 'traveling to and living in foreign countries so as to have greater access to performance and image enhancing drugs'. Their study, which drew upon data from public forum posts from Australian users, found that users commonly travelled to Thailand to circumnavigate their domestic regulations. This chapter therefore aims to build upon Dunn et al's (2020) work and examine steroid holidays in the popular destination of Sharm El Sheikh in Egypt by UK steroid tourists.

Sharm El Sheikh as a steroid holiday destination

The Egyptian Tourism Authority (2017) describe Sharm El Sheikh as a place to 'soak up sun, dive amazing coral reefs, and enjoy the sea'. Indeed, even in the midst of the COVID-19 pandemic in the summer of 2020, over 50,000 tourists visited the city (Ahram Online, 2020). More poignantly, however, Egypt allows popular AAS like testosterone propionate and testosterone enanthate, as well as a number of PCT drugs, to be sold over the counter without a prescription. Echoing Dunn et al's (2020) findings, users on a popular British bodybuilding forum discussed the ease of acquiring such products in the resort:[1]

Bigbeast43: I'm going on holiday to Sharm [El Sheikh] and want to buy some Test[osterone] Prop[ionate] along with the rest of my cycle and PCT while away. Was just wondering if anyone on here has bought it from there before and whether it's all above board?

Roid_rager: Yeah it's legal, and easy enough to source. Best bet is to speak to a local and ask him where to go, otherwise you can just try your luck in

[1] Pseudonyms have been used to protect users' real identities. Further, to reduce searchability, phrasing has been altered in line with Markham (2012).

> a pharmacy. I got [testosterone] prop[ionate] from there and it was good stuff.

As is evident from this extract, forum users spoke encouragingly about the availability and legitimacy of purchasing pharmaceutical-grade products over the counter in Sharm El Sheikh. Similarly, amateur bodybuilder Jake recalled his friend's routine visits to Egypt to purchase AAS, medicinal fat burners and the PCT substances he used after each AAS cycle:

> 'I've got a friend who gets all his gear from Egypt. He brings a lot of the over-the-counter stuff back from there, like your clen[buteral], T3, Arimidex [Anastrozole], Winstrol [Stanozolol] as well. You can get all that over the counter over there … he'll ring them up two weeks before and they'll set stock aside for when he's coming.'

The attraction

But why travel to another continent to procure these drugs when a serviceable domestic market operates in the UK? First, and most obviously, steroid holidays allow users to bypass the illicit economy and feel secure that they are operating within the law and, as 'Maxmuscle93' stated, 'not giving money to the bad guys'. Thus, given the mainstreaming of AAS as a lifestyle drug (Hall and Antonopoulos, 2016), most users would not otherwise engage in illicit behaviour and therefore welcome the opportunity to remain law-abiding.

Further, Dunn et al (2020) note that steroid holidays are motivated by the products' relative affordability in such destinations. To acquire legitimate pharmaceutical-grade AAS in the UK, consumers often pay a heavy premium given the risk involved in removing licensed medicines from the licit supply chain (Fink et al, 2019). However, by travelling to steroid holiday destinations, users dispel this risk, as well as benefiting from favourable exchange rates, as 'The_Freak' explained: 'The Egyptian pound has massively been devalued in the last few years. You'll literally get twice as many Egyptian pounds for your Great British Pound as you would have done.' Similarly, 'TrishSimms1961', answering an enquiry about Egyptian AAS export laws on popular review website Tripadvisor, counselled 'my son uses steroids and last year he asked me to bring him some back from Sharm [El Sheikh] … I ended up bringing him about 30 boxes back because they were so cheap'. Clearly, 'TrishSimms1961' was in breach of the law given that steroid holidays rely upon imports for personal consumption; however, both accounts speak to the cost efficiency of this purchasing strategy. As a result, even taking into account the air fare and associated accommodation expenses, steroid tourists can reduce their overall expenditure when purchasing their cycles.

Dunn et al (2020) further describe how steroid holidays in destinations like Sharm El Sheikh provide buyers with assurances of product quality and legitimacy. As noted, many users favour pharmaceutical products to those that are produced in UGLs on account of the stringent regulations in licit manufacturing facilities. Ben, an International Federation of Bodybuilding and Fitness Pro bodybuilder, for example, only consumed pharmaceutically produced AAS and derided UGL products, which he perceived to be 'cooked … up in a bathtub'. Visiting countries like Egypt on steroid holidays therefore satisfies users' desire for officially regulated products, which are more challenging to source domestically. Finally, bringing this chapter more in line with this collection's focus on *destinations*, Sharm El Sheikh not only facilitates steroid tourists' purchasing and consumption but also provides them with a sunny paradise within which to show off their enhanced bodies, as Ben explained when recalling his experiences of buying AAS in the Egyptian resort:

> 'I've been abroad to Cyprus and Egypt and things like that, and you can just buy it over the counter, you can go to a chemist and just buy it. Plus it's a decent place to get a bit of sun with the Mrs or the lads or whatever. So it's [killing] two birds [with] one stone when you think about it – you get your gear and also get to be in the pool or in the clubs looking decent. I went to Sharm [El Sheikh] to get it and it was just like bringing some souvenirs back [laughs].'

Here, Ben's description of his steroid holiday in Sharm El Sheikh captures the impact of the 'gear' that he purchased there on his experience of the destination itself. The resort's idyllic beaches and hedonistic nightlife therefore offer steroid tourists like Ben a means of sharing their bodily capital (Wacquant, 1995), effectively completing the circle of demand and consumption.

The risks

Although steroid tourism offers users a means of legally purchasing affordable, high-quality AAS, Dunn et al (2020) highlight a raft of harms associated with the practice. First, despite steroid tourists' claims of the legitimacy of their products, the licit AAS market in places like Sharm El Sheikh is awash with fake and counterfeit AAS. This was a persistent theme on the forums under study, as 'Deltsnglutes' warned other members to 'only buy from a reputable pharmacy like El Ezaby and make sure they are packaged in single boxes that haven't been tampered with'. Echoing this, 'The_Freak' advised, '[a]s a rule, trust nothing other than El Ezaby if you want guaranteed products at the correct price – it's a legit chain and there's loads around in all the tourist towns'. As these excerpts demonstrate, steroid tourists face being scammed or over-charged during their visits if they are not informed of the local market. Further, although unlikely in practice, the legal definition of 'personal consumption' is decidedly vague, and therefore steroid tourists risk a lengthy prison sentence if they attempt to import a large volume of drugs or show intent to supply (Home Office, 2021). This grey area is potentially problematic, particularly if users fail to declare their products at customs. Finally, from a more societal perspective, even if steroid tourists acquire legitimate products and successfully return home, they are removing licensed medicines from Egypt's market and potentially denying a local resident treatment for an actual malady.

Conclusion

Ultimately, steroid holidays to destinations like Sharm El Sheikh represent a niche, but nonetheless significant, form of dark leisure. Although something of a departure from this collection's account of places of deviant or illicit leisure, the UK's legal loophole around in-person importation for personal consumption allows users to create something of a one-man supply chain, leaning upon destinations like Sharm El Sheikh to provide them with a licit means of purchasing AAS. Simultaneously, steroid tourists like Ben can soak in the sun while they procure their products, and can even put their physique's enhanced bodily capital to work in the resort's spaces of pleasurable, stupid consumption (Žižek, 2008). After all, why not take advantage of this destination of sun, sea and anabolic steroids?

31

The souks: Tunis, Tunisia

Kyla Bavin and James Treadwell

Staffordshire University

Introduction

A lot of tourism is tied to contemporary dominant forms of capitalist consumption. Finding a bargain and shopping so frequently feature as motivations underpinning travel, the desire to find a bargain and indulge in forms of retail therapy. Consumerism is now integral to our global political economy yet few have offered critical accounts of the vital functional and ideological roles consumerism has played throughout the history of capitalism (Winlow and Hall, 2017). While conspicuous consumption is stratified, as is the ecological footprint that arises from such practices, the places and sites of the consumption of 'luxury commodities' in criminology and social science more broadly remain little recognised, as does the everyday way that such forms involve advantage and privilege that are often not seen as such. While we can draw attention to the heightened ecological footprints of super yachts, super homes, luxury vehicles and private jets, so too, the ability to travel globally and find meaning in markets of all sorts is often under-considered. Yet the place of markets in generating harm is worth consideration. It was the wet markets of Wuhan that were first blamed for the COVID-19 pandemic, while the counterfeit markets travellers visit rarely gain attention. Be it buying 'genuine fakes' cheaper than Asda price in Tunisia or Turkey, the go-go bars, scorpion eating and snake blood drinking of Thailand or smoking vulture brains in Johannesburg, markets and visiting them tell us much more than just what is being sold and consumed.

The souks of Tunis and abroad

The souks of Tunis are a set of shops and boutiques located in the medina of Tunis, the capital of Tunisia. Most of the souks were built in the 13th century and are located near the old part of the city. Fittingly, they still have a feel of the medieval medina. Today, its architecture divides the medina from the rest of the city – you can see where the medina begins just by looking at the buildings. The streets in the medina are narrow and winding, full of covered souks, artisans' workshops and residential buildings with colourful painted doors. These souks, as with similar destinations, are not so much dark and dingy but bright, vibrant places of hustle, bustle, haggle and barter, where an array of goods are traded. The value of travelling and studying places of trade or marketplaces for social scientists is, arguably, self-evident, for within them, all manner of human interactions play out, offering an insight into an eclectic host of varying aspects and facets of behaviour. In a souk in Hammamet in Tunisia, I (James) once saw an impoverished local attempting to sell odd shoes.

The trade in spices, fabrics, perfumes, fruits and meats is arresting on a sensory level. The cow's head dripping blood onto cobbles, flies and pungent aromas coupled with vivid colours and smells assault the senses. Souks are a maze of alleys and narrow streets, and it's easy to get lost. It is always advisable to look out for landmarks such as a flight of stairs or an archway, so if you need to return after dark, they can easily be picked out. In terms of security and safety, numerous travel guides will counsel that it is not a good idea to walk around on your own after dark in places such as Casablanca or Tangier. Aside from the obvious risks of criminal victimisation, mopeds ridden at high speed are an additional and persistent risk. So too, photography is not something the communities generally like, and this needs to be considered as you explore the various stalls and alleyways. In crowded areas, pick pocketing and petty theft is very common, so expensive jewellery is always best left in the hotel room. Keeping your valuables out of sight and a firm grip on your bag is sensible. Such precautions could perhaps be seen as daunting, but they are worthwhile.

The cacophony of haggles and stall owners shouting combined with the smell of spices and fumes from motorbikes delight the senses. The feel of the heat surrounding you as you explore the brightly coloured stalls piled high with an array of pottery and leather bags is overwhelming. Souks are the heart of the Marrakech medina and have been the centre for trade in the city for a thousand years. Today, the souks of Tunis as well as Marrakech are as much a mainstay tourist attraction as a place of local life, and yet they still have the exotic, even chaotic, feel. But the souk is a segway into the notion of the market more widely, and that is a vital notion when it comes to crime. For example, the question could be asked, 'why have we chosen the Tunisian souk and decided to reflect on Yemen's largest arms market?' It is located in the village of Jihana, a mere 40-minute drive from the Yemeni capital of Sanaa, where here buyers could find a dizzying array of small and medium arms and it is suggested extremist Islamists did a ready trade. So too, it is common knowledge, and guides will often use it as a way to pique tourists' interest, that Al Qaeda were heavily active within the souks of Marrakech.

Colonial consumption

The heady scents of these markets, while pungent and intoxicating, do little to mask the overwhelming stench of colonialism that has cultivated much of the trade meant for Western appetites. Since the HMS *Endeavour* sailed across the South Seas in 1768, our Western palates have developed the taste for the delicious cultures of the freshly acquired territories that we have long since converted and exploited. From trinkets to the sun-kissed flesh of the most vulnerable in their society, the occupied have survived such tyrannical rule by trading whatever they had left after we had forcibly taken everything else.

A sexualised fantasy of the rest by the West has persisted (Gieben and Hall, 1992), creating a symbiotic relationship that fuels dark tourism and illicit markets around the globe. From the go-go bars of Bangkok to the 'genuine fakes' of Istanbul, these markets exist to provide the goods and services that the West fetishise. Instead of rationalising that the criminogenic features of dark tourism are an issue at source, the discerning criminologist needs to look more inwardly at our own relationship to capitalism and our own desire for exotic flavours regardless of their costs.

At this point, it is prudent to not to be historically naïve and suggest that it is only the West that has reaped the benefits of colonial brutality. However, when looking at the contemporary marketisation of the darker offerings of countries that survive on tourism, we must recognise that the cash-rich West is at the forefront of their development. It is our darkest desires that are catered for by the populous of countries that have been ravaged by colonialism, seeking to claw out an existence in a global capitalist economy that thrives on exploitation.

The way that we consume may have changed, especially since the start of the COVID-19 pandemic; however, consumer appetites persist, especially for sex, intoxication and indulgence. Whether it be the lads on holiday trawling local watering holes for gratification or the mum buying ten snide Nike t-shirts for her kids, as the Manic Street Preachers stated, 'everything is for sale'. Moreover, if we tolerate this then perhaps it will not be our children that are next, but someone's will be.

The merits of markets

In many ways, criminologists should look at markets wherever they are found. The criminal market spans the planet: illicit goods are sourced from one continent, trafficked across another and marketed in a third, and yet how we conceive of licit and illicit is in and of itself interesting. By 2010, the United Nations were suggesting that the number of counterfeit goods detected at the European border had gone up by a factor of 10 since 2000. As much as half of medications tested in Africa and Southeast Asia are counterfeited and substandard, increasing, rather than reducing, the chance of illness. Counterfeit items consist of everything from pharmaceuticals to safety critical vehicle parts. Illegal exploitation of natural resources and the trafficking in wildlife from Africa and Southeast Asia are disrupting fragile ecosystems and driving species to extinction. The United Nations Office on Drugs and Crime estimates that illicit wood products imported from Asia to the European Union and China were worth some 2.5 billion dollars in 2009.

Of course, not all of this is seen in the traditional marketplace, bazaar or souk. In his text *Crime in Markets*, Vincenzo Ruggiero (2000) sought to promote a unified theory of crime and highlights the interpretive oscillations, which always occur when we are faced with criminal behaviour. The anti-criminological tradition to which he claims affiliation, he suggests, allows a greater insight into the nuances of the world. But markets, real world and online, can be a place for criminals to operate (Treadwell, 2012). Whether they be open to the world or secretive and accessible to only the knowing few are the very stuff of so much criminology but are often not considered thus. This brings to the fore the key value for social sciences and criminologists. Crime is a human activity, and at the root of much of how we conceive of and consider crime is trade and exchange in goods and services. More obviously, different criminal markets such as sexual exploitation, drugs and illicit cigarettes often form the backdrop to that we see in the foreground. For example, consider how physical markets can be the backdrop to crime or violence, protest and resistance. How shelling of markets during the war in the Balkans in the 1990s targeted civilians, or how it was a protest by Tarek el-Tayeb Mohamed Bouazizi, a street vendor who set himself on fire on 17 December 2010 in Ben Arous, Tunisia, which became a catalyst for the Tunisian Revolution and the wider Arab Spring, just 30 kilometres away from Tunis.

Conclusion

Just as how recent technological developments, such as cryptocurrencies, have seen rise to dark web-based illegal markets, the sometimes fine lines between illicit and legal are apparent within these contexts. Illegal markets are defined as such because they either avoid the local government market regulations or they trade in illegal goods, such as drugs or weapons, and hence consideration of this benefits the aspiring criminologist. The answers to the questions of the reasons why individuals may buy, sell or otherwise engage in these markets can also be found within them, and can provide reasonable understanding of how we might consider their proliferation, especially when taking into consideration the history of their locales. So perhaps criminologists should head to the market, of which there are many, but the souks of Africa remain among our favourites to offer an insight into human nature and how black markets in their various forms proliferate across the globe.

32

Mezhyhirya Residence Museum: Novi Petrivtsi, Ukraine

Tereza Østbø Kuldova and Jardar Østbø

OsloMet – Oslo Metropolitan and Norwegian Institute for Defence Studies

Note

This chapter was written in Summer 2021, months before the Russian invasion of Ukraine. At the moment, we can only preface it by noting that Mezhyhirya's symbolic significance is not likely to recede. On the first day of the war, a bomb landed near the lake, reportedly killing two swans – a highly symbolic event, as *Swan Lake*, in the post-Soviet context, connotes political meltdown in Moscow (it was aired on TV during the 1991 coup attempt, after which the Soviet Union quickly dissolved).

Introduction

On 21 February 2014, in the last days of the Ukrainian revolution, violence escalating and police snipers killing protestors, Victor Yanukovych fled the estate of Mezhyhirya in a helicopter, an estate where he has lived since 2002, first as prime minister and then as president of Ukraine (2010–2014) – after having spent the last three days stuffing his bags with luxury items, that is. The regime was overthrown. The next day, Euromaidan protestors stormed the Mezhyhirya residence: "everyone wants to see the humble home of their legitimate leader", as one of them put it. While everyone knew of the kleptocracy, corruption, fraudulent schemes, tax evasion and money laundering even well prior to the revolution, many were still in shock and awe when seeing for themselves what has been hiding behind the previously impenetrable gates of the Mezhyhirya residence. In Novi Petrivtsi, 25 km from Kiev, carefully hidden from the public view behind guarded gates, the obscenely lavish Mezhyhirya complex turned out to feature golf courses, a swimming pool, tennis court, yacht club and artificial lakes, racecourses and stables, a luxury five-storey residence and three-storey guest house, winter garden, a zoo (with kangaroos who did not survive the winter), greenhouses, collections of over 70 cars and of weapons and bullets, a private chapel, karaoke bar, bowling alley, gyms, massage salons and more, much of it gold-plated and equipped with antiques and an enormous wealth of luxury goods. The cost of fittings, fixtures and chandeliers, as well as the golden loaf of bread, has shocked many:

> Each of the mansion's Lebanese cedar doors cost \$64,000. Three sets of wooden panelling for staircases came in at \$200,000, wall panelling for the winter garden at \$328,000, and cladding for a neoclassical column and parapet for a flight of steps at \$430,000. In the course of one and a half years the overall cost of fittings imported for Mezhyhiriya was \$9,416,000. The price of the chandeliers in Viktor Yanukovych's new residence has shocked Ukrainians. In a country where 35% of the population live under poverty line, spending 100 000 dollars on each individual chandelier seems excessive, to say the least. (Leshchenko, 2012)

Mezhyhirya is 'key to understanding the elite's self-destructive greed. Their schemes drove the Ukrainian economy into the ground' (Wilson, 2014: 60). Yanukovych and his close allies, or rather (mafia-style) 'Family' (Wilson, 2014), siphoned 'at least \$37 billion of government money into offshore bank accounts' (Schuster, 2019), Mezhyhirya being just one of the opulent, kitschy and conspicuous properties owned by the clan, and perverse displays of insatiable 'conspicuous consumption' (Veblen, 2007). One of the Euromaidan activists, Denys Tarakhkotelyk, quickly decided to prevent the looting of the palace, turning it instead into a 'museum of corruption' and taking care of the property ever since, with the help of around 200 employees, including former self-defence group members providing security, supported further by '[s]pecial unit soldiers from the Ministry of Internal Affairs and National Guard [who] provide public order'. Since then, a great number of tourist agencies have been offering guided tours to tourists (prices range between US$65 and 100 for a four-hour tour, in addition to entry fees to the park and individual buildings, and fees for renting bikes and golf cars, necessary to get around the vast property), encouraging the visitors to 'plunge into a rich life and be surprised at how limitless human greed and desire to be in power are' (Capital Tours and Transfers Kiev, 2021). Visitors often end up both repulsed and attracted, as one of them put it on Tripadvisor: 'The sheer vastness of the looting from the nation of Ukraine by Yanukovych and his cronies was at the same time fascinating and disgusting, just as the house is both impressive yet incredibly cheap and tacky in places. It's a unique attraction' (KNL999, 2019). Mezhyhirya is one of the most striking expressions of the greed and corruption at the heart of the economy, an economy underpinned by the 'the moral economy of fraud' (Whyte and Wiegratz, 2016) – an arresting manifestation of the inequalities, harms and criminal and criminogenic nature of neoliberalism, all 'condensed' at 140 hectares. While at first sight not as obvious a site of 'dark tourism' – such as the sites of mass death, suffering, disasters and tragedy, strikingly morbid and macabre (Stone et al, 2018) – the luxury of the residence should not blind us to the crimes and infliction of harms on the many by the few, without which this wealth would have been impossible to amass. Nor should we forget the function of luxury as a quest for secular immortality (Hirschman, 1990), one that fuels consumer capitalism, with all its powers of destruction – of human lives, nature and meaning.

Violence, death and immortality

Mezhyhirya is intimately connected to death, and to the desire for biological, secular/symbolic and even religious immortality. Yanukovych, who, when explaining how he came to move there, referred to his personal safety after an attempt on his life, and made the residence a fortress in the literal sense, surrounded as it is by a 6.5-metre-high fence. Ironically, he eventually also fled from there out of fear for his life. Virtually all the fruit and vegetables that its inhabitants consumed were grown on-site in advanced greenhouses, and there is also a special laboratory, estimated to cost US$15 million, tasked with checking every food item served to Yanukovych, as well as presents given to him, for poisons. The air inside the house was constantly cleaned by a special, multi-step device, securing laboratory-grade, clean air in all rooms – in the country of Chernobyl and coal mines. As if that was not enough, there is also a 'salt room' for halotherapy. The narcissistic quest for symbolic immortality is materialised in numerous pompous portaits of Yanukovych, some of which are made of expensive materials. On the occasion of the president's birthday in 2013, the National Bank of Ukraine made him a memorial coin of half a kilo of gold, decorated with emeralds and with the illustrative imprint 'May you live long!' (Bozhko, 2013). 'Traditional', Orthodox Christian immortality was far from forgotten, but also sought to be achieved through luxury, as the residence contains a chapel with a lavish iconostasis, not to mention an antique bible and numerous expensive icons. Of course, considering Yanukovych's failure not only to stay in power, but also to uphold the state's integrity, the contrast between these items' heroic imaginary and reality is striking. The former president's luxury-fuelled pursuit of immortality also gains dark tones against the background of the death and destruction directly contributed to – at the very least – by his incompetent leadership in a severe national crisis: more than one hundred people died in street fighting during the 2013–2014 Euromaidan uprising, and the ongoing war in the east has so far taken 14,000 lives.

The predilection for violence that lies at the base of conspicuous consumption is obvious in Mezhyhirya. As Veblen reasons, whereas the early barbarians had to resort to simple aggression and unrestrained violence as a means of dominance over others in order to accumulate wealth, at later stages, the upper classes rely on more subtle means than direct aggression, such as 'shrewd practice and chicanery', betraying a 'quasi-peaceable regime of status'. But the 'barbarian temperament', with its emphasis on prowess, is conserved to a large extent (Veblen, 2007: 155–157). The propensity for violence surfaces elsewhere, such as in the predilection for certain kinds of sports, or in cultural artefacts. At Mezhyhirya, this is exemplified by Yanukovych's collection of weapons consisting of 700 pieces of arms old and new, and an impressive amount of bullets framed in glass boxes. There is also a shooting range, and, in the well-equipped fitness room, a full-sized boxing ring. That said, Yanukovych himself has, according to several media reports, repreatedly acted on the impulse to respond violently to insults (Perovoznaya and Yakimenko, 2010), evincing an essentially archaic 'martial spirit' that Veblen observed among the upper classes as well as among the 'lower-class delinquents' (Veblen, 2007: 161–162).

Special liberty and transnational corruption

Mezhyhirya is a physical manifestation of 'special liberty' (Hall, 2012), its former resident being both a criminal and member of the elite (the two increasingly overlapping, globally speaking) – who believes himself to be above the law and above any ethical, moral and normative codes, willing to inflict harm and exploit others in order to maximise his self-interest, quest for profit, symbolic immortality, distinction and 'toxic sovereignty' (Tudor, 2018; Lloyd, 2019). At the same time, it is striking how banal and normalised the fraud is. Among the documents first discovered after Yanukovych fled, there was a printed book-keeping record stating the exact amount of what was explicitly termed a bribe, down to the last *kopek*, as well as hand written acknowledgements of the receipt of millions of dollars. Well-known parts of Yanukovych's early biography are illustrative of this combination of special liberty and normalisation of crime. Twice sentenced in his youth, first three years for robbery, and then two years for violence, he served only a fraction of the prison terms, thanks to connections and 'good behaviour'. A few years later, a regional court quashed the decisions at the request of his patron, the cosmonaut and member of the Supreme Soviet, Georgiy Beregovoi. Having powerful connections, he could get away with it. Also, Yanukovych grew up in Pivnovka, a particularly bad neighbourhood in Yenakieve, Donetsk region, where law enforcement was weak, violence was omnipresent and crime often paid. According to an elderly woman interviewed by *Moskovskii Komsomolets* (Bobrova, 2010):

> Everyone who sat in prison is now at the top … in Pivnovka they arranged terrible fights. 200 people converged in the lowland. The police did not intervene in this showdown … as for Yanukovych, I'll tell you this – whoever was not small was not bad. I myself stole apples until my hair was gray. And for Vitka, we all from Pivnovka voted for him.

Crucially, these details, as well as Mezhyhirya, should not be interpreted merely as symptomatic of Yanukovych's personality or Ukraine's culture of corruption. On a global scale, Yanukovych is in no way a lonely figure, nor does his embrace of 'special liberty' make him special. The line between Yanukovych's youthful crimes and his later corruption schemes as president has been drawn by many of his opponents, but the line between the petty violence of Pivnovka and the grand corruption revealed in the Panama papers is practically ignored. Nevertheless, the stories from Pivnovka can easily be read as an allegory about the neoliberal, globalised world economy. Already, Thorstein Veblen observed the clear parallels between the mentality and modus operandi of the upper classes and the 'lower-class delinquents', the difference being mostly about the scale and the resources at hand:

> The ideal pecuniary man is like the ideal delinquent in his unscrupulous conversion of goods and persons to his own ends, and in a callous disregard of the feelings and wishes of others and of the remoter effects of his actions; but he is unlike him in possessing a keener sense of status, and in working more consistently and far-sightedly to a remoter end. (Veblen, 2007: 156)

Conclusion

Even though the tourist agencies entice us to 'learn the details of modern history of Ukraine, and see with your own eyes the loot of Yanukovych over the years of corruption' (Capital Tours and Transfers, 2021), Mezhyhirya is better understood as a physical manifestation of transnational and opaque networks of corruption enabled by neoliberalism, globalisation, consumerism and the chronic state of 'anomie' (Durkheim, 2006). One should not forget here Yanukovych's helpers – members of what we term the transnational 'defiance industry' which serves the needs of the corrupt and operates at the borders of the legal and the illegal. Or else, the many individuals belonging to the transnational networks of lawyers, compliance officers, advisers, real estate brokers, financial experts, 'evasion experts' (Zucman, 2015) and actors within the luxury industry laundering money through art, antiques and other valuables (De Sanctis, 2013) – all willing to compromise their professional ethics for private gain and to facilitate large-scale fraud and crime, and further fuel the harms of neoliberal economy. This transnational defiance industry not only serves those who believe themselves to possess 'special liberty', but itself consists of those who equally believe themselves to be above laws and morals. We should not let ourselves be blinded by the figure of Yanukovych, and by the spectacular images of illicit wealth used to mobilise popular passions, or by the borders of Ukraine. Instead, the visitor should take the 'dark tour' through Mezhyhirya as an opportunity to contemplate the systemic and transnational nature of corruption (Pasculli and Ryder, 2020).

Funding

This work was funded by the Research Council of Norway under project no. 313004, 'Luxury, Corruption and Global Ethics: Towards a Critical Cultural Theory of the Moral Economy of Fraud' (LUXCORE).

33

The great British seaside: various locations, UK

Neil Chakraborti

University of Leicester

Introduction

It started with a warm doughnut. Like any other 8-year-old city-based kid with only grown-ups in tow, a day trip to the seaside could feel infinitely less appealing than parents might assume (Why the boring long car journey? Why couldn't I be at home playing Subbuteo with my mates?). But with an air of confidence, my dad whisked me off towards the seafront, bought us a bag of warm doughnuts and sat us down on a secluded part of the beach. In my 8-year-old head, everything about that moment felt both unfamiliar and utterly perfect: the sand in my toes, the lapping of the waves, the warmth of the sun and, of course, the sugary gorgeousness of those doughnuts.

It's a memory that kick-started my love affair with the seaside and has lived with me for many decades since. It feels relevant here, not just for the waves of nostalgia that it evokes but also for the rather more sinister encounter which followed soon afterwards. My dad and I walked back along the seafront to meet the rest of our family for a stroll down to the funfair. What should have been the springboard for more happy memories soon took a different turn when the family behind us in the queue used insulting language to belittle us in deliberately loud voices. References to our 'curry smells', 'Paki' heritage and 'funny' accents were all invoked in a way which felt both humiliating and alienating in an environment in which no bystanders stepped in to offer support. At the time, I recall myself longing for us to leave straight away and feeling furious with my father for silently doing nothing except stand his ground in the queue. In hindsight, I know that his actions will have been inspired by a sense of defiance in the face of racist hostility and a sense of weary resignation that would have been familiar to countless other minority ethnic households in the 1980s.

These recollections are illustrative of the 'hidden' harms that present themselves in places which are typically romanticised as problem-free spaces in an increasingly problematic world. Seaside towns and villages, like much of rural England, tend to be portrayed as sanctuaries of tradition, virtue and timelessness in sharp contrast to the anonymity associated with urban environments (Chakraborti and Garland, 2004a; Neal and Agyeman, 2006; Fowler, 2020). However, the great British seaside is a much darker destination for many of its inhabitants and visitors. Describing it as a repository of White values, ideologies and lifestyles, Burdsey (2013) observes that the seaside has always been an inherently, albeit subtly, racialised environment as a site for the consumption of Orientalist, neocolonial and sometimes overtly racist-themed entertainment (see also Hubbard, 2005). Within this context, the seaside's nostalgic and quintessentially English overtones can present an insular, jingoistic and exclusionary feel to those who don't 'fit', as we shall see in the sections that follow.

Hidden darkness

In an age where the diversification of rural space has become increasingly commonplace, it is clear that the challenges associated with racism and other forms of exclusionary behaviour are not confined just to larger towns and cities. 'Picture-postcard' depictions of the seaside mask both the plurally constituted nature of their communities and the processes of 'othering' which serve to ostracise those who do not align with the Anglocentric stereotypes which come with those depictions (Neal and Agyeman, 2006; Kerrigan, 2018). The denigration of minority ethnic 'others' is often defended as a form of preservation of local customs, and sometimes overtly celebrated, as is the case with the 'Darkie Day' festival held in the Cornish fishing port of Padstow. Part of an ancient tradition of Pagan midwinter festivals, this annual event sees locals parade through the town in blackened faces, donning 'afro' wigs and performing minstrel songs which make regular reference to the 'N word' (Chakraborti, 2010). Despite being re-badged as 'Mummers Day' by festival organisers in an attempt to quell growing criticism from senior politicians and campaigners during the early 2000s, the festival continues to be promoted as 'Darkie Day' within local tourist guides and is illustrative of the way in which racist stereotypes can be legitimised and celebrated in communities unfamiliar with cultural, religious and visible differences.[1] Processes of othering are also sustained through a propensity to blame newcomers (and minority ethnic newcomers in particular) for the range of perceived and actual problems which affect many coastal communities, including escalating crime rates, dwindling local services and a lack of community amenities (Neal and Agyeman, 2006; Burdsey, 2013).

The 'othering' of minority ethnic rural households reinforces a double form of isolation where, in effect, those households can be marginalised from the sense of community shared by their urban-based counterparts *and* from the conventional activities of their local communities (Henderson and Kaur, 1999). It can create what Giddens (1994: 126) refers to as a 'compelling pressure towards conformism' which is heightened for anyone perceived to be somehow 'different' (see also Magne, 2003). It can also generate damaging and repeated experiences of racist harassment. Research evidence has shown how these experiences form an unremitting continuum of victimisation for many minority ethnic families, comprising of frequent encounters of 'low-level' harassment such as racist epithets, verbal threats, stone throwing and physical intimidation, in addition to harrowing experiences of physical attacks, racist graffiti and other forms of criminal damage to homes and businesses (Chakraborti and Garland, 2004b; Chakraborti, 2010; Burdsey, 2013). Moreover, the cumulative 'drip-drip' effect of these experiences compounds

---

[1] See, for example, https://www.cornwalls.co.uk/events/darkie_days.htm (accessed 14 December 2021).

their harrowing impacts but can often be overlooked by third parties because of a lack of understanding, a lack of empathy or a lack of familiarity with the more subtle, less overt expressions of racist behaviour (Chakraborti, 2010). As such, it is the 'intangible, implicit and in some senses "unreportable" nature of this process of victimisation that exacerbates the problems facing rural minorities' (Chakraborti, 2010: 507).

Hidden harms

It is well documented that the harms associated with racist hostility and other forms of hate crime are wide-ranging and damaging (Williams and Tregidga, 2013; Chakraborti et al, 2014; Paterson et al, 2018). In addition to physical injury, many victims of hate crime suffer high levels of psychological and emotional trauma as a result of their experiences, with increased levels of anxiety, depression, loss of confidence, nervousness, anger and fear of repeat victimisation commonly documented by researchers (Perry and Alvi, 2012; Hardy and Chakraborti, 2016; Burch, 2021). Moreover, Craig-Henderson and Sloan (2003: 482) suggest that these harms are 'qualitatively distinct' from the emotions that victims of parallel crimes may experience because of the deeply personal nature of the attack on their core identity. Victims are especially likely to experience greater harms when, as a member of a stigmatised or marginalised group, their victimisation brings to the fore the fear and pain caused by historical, systematic discriminative attacks on their identity group (see also Hardy and Chakraborti, 2019). Research has also highlighted the way in which flawed criminal justice responses can exacerbate these harms, with fault lines in reporting, recording, investigative and prosecution pathways all compounding victims' sense of isolation and injustice (Chakraborti, 2018).

These issues are equally relevant to coastal towns and villages (see, inter alia, Magne, 2003). However, the harms described here are rendered all the more invisible by virtue of the fact that so few racist incidents are reported to the police and other service providers, typically because victims have less confidence in their local police force's willingness or ability to respond effectively (Garland and Chakraborti, 2006). In essence, this results in a 'vicious circle' scenario wherein the police are reluctant to acknowledge the seriousness of the problem given the paucity of victims stepping forward to report, and where victims are reluctant to report given their lack of faith in police responses. Continued cuts to police resources, and a prioritisation of other challenges perceived to have greater relevance to local communities, have reinforced this problem in recent years. As such, those who encounter racism either as seaside residents or as tourists are likely to face an uphill struggle to elicit meaningful support in towns and villages where awareness levels are invariably lower, and where prevailing economic, political and social conditions act as enabling factors for the othering of 'outsiders'.

Conclusion

This chapter has highlighted some of the everyday realities facing ethnic minorities who live, work and holiday in coastal towns and villages. In doing so, it challenges some of the assumptions which underpin the imagery of the great British seaside. Experiences of racism are by no means an inevitability in such environments, and many minority ethnic residents and visitors will, like me, continue to have their own cherished memories of their time by the seaside. However, these locales are not immune to problems of racism but instead have distinctive cultures which shape the way in which 'difference' is understood and engaged with. Within this context, it is important to recognise the seaside as a marginal space, with its marginality constructed in relation both to its spatial location and its cultural associations. As Burdsey observes, this allows us to see beyond the nostalgic stereotypes of the seaside towards its darker reality as a place beset by multiple challenges, namely:

> its geographical position as a place literally on the edge of the nation; a declining tourist industry … the effects of seasonality that impact directly on the essential character of the town … its limited history of living with difference … and a sense of residential stasis that restricts the wider mobility of its communities and promotes a local-centric world-view. (Burdsey, 2013: 114)

These challenges also feed into the social conservatism, nationalism, outsider scepticism and resurgence of Britain's colonial era ambitions which were central features in the widespread support for Brexit across coastal and other rural communities (Goodhart, 2017; Brooks, 2019).

Acknowledging these multiple realities enables us to move away from problem-free notions of coastal life which ostracise those who do not fit within conventional, outdated frameworks of belonging. Instead, it nudges us towards a more nuanced, and potentially more hopeful, way of framing the great British seaside: a place which we acknowledge as problem-laden, as complex and as dark as all destinations can be, but one which continues to appeal and to evolve.

34

The Biggie mural: Brooklyn, New York, USA

Natasha Pope

Birmingham City University

Introduction

Venturing to Bedford Avenue, Brooklyn, New York, avid hip-hop fans worldwide seek to capture glimpses and take photographs of the mural dedicated to the late King of New York, Christopher Wallace, aka Biggie Smalls or the Notorious B.I.G. Listed as being number 54 of things to do while visiting Brooklyn by Tripadvisor (2022), the 'King of New York mural' appeared in 2015, designed by artists Scott Zimmerman and Naoufal Alaoui (George, 2019). Reaching an impressive 38 ft, the imposing mural showcases an image of Biggie wearing a crown alongside verses from his first demo record, 'Microphone Murder' (George, 2019). More than 20 years after his untimely death, some may wonder why this mural is of importance to tourists visiting Brooklyn, and the answer lies not only in the accomplishments of Biggie, but in everything his life and death reflects and symbolises.

The murder of then 24-year-old Biggie in March 1997 (Rowlands, 2011), in a manner reminiscent to that of a Shakespearean play, the result of a feud between two coasts turned deadly, left a lasting impression on the wider Brooklyn community that exists to this present day. Such is his legacy that not only are there other murals dedicated to Biggie and walking tours around Bed-Stuy (Do N.Y.C., 2022), but the flat in which he lived as a child is now available to rent (Weiser, 2019) and a basketball court in Brooklyn has been named after him (Remnick, 2017).

Gentrification

Brooklyn was once an area representing diversity (Sherman, 2016). In the 1990s to the 2000s, the borough possessed the largest Black community of all the boroughs in New York (Giuliani and Rose, 2001). With a total population increase of 7.2 per cent in the 2000s, immigration levels within the borough had been consistently high for decades (Giuliani and Rose, 2001). However, once demarked by its industrial economy, Brooklyn fell into deprivation and poverty as the result of the closure of manufacturing premises by the 1970s (Sherman, 2016). The consequent living conditions within Brooklyn enticed many young Black men into lives permeated by drugs and violence in an attempt to free themselves from the constraints of deprivation (Malone, 2015). East Coast hip-hop was specifically inspired by and depicted the nature of the environment these men grew up in, with its extensive references to violence and criminality (Collins, 2006), but also the aspirations and desires to be successful to support their families and uplift their peers (Collins, 2006).

The conditions in which gangsta rap and hip-hop once thrived and inspired the legends of today such as the Notorious B.I.G. are transforming due to prevalence of gentrification (Westhoff, 2015). The facilitation of gentrification requires the redevelopment of urban communities to satisfy the demands and preferences of wealthier newcomers (Benediktsson et al, 2015). As Stabrowski (2014) notes, displacement of local residents is beneficial for developers as there is less resistance to redevelopment and remodelling (Stabrowski, 2014), meaning that the issues polarised by Biggie are continuously neglected, with native Brooklyn residents pushed out of their own communities in favour of wealth and the economy. Looking at more recent figures pertaining to Brooklyn, the inference of gentrification becomes clearer with the percentage of foreign-born residents at 23.8 per cent and the percentage of residents speaking languages other than English within the home at 33.5 per cent. The number of ethnic minority-owned firms stood at 882 in comparison to 1,135

White-owned firms, and 15.1 per cent of residents were living in poverty between 2015 and 2019 (United States Census Bureau, 2022). Further, when looking at Greenpoint, East Brooklyn, more specifically, we observe an increase in young populations (8 per cent) and a decrease in the availability of family occupancies (25 per cent), while income levels increased by 5 per cent between 2000 and 2010, and the average property values increased by 13.8 per cent between 2010 and 2012 (Stabrowski, 2014).

More importantly, these events signify the erosion of culture emerging from gentrification and may be no better demonstrated than by the controversy that continues to plague the legacy of Biggie to this day. Attempts to name a street after the artist were blocked by residents who perceived him to be a poor 'role model', citing his extensive criminal history, lyrics advocating violence and misogyny, the manner of his death and his appearance (Santora, 2013). The same majority White residents would later try to prevent the basketball court being named after him (Remnick, 2017). The 'King of New York mural' also faced being destroyed in 2015 in favour of window installations to increase rent for the property it is located on (Walker, 2017). The landlord further attempted to incur monthly charges for the mural to remain, before succumbing to intense public pressure to preserve the mural (Walker, 2017). To the local community, Biggie inspires hope through his own experiences of adversity and admissions of his wrongs. His love for his community and his peers was indisputable.

Conclusion

Whatever your stance on Biggie, his influence upon the hip-hop generation and Brooklyn community is evident and inescapable. Not only did his music inspire a generation of artists including Drake and Kendrick Lamar, Biggie successfully commercialised and revolutionised hip-hop for mainstream audiences. He provided an insight to White audiences of the conditions and trauma that many Black young men face in pursuit of the 'American Dream' (Lynes et al, 2020), and how in real terms, the pursuit for betterment can still not be enough for these young men to escape the 'street life' (Malone, 2015). Consequently, his lyrics stand the test of time with many of the issues and themes discussed still resonating within today's society (Collins, 2006; Abt, 2019). The talent permeating from Brooklyn, which stands the test of time, producing hip-hop giants such as Big Daddy Kane and Jay-Z (Westhoff, 2015), faces being displaced and eradicated due to the devolution of communities such as these.

35

The Rebus guided tour: Edinburgh, UK

Ian R. Cook and Michael Rowe

Northumbria University

Introduction

This chapter explores 'dark destinations' associated with crime fiction. It focuses on Ian Rankin's Rebus detective novels, set in Edinburgh, and the guided tour of Edinburgh that is inspired by the novels. In doing this, the chapter reflects on the portrayal of urban life, crime and policing in the novels and tour.

Edinburgh in the Rebus novels

Cities are important settings – and arguably characters too – within crime fiction. Think, for instance, of Brighton in Peter James' Roy Grace series, Chicago in Sara Paretsky's V.I. Warshawski novels or Reykjavík in Arnaldur Indriðason's Erlendur series. Like their equivalents in crime drama and crime film, cities are usually depicted in a negative light, frequently as '[d]angerous, violent and squalid' places (Willett, 1996: 4), replete with social harm (not limited to murder) and threatening atmospheres (cf Cook and Ashutosh, 2018; Plain, 2018; Sandberg, 2020). Readers of crime fiction can 'visit' these cities using their imagination without physically travelling there.

The Edinburgh in Ian Rankin's long-running John Rebus series is vividly painted. It features many real streets, neighbourhoods, police stations and pubs – for instance, Rebus' haunt, the Oxford Bar, and the street that Rebus and Rankin have lived on, Arden Street – alongside a few fictional places in the city such as the estates of Knoxland and Pilmuir. It portrays Edinburgh as a complicated, confusing and claustrophobic city (Marshall, 2018) where social, economic and political divisions are ingrained.

The tourist plays an important role in Rankin's vision of Edinburgh. For Rankin, the city has been beautified for tourists, disadvantaged groups have been ushered away from the tourist hotspots and tourists remain ignorant of the city's social problems – problems that Rebus knows only too well. Rankin's frustration with this sanitised view of Edinburgh influenced his decision to write the Rebus books. Too often, Rankin told *The Sunday Telegraph*, tourists would:

> [G]et off the bus and take a picture of Greyfriars Bobby and of the Scott monument. You felt they weren't seeing Edinburgh – they were seeing what the City of Edinburgh wanted them to see – the public statues and edifices, the galleries, bagpipers and the Castle. But they weren't seeing the unemployment, the drug problems, the deprivation and the prostitution. (Bruce-Gardyne, 2002: np)

The Rebus novels peer at this hidden side of Edinburgh, examining its deprivation, exploitation, corruption, racism and murder. It is a 'cruel city' (Rankin, 2000: 341), a 'city of short tempers' (Rankin, 2018: 153) and a city that is 'lethal when crossed' (Rankin, 2000: 293). Readers are shown a city haunted by its past (Cook, 2022) whose problems are repeatedly swept underneath the city's metaphorical carpet. Rankin urges us to view the duality of Edinburgh: its light and dark, its affluence and poverty, its Jekyll and Hyde. The following passage from *The Falls* speaks to this view of Edinburgh as a dual city:

> He'd parked the Saab on North Bridge. There was a cold wind blowing, but Jean stopped to look at the view: the Scott Monument, the Castle, and Ramsay Gardens.

> 'Such a beautiful city,' she said. Rebus tried to agree. He hardly saw it any more. To him, Edinburgh had become a state of mind, a juggling of criminal thoughts and baser instincts. He liked its size, its compactness. He liked its bars. But its outward show had ceased to impress him a long time ago. Jean wrapped her coat tightly around her. 'Everywhere you look, there's some story, some little piece of history.' She looked at him and he nodded agreement, but he was remembering all the suicides he'd dealt with, people who'd jumped from North Bridge maybe because they couldn't see the same city Jean did.
>
> 'I never tire of this view,' she said, turning back towards the car. He nodded again, disingenuously. To him, it wasn't a view at all. It was a crime scene waiting to happen. (Rankin, 2001: 153)

Rebus acts as the reader's knowledgeable tour guide of the city; he has the power to not only gain access to places that readers are unable or unwilling to go but also expose the hypocrisy of the dual city.

Edinburgh in the Rebus guided tour

> We're standing in the blazing sun, an odd-looking band of people, gathered around a man who, moments ago, was wildly waving a novel above his head in a bid to attract our attention. The Old Quad at Edinburgh University, just off South Bridge, is the venue, and I'm surrounded by 15 detective story buffs. They're here to spend the next two hours pounding Edinburgh's streets, following in the footsteps of their fictional hero, Inspector John Rebus, the man first created in print by Ian Rankin and recently portrayed on the small screen by John Hannah. They know the books inside out, and have the light of the zealot in their eyes as the tour sets off, led by John Skinner, 47, a man whose passion for the fictional Edinburgh cop – and old Edinburgh – knows no bounds. (Clapperton, 2000: 15)

Two decades later, Rebus tours are still running. A form of literary tourism, they echo many crime fiction and crime drama-themed guided tours worldwide (Sjöholm, 2010; Tzanelli and Yar, 2016; van Es and Reijnders, 2016). The Rebus tour is a walking tour that lasts for approximately two hours with a series of stops when the guide addresses the attendees and reads aloud a series of extracts from Rankin's published work.

Crime fiction guided tours are often marketed as opportunities to follow in the footsteps of the detectives and their authors. Where better, in the case of Rebus and Rankin, than the city where the novels are set and the author and detective live? The tour, like the novels, takes an alternative perspective on the 'hidden' Edinburgh and this is perhaps why the tour's route echoes other crime fiction tours: 'getting off the beaten track' (van Es and Reijnders, 2018: 517) and '[z]igzagging through the city, frequently turning left and right and generally avoiding main roads in favor of side-roads and alleys' (van Es and Reijnders, 2018: 510). The stops and routes on the Rebus tour have changed over the years. No longer does the tour take in the Oxford Bar or Arden Street, for instance; now it concentrates on a part of the city where few tourists venture, south of its Old Town and east of Salisbury Crags, traversing through university and residential areas.

A sense of place is cultivated through the guide's readings, script and improvisation. During a tour we went on in July 2021 (henceforth, 'our tour'), the guide seemed to want attendees to view Edinburgh as a city to be *impressed by* (a literary city), *intrigued by* (a mysterious, secretive city) and *frustrated by* (a divided, troubled city). Yet the sense of place that is crafted during the tours is not solely crafted by the guide; it is also shaped by attendees' pre-existing experiences and knowledge of Edinburgh and through the routine and unexpected sights, sounds and smells of the city that the tour encounters – for instance, the group loudly shouting at each other across the street as the guide attempted to conclude our tour.

The Rebus novels blend detection, death and social commentary. Let's examine these three issues in relation to the Rebus tours. Turning to detection first, Rebus is at the centre of the tour, the guide and his readings speaking of Rebus' personality, attitude towards policing, style of policing and place of work. This was most apparent when we stopped outside the rear of the St. Leonard's police station, where Rebus worked for many years. We were encouraged to look over the wall into the station car park and to imagine Rebus working next to a certain window – the one with an extractor fan set in the pane of glass, to extract his cigarette smoke (it was implied) – on the top floor of the station. Perhaps the rear-side view was to avoid the group clustering outside the main entrance of the police station, but it also enabled more of a 'back stage' perspective of a largely unremarkable station.

Death is central to dark tourism (Lennon and Mitchell, 2007) and murder is the 'preferred crime' of much crime fiction (Harris-Peyton, 2020: 141). In the Rebus series, murder is a device used to encourage readers to consider, on the one hand, the duality of good and evil that is present in every person and, on the other, various social problems and social inequalities. Unsurprisingly, then, death features heavily in the Rebus tour. The first stop on the tour is at the city mortuary on Cowgate that Rebus regularly visits in the novels. Later, we were told outside St. Leonard's that Glasgow has a much higher murder rate than Edinburgh (as the guide underscored its relative gentility and the long-held rivalry between the cities). A few minutes later, stood in a small park, we were asked to imagine that we were in a graveyard as the guide began another reading.

Conclusion

Social commentary was more implicit than explicit on our tour. The social divisions and spatial inequalities that Rankin repeatedly bemoans in the Rebus series (McDonald, 2020) were evident in the places we walked through and stopped as well as the people we encountered on the tour. We were guided through different residential areas with varying levels of affluence and deprivation. Midway through the tour, the tour stopped so the attendees faced an apartment block with a concrete exterior while the guide read an extract from Rankin's novella *Death is Not the End* in which Rankin reasoned that '[t]he city hid its secrets well, and its vices. … Potentially troublesome elements had been moved to the sprawling council estates which ringed the capital' (Rankin, 1998). The apartment block acted as a signifier for these distanced estates, and for those familiar with Rankin's outlook on Edinburgh, it may have served as a reminder of Rankin's maxim that there is much hidden away behind the glossy veneer of Edinburgh.

36

Volunteer tourism – 'doing it for the 'gram': Cambodia, Southeast Asia

Orlando Woods

Singapore Management University

Introduction

In recent years, volunteer tourism – or 'voluntourism' – has become an increasingly popular way for relatively privileged individuals to access and 'give back' to those deemed to be less privileged. While the motivations for such practices are often benign, so too is there a tendency for the distinctions between 'volunteering' and 'tourism' to become blurred. With this blurring, the humanitarian logics upon which volunteerism is assumedly based can become commodified in ways that close down the potential to effect change (Sin, 2009). Exacerbating these closures is the mediatory role of digital photography in documenting voluntourist experiences, and representing the humanitarian self (and disadvantaged others) to dispersed networks of followers via social media. These digital mediations can be seen to 'complicat[e] simple models of subject and object, representation and reality, image and process' (Crang, 1997: 366) as voluntourists are invariably implicated in the new representational politics of 'doing it for the 'gram' (Woods and Shee, 2021a; 2021b). By this, I refer to the obfuscatory role of digital media (an expansive term that captures practices of digital photography and the circulation of images via social media) in both motivating engagement with humanitarian projects and structuring the encounters that voluntourists have with the people and places they are meant to be serving. Indeed, given the assertion that 40 per cent of British millennials 'choose their travel destination based on the Instagrammability of the locations' (Wearing et al, 2018: 503), the potential for digital media to reify, and possibly exacerbate, the development differential that voluntourism is designed – in theory at least – to help overcome becomes more apparent.

These reifications and exacerbations encapsulate the ethical ambiguity that is evoked in the title of this chapter. They not only cause the meaning of voluntourism to become diluted; they also cause it to become a more 'morally ambiguous construct that can be leveraged for its representational value' (Woods and Shee, 2021a: 48). In this vein, the act of 'doing good' itself becomes a self-directed form of value creation in which the voluntourist has much to gain from embedding themselves and their beneficiaries within the visual narrative of humanitarianism. Over the past decade, the implications of these 'alternative commodity cultures' (Bryant and Goodman, 2004) have become a focus of scholarship, with Wearing et al (2018: 502) even suggesting that voluntourism has reached the level of a 'fully commodified experience where both hosts and tourists become exploited forms of labour and capital'. Zooming out, the commodification of the voluntourist experience might well be enabled by digital media, but so too does it reflect the extent to which a neoliberal ethic has led to the ongoing 'privatization and commodification of development and global justice agendas' (Mostafanezhad, 2013a: 321). In this sense, not only does 'doing it for the 'gram' motivate *dis*engagement with the people and places that define the landscapes of voluntourism, but so too does it implicate them in an aesthetically driven narrative of marginality that can be read as one of neoliberalism's more insidious effects. Before illustrating these ideas empirically, I first provide a brief theoretical overview of how debates concerning representations of the 'suffering subject' and 'hero humanitarian' have evolved in recent years.

The aesthetic value of the 'suffering subject' and 'hero humanitarian'

The visual has come to occupy a hegemonic position in the informational economy. Visual media – especially those that are digitally produced, shared and consumed – thus play an integral role in 'galvanis[ing] popular interest in the world and its representations' while simultaneously 'suppress[ing] the critical faculties needed to identify injustices and enact change' (Woods and Shee, 2021b: 3). As much as the visual can be seen to obstruct the potential for positive change to be made, so too have these obstructions evolved in meaning and manifestation in response to technological advances. Dependence on smartphones and social media, and the ever-growing penetration of broadband connectivity, means that acts of voluntourism are structured as much by ongoing social connection as they are spatial *dis*connection. Technology, then, can be seen to 'thoroughly fictionalize reality' (Chouliaraki, 2006: 3) in ways that might motivate engagement with less developed peoples and places, but also obstruct the potential for meaningful exchange. The reasons for these motivations and obstructions can be traced back to the 'popular humanitarian gaze' in which acts like voluntourism are 'reframe[d] … as an empathetic gesture of commoditized concern' (Mostafanezhad, 2014: 111). Offering the same sentiment but in a more critical light, Chouliaraki (2012: 1) negates the idea of 'concern' and asserts instead that photographic representations reproduce a 'narcissistic disposition of voyeuristic altruism rather than commitment to a humanitarian cause'. Further galvanising this dynamic is the emergence of the celebrity humanitarianism, in which celebrities like Angelina Jolie and Madonna have helped to create a theatre of popular 'humanitarianism [in which] the 20 something female has taken center stage. … As celebrity's most allegiant audience, young women have dutifully appropriated this role where they comprise more than 80% of all volunteer tourists' (Mostafanezhad, 2013a: 332).

The 'appropriation' of a 'role' refers here to the idea that voluntourism has become a pathway to some level of celebrity status for voluntourists. A unique feature of digital media is not just the potential to capture images anytime, anywhere, but also to share them among networks of followers. Sharing can create influence, which in turn can elevate the sharer within their networks. The motivations for these practices stem from the emergence of a 'celebrity-consumption-compassion-complex' that is forged at the nexus of digital media and celebrity culture, and involves participating in, representing, and sharing 'poverty tours, photoshoots, textual and visual diaries, websites and tweets' (Goodman, 2011: 82). Through these acts, voluntourists have been shown to 'enjoy a renown or pseudo-celebrity status in their own right' (Mostafanezhad, 2013b: 491), the knowledge of which can recursively serve to motivate participation in voluntourism in the first place; or, to 'do it for the 'gram'. I now offer an empirical illustration of what I mean by this. I draw on 20 semi-structured interviews conducted in late 2019 among Singaporean voluntourists. Most of my interviewees (14) were university students, while a minority (six) were with representatives of non-government and government-linked organisations that organised overseas volunteer trips. I focus explicitly on projects undertaken in Cambodia, mainly because of its geographical proximity and tangible difference in development level to Singapore, and, therefore, its popularity as a destination for Singaporean voluntourists.

'Doing it for the 'gram' in Cambodia

In the empirical illustrations that follow, I offer two examples of the ethical ambiguities that can arise from voluntourists 'doing it for the 'gram'. The first involves Ming,[1] a university student who visited Cambodia to help build houses for the charity Habitat for Humanity. She spoke openly about how physically tiring the work was, and soon came to the realisation that local Cambodians are much better equipped to be doing it than Singaporeans. More revealing, however, were her observations of her fellow voluntourists. Joining her and her group mates on the trip were a few female voluntourists in their 30s representing the Young Women's Christian Association (YWCA). Ming was critical of their work ethic and believed that their tangible contribution to the project was negligible:

Ming: Some of our guys went over to help them. … Then they started posing for photos, the women did. So maybe we're taking a break …

[1] All names have been changed.

	everyone ceased work, ceased operations, so the women were like holding the shovel or something, like posing for photos. ... So, [we] find that it's not being done by you guys, but you're so proud of it.
Interviewer:	Why were they doing that, do you think?
Ming:	I would say for the 'gram, maybe? ... [They are] typical millennials, just posing for photos, trying to put them on Instagram and getting likes or exposure and saying 'hey, I've been doing this cool stuff'.

Interesting is Ming's rationalisation of the value of such practices, which is indexed to the novelty of the material – representing "cool stuff" – that can be posted on Instagram. As she put it, "[they're] posting for the impression that [they're] doing this. It's just about feeding all your followers what I'm currently doing now". The idea of "feeding all your followers" reveals the social cachet that comes from doing something different. The voluntourism experience is used to elevate the status of the voluntourist, even if they did relatively little work in the first place. This aggrieved Ming, who concluded that "we just don't find that they deserve the photos ... they didn't come here for the purpose of serving the community ... it's not a genuine kind of voluntourism they're doing".

The second example involves Zann, an employee of a non-governmental organisation who was responsible for arranging volunteer trips for families to Cambodia and Nepal. While Zann echoed the sentiment shared by Ming, more unique was how she engaged with local beneficiaries for the purposes of fundraising. She shared how she transformed one of the beneficiaries of her projects – a young Cambodian boy called Vong – into an influencer who could be used to solicit donations for her organisation. As she explained:

Zann:	This guy, he is very cute. I follow[ed] him in Cambodia. His name is Vong, he's my favourite child. I started to put his name [when posting photos of him on Instagram], and I see a lot

of people are, like, 'ohhh, Vong, he's so cute!'. … They have a connection.

Interviewer: Does that translate into anything like donations?

Zann: Yes, it does. So, for a period of time we had these hygiene packs for kids, and Vong was the star of the whole campaign. I had friends wanting to donate money because Vong is cute.

Yet, while Vong proved to be popular – and successful in eliciting donations for the organisation – his popularity quickly waned. As Zann went on to explain:

Zann: We cannot keep using Vong … [or else] people will get tired of seeing his face. When I check other social media, they don't reuse [their 'influencer' beneficiaries]. … My colleague, she encourages it. Like, she'll say 'it's not very nice to keep reusing the same photos' because it's, I don't know. Not new?

Interviewer: Did they [the followers] get upset? Did they ask 'where's Vong?'

Zann: No, no one asked.

Interviewer: But they liked him, right?

Zann: Yeah, I think the social [media] relationships are very fleeting. Once he's inside [the feed] he's cute, but once he's out of mind, he's really out of mind.

The examples shared by both Ming and Zann reveal two types of influence that is reproduced through digital media. The first relates to the YWCA women trying to elevate themselves by drawing on the uniqueness of their experience. The second relates to how the 'cuteness' of Vong is used to galvanise followers for fundraising purposes. The ethical ambiguities of these practices stem, respectively, from the fact that the YWCA representatives went to Cambodia to 'volunteer', but contributed little in terms of actual work, while Vong's image was used in a casual and non-consensual way to attract the attention of, and donations from, followers but then dropped once the purpose was served.

Both implicate humanitarian actors, their beneficiaries and their networks of followers in the politics that emerge when voluntourists 'do it for the 'gram'.

Conclusion

Digital media is a fact of everyday life, but its (dis)empowering effects can become problematic when used to represent people and places that are different. While this sentiment holds true in any situation, it becomes *more* problematic when enacted through ostensibly humanitarian practices like voluntourism. When digital mediated, these practices reveal the 'apparent tension between the messy world of place-based experience … and a more abstract world of ideals, mediated representations, and knowledge production' (Sin et al, 2014: 124; see also Woods, 2021a and b). The full effects of this tension must be explored if the generative effects of social media are ever to be fully realised.

37

The staycation: home

Jack Denham

York St John University

Introduction

'r/watchpeopledie' was an internet forum dedicated to viewing and commenting on user-uploaded video content of real-life deaths. At its peak, it held almost half a million subscribers, tuned in to watch brutal killings or particularly gruesome fatal accidents. It was banned from the host website, Reddit, in 2019 after the mass shootings that took place in Christchurch mosques, New Zealand, attracted critical media attention – highlighting the forum's breach of Reddit's rules for 'glorifying or encouraging violence'. But r/watchpeopledie was not the first or only online space for consuming violence and death, as evidenced by Wood's (2016) article on Facebook's similar street-fighting pages, provocatively titled 'I just wanna see someone get knocked the fuck out' – they are relatively widespread. It was the spiritual successor of Rotten.com, an early internet shock site of similar character. And a cursory Google search performed today will reveal a deluge of websites still hosting the most graphic and infamous deaths, such as photos from the crime scenes of serial killers Ted Bundy and Jeffrey Dahmer.

This work will treat the internet as a space, and consider in what ways visiting that space can be understood through the lens of 'dark tourism'. After that, it will consider the hidden harms attached to online dark tourism, using the lens of 'violence', and highlight two specifically: the trauma and offence caused when this content is consumed accidentally, and the ways in which a focus on this type of violence obscures its causal harms.

Surfing from the sofa

Seeing online content sharing as dark tourism isn't immediately easy because theories of dark tourism have been rooted in physical space. A clear place to start is Phil Stone's 'dark tourism spectrum' (2006) that differentiates 'sites of death and suffering' from 'sites associated with death and suffering', the latter of which is 'less dark', but could certainly be applied to r/watchpeopledie. Stone cites 'location authenticity' as being a key factor in how valid, and how 'dark', a dark tourist site is – with places where atrocities did not actually occur being maligned in this dichotomy – that's strike one against the internet. These sites are also not particularly educational in their framing (although it would be difficult to make the argument that one isn't learning something by viewing), and they are usually not of historic or commemorative importance – strikes two and three.

r/watchpeopledie did lack tourism infrastructure, though. It was an organic space where users would come together to voluntarily share and view images of all human atrocity relatively indiscriminately, as long as it depicted the loss of life. It also benefited from a shortness of timescale from the tragic events themselves in a way that traditional dark tourist attractions could not compete – people would be able to capture human suffering on a smartphone and have it viewed by the world in a few minutes. Because of this short timeframe and lack of curatorial scaffolding, it could be perceived by the user that this product is quite authentic – but authenticity is a challenging concept with too many meanings to discuss here (Enli, 2015) – suffice to say that it hasn't been tampered with, and users experience a perceived authentic product interpretation. That's three more of Stone's qualities of dark tourism that the internet provides well.

Online sites of death are certainly pretty 'dark', then – but are they tourist attractions? Now that r/watchpeopledie is banned, the site itself is dead. It has become a historic artefact with users regularly posting elsewhere on the host site, Reddit, to collectively sleuth out cached content on sites such as 'webarchive'. This development represents another turn in r/watchpeopledie's trajectory, where content can still be viewed but barriers to entry have been erected, superimposing the element of pilgrimage, travel and ponderousness attached to traditional dark tourist visits.

There's confusion in dark tourism studies as to whether a site being purposefully created for the consumption of death makes it darker, or somewhat less dark – with Sharpley (2005) arguing that the deliberate curation of encounters intended to satisfy a desire to consume death is much darker – but Stone (2006) countering with the idea that these types of site are often highly mediated, and the darkest experiences are conversely more organic. Online, we have a meeting of the two poles – with user-generated content appearing in almost real time being extremely organic, but curated in a contrived and artificial 'space' and setting. Stone refers to dark tourism as 'a diverse and fragmented … product' (2006: 157) – and nowhere is the product more fragmented than the internet. Certainly, the internet is a place that some users go to in order to recreationally consume death – and by that definition, we can understand some internet spaces as dark tourist attractions.

There are some obvious harms that could be applied to online dark tourism – to mention a few, the potential emotional distress suffered by relatives or friends of victims if it is known that their demise is being consumed, the potential desensitising effect of consuming death regularly, the potential for content creators to put themselves in harm's way for 'likes' or the general questionable morality of watching death online that *The Guardian* has referred to as 'exploitation' (Dahl, 2018). What I draw attention to here is the second-hand objective violence that can occur when this type of content is deceptively shared as a source of dark humour, stumbled across or maliciously inflicted on unwilling participants – all uniquely enabled by the networked and shareable nature of online dark tourism – and the ways in which this focus on gruesomeness distracts from more prominent forms of harm.

Several high-profile incidents of content spilling out from r/watchpeopledie have drawn attention to one key way in which this form of dark tourism differs from the traditional: it lacks definable borders. On social media sharing sites, especially ones with the anonymity of Reddit, content can break free of the usually reliable algorithms that constrain the internet user's experience by being 'crossposted' (into a segment of Reddit that you do usually frequent), or 'upvoted' into your line of sight on Reddit's catch-all homepage, r/all. This coupled with well-established bait-and-switch meme tactics tantamount to a gruesome 'rickrolling' have meant that the bulk of this morbid content can drip on the average user through social media's leaky sieve. Perhaps the most prominent example is the post titled 'Teenager waves bye, then blows head off with a shotgun on YouTube Live', which was featured on r/watchpeopledie and quickly spread through other, more mundane corners of the host forum, outrage and trauma along with it.

Ellis (2009) has referred to the viewing of moments of crisis through traditional media as 'mundane witnessing', something which demands a moral reflection and engagement from the viewer – but Silverstone (2007) draws attention to the mediating work that these outlets conduct, often framing the events as 'distant', or toying with concepts of 'otherness' which can result in a muted, packaged or predictable reaction from the viewer. In the case of the content that spills out from sites like r/watchpeopledie, witnessing is often unpackaged, unexpected and brutally uncensored. It is harmful in the absence of packaging, and lack of ability for the viewer to be prepared, in its shocking nature without a trigger warning as an act of discursive symbolic violence.

We can turn to Žižek's (2008) call for us to resist the fascination of subjective violence (like these gruesome deaths, stabbings and killings) in favour of the objective (like structural violence, or the violence embedded in discourse and language) to understand the second harm attached to online dark tourism. The creators of r/watchpeopledie justified its existence as an educational space in which to 'document and observe the disturbing reality of death' – they position themselves, against the host forum's rules, as an emancipation of 'real' violence that is so often constrained by media – tantamount to what Benjamin (2007/1921) would call a 'divine violence', something which represents a strike at power in favour of justice. But they trade in subjective violence, drawing attention to the very form of harm which is distracting from what Žižek refers to as the 'true locus of trouble' (2008: 9), objective violence, which for the purposes of this chapter can be understood as systems which exploit and oppress. Žižek

(2008: 3) writes that 'the overpowering horror of violent acts and empathy with victims inexorably function as a lure which prevents us from thinking' – precisely of the underlying systemic causes of such horror. r/watchpeopledie, then, is a clean and literal example of an objective violence, exploiting of its characters and oppressing of its accidental viewers, which hides behind the distraction of the subjective.

Conclusion

The presence of death material online, then, is doubly harmful: in its involuntary consumption, offensive nature and ability to elicit potentially traumatic, disturbing and distressed reactions – or the ensuing fear when navigating the internet, sometimes referred to as a 'risky click'. And second, in its distracting glorification of instances of subjective violence without acknowledging the objective harms which hide behind them.

The internet has been studied alongside dark tourism predominantly as a mode to improve or supplement the dark tourist experience for traditional, physical sites (see Bolan and Simone-Charteris, 2018) – but there is scope to consider the internet's role more broadly, as a destination in and of itself. When we do, the networked nature of the space makes a zemiology of online dark tourism challenging, but here I have proposed one lens – violence – through which to understand its negative or harmful outcomes.

38

The 'suicide forest': Aokigahara, Japan

Max Hart

Birmingham City University

Introduction

On 31 December 2017, famous YouTuber, Logan Paul, received widespread criticism after posting a video to the social media site that showed the body of a man who had allegedly committed suicide (BBC, 2018). The video, which gained over six million views before it was removed by YouTube (Rosenblatt, 2020), also showed Logan Paul and his entourage jokingly discussing suicide. While this publicisation of a tragic event triggered a display of shock and disdain on social media (BBC, 2018), the wider context of this video paints an even darker picture than the one offered by Logan Paul.

This chapter attempts to shed light on not only this darker reality and subsequent attraction this offers, but also, using Derrida's (1994) concept of hauntology, puts forward an argument to help understand both the fascination with Aokigahara Forest and 'Japanese suicide culture' (Flaskerud, 2014) itself. This work seeks to build on previous discussions of Japanese suicide culture (McKenna, 2015) and argues that media representations over time not only act as a vehicle for tourism, but simultaneously function as a mechanic for the deeper level of disavowal that both banishes any ethical and moral consideration of dark leisure practice and cements the forest as a visual crypt of the 'haunted' past experienced in Japanese culture.

Aokigahara Forest: a dark history

At the base of Mount Fuji, Japan, lies a forest that stretches for an estimated 13.5 square miles and has existed for approximately 1,000 years (Keefe, 2017). Aokigahara, or 'Jukai' meaning 'Sea of Trees', gets such a name due to its dense canopy of trees which, when swaying in the wind and viewed from above, offers visuals akin to that of the ocean (McKenna, 2015: 293). On entering the forest, individuals experience a loss of light, sound and direction (McKenna, 2015). This can be explained by the forest's large floral canopy and iron concentration found in the ground that interferes with compasses and Global Positioning System signals (McKenna, 2015). However, when you combine this with the forest's natural mystic beauty, it is no surprise that Aokigahara has become topical for those interested in the supernatural. A simple Google search of 'Haunted Aokigahara Forest', at the time of writing, will return 43,000 results offering examples of eerie experiences, creepy stories and even YouTubers spending the Halloween night of 2021 in the forest to 'drink and debunk' its haunted reputation (see Ronin Dave, 2021).

This attachment of the dark and paranormal to Aokigahara is not simply a side effect of imagination and scenery alone; rather, the forest has historically been the backdrop for sinister Japanese folklore. It is alleged to have once been a place in which Japanese citizens would practise 'geronticide', often referred to as 'Ubasute' in Japanese culture. This refers to abandoning elderly relatives in such desolate places and leaving them to die (Killilea and Lynch, 2013). Furthermore, Aokigahara is said to be haunted by 'Yūrei'. These are spirits who have been denied access to a peaceful after life, allegedly due to having some form of unresolved conflict, for example, having died in a sudden or violent manner (Peñascal, 2020). Ultimately, the forest has historically become a focal point for Japanese folklore, arguably providing some of the foundations for its now dark reputation and subsequent attraction.

From folklore to media fixation

Such sinister and supernatural tales, however, have continued throughout time with representations, stories and understandings shifting through different forms of media as they have advanced, making Aokigahara a common reference point throughout popular culture in Japan and globally. For example, in the late 17th century games such as *Hyakumonogatari Kaidankai* became a cult phenomenon in Japan (see Davisson, 2020), in which 'supernatural experiences' are a key focus of the game – including the 'Yūrei' who roam the forest. Aokigahara is also used as a setting in modern games played on consoles such as *Tokyo Dark* (Cherrymochi, 2017) that utilises Aokigahara as the setting for its penultimate level. The forest is a staple of anime and manga, with the series *Tokyo Ghoul* including scenes in which bodies found in Aokigahara are used as food for ghouls as supplement to live humans (IMDb, 2014). References are also frequent in literature, ranging from: *Suicide Forest (World's Scariest Places)* (Bates, 2015), *Namo no Tō (Tower of Waves)* (Matsumoto, 1960), *The Sea of Trees* (Murphy, 1998) and *The Complete Manual of Suicide* (Tsurumi, 1993). Of note here, and of particular importance to later discussions in this chapter, is that Matsumoto and Tsurumi both refer specifically to the forest as a popular suicide spot and in Tsurumi's case, 'the perfect place to die'. Aokigahara has also offered inspiration for movies such as *The Sea of Trees* (IMDb, 2015) and *The Forest* (IMDb, 2016). As a result, the forest has not only been popularised in film, text and storytelling, but also as a tourist destination. At the time of writing, individuals can book 'Dark Holidays' that include tours around Aokigahara with price ranges varying between £600 and £900 depending on date and type of experience you want. A simple search for 'book trips to Aokigahara' alone returns 97,500 results. It is important to note that some of these results describe the forest's natural beauty – including its numerous caves and excellent views of Mount Fuji. Suggesting that while the forest may be a popular tourist spot, this is not solely due to its haunted reputation. Ultimately, the previous discussion of Logan Paul pushing the forest into the realms of social media – both as a vehicle of representation and the subsequent discussion – provides but one example of Japanese culture appearing in newer forms of media. A deeper exploration in fact highlights the forest as an inspiration point historically that has simultaneously garnered attraction worldwide and has since become a key dark destination.

Aokigahara Forest in context: Japanese suicide culture

There is another element to the attraction to Aokigahara that stretches beyond questionable tales of the supernatural. A dark reality that also mirrors wider Japanese society itself. For a long time, suicide has been a serious issue in Japan with the country having one of the highest suicide rates in the world, with 24,025 suicides in 2015 alone (McKenna, 2015; Kettenhofen, 2021a). Prior to this, in 2011, Japan suicide rates hit highs of 30,651 (ibid). In recent years, however, Japan's suicide rate started to decline before rising again in 2020 (ibid). Currently, Japan does not fall into the top ten countries regarding suicides (World Population Review, 2021), but remains a significant cause of concern as suicide is the leading cause of death for men aged between 20 and 44 in Japan and for women between the ages of 15 and 34 (World Population Review, 2021). Furthermore, the slight increase in suicide in Japan is estimated to have been the result of a general increase in female suicides (Kettenhofen, 2021b). This resulted in numerous commentators referring to the term 'Japanese suicide culture' (Flaskerud, 2014). However, it is Aokigahara Forest itself that has arguably highlighted the sheer seriousness of the issue as it has become somewhat emblematic of suicide in Japan. At the entrance to Aokigahara, a sign can be seen that reads 'please reconsider' and 'think carefully about your children, your family' (Flaskerud, 2014). This is because it is deemed as a suicide 'hot-spot' (Keefe, 2017). The exact number of suicides that take place at Aokigahara is unknown as Japanese officials have stopped publishing such data in attempts to avoid encouraging those thinking of taking their own life (Keefe, 2017). However, it was reported that in 2010, 247 people attempted suicide in the forest (Gilhooley, 2011), and roughly 100 people die at Aokigahara each year (McKenna, 2015). McKenna (2015) also explains that ribbons can be seen tied from tree to tree at Aokigahara offering a trail back to society, often a trademark for an individual who remains undecided on whether to end their own life; thus, it is not uncommon to find a dead body at the end of these ribbons. Furthermore, the forest itself is said to be littered with small campsites, personal belongings and ropes owned by those who have contemplated suicide or even the corpse of someone who followed through with the final act (Vice, 2012). Due to this, security cameras, signposting and 'suicide patrols' can now be seen throughout Aokigahara to help prevent further suicides (Gilhooley, 2011). Evidently, then, Aokigahara offers much more to tourists than a chance to see mystic beauty steeped in supernatural anecdotes. It also provides opportunity to would-be dark tourists to explore an area shadowed by one of the most taboo subjects – suicide.

Aokigahara Forest as a visual 'crypt'

Japan's 'culture of suicide' has been explored and explained in multiple ways. Economic pressures and over-work combined with a sense of responsibility enshrined in Japanese culture (Beam, 2007; MacFarquhar, 2013; Flaskerud, 2014), a lack of religious prohibition against the act (Flaskerud, 2014; McKenna, 2015) and debates regarding the over-stigmatisation of mental health, poor mental health support services and the over-romanticisation of suicide (French, 2002; Gilhooley, 2011; MacFarquhar, 2013) have all been offered as explanations. Observers have also explored environmental impacts on the psyche, for example, 'blue lighting' (Matsubayashi et al, 2013) and 'Green Space' (Jiang et al, 2021). Attention has also been given to historical Japanese suicidal traditions which are said to still linger in the cultural make-up of Japan (Gilhooley, 2011), such as *Seppuku*, a ritual suicide carried out by feudal samurai warriors in which self-disembowelment rather than dying at the hands of the enemy was enacted to achieve an honourable death (Flaskerud, 2014).

McKenna (2015) offers an insightful discussion that draws upon Japan's political, cultural and historical development. Utilising Durkheim's (2002) concepts of integration and regulation and Trotsky's (1997) 'privilege of historical backwardness', McKenna argues that the development of Japan's political system is peculiar in the sense that its turn to capitalism was shadowed by a 'quasi-feudal hangover' (McKenna, 2015: 299) as it was not done so in the same order as other advanced countries. He explains that the Meiji revolution in the late 19th century can be viewed as a revolution from above, that is, it was carried out by feudal landlords. This is because it had become apparent to them that to compete with other advancing countries in the West, a top-down modernisation was needed. Such modernisation allowed Japan to become a major industrial and military power by the close of the century – providing the foundation for its contemporary capitalist form and ultimately undergoing a 'privilege of historical backwardness' (see Trotsky, 1997). Therefore, unlike other advanced capitalist countries, Japan had undergone a unique but rapid transition that kept some of its feudal traditions and culture intact, arguably catalysing its issues with suicide. As a result, Japanese citizens are susceptible to excessive integration, a sense of attachment overwhelming to the point that individuality is dangerously insufficient (Durkheim, 2002), unlike other capitalist countries, whose citizens are said to experience excessive regulation and a lack of integration (see Durkheim, 2002). For McKenna, this is demonstrated in Japanese labour practices that offer resemblances to the older guild mentality through the practice of *Shafu*, meaning a job for life and a connection to your company. Therefore, a Japanese worker is likely to commit suicide not only due to the capitalist labour market which encourages over-working and competitiveness, but also due to the excessive integration of the ghostly presence of *Shafu* within such an unstable market where one may feel the personal burden of not only their own debt but also their company's.

There has also been ample commentary on society's interest in dark tourism. Some have attempted to explain the practice by offering categories, typologies and classifications. Verma (2021) offers subcategories of dark tourism, for example: grave tourism, genocide tourism, Holocaust tourism, nuclear tourism and haunted tourism. Kuznik (2018) offered seven motivations for visiting dark tourism sites, including: curiosity, empathy, horror, education, nostalgia, remembrance and survivors' guilt. While Sharpley (2005) put forth 'four shades of dark tourism', based on previous assertions that attractions and experiences of dark tourism are supplied both accidently and exploited for profit. The four shades include: pale tourism, grey tourism demand, grey tourism supply and black tourism. Others have explored the role of dark tourism within the remit of *Thanatopsis*, discussing the opportunity it offers for individuals to 'avoid death' (Korstanje, 2011; Korstanje and Ivanov, 2012), as well as acting as a social mediator between life and death and offering understandings of 'ontological meanings of morality' (Stone, 2012).

However, within all these discussions sits a consistent suggestion that dark tourism is either an outcome of, or has been influenced by, 21st-century capitalism. As Verma (2021: 54) states, dark tourism can be viewed as a 'commodification of anxiety and doubt' – feelings that are central to a functioning capitalist system (Hall, 2012). Additionally, the commodification of tragic events that turn sites of disaster and sorrow into financial opportunity, both physically and virtually, is itself an illustration of a system that places importance on profit over ethical and moral boundaries and wider harm (Raymen and Smith, 2019). It is through this understanding that we can begin to draw from criminological theory to better explain the actions of tourists visiting sites such as Aokigahara Forest – specifically, Hall's (2012) 'pseudo-pacification process' and 'special liberty'. The first referring to the way in which society's violent tendencies of the past have been subdued into more practical forms to exist within the capitalist market to ensure economic growth. The latter referring to a perceived right an individual feels to surpass rules and socio-ethical norms to express their own desires as something substantial is being provided in return. Leaving behaviours such as individualism, competitiveness, greed and envy at the forefront of society (Raymen, 2017). Therefore, we can view the actions of Logan Paul as an outcome of the pseudo-pacification process and one of special liberty. Paul was able to obliviate any moral and ethical consideration of his actions in his request for social media popularity as he was providing 'content' back to the wider public.

Although not all those who visit Aokigahara Forest generate such controversy, nonetheless, an interest remains. Such an interest can be explained by Kelly et al's (2022) 'graze culture'. Briefly, graze culture argues that society's fascination with horror is an unknowing attempt to consume a more tangible form of violence. A subjective violence (a physical manifestation of violence) that is somewhat comforting as opposed to recognising objective and structural violence (social harm such as job insecurity and insufficient social welfare that can be deemed violent in nature). Consuming horror-related media, for the authors, allows for a fetishistic disavowal (referring to the process of denial in which we dismiss what we know, because we don't want to know – see Žižek, 2008) of this objective violence. Thus, in the context of dark tourism, we can argue that the exploration of such sites is a further subconscious attempt to disavow objective violence by experiencing a known and more obvious form of it. Therefore, the fascination with Aokigahara Forest can be best understood as a side effect of 21st-century capitalism. The commodification of the forest has simultaneously allowed individuals to consume palpable violence that can also demonstrate behaviours attributed to the dark undercurrent of capitalism.

It is here, however, where Derrida's (1994) concept of hauntology, as well as work that draws from it, can be interjected to offer a final consideration. Hauntology refers to ways in which our present, past and future are continuously merged, as making sense of a present moment relies on contemplating the past and anticipating the future. Our experiences are haunted by what already exists and what is yet to. Fisher (2009), drawing upon Derrida, adds that capitalist society has since reached a 'cultural impasse', in the sense that we are no longer trying to envision the future and instead paradoxically try to recapture this anticipation of the future by revisiting the past, often through media. Building on this notion, Abraham and Torok (1972) discussed the concepts of 'incorporation', the 'Phantom' and the 'Crypt'. Incorporation is a psychoanalytical term used to explain the process in which a lost object (anything from a place, individual or an ideal) is internalised within a subject to become part of their identity as a means of mourning that object – ultimately denying the loss of it (Abraham and Torok, 1972; Scott and Bengtson, 2021). A phantom, therefore, is this now ghost-like presence of the object haunting that person's behaviour (Scott and Bengtson, 2021). Scott and Bengtson (2021) add that this incorporation happens unconsciously and is therefore hidden within a crypt, what they refer to as an 'isolating structure' that is 'doomed to endlessly repeat the trauma, the loss, for which it was originally incorporated' (Fiddler, 2019: 467).

Placing this within the context of Japan and Aokigahara Forest specifically, the 'lost object' or 'phantom' can be understood as the lost futures of Japanese citizens. As capitalist societies advance, a deficit is often a loss of culture that once offered opportunity to its inhabitants (Winlow, 2001). However, as McKenna has acknowledged, Japan's capitalist structure is merged to an extent with its feudal past, arguably intensifying this loss as elements of it can still be seen, but not completely experienced. However, Scott and Bengtson (2021) state that this 'haunting can be transferable', thus we can also view the 'crypt' in this context as shifting from the confinements of the individual's identity and becoming incorporated within Aokigahara Forest itself – making the forest somewhat a visual crypt instead of one that remains in the subconscious. Essentially, due to its frequent reference within popular culture, from historical folklore stories to modern-day entertainment outputs, the forest has become a constant reference point for violence in a subjective and objective sense, simultaneously allowing for 'trauma to be endlessly repeated'. As such, these media outputs are 'texts in distress' as they contain secrets of past traumas (Rashkin, 1992; Scott and Bengtson, 2021). Furthermore, Derrida (1994) described the crypt as being constructed by violence as its enclosures are built by the social violence experienced by the individual. He adds that to unearth any trauma and loss, we need to unlock the crypt. However, as explained, graze culture means that individuals unknowingly engage with the subjective and palpable violence rather than the objective (Kelly et al, 2022). Thus, rather than simply denying the loss of the phantom, individuals are instead fetishistically disavowing the objective violence that creates the lost futures. Instead, visiting places such as Aokigahara Forest that have become a beacon for violence literally and metaphorically, as well as a place in which the phantom has been transferred – somewhat making it a fixed point within an ironic but tragic cycle.

Conclusion

Ultimately, then, visitors to Aokigahara are influenced by multiple factors. Some seek to experience nature's beauty, while others are attracted to the supernatural and mystic aura of the forest that is rooted in Japanese folklore. However, not all those who visit the forest do so with the intention of leaving. The forest, to some of these individuals, is a means of escaping their own quasi-capitalist reality. It is a familiar destination that has offered consistency and attachment to the past throughout times of rapid but semi-complete change. It is a destination that has remained in place, but simultaneously travelled through different media forms picking up greater and more global interest along the way, each stop furthering the disavowal of the deeper levels of harm within its wider context, allowing influencers such as Logan Paul to subconsciously justify their dismissal of this context and their own in the name of providing content to a wider audience. In doing so, it has also cemented itself as a visual crypt for the lost future of Japanese citizens. Indeed, it is not the Yūrei that haunts the grounds of Aokigahara Forest, but in fact the forest itself is what haunts Japanese culture.

39

Pitcairn Island: Pitcairn Islands, Pacific Ocean

Steve Wadley

Birmingham City University

Introduction

With New Zealand 3,324 miles to the west and Chile 3,587 miles to the east, the outcrop of four volcanic islands forming the Pitcairn Islands group are some of the most remote in the world. Situated in the Southern Pacific Ocean, the islands of Henderson, Ducie, Oeno and Pitcairn are an idyllic location for travellers looking for that remote getaway experience. With picturesque cliffs, rocky outcrops, clear blue waters and an average yearly temperature above 70 degrees, it is hard to look past Pitcairn Island as the ultimate location for the more adventurous traveller. September 2016 saw the introduction of the Pitcairn Islands Marine Reserve, a 320,465-square-mile protection of the isolated waters that are home to 1,249 identified species in one of the most intact marine ecosystems on the planet (The Pew Trusts, 2015), further demonstrating the scale of beauty on offer.

Most famous for being the end destination of the 17 mutineers of HMS *Bounty* in 1789, the Pitcairn Islands are often lost in the annals of history. While subject to some fluctuations due to classification type, Pitcairn is arguably one of the most (if not the most) remote inhabited islands in the world. As outlined in the *British Medical Journal* (1921), the island had 176 inhabitants in 1921; 100 years later and now with a population of 46, seven of whom live off the island long term (The Government of the Pitcairn Islands, nd), it is evident to see that a minute number of citizens occupy this tiny and isolated island.

Travel to the Pitcairn Island is not an easy affair – the determined tourist will need to be well organised and have deep pockets to secure passage to the island. Currently serviced by a working freighter, MV *Silver Supporter*, it is possible to book one of six cabins on board for a relatively comfortable journey to Pitcairn, though travellers must make their way to Mangareva in French Polynesia first to board the ship. As there is no dock on Pitcairn, all ships need to moor away from the island and are reliant on locals using longboats to navigate the often choppy seas to the ship to allow passengers to disembark. While this adds to the excitement of arriving at the island, it is possible that the conditions would be too adverse, and passengers may have to stay on board MV *Silver Supporter* until another attempt can be made. The remoteness of the island is adequately summed up by Dauchez and Perrot (2008: 21), who stated, following a visit in 2007: 'It is an understatement to say that Pitcairn is not easily accessible: there is no beach, no creek, no bay, no dead end, and its oval form offers no protection from the wind and the waves.'

Due to the size of the island and number of inhabitants, Pitcairn's 'nano-economy' relies heavily on tourism as its main source of revenue, with visitors buying wood carvings, honey, stamps and other island-related paraphernalia as mementos of their visit. Alongside the artisan creations, the earning potential of islanders is boosted via its accommodation offerings. There are 12 registered accommodation providers on the island, many of whom offer the opportunity to 'live in' with a local family, sharing all meals and facilities, and a chance to immerse yourself in island life. For those seeking a private residence, a three-bedroomed chalet with ocean views can be rented for $120 per person per night (PPPN). An additional $55 dollars PPPN in the accommodation fund will get you one extra bedroom and partial ocean views, plus the opportunity to stay in the property owned by Olive and her husband Steve Christian, the great-great-great-great-great-grandson of *Bounty* mutineer Fletcher Christian. A key patriarchal figure on the island and holding the position of island mayor from 1994 to 2004, Steve Christian is one of the most influential and competent men on Pitcairn. Alongside his mayoral duties, Christian worked as the island's dentist, engineer and long boatman and had great influence on the island and its inhabitants as a man of authority and power.

Pitcairn's dark past

Initial reports of sexual assault on young Pitcairn girls were made in 1999 to Gail Cox, a serving police officer from Kent Police on secondment in Pitcairn. 'Operation Unique' went on to uncover a 40-year history of sexual abuse on nearly every girl growing up on the island and that nearly every man had been an offender. The ensuing investigations, culminating in the highly publicised 2004 sex abuse trial, brought Pitcairn once more into the global mainstream, highlighting its dark past, archaic laws and seeming unwillingness to accept the concept of statutory rape. The trial highlighted the severity, magnitude and level of abuse children on the island were subjected to, with girls as young as five years old being forced to perform oral sex on at least one male inhabitant. In total, seven of the 12 male islanders were brought to trial; at the forefront of the investigation were Steve Christian, his son Randy, Terry Young and a fourth man, Len Brown (Marks, 2004). Together they were found guilty of 13 rapes and 15 indecent assaults, with Randy Christian and Terry Young being dealt the 'harshest' of punishments at just six years. Due to his age at the time (79), Len Brown was able to avoid prison, being granted two years' home detention instead. Dave Brown, convicted of nine accounts of indecent assault on three different girls, and Dennis Christian, found guilty of two charges of sexual assault and one of indecent assault, avoided imprisonment, receiving 400 hours and 300 hours of community service respectively.

Adding to the curiousness of the working practices of such a small island, and to the integral role the male inhabitants play in its day-to-day running, the three men began their prison sentences in a prison that they had built themselves (arriving in kit form from Britain) and that was specifically constructed to house them. As stated by McKie (2006: 1): 'It turned out to be the most luxurious building on the island. It even has plumbing.

A Pitcairn extravagance.' As experienced long boatmen, again demonstrating the vital role they played in the survival of the island, they were regularly released from prison so they could man the boats, ferrying new visitors to Pitcairn and helping to resupply the island.

Some ten years later, Pitcairn Island was again struck another blow and spotlighted in the media when the mayor (serving from 2008 to 2013), Michael Warren, was convicted of possessing more than 1,000 images and videos depicting child sexual abuse, ironically downloading the images as early as 2004 at the height of the criminal proceedings against many of the island men. Warren went on to serve only 20 months for his crimes – this time the sole occupant in the island jail – arguing to be tried under 'local law' (Ainge Roy, 2016) and reinforcing the lenient sentencing imposed for such horrific offences. At his time of arrest, Warren was working in child protection, exploiting the very people he was duty-bound to safeguard. As recent as 2020, Warren was once again arrested, facing three charges of behaving in an indecent manner in a public place (RNZ, 2020) – an offence which is punishable by up to 100 days in jail.

What is Pitcairn's appeal?

So, what is it that draws visitors to Pitcairn? As previously discussed, you cannot simply stumble across the island by chance as it is too remote and too arduous a journey to get there – for those looking to visit, there needs to be a good deal of planning involved. Any research conducted on Pitcairn will flag up two main areas: first, the obvious historical links to HMS *Bounty*, and, second, the child sexual offences cases, suggesting that the type of person who may want to visit the island may do so out of morbid curiosity or for the more controversial end of extreme tourism.

Visiting a location where there is an almost guaranteed certainty that you will cross paths or rub shoulders with known sexual offenders pushes the boundaries of extreme tourism (Picken, 2018). Akin to visiting serial killers in prison, or to visiting sites of mass atrocities, this practice for some may challenge social norms, provide that ultimate sense of adventure and potentially afford some degree of sexual gratification over and above simple curiosity. Blurring the lines of sex tourism, potential Pitcairn visitors may hold several of the known personality traits of child sex tourists (CST) (Koops et al, 2017), such as paedophilic sexual interests or previous sexual contact with children. The extremely lenient sentences imposed on the men of Pitcairn may provide further interest to potential visitors and easy access to known offenders may offer the opportunity to explore what had mostly been written about in newspaper articles or publicised on the internet.

Of course, it would be wrong to assume that all visitors to Pitcairn do so with an ulterior motive and with some dark, underlying fantasy – the scale of beauty on offer in a genuinely inaccessible part of the world is evidence to this – but the world is full of remote islands waiting to be explored so why settle on Pitcairn?

Conclusion

In researching this work, it became apparent that the Pitcairn Islands are multifaceted; on the one hand, it is impossible to argue against the attraction of the remoteness of the island and its setting within a stunning marine reserve, and so too is it difficult to ignore the hospitality of the locals and that personal experience you will receive while visiting.

For such a small island, with such a small population located in one of the most inaccessible places on Earth, the future of Pitcairn is in the balance. As one of only 14 UK Overseas Territories (OTs), much of the survival of the island is down to annual aid payments as detailed by the Foreign Commonwealth and Development Office (2021). The 2020–2021 budget, totalling £4,520,000, provides financial aid, running costs and power generation, as well as pensions and welfare aid. With slowly dwindling numbers of inhabitants and an ageing population, the future of Pitcairn could be seen as hanging in the balance. With only a few children left on the island, the chances of natural repopulation looks slim, suggesting that in years to come, Pitcairn may eventually lose all of its inhabitants and be returned to nature as it was prior to the visit from the *Bounty* mutineers in the late 1700s. A short 250-year history.

It seems fitting that the final remarks should fall with 'Isobel': 'Because really, all the money Britain's putting in is for what? What are they keeping it for? I mean, what future has the island got?' (Marks, 2009: 304).

40

Favela tours: Rio de Janeiro, Brazil

Duncan Frankis and Selina Patel Nascimento

Newman University

Introduction

Expedia's 'Rio de Janeiro Vacation Travel Guide' has been viewed two million times on YouTube (Expedia, 2014). It opens with joyful Bossa Nova music and describes the city as 'one of South America's most famous hubs of energy and excitement' (Expedia, 2014). Images of the Cristo Redentor statue on Corcovado Mountain, as well as Ipanema beach, flash across the screen; the latter is described as possessing a 'seductive and rejuvenating effect that appeals to everyone' (Expedia, 2014). It is a familiar image of the city that is projected to global tourist markets, which may explain why Rio de Janeiro attracted 2.65 million visitors in 2019 alone, averaging over 220,000 tourists every month (Lopez, 2021). However, despite these numbers, the reality is that Rio de Janeiro does not appeal to everyone; and in fact, there are many within Brazil that treat the city with extreme caution.

Favela tours as a tourist destination

Brazilian anthropologist, Roberto da Matta, offers an alternative explanation for the energy of the city, calling the famous carnival of Rio de Janeiro a 'space for forgetting', arguing that the party culture of Brazil would not exist if Brazilians insisted upon thinking about the 'secular and problematic aspects of their lives, such as the country's formidable debt, the high rates of infant mortality and illiteracy, the chronic absence of civil and political liberties, and the shocking socioeconomic contrasts' (Da Matta, 1983: 231). This subversive observation is popular among parts of the Brazilian academic community, who have traditionally explored the ludic sociality, ribald sexuality and defiant optimism of Rio de Janeiro that offers a stark juxtaposition to repressive political regimes and extreme poverty (Scheper Hughes, 1993: 481). Whether the tourists who flock to the city know of, or agree with, this philosophical perspective is unclear; but what is apparent is that there is a voyeuristic quality to the tourism that has emerged in Rio de Janeiro – where the wealthy flock to watch locals dance in favela parties, many with little idea of the dangers that face locals, or them.

In contrast to many of the other destinations discussed in this book, Rio de Janeiro is not always considered to be an intrinsically dangerous and 'dark' tourist destination outside of Brazil: favela tours and parties are believed to be relatively safe by foreign tourists. Rocinha, advertised as 'the largest favela in Latin America', attracted more than 3,500 international tourists on average every month over the last decade (Freire-Medeiros, 2011: 22). Interestingly, the authors' own experiences in Brazil, as well as a cursory glance over the headlines of the largest Brazilian media outlets, and interviews with favela residents, indicate that favela tours are most certainly not part of Brazilian tourists' 'must-do' list. Lina, a 55-year-old house cleaner living in Rocinha, contrasted Brazilian nationals' stance against visiting favelas with the enthusiasm displayed by foreigners: 'people from here look down at Rocinha, and now people come from abroad and make a point of visiting – look how splendid! Meanwhile people from here are afraid, right?' (quoted in Freire-Medeiros, 2012: 180). Having owned a travel agency in the state of São Paulo, one of this chapter's authors frequently heard customers' fears and prejudices of Rio de Janeiro, based fundamentally on Rio's notorious reputation for gun violence, drug trafficking and extremely high murder rate. Despite being the cheapest option for Brazilian tourists, not a single client booked a holiday to Rio de Janeiro. The daily media news cycle extensively covered drug- and gang-related assassinations, and customers were convinced they would never return home alive (Araújo, 2021).

The romanticisation of the favela

From a foreigner's perspective, however, the glamorisation and romanticisation of Rio de Janeiro's vibrant cultural landscape has nullified the trickle of news coverage of bloody violence that *cariocas* (residents of Rio) have come to live alongside. While most Western travellers to Latin America will have some awareness of the endemic violence that characterises much of daily life, there is a widely held belief that tourists are safe from harm. Cinematic renderings of favela life in the critically acclaimed films *City of God* (2003) and *Favela Rising* (2005) have been instrumental in popularising and romanticising the poverty, hardship and social inequalities that frame the lives of nearly 1.5 million *favelados*, giving rise to the imagined 'travelling favela', which Freire-Medeiros (2011) describes as 'a global trademark and a tourist destination'. Although it is generally accepted that favela tours sprang from politically minded tourists seeking greater awareness of Brazil's social ills during the 1992 Earth Summit, they soon became commercialised into mainstream tourism, much of which has little or no political or community engagement. While some academics have complicated the voyeuristic gaze of the foreign tourist as more than simply 'poverty porn' and have suggested that favela tours be considered as 'political tourism' with an interventionist motive, or 'educational tourism' that can enrich the visitor's own worldview, the ethical backdrop of colonialism and power relations in poverty tourism remains stubbornly in view (Selinger and Outtersen, 2010; Basu, 2012; Frenzel, 2012). It might be a moral duty to alleviate or eradicate mass poverty and slum dwellings, but from the other side, such interventions may appear as part of a post-colonial logic of condescension in which the West knows best (Frenzel, 2012). Basu (2012) also concedes that although more work is urgently needed on favela and slum residents as participatory stakeholders in slum tourism, it is 'vital that the poor do not feel demeaned by the visits, regardless of operators' and tourists' good intentions'. Indeed, she believes that knowledge and consent of the people visited is most critical, 'without which slum tourism would be reduced to voyeurism' (Basu, 2012: 78). Considering how the majority of tourists take a guided tour with an operator and interact only minimally with residents, due primarily to language barriers, it is easy to see how favela tours are inherently voyeuristic, although they may also be educational or political.

The tourists' search for 'authenticity'

That voyeurism is not always well intentioned, however. It can be partially conscious and self-serving, fulfilling an individual's own equation of poverty with 'authenticity' in poorer countries. Freire-Medeiros (2012: 179) describes how favela tour operators have to navigate the challenges in squaring visitor expectations of homogenous poverty with the differences in wealth and access in different parts of the favela Rocinha, concluding that 'poverty does not need to essentialized and fetishized (and often "ethnicized") in order to be marketable'. Conversely, or perversely, it is often the moral repulsion/attraction of favelas as places of intense and illicit pleasures that grounds many foreign tourists' processes of othering (Frenzel, 2012: 58). These sought-after, and supposed, locations of illicit pleasures are marketed to tourists as being 'transformed in recent years, moving away from the stereotype of a slum and into a creative, artsy hub, coining the phrase favela chic' (Sarah Brown, 2018). Guides to favela tours and parties downplay the latent dangers facing tourists: *The Culture Trip*, in its 'Top Favela Parties in Rio de Janeiro' guide, states that 'the dangers of the favelas in Rio de Janeiro are often widely exaggerated in international media' (Sarah Brown, Culture Trip, 2017). Despite such claims, the threat to tourist safety, and crime in general, have not diminished in the last decade: tourists' searches for authenticity in the favelas of Rio de Janeiro continue to end in tragedy.

Tourism and violence in the favela

In 2013, there was a kidnapping involving an American tourist who was subjected to a six-hour gang rape after she boarded a minibus to take her to a samba party (BBC, 2013). Alexandre Braga, the police officer in charge of the investigation, said that, rather than being taken to a popular tourist spot, the victim had been subjected to a 'party of evil' in which her French partner had been forced to watch as she was violently, and repeatedly, sexually assaulted (Pereira, Lehman and Sibaja, 2013). Fearful of negative international coverage, there was an attempt by police to secure the city following the violent attack and before the 2014 FIFA Football World Cup – mainly to keep foreign visitors safe. Despite the huge financial injection into city security forces, muggings still increased by 44 per cent during 2014 (Francesca Trianni, TIME, 2014). Since the 2016 Olympics, it has been impossible to maintain the 85,000-strong security force that had been deployed (Kaiser and Jacobs, *The New York Times*, 2016), and there has been a wave of violence returning to the favelas. In recent years, there have been several high-profile incidents involving tourists: in 2017, 15 shootings a day were recorded, and hundreds of locals and visitors were hurt or killed in the crossfire of rival gangs (Brito, Chicago Tribune, 2017). It is not only the gangs which are a threat to tourists, however. In October of the same year, a Spanish woman on a favela tour was accidently shot by police, after her tour guide went down the wrong street, the third tourist to have died in similar circumstances within a year of the incident (Phillips, *The Guardian*, 2017). In 2019, a police sting to stop a *baile funk*, a type of favela rave, left three dead and five arrested in the Cidade de Deus area. Also in 2019, an elderly Swiss tourist was shot during a mugging after mistakenly entering the Cidade Alta favela. The police emphasised afterwards that the shooting 'occurred in a zone dominated by criminals … tourists should avoid the area' (De Sousa, ABC News, 2019). In May 2020, at least 25 people died in a shootout between gang members and police in a favela in the Jacarezinho area of the city (BBC, 2020). New technology is also proving to be a problem, as a surge of 'lightning kidnappings' are taking place in 2021, where wealthy locals and tourists are forced to transfer money from their phones to armed criminals via apps on their phones (Harris, 2021). Contrary to the tourist guides' reassurances, the list of violent incidents continues to grow in the favelas of Rio de Janeiro.

The potential harms to locals

It is also important to note that tourists' desires to experience the 'authentic' Rio de Janeiro favelas do not only hurt the visitors, but also the visited. Much of the focus of European and American media takes an Americentric or Eurocentric perspective and focuses on how crime experienced in Rio de Janeiro impacts White tourists, as opposed to how Brazilians are impacted by travellers. The favelas of Rio de Janeiro are one of the capitals of the world market for sex tourism, which has had a variety of detrimental impacts on feminised labour, as well as an increase in gender-based violence against Brazilian nationals (Blanchette and Da Silva, 2011). Blanchette and Da Silva discuss how government policy pushes commercial sex workers out of the public eye and into dangerous parts of favelas run by pimps who often cater to foreign travellers (Blanchette and Da Silva, 2011). Lorenzo Moscia interviewed several Rio de Janeiro-based sex workers to get their perspective of tourists from Europe, Australia, Asia and North America. He found that it is commonplace for tourists to visit for ten-day trips to experience Latino and Mulatto prostitutes, in an 'authentic' setting. One of the sex workers, Maria, states how she makes a living from sex tourists and how commonplace violence against her is: 'I only make love to a man for money, at least then it's worth it and if I get hit as well, at least I have earned something' (quoted by Moscia, 2005). Transexual sex workers are also affected. A trans-woman known as Amanda told Moscia that an Italian pimp moved her to Italy for work (Moscia, 2005). These stories of tourist violence and sex trafficking are common, but not well publicised in Western media.

Conclusion

The incidences of sexual, economic and physical violence against tourists in the favelas of Rio de Janeiro, as well as the violence experienced by Brazilian nationals, may be enough to deter some from visiting. However, for others, the danger continues to be an important part of the appeal. Days after another Spanish tourist died on a tour of Rocinha in October 2017, Michael Wijnstok, a finance manager from the Netherlands, decided to go on a favela walking tour in the same area. He said 'you hear the stories … but I wanted to see it with my own eyes' (quoted by Brito, 2017). His tour guide on the day, local resident Marcelo Armstrong, concluded that 'the question is very complex to simply say if it is safe or not … depends where, depends what day' (Brito, 2017). The tour, which ended with caipirinhas in a local bar, starkly juxtaposes the momentary voyeurism of wealthy Europeans with the uncertainty of the everyday lives of favela inhabitants – a dynamic that continues to confuse many, including the head of tourism police in Rio de Janeiro, Valeria Aragão. Aragão lamented that 'I understand the tourists' curiosity … what I don't understand is the irresponsible attitude … when even residents feel unsafe' (Brito, 2017). As Enrique Arias and Corinne Rodriguez have concluded, there is a 'myth of personal security' in the favelas of Rio de Janeiro (Arias and Rodriguez, 2006), a fact of which any tourist should be aware.

41

Skid Row walking tours: Los Angeles, California, USA

Craig Kelly

Birmingham City University

Introduction

Invariably, when tourists think of Los Angeles, images of bright lights, movie stars, Hollywood Boulevard and the sun-kissed Californian beaches come to mind. The city is strongly associated with the worst and most garish excesses of late capitalism. Los Angeles is a city of extreme parallels. Behind the glitz and glamour of Hollywood, away from the mansions looking down upon the valley, and outside the door of its many exclusive restaurants and private member clubs, the solipsism of the City of Angels functions upon the shoulders of the invisible poor (Young, 2007) who drive forward the service economy, the disenfranchised gang members who ensure illicit substances are always available (McLean et al, 2018) and the extreme material deprivation of residents of Skid Row. These residents are perhaps the most important cog in the late capitalist ecology of Los Angeles. Without this perpetual reminder of extreme poverty, the working poor who drive the limousines, wait tables while being paid so little they are dependent on tips and hand out flyers for the latest event may begin to question why they continue to work numerous jobs yet still struggle to get by – trapped in the zone of humiliation posited by Young (2007).

The homeless capital of America

Skid Row is a four-square-mile, 50-block area of the east downtown area of Los Angeles sandwiched between the historic downtown, fashion district, arts district and Little Tokyo. Since the 1930s, the area, which comprises of many low-income apartments, hotels, motels and hostels, has been the epicentre of the US homeless problem. At the time of writing and over the last few years, the area has been host to anywhere between 2,000 and 8,000 homeless men, women and children at any one time. Many of these individuals are homeless in the most literal sense, with their only protection from the warm California heat and smothering smog being makeshift cardboard structures or, if they are lucky, tents. The area is widely considered the homeless capital of America, with around over 1,600 people sleeping rough on its streets each evening (Stuart, 2018). In recent years, the area has seen rapid redevelopment and is surrounded by the sight of progress, with trendy coffee bars and exclusive apartments springing up. The benign neglect that has characterised the area since the concerted effort of city officials to relocate low-income housing, shelters and soup kitchens into the area in the late 1970s with industrial buildings intentionally developed around the outskirts of the Skid Row to 're-enforce' the boundaries of Skid Row, dissuading the impoverished residents from straying out of the area and into the wider metropole (Davis, 1990). Within this, the Skid Row area of Los Angeles was, as Stuart (2018: 52) details, designed to act as a magnet to the destitute, impoverished and problematic residents in surrounding areas.

There are three main missions that offer services to the residents of Skid Row, with various other organisations in addition (usually subcontracted to the three most dominant missions). The area has, over the decades, been the epicentre of much scandal, often in the pursuit of profit or meeting targets. Between 2005 and 2007, police departments outside of the area, as well as hospitals, were accused by the Los Angeles Police Department of 'dumping' homeless people under their care in Skid Row, thus transferring the 'problem' (Dimassa and Winton, 2006). The area is the most common area of prison re-entry in the whole of the Southern California region, with one third of the citiy's prisoners being released on parole to Skid Row. Release from the Southern Californian penal system into the hustle and bustle of Skid Row is so common that shuttle buses operate between Skid Row and nearby jails and prisons (Stuart, 2018).

Being homeless in America is a tough life and existing on Skid Row is no different. Problematic drug use (Padgett and Struening, 1992) and mental health issues (Fischer et al, 2008; Dunne et al, 2012) have long been documented as being highly prevalent within homeless communities. Experiences of criminal victimisation and violence are commonplace (Ellsworth, 2019). So too are more structural forms of violence such as overt and often overzealous policing tactics as a means of control over and dispersal of the population (Schneider, 1988; McCulloch, 2017; Stuart, 2018; Robinson, 2019). The residents of Skid Row live precarious lives on the margins of the capitalist dream. Upon entering the area known as Skid Row, or more locally 'the nickel', you could be forgiven for thinking you have transitioned into a Hollywood film set. A dystopian portrayal of late capitalism where the disillusioned, downtrodden and disenfranchised are swept away and discarded. Somehow, this heavily defined area that optimises the worst of Western excess and economic marginality has become somewhat of a tourist hotspot. Often, tourists leave the beaten track of the arts district and participate in tours of Skid Row, hosted by third-sector charities that support the beleaguered residents.

Charity as a leisure pursuit

Of course, elsewhere in this book, contributors discuss various forms of what is commonly referred to as 'poverty porn' across the globe, such as the favela tours discussed in Chapter 40. In the same vein of these tours, the profits are diverted into helping the residents of the nickel. This, at first glance, appears to be a rather commendable form of tourism, a way to offset the lavish nature of a holiday in LA. Obviously, the hosts of the tours run them with good intention (it would be hoped), with the aim to generate funding and bring attention to the plight of those they aim to serve. But what drives us to seek out the most marginalised, destitute and damaged while on holiday? This chapter seeks to question this.

While discussing doing charity work as a leisure pursuit, Large (2019) draws upon the notion of *amour-propre* put forth by Hall et al (2008). *Amour-propre* is, they detail, a particular form of egoism in which individuals elevate themselves above others through the distinction from and denigration of others. Within the context of the Skid Row walking tours, the application of *amour-propre* as a lens from which we can understand participation is clear. As referred to earlier in this chapter, Young (2007) discusses the zone of humiliation that is inherent to much of the service economy within Western culture (see also Lloyd, 2018, for discussion around wider precarious employment in the service economy). This service economy underpins much of the typical tourist participation of those that visit Los Angeles for many of its known tourist attractions. Within this, the distinction between the consumer and the service provider is abundantly clear. While the tourist indulges in the most lavish of late capitalist excess, the facilitators of this undergo the routine and systematic humiliation involved in low-paid, precarious jobs within the service sector. A walking tour of Skid Row, however, offers a further extension of the *jouissance* (excessive and transgressive pleasure) derived from the excessive consumption the tourist is ordinarily participating upon. This *jouissance* (Hall et al, 2008) is heightened by the extreme form of *amour-propre*. The opposite ends of the capitalist project are experienced in their most stark form. The 'haves' take a literal tour around the living conditions of the 'have nots'. As Large (2019: 331) details, 'in a society of competitive individualists, distinguishing oneself from the masses is a key cultural drive'. Large expands upon this, noting that charity tourism allows the consumer to show their cultural awareness and display their politics in an overt way while not having to depart from a mode of consumption. A walking tour of Skid Row, therefore, that raises money to support those living within its confines, is an extreme example of this. Within other forms of charity tourism, the consumer is expected to participate in some form of charity work for an extended period of time, though it is normally just a day or two. On the tours of the nickel, however, this overt form of social justice through consumption is at its most opaque. The consumer walks the streets and observes (perhaps interacting in a limited way with) capitalism's causalities as if it was an interactive museum or even a zoo (not forgetting the intentional design of Skid Row to keep the residents contained).

Graze culture and the commodification of familiar violence

Within this, we can begin to see how modes of transgression, egoism, cultural drives and thinly veiled social justice culminate within the confines of consumption. Consumers pay a nominal fee to be guided through the lives of the starkest forms of structural violence within late capitalism. This is, of course, not the only example of such tours within the Los Angeles area, with various 'gang' tours available that take tourists around infamous neighbourhoods in which gang activity, driven by structural violence, are common. This raises the question of why such tours are so popular. I propose the answer lies, at least in part, within the notion of graze culture (Kelly et al, 2022).

In 1998, Seltzer argued that the rise in serial killer-themed media was due to society's obsession with what he termed 'wound culture'. Seltzer suggests that wound culture describes a collective that is addicted to violence, 'not merely [as] a collective spectacle but one of the crucial sites where private desire and public space cross' (Seltzer, 1998). Seltzer suggests that society consists of a pathological public sphere, which is underpinned by a fusion of the public space and an individual's private fantasy, ultimately blurring the line between what is public and what is private. However, we refute this and offer the notion of *graze culture*. Whereas Seltzer (1998) contends that we as a society are drawn to the 'torn and open bodies', I contend that this is not the case. In an era of ever-increasing uncertainty and anxiety, society is drawn to forms of violence we understand and feel, while distasteful, familiar. As individuals in society struggle to conceptualise the realities of violence in the contemporary world, a world that has been gripped by both economic crisis and increasingly the ecological crisis, we find solace in both consumerism and overt forms of violence we can easily understand. This is why the true crime genre, which is overladen by simplistic analysis of serial murder, is a popular staple within contemporary media. We can choose to consume violence in a palatable and controllable manner.

Conclusion

Tourism, therefore, is, within the context of tours of a Crip neighbourhood or a walking tour of Skid Row, just a more interactive version of graze culture. Participants expect to come across visual representations of overt violence on such tours including the scarred and weather-beaten bodies society has cast aside. It allows them to glimpse into the realities of structural violence that late capitalism has allowed. The donation enables the tourist to disavow their role within the system, to virtue-signal their politics, all within the safe confines of depoliticised consumption. *Amour-propre* is achieved in an extreme form, forgoing the usual zone of humiliation and offering a much more visceral form. In doing so, a form of *jouissance* typically achieved through criminal transgression or vicarious thrills through the consumption of media is achieved in synthesis with the ability to project being a conscientious traveller.

42

The 2019–20 anti-extradition protests: Hong Kong

Jane Richards

The University of Hong Kong

Introduction

The 2019–2020 anti-extradition protests in Hong Kong marked the beginning of the rapid erosion of fundamental political and civil rights so striking as to take on international political significance. Global broadcasting of dramatic scenes of tear gas, water cannons and black-clad protestors facing off against armed riot police attracted the attention of politicians, activists and international and domestic tourists. In an article published by the *Washington Post* on that topic, one medical and security professional was quoted as saying that 'culturally, it's not insensitive to visit … you can experience the pursuit of democracy' (Sachs, 2019). But is making a holiday out of the injustice faced by locals really just harmless voyeurism? Or does tourists' failure to engage signal complicity with an unjust and repressive government? Can snapping a picture of police beating a protestor be equated with a ride on the iconic Star Ferry for a dim sum lunch? These are awkward questions; as tourists, many of us have found ourselves proximate to a protest. But what of tourists who seek out situations of civil unrest for their summer break? Do tourists have ethical obligations when they seek out a protest, or does tourism become dark if its destination is a situation of civil unrest?

This chapter analyses the different tourists that travelled to Hong Kong during the 2019–2020 protests and argues that in situations of injustice, more than just being passive bystanders, the proximity of tourism triggers an ethical obligation of Samaritan rescue to call out and resist injustice (Delmas, 2018). Many tourists to Hong Kong satisfied this obligation. However, others engaged in tourism of a more sinister nature, either for their own ends, because their presence potentially undermined the cause by subverting the protestors' demands for democratic freedoms or by playing into the narrative propagated by Beijing that the Hong Kong protests were the product of 'foreign collusion'.

Hong Kong: not a typical dark destination

At least until 2019, Hong Kong was not an obvious 'dark destination' for tourists. Like many big Asian cities, Hong Kong does have a nightclub scene where Asian sex workers are an attractive commodity for a particular contingent of foreign tourists. However, for the most part, Hong Kong is a safe, clean, easy and exciting tourist destination for visitors from all over the world (Li and Ives, 2019).

However, the 2019–2020 anti-extradition protests resulted in a dramatic downturn in tourism to the city (BBC, 2019; Kim et al, 2020; Poon and Koay, 2021). For many, the primary concern was safety (Australian Government, 2019; BBC, 2019; Mullany, 2019), and also the utility of visiting a city which experienced weekly, and often daily, civil unrest which lasted for months on end. Dramatic scenes of pitch battles between protestors and police, engulfed by tear gas in an altered cityscape replete with protest graffiti, artworks, Lennon Walls and torn-up roads were beamed in real time in the international media and via social media around the world. However, not all tourists were put off and for some this was the attraction. The next section considers which tourists came to Hong Kong for the protests and why. It is shown that while some tourists came to satisfy a duty of justice by a Samaritan duty of rescue, others were arguably dark tourists which were unwelcome by protestors in their potentially sinister intents. The juxtaposition of the different tourists provides insight into whether and when tourism to situations of civil unrest are ethical.

The ethics of protest tourism: satisfying a duty of justice or dark tourism?

The immediacy of news reporting and social media connects citizens around the world instantaneously (Delmas, 2018: 149; Veitch, 2021: 109). At least until the COVID-19 pandemic, international travel removed barriers of distance and difference, meaning that in some cases, domestic issues were able to be tackled because their immediacy made them issues of global concern. For some, Hong Kong's street clashes metaphorically represented the clash of geopolitical tensions between liberal democracy and expanding Chinese authoritarianism; the bodies of protestors being beaten by the Hong Kong Police Force stood in for the beating down of democratic rights and freedoms of Hong Kong citizens by an oppressive and merciless government. Satisfying ethical duties of justice, one category of visitors came in staunch support of the movement and made efforts to raise international awareness and stimulate a political response by foreign governments. American Republican Senators Ted Cruz, Rick Scott and Josh Hawley (Cheung, 2019; Lendon, 2019; Scott, 2019), British conservative politician Luke de Pulford and human rights campaigner Brian Dooley joined the protests and bore witness to some of the most dramatic events, such as the siege on Poly U, and then shared their time on Twitter. Welcomed by protestors, their presence positioned the West in support of the struggle for democracy against an advancing wave of authoritarian rule being dictated by Beijing. The international visibility of their presence helped inspire foreign legislation,[1] immigration pathways and sanctions against China by Western governments, while increasing fricative relations between China and the West.

In fact, perceiving an imminent risk to the fundamental interests and rights of the people of Hong Kong, these politicians and activists satisfied a Samaritan duty of rescue by doing what they could to lend assistance to the pursuit of democracy. To

[1] For example, see s. 1838 – Hong Kong Human Rights and Democracy Act of 2019 (U.S.); Hong Kong British National Overseas (BNO) visa.

explain, in the words of Candice Delmas, a duty of Samaritan rescue may compel acts of disobedience, which 'grounded in our nature as moral beings … binds us all equally, regardless of our relations or voluntary undertakings' and obligates all of us to 'aid persons in peril or dire need when we can at no unreasonable cost to ourselves' (Delmas, 2018: 138).

These visitors to Hong Kong are illustrative of how this duty may be satisfied. In travelling to Hong Kong to join protests, speak at rallies, speak to the international media and lobby their own governments upon their return to their countries of origin, as 'tourists' these figures actively satisfied this duty of justice. They were not 'dark tourists', but rather authentic supporters of a movement designed to resist injustice.

Motivated more by a duty of solidarity (Delmas, 2019; Veitch, 2021: 102), as opposed to being politically motivated per se, Masanori Nishikawa is a Japanese cyclist who travels around Japan and overseas and 'creates connections with people through coffee' (Nishikawa, 2019; @earthride.jp). To Hong Kong, Nishikawa brought his spirit, his 'Free Coffee for Peace' and he was welcomed by civil society. Though perhaps his free coffee and good nature were ultimately less impactful than that of the higher-profile protest support group, Nishikawa's act of solidarity is illustrative of exceeding the reasonable personal cost threshold required to satisfy a duty of justice (Finnis, 2011: 304; Delmas, 2018). Travelling to Hong Kong at his own expense, living cheaply to afford to do so and then extending messages of solidarity via the gift of coffee was a significant personal cost in aid of the cause. This example is perhaps the antithesis of what might be considered dark tourism to situations of civil unrest. In the context of tourism to sites of civil unrest, this example helps to establish what dark tourism is not, and by doing so, establishes space to understand what it is and the ambiguous spaces between the ends of the spectrum.

Less equivocal as to whether they were dark tourists were those who joined guided tours of the protests. Seemingly consistent with its ethos of showing the real Hong Kong – in all its grit and diversity – Free Hong Kong Tours guided interested folk past riot police while avoiding the tear gas of Victoria Park (Han, 2019). Though foreign faces were usually welcomed by local

Hong Kong protestors,[2] it is arguable that if the protests were consumed for entertainment as opposed to education, then the intentional and proximate witnessing of another's trauma verges on dark tourism. It is difficult to quantify precisely what a duty of Samaritan rescue would require of these tourists. However, confronted with scenes of injustice and even violence, it might be reasonable to expect that tourists would make some efforts to educate themselves about the political situation, and to increase awareness of the events in their home countries by sharing what they witnessed on social media. This low-cost action could draw attention both to the direct threat to bodies on the front lines, and also to the underlying issues being protested. Alternatively, upon returning to their home country, tourists could join a Hong Kong protest in their own city – particularly now because Hong Kongers in Hong Kong cannot protest. Lobbying one's own government to apply political pressure in aid of resisting injustice is one way to indirectly influence Chinese politics and is easily in the reach of many tourists. The alternative, of passive voyeurism of political and civil injustice for entertainment purposes, verges on the dark; at best, it turns a blind eye to injustice; at worst, it provides tourist dollars to authoritarian governments which may assist in sustaining systemic injustice.

The unequivocal dark tourists of the Hong Kong protests were a group of Ukrainian fascists, bearing Swastika and White power tattoos (Hume, 2019). The leader of this group known for its far-right ideology and Nazi sympathies, Serhii Filmonov, was quoted as saying that they had come not to participate but to potentially learn from the protestors (Hume, 2019; Lum, 2019). However, analysts expressed concern that their involvement was an attempt to expand their brand (Hume, 2019) and they were not welcomed by Hong Kongers. It was never entirely clear why Ukrainian fascists travelled to Hong Kong to join the protests. But their presence elucidates what dark tourism actually is in situations of civil unrest.

---

[2] As a participant observer at many protests, I can attest that my foreign face brought multiple thanks, warnings as to what was about to take place, gifts of eyedrops, tissues and masks to defend against the effects of tear gas and extensive explanations about the cause.

Hong Kongers were protesting against a series of perceived injustices, largely based on political and civic inequality and an erosion of their democratic rights and freedoms which were guaranteed in Hong Kong's mini-constitution and under international law.[3] The politics of these Ukrainian fascists stand in marked contrast to this struggle for democracy. And their assumed partiality for violence played into the official, but largely inaccurate, government narrative of the protests being the work of a violent but largely isolated minority, unsupported by the majority of civil society (Graham-Harrison, 2019; Lahiri and Hui, 2019; Lam, 2020).

Beijing characterised all foreigners as guilty of interfering in internal matters, and some critics argued that the presence of foreigners at protests lent credence to Beijing's narrative that the protests were the work of foreign forces who had ulterior motives in organising the rallies (Myers, 2019). In fact, there was no credible evidence to suggest that the Central Intelligence Agency or any other foreign institution was orchestrating from behind the scenes, or corrupting Hong Kong's youth. Still, under the National Security Law, enacted in 2020 and imposed on Hong Kong by Beijing without public consultation, foreign collusion became one of the four offences.

These contrasting examples show that protest tourism is not value neutral: if tourists come for their own benefit – to learn, or as voyeurs, and becoming aware of ongoing injustices, remain silent or even inflame tensions – then that tourism crosses the line of being unethical and may even manifest in harm to dissidents because tourist dollars and voyeuristic observation may serve to legitimise and fund unjust regimes. This can be contrasted to tourists who attend protests to express solidarity or to resist indignity and inequality. The Hong Kong anti-extradition protests demonstrate that tourism to situations of political unrest may trigger ethical duties of calling out or resisting injustice, failing which tourism may become dark.

---

3 Hong Kong Basic Law; Hong Kong Bill of Rights Ordinance (Cap 383); International Covenant on Civil and Political Rights; Joint Declaration of the Government of the United Kingdom of Great Britain and Northern Ireland and the Government of the People's Republic of China on the Question of Hong Kong (Sino-British Joint Declaration).

Conclusion

This chapter has made the case that not all forms of protest tourism are equal: when tourists travel to situations of civil unrest, they have a moral obligation to make efforts to understand the cause of action, and in situations of injustice, engage in some efforts to satisfy a Samaritan duty of rescue – whether that be by expressing solidarity, raising awareness about the situation, joining a protest at home or abroad, applying political pressure on governments to agitate for reform or bringing about legislative change. Tourism which has the potential to undermine or confuse the message of protestors, or is motivated by some sort of gratuitous fascination, likely constitutes tourism of a much darker nature which breaches ethical obligations of Samaritan rescue and even has the potential to undermine a protest movement.

43

The Maldives: Republic of Maldives, Indian Ocean

Emiline Smith and Oliver Smith

University of Glasgow and University of Plymouth

Introduction

Maldives is an archipelago of 1,192 islands grouped into 26 atolls in the Indian Ocean. Like other Small Island Developing States (SIDS), Maldives is increasingly economically reliant on tourism and related industries, marketed around the unique natural beauty of the area, both above and below the waterline. Those better versed in the language of luxury tourism speak of 'unrivalled luxury, stunning white-sand beaches and an amazing underwater world … an obvious choice for a true holiday of a lifetime' (Lonely Planet, 2021). The 'Visit Maldives' (2021) website promotes 'unique geography that mesmerises the visitor. Reefs that offer bands of colour, tiny jewel-like islands rimmed with the whitest of soft sand surrounded by the clearest shallow waters that one can imagine'. Snorkelling and scuba diving are therefore among the most popular tourist activities in Maldives due to its extensive coral gardens and variety of marine mega fauna. Maldives is a status destination for many, where they get to experience luxury and exclusivity, with a premium paid for seclusion and privacy.

The Maldives: truly dark tourism?

Maldives is not an obvious subject of a chapter on dark tourism. In fact, proponents or students of sustainable tourism would argue the opposite. Tourists to the area appear to be drawn to the life and the vitality of the coral reefs, and tourism is generally positioned as an unmitigated good for the region and for the wildlife that lives there. Sustainable use and conservation of the environment are therefore of paramount importance to the Maldives, evidenced by a range of relevant environmental laws and policies the country has implemented (Techera and Cannell-Lunn, 2019). Furthermore, Maldives has been the recent recipient of several awards for sustainable tourism and has a number of government-backed programmes to foster sustainability and conservation efforts within the tourist industry. In order to position Maldives as a site of dark tourism, then, we need to look again at our understanding of the term, and interrogate the existing tourist industry within the islands in the context of a criminological understanding of harm.

As other chapters in this volume have illustrated, dark tourism is usually defined as travel to particular sites or locations that are synonymous with or otherwise linked to death, trauma and suffering (Stone and Sharpley, 2008), a broad category that encompasses both tragedies of human creation and natural disasters. The focus tends to be anthropocentric, commodifying the human victims of suffering, and incorporates sites of brutal or inhumane incarceration, crime scenes of serial killers, genocide and disaster. For us, this definition is incomplete. Whereas dark tourism is a term applied to those sites where profits are drawn from the commodification of suffering that has occurred in the past, Maldives provides an example *par excellence* of the commodification of an evolving and current crime scene. This is a crime scene that has begun to emerge in step with the Anthropocene – the indelible signature of human progress scarring landscapes, polluting ecosystems and driving climate change. The crime that is unfolding in front of our eyes is ecocide, the contamination, desecration and destruction of the natural environment, reducing its ability to support life (South, 2009). Within this short chapter, we only have space for a cursory exploration of some of such harmful activities associated with tourism and the tourist industry, to illustrate the importance of developing our understanding of dark tourism to include destinations that are experiencing ecocide.

Despite only being introduced in the early 1970s, tourism is the backbone of the Maldivian economy, accounting for 24 per cent of GDP, 32 per cent of direct employment and 41 per cent of government revenue in 2015 (Shakeela and Weaver, 2018), attracting in excess of 1.7 million international tourists in 2019 (Ministry of Tourism, 2019). Amid the global pandemic, Maldives even became the World's Leading Travel Destination in 2020 (Shaany, 2020a). This successful model is based on the commodification and fictionalisation of Maldives as a luxury paradise. But it also relies on spatial separation: tourists spend their time on resort islands and diving from liveaboards while the local population are located on different islands, with minimal interaction between these two parallel worlds that are vastly different and often conflicting cultural and political spaces. While basic services were centralised in the capital of Malé and in resort islands, other islands were deprived of necessities like drinking water and sewage facilities. Consequently, natural resources – including land and marine environments as a source of income and food – have become a privilege for wealthy local and foreign investors, not for island populations. Instead, islands are left with the consequences of limited safe water supply and an ever-growing tourism industry: plastic pollution.

Plastic pollution is a global threat to biodiversity, food security, ecosystems and human health. It has now become clear that the planet is unable to deal with the rapidly increasing production and disposal of plastic, of which much accumulates in the marine environment (Browne et al, 2011). Due to its geographical location, Maldives is therefore quite literally drowning in plastic. In 2020, researchers recorded the highest level of marine microplastic pollution on the planet in the Maldives (Patti et al, 2020). Most Maldivian beaches are filled with plastic waste. These plastics are transported by ocean currents from neighbouring countries, but also originate from within the Maldives, due to insufficient municipal waste facilities, poor sewerage and unsustainable land reclamation policies.

The waste problem in Maldives is so dire that a special artificial island was created in the early 1990s: Thilafushi is now the world's largest rubbish island. Yet there are no state-managed recycling facilities in the country. Instead, plastic ends up on ever-expanding mountains of rubbish on each island and is subsequently burned, or shipped to Thilafushi (Kapmeier and Gonçalves, 2018). This has resulted in Maldives being ranked the fourth largest producer of mismanaged waste (waste disposed of in an uncontrolled way) per capita on Earth in 2019 (Barnes, 2019). Recognising the detrimental impacts of the plastic crisis on the marine environment and local livelihoods, several resorts, non-governmental organisations and island communities have taken steps to eradicate plastic pollution on their islands, for example through 'waste-to-wealth' and other sustainability initiatives (for example, Shaahunaz, 2020). Moreover, Maldivian President Ibrahim Mohamed Solih has announced his desire to phase out single-use plastics by 2023 (Shaany, 2020b). However, these efforts are challenged by an overall lack of coordination, public awareness, corruption, human and financial resources, an overreliance on imported products and an ever-increasing tourism industry. Plastic pollution therefore continues to threaten Maldivian livelihoods and marine life.

The epitome of a luxurious holiday, away from both daily reality and the local population of your holiday destination, is the concept of the scuba diving liveaboard. These boats, often owned by foreigners and able to accommodate up to 24 guests, take tourists straight from the airport to the most secluded, exclusive dive spots. When out of the water, guests can enjoy the air-conditioned suites, sun deck, open-air dining room, bars and even jacuzzis and swimming pools on board. Local island populations whose waters these boats dive in do not typically benefit from the liveaboard experience. Instead, plastic waste and cigarette butts wash up on their shores, marine wildlife alters their behaviour because of diver interactions and anchors (and divers) damage the coral reefs. This constant pursuit of luxury within the Maldivian tourist industry has the effect of exacerbating waste and excess, while paradoxically rendering harm invisible to the extent that elite tourists are paying a premium to experience nature in a pure and unaffected state.

Maldives has been constructed as a bucket list destination, featuring regularly on lists of 'places to see before you die', an accolade that confers a level of status and aspiration for discerning tourists, and which draws a first link to the macabre and death. It reminds us that our worth in life is measured through our participation in consumer markets and by our accumulation not just of goods, but of experiences, whereby 'luxury' equates with 'better'. However, more recently, Maldives can be found topping new lists, reorienting its connotation with death from a place to see before *we* die, to a place to see before *it* dies. With tag lines such as 'Visit the Maldives before it sinks into the ocean' (Sorte, 2018), Maldives is reduced to an eerie spectacle of ongoing deterioration preceding a death that is yet to come. Importantly, while climate experts warn us of the rapidity of environmental change, the truth is that the visitor to Maldives, seduced by the exclusivity, the luxury and the beauty of the natural surroundings is not going to witness extinction in real time. For the wealthy and privileged visitor, the carefully packaged and presented consumer experiences that they will enjoy steer them away from any signs that something is wrong. Resorts will present pristine, plastic-free beaches. Dive guides will assiduously ensure that the reefs they explore are teeming with wildlife, vibrant in colour, while the skeletal, ghostly shapes of dying corals are hidden from view. Put simply, the tourist industry is committed to presenting a view of Maldives that suggests purity, balance and untouched beauty, and yet almost every aspect of tourism in this area drags the tourist into an active role of violence perpetrated against its environment, whether through the emissions generated in reaching the islands, marine pollution generated by the use and maintenance of outboard engines or the waste discarded through the act of holidaying.

Conclusion

Despite the urgency of the climate crisis, this is a crime scene that is dominated by a slow violence (Nixon, 2011), one which is experienced by the inhabitants of Maldives through displacement, land grabbing, poverty, cultural erosion, economic inequality and the impending precarity of sea level rise, and upon the natural environment through species depletion, coral bleaching and pollution. All the while, the inhabitants of Maldives are told that they are lucky to have a thriving tourism industry.

44

Death Road: La Paz to Coroico, Bolivia

Joe Garrihy

Maynooth University

Introduction

The central role of leisure in contemporary cultures and societies continues to develop in expected and unexpected directions. While analyses differ in their definitions of the nature of leisure – often in 'good' versus 'bad' binaries – such analyses can be expanded with the inclusion of less-considered harms in social contexts (Williams, 2009; Stone, 2013). The urge, desire and the asserted necessity to experience 'sensation' comprises a most valued and valorised form of cultural capital (Bourdieu, 1993) while integrating a broader array of deviance which warrants examination through the lens of dark tourism (Sharpley, 2009; Williams, 2009; Smith and Raymen, 2018).

In May 2009, I embarked on a ten-week trip comprising six countries in South America. Though many days featured tourist attractions and experiences packaged for our consumption, there was one experience that remains foremost in my mind: cycling down the 'Death Road'. The fact that this experience prevails over a decade later is striking and arguably a testament to the exhilaration and uniqueness of the Death Road which aligns with the surrounding marketing discourse (Viator, 2022). However, it is not the primary source of its lingering in my consciousness. On the day, and every time I think of it since, there is a discomfort with the symbolism and signification of death inherent therein. This chapter will briefly outline the background of the 'Death Road' and the offered experience before examining this within the broader context of deviant leisure and dark tourism.

Death Road details and context

With an elevation of 'between 10,650 and 13,250 feet (3,250 and 4,100 metres) above sea level', La Paz is the highest capital city in the world (Britannica, 2021). The 'Carretera de La Muerte' or 'Death Road' (also 'Road of Death'), as it is commonly known, is the North Yungas Road. It stretches from La Paz – the administrative capital hosting the executive and legislative branches of government – to Coroico in the tropical Yungas region of Bolivia. At approximately 37 miles (approximately 64 km), the North Yungas Road descends precipitously from 11,800 feet (3,596 m).

The promotional material of multiple tourist agencies presents the opportunity to tackle the 'world's most dangerous road' while travelling (at great speed) through 'Bolivia's most breath-taking landscapes, beautiful mountains and sparkling waterfalls' (Viator, 2022). The road offers breathtaking natural beauty as it snakes through the Andes hugging the side of sheer mountain reliefs often enveloped by the flora and occasional waterfalls. In 2006, a new highway was constructed on the upper section while the lower section remains undeveloped. The paved portion consists of approximately the upper third of the journey allowing for a smoother and faster descent while the remaining two thirds is defined by its gravel surfaces accompanied by precipices of nearly 3,000 feet (900 m) in places. The requirement to 'pass on the left' – justified to allow travellers to gain the most vantage of oncoming vehicles or bikes – adds further apparent gravitas to the sheer drop touted by the tour guides and ramped up by the riders.

While the beauty of the Andes Mountains is not in doubt, it is the frisson of danger that infuses the title and the corresponding conversations with fellow travellers throughout the journey. Moreover, the fast pace of the descent – '30mph (48km/h)' (Geoghegan, 2010) – demands such attention, even with the constant use of brakes by many, that the scenery fades into insignificance while riding. Its draw is felt far beyond Bolivian borders and permeates backpacker discourse across South America in my experience. Although not included in the brochures and webpages, the number of deaths – those approximating accuracy and those wildly exaggerated – were never far from the lips of tour operators and their wilful clients. This is the crucial element that draws a morbid distinction of this leisure pursuit in comparison with other mountain biking routes, or indeed other outdoor sporting pursuits more generally. Geoghegan (2010) reports these words from one of the early tour operators offering the trips: 'Simply put, it's all about "bragging rights".'

Death Road and thanatourism: a reflection

Dark tourism, generally conceived, is defined as 'any form of tourism that is somehow related to death, suffering, atrocity, tragedy or crime' (Light, 2017: 277), which is certainly applicable to Death Road tourism. Additionally, it must also be considered as a form of thanatourism – the more specific concept about long-standing practices of travel motivated by a particular desire for an encounter with death (Light, 2017: 277) – not least due to the explicit nomenclature in its title.

The nature of Death Road tourism encompasses three overlapping pursuits. People wishing to engage in dark tourism generally are attracted to the site while it is all the more appealing for those of a thanatouristic persuasion. However, there is a nuance, not uncommon to other dark tourism sites on backpacker routes, that many are directed to it along with a list of other attractions ('must-sees'/'must-dos') that populate tourist routes, attractions lists and publications. The precise motivation of each traveller is beyond the scope of this chapter but the implicit and explicit characterisations of the title, promotional materials and representations of the experience situate death at the heart of the attraction.

My recollections are both seared into my consciousness while others appear somewhat underwhelming. The high numbers of fellow riders in the various organised company tour groups brought a sense of mundanity to the interludes between intense concentration and speed. Moreover, the suspension of paradox necessary for countless riders to queue and pose for the cliff-edge panoramic shot to represent their unique experience was more palpable than the promised fear generated by the risky ride. However, this is precisely the point where the experience intersects with the dark and deviant. The caustic subjectivity and superficiality of contemporary capitalism's imperative to curate identities according to experiences presented as unique while being more accurately characterised as conventional and conspicuous consumerism in exchange for presumed cultural capital (Bourdieu, 1977).

The descent from altitude mirrors the descent from higher moral and social values. Each cross, shrine, memorial, bouquet, set of rosary beads, placed to commemorate the loved ones lost, have become 'experience enhancers' in the macabre tally of deviant leisure. The frisson of danger is fuelled and heightened as riders pass each of these frequent demarcations of death that punctuate the descent. Bolivian cultural meanings related to death and their commemoration are noticeably absent from any discussions in the hostels or tour agencies. While each lost life is tragic, there is a juxtaposition between those local persons who have died during their daily activities and the riders who have lost their lives in pursuit of a socially corrosive individualism by consuming commodified significations of death. This exchange takes place in one of the least economically developed, poorest and most unequal societies in Latin America (United Nations Department of Economic and Social Affairs, 2020). The gravitational pull of the Death Road appears to correlate with the pull upon swathes of largely middle-class international travellers, myself included, to experience this 'sensation' but, more importantly, to produce the culturally valorised artefact to buttress this identity. A most valued form of cultural capital (Bourdieu, 1993), this process has intensified exponentially in the intervening years with the rise of social media (Fuchs, 2021). Many riders were paradoxically seeking to emulate the photos in the brochure and online while also seeking to distinguish themselves and convince themselves, and indeed the viewers of their impending photographs, that they are unique, individually adventurous souls.

There is a contradiction between the rebellious and thrill-seeking striking out on the death-defying road – which local people traverse out of necessity – and the kind of 'alternative' ideology espoused by many travellers while touring South America. Travellers' ubiquitous alpaca wool clothing and other forms of local 'folk' attire grates with the prominent demonstration of pecuniary affluence facilitating their presence in Bolivia to pursue this morbid adventure. It is noteworthy that backpackers – who make up the majority of the apparent rider demographic – often characterise their journey as being representative of a voyage of self-discovery complete with an opportunity to step away from the everyday cynicism of consumer culture in advanced, distinctly 'Western' societies. Their 'anxiety, unhappiness and despair' (Smith and Raymen, 2018: 72; see also Stiegler, 2013) is quelled by escapism, edgework (Lyng, 2004) and exhilaration provided by the sensational, and associated cultural capital, of engaging in the deviance afforded there. The commodification of death is not new, but here, the currency is not merely the legacy of historic deaths but the contemporary deaths such as the Israeli biker who perished the week before Geoghegan's (2010) article, a year after my departure. This corrosive social harm comes into sharp relief when considering that this source of prestige and cultural capital – essentially trading on the death of poor people and/or fellow travellers – is beyond macabre and testament to the commodified modern consumer culture and vacuous nature of social media.

Conclusion

In societies where relentless social comparison and competition are ever-increasing, the Death Road offers an opportunity for thrilling individualism infused with the macabre of dark tourism or thanatourism. Moreover, it is reasonable to argue that the experience pales in importance as compared to its capture and curated reproduction through the lens of the well-placed camera shot, with the additional immediacy of social media proliferating in the intervening years since my trip. There is limited scope for considerations of the subjective and socially corrosive harms of identities built on such significations and symbolism (Smith and Raymen, 2018). It would be dishonest to present my consciousness of the time as attuned to the extent of these factors at play but it is our responsibility to reflect on our experiences, their contexts, our role in them within the inexorable social structures as much as we analyse those of others. Sites such as the 'Death Road' offer opportunities to examine broader social, economic and political trends while addressing the central premise of doxic (Bourdieu, 1977) endeavours such as the 'visitor economy' (Stone, 2013: 307) and leisure. Though brief, this chapter instigates further analyses of this specific example such as the relationship between local people and the mountains, the road and death. Additionally, the intertwined nature of globalised economies, environmentalism and social harm through myriad lenses invites further inquiry.

45

Vulture brains and *muthi* markets: Johannesburg, South Africa

Angus Nurse

Nottingham Trent University

Introduction

The use of animals and plants as traditional remedies for both medical afflictions and social or spiritual concerns issues is well established in South Africa, and it has been estimated that a large proportion of the population will consult a traditional healer at least once in their lifetime (Williams and Whiting, 2016). The umbrella terms Traditional Asian Medicine (TAM) and African Traditional Medicine (ATM) are used in respect of traditional healing that makes use of 'natural' rather than chemical and pharmacological compounds to promote health and wellbeing. The term 'African Science' also conveys incorporation of spiritual beliefs and indigenous knowledge as aspects of traditional healing approaches specific to the African diaspora (Ashforth, 2005). '*Muthi*' is a blanket term applying to ATM in South Africa and while in one sense *muthi* refers to herbalism and the use of herbal remedies is an expanding part of wellbeing and healthcare in Africa, it has broader application to traditional healing (Mbendana et al, 2019). The consumption of non-human animals is part of a long-held cultural belief and animal use is incorporated into *muthi* practices. Thus, in both TAM and ATM, 'non-human animal and plant material are ground up, dried or manufactured into plasters, pills or tablets' (Nurse and Wyatt, 2020: 114). The compounds produced can be considered to have direct medicinal properties such as 'the treatment of eczema, acne, scabbing, skin allergic reactions, and genital infection' as well as for use as cough syrup (Ngyuen and Roberts, 2020: 9). *Muthi* medicines derived from animals are also consumed for more generic and arguably spiritual properties, such as promoting 'strength' (both physical strength or overcoming fear), but also as love charms, and for either warding off bad luck (or bad spirits) and potentially improving one's luck (Williams and Whiting, 2016).

As part of TAM and ATM, the Faraday *muthi* market in Johannesburg, South Africa, is one in which tourists and locals go for animal-derived *muthi*. The focus of this chapter is on the smoking of vulture brains as a form of drug consumption linked to ATM practices. Traditional healers use or prescribe certain parts of vultures within their medicinal work, mainly the head and brains. Consumption of vulture-derived *muthi* is believed to have beneficial properties, specifically mind-opening capabilities, with the potential for users to develop clairvoyance. Vulture-derived *muthi* are also considered to be 'lucky' to consumers. Yet, consumption of endangered animal parts for TAM has been identified as a significant driver in wildlife trafficking globally and is arguably a cause in the decline of some species. As a result, a green criminological conception on such markets would argue for their strict control and an appropriate enforcement response (Nurse, 2015).

The Faraday market as a dark destination

The reality of the Faraday market is that legal sale of traditional medicines (for example, purely plant-based remedies) appears to operate alongside illegal uses. McKean et al identify that 'use of vultures is an important component of traditional medicine, particularly in South Africa and there is evidence to suggest that traditional use is at least partly responsible for the rapid decline of vulture populations in this country' (2013: 15). Their 2013 analysis estimated that between 106 and 240 vultures were traded per year in South Africa and suggested 40 vultures per year were traded specifically through the Faraday market (McKean et al, 2013: 24).

Selling poached vultures is illegal in South Africa, yet the protected bird is regularly found in markets despite its protection under the law. Thus, through purchasing vulture products and smoking or otherwise consuming vulture-derived *muthi*, consumers potentially contribute to the potential decline of vulture species and their continued illegal exploitation.

The reality of legal protection for vultures and potential penalties for illegal trade in vultures contextualises the Faraday market as an illegal wildlife market. Arguably 'the "ideal" wildlife victim is the critically endangered charismatic mega fauna, like the tiger, whereas other less appealing animals, such as the pangolin, are less "worthy" victims' (Wyatt, 2013: 59). Vultures are perceived as scavengers and fall outside of contemporary conceptions of charismatic megafauna and are thus largely ignored within contemporary discussions of necessary animal protection. Yet there is considerable conservation-based literature arguing for increased vulture protection and to address threats to vulture populations. The conservation and wildlife protection literature also identifies TAM and ATM as threats to vulture populations.

McKean (2004: 214) identifies that 'the trade in animal parts is secretive and mostly illegal in South Africa. This makes it extremely difficult to obtain reliable information on amounts and turnovers of species traded, which is essential to assess potential impact on species populations'. Morelli et al (2015) suggest that with the intensification of farming and modern sanitary restrictions, as well as the spread of human populations, there has been a radical decline in vulture populations throughout the world. Thus, while the popular conception of vultures may be one of a predatory carrion-eating species, akin to vermin, it is important to consider vultures as a potentially threatened species and one requiring protection under the law. Indeed, talk of an African vulture crisis has emerged within the conservation literature. In 2015, Ogada et al identified that '69% of vultures and condors are listed as threatened or near-threatened by the IUCN, the majority classed as Endangered or Critically Endangered' (2015: 89). Their analysis of the population status of eight vulture species in Africa concluded that 'of 95 national populations assessed, 85 (89%) were either nationally extinct or had experienced severe declines (>50%) or strong declines' (Ogada et al, 2015: 91).

Thus, the Faraday market is problematic as an underground market for vultures where illegal exploitation of vultures takes place and where the practice of vulture consumption takes place outside of mainstream tourism and medicinal practices.

Species justice and exploitation of nature

The exploitation of vultures falls within green criminological consideration of animal harm, which has been defined as follows:

> Animal harm is any unauthorized actor omission that violates national or international animal law whether anti-cruelty, conservation, animal protection, wildlife or general law that contains animal protection provisions (including the protection of animals as property) and is subject to either criminal prosecution and criminal sanctions, including cautioning and disposal by means other than a criminal trial or which provides for civil sanctions to redress the harm caused to the animal whether directly or indirectly. Animal harm may involve injury to or killing of animals, removal from the wild, possession or reducing into captivity, or the sale or exploitation of animals or products derived from animals. Animal harm also includes the causing of either physical or psychological distress. (Nurse, 2013: 57)

While on the face of it, consumption of parts or derivatives of animals might seem relatively benign, the definition of animal harm employed in green criminology identifies that exploitation of parts of dead animals is as much a concern as the exploitation and trafficking of live wildlife. This is especially the case where animals are killed for their use, such as the killing of rhinos for their horns, elephants for their ivory and, here, the killing and exploitation of vultures. Thus, the 'hidden' harms arising from vulture smoking are those of the ongoing killing of vultures for ATM use and exploitation. There is evidence of vultures being poisoned and the heads and feet then being sold for use in ATM, which tourists may not be aware of. Arguably, such continued use and exploitation also feeds into ongoing anthropocentric perspectives of wildlife as being primarily available for human exploitation. Green criminologists consider such views to be speciesist (Sollund, 2012) both in terms of failing to recognise the intrinsic value of wildlife and also reflecting a failure to recognise that man owes a responsibility to other species. In addition, vultures arguably provide an important ecosystem service where some studies have suggested that vultures can provide a key regulating service by disposing of up to 22.4 per cent of the organic waste annually produced in towns (Gangosa et al, 2013) as well as potentially being useful for locating dead livestock (Craig et al, 2018). Thus, the removal of vultures from the ecosystem has potential negative consequences for both human populations and non-human nature.

The Faraday *muthi* market also raises questions in respect of ethical tourism considerations. Local or indigenous beliefs around animal use may resist efforts to move practitioners and users to synthetic compounds rather than animal-based ones. But animal exploitation continues largely as a consequence of consumer demand and in other areas of animal exploitation, for example, zoos, safari parks and tourism more generally, efforts have been made to educate consumers to understand the reality and implications of their purchases (Fennell, 2011; Tablado and D'Amico, 2017). Where education fails, there is arguably a case for making the consumer activity the target of dedicated enforcement activity to reduce demand and discourage consumption.

Conclusion

The consumption of vultures for medicinal purposes represents a form of animal harm with the Faraday market being a form of dark destination situated within conceptions of tourism-based exploitation of wildlife. As this chapter identifies, vultures are protected by law in Southern Africa yet continue to be exploited within a medicinal context that considers such use of animals to be acceptable, despite the illegality involved. McKean et al (2013: 34–35) identify that continued use of vultures for traditional healing needs to be reduced, as do other negative pressures on the vulture populations in the region, if vultures are to be conserved in eastern South Africa. McKean et al (2013) argued for an intervention strategy that would reduce the consumption and demand for vultures in ATM and TAM practice through awareness raising, promoting the use of alternatives and improving the regulation of the trade. From a green criminological perspective, interventions targeted at consumers and that identify the problematic nature of visiting such markets to consume animal products should also be attempted to discourage vulture exploitation.

46

Dark tourism, ecocide and Alpine ski resorts: the Alps, Europe

Oliver Smith

University of Plymouth

Introduction

As much as 20 per cent of the world's tourist industry takes place in the world's mountainous regions, and ski tourism has proved itself to be a relatively rapid route to profitability. It generates tourist income, employment and, for some, a ready-packaged experience of natural wilderness that can be truly exhilarating. Mountain ecosystems conjure up evocative images of pristine mountain vistas, blue skies, clean air and uninterrupted tranquillity, imagery capitalised upon by resort operators and booking agents alongside connotations of health and wellbeing. However, Alpine ecosystems are fragile, and are adversely impacted by the proliferation of purpose-built ski resorts and the infrastructure that is necessary to support them. While resorts appear to adopt some of the tenets of sustainability, in reality, ski tourism is an industry predicated upon an exploitative relationship with nature against the backdrop of shortening ski seasons, less reliable snow cover and biodiversity loss which threatens irreversible damage to this fragile ecosystem.

Ecocide and Alpine ski resorts

It is the environmental impact of skiing, combined with the climate change-induced slow motion collapse of the industry, that warrants its inclusion in a collection oriented around the notion of dark tourism. A widely utilised definition of dark tourism includes a touristic fascination with death or mortality (Bathory, 2018). For me, this definition does not really go far enough. As we shall see through the course of the following pages, the ravaged landscapes of purpose-built ski resorts, the impacts of pollution generated by the need to service millions of visitors in Alpine luxury and the contribution to global heating suggest a tourism experience that encompasses an astonishing amount of violence. In this sense, ski tourism is not simply skirting on the periphery of death and misery, but monetises the exploitation of nature, while causing increasing amounts of harm as it seeks to stave off the effects of climate change through technological means that continue a spiral of destruction through contributing to climate change and pollution.

In essence, Alpine ski resorts should be viewed as sites of a legalised and socially permissible form of harm, that under a more environmentally oriented social order might be reclassified as a crime of ecocide. A decade ago, Polly Higgins introduced this term to explain 'the extensive damage, destruction to or loss of ecosystems of a given territory, whether by human agency or by other causes, to such an extent that peaceful enjoyment by the inhabitants of that territory has been severely diminished' (Higgins et al, 2013: 255). The impact of ski tourism as an industry, alongside the cumulative impacts of individual tourists, suggests that it is not unreasonable to equate the perpetuation and expansion of this industry as a form of ecocide. Ski tourism (as is the case with other forms of tourism) is largely reliant on the proliferation of cheap air travel, significantly reducing travel times to Alpine resorts for Europeans and beyond. Furthermore, research suggests that those who live closer to ski resorts are unwilling to trade the convenience and increased luggage space offered by their car for lower-carbon forms of transport (Wicker, 2018). Of course, carbon offsetting schemes are available to reduce the carbon footprint of a given trip, but aside from huge question marks around the efficacy of such schemes, there is reason to believe that there is little appetite among many travellers, convinced that they deserve their holiday regardless of its environmental impact, to stretch holiday budgets further by signing up to carbon offsetting options. Beyond the air travel component of the ski holiday, there is also a huge influx of traffic, as tourists vie to make their way up the mountain in a cavalcade of motor vehicles.

Furthermore, once tourists have reached their destination, they continue to consume energy and contribute pollutants at an alarming rate. This is not a closely guarded secret by any means – building the infrastructure of a ski resort is a logistical challenge, and one that bears economic and environmental costs. Demand for luxury within the ski tourism industry also exacerbates a range of existing harms. Consumer expectation from a resort is increasingly likely to include carbon-intensive experiences – saunas, swimming pools and shopping centres, as well as fine dining experiences on the summit of the slopes (Smith, 2019).

Mountain sports are intrinsically cumbersome – consider, for example, the bulk of equipment and clothing that must be stuffed into suitcases. Combined with the awkwardness of moving in ski or snowboard boots, these factors dictate the willingness of consumers to pay a premium for 'doorstep skiing'. This demand for accommodation right on the ski slope precipitates the development of ever higher altitudes for hotels, chalets and the infrastructure that supports them. Furthermore, the sport is closely linked to other wasteful forms of consumption. Ski tourism collides with fast fashion both on and off the slopes, as skiers compete to stay on trend. Consider for a moment the clothing associated with skiing. From base layers to the latest in hi-tech cold weather gear, we swaddle ourselves in man-made fibres which inevitably shed microfibres, becoming part of the global scourge of plastic waste (Napper and Thompson, 2016). Ski clothing is particularly susceptible to falling out of favour and being cast aside well before its useful life is finished – the velocity of fashion far outstrips functionality. While some of these items might find a new home in the second-hand clothing market, many will simply languish in the back of closets, or be discarded after only hours of use. A similar fate awaits much of the ski equipment – skis, snowboards, boots and bindings – that are integral to the sport, but not easily recyclable. The industry is driven by generating desire for incremental shifts in equipment design and technology, which consigns unrecyclable, bulky items to landfill.

A further consideration is the waste created in the development, operation and maintenance of Alpine ski resorts. In the second half of the 20th century, across the Alpine region, small farming communities were rapidly transformed into tourist centres (Denning, 2014). Aside from the rapid erosion and displacement of traditional ways of life and culture, this touristification has necessitated large building projects or infrastructure such as accommodation, car parks, leisure activities and so on. Such large expanses of concrete doubtless provide a number of challenges for water run-off, as well as environmental disruption. Architecturally, ski resorts tend towards the incongruous, brutal and functional in contrast with the majesty of the mountains they colonise. At best, they represent a clumsy attempt at what might pass for traditional Alpine living, resulting in a sense of hyperreality in which all remnants of authenticity are lost. This is an issue that is even more stark in many of the resorts in the US, which have been accused of a cynical Disneyfication of mountain wilderness as ski areas fall under the control of a decreasing number of corporations, who seek to provide customers with an increasingly homogenised experience.

The ski runs themselves are responsible for much of what we might consider ecocide. Heavy machinery flatten forests and carve out pistes, leaving indelible scars on the landscape, and disrupting unique fragile ecosystems (Rolando et al, 2007). The creation and maintenance of ski runs has been linked to the decline in numbers of several species of animal and birds. The soft silence of the snowscape is punctuated by the electric hum of ski lifts and cable cars, which cross the mountainside like sutures on a wound. These sounds, and the calamitous noise of skiers making their way down the mountainside, represent an invasion of the habitats of a range of small creatures adapted to living in the unforgiving winters but unprepared for the impact of skiers traversing the terrain (Thiel et al, 2008). Furthermore, the impact of global heating has begun to dictate an increasing reliance on snow-making machines for the majority of ski resorts. Obviously, a ski resort without snow is going to suffer on the bottom line, which generates a survival spiral of environmental destruction, regardless of any apparent commitment to sustainable practice. This is perhaps most clearly exemplified by the decision made by a resort in the Pyrenees recently to bring in snow by helicopter in order to save their ski season (Willsher, 2020). Snow-making machines offer a more practical solution for many resorts, but are dangerously inefficient, using huge amounts of water and energy, as well as posing a threat to human health (Lagriffoul et al, 2010). While it is not unreasonable to suggest that technological advancements will increase the efficiency of snow machines, the Jevons paradox dictates that the net effect is unlikely to be positive, as cheaper snow machines will mean that they will be used more frequently and adopted with more enthusiasm by resorts eager to offer optimum skiing conditions.

Conclusion

Mountain sports such as skiing and snowboarding are broadly viewed in positive terms. They generate income and create jobs, they bring people into contact with wilderness ecosystems that they might otherwise never experience and they promote a lifestyle of fitness and wellbeing. However, the rapid development of ski tourism as an industry has generated business models and normative practices that bring humans into direct conflict with nature. As this brief chapter has argued, the skiers flocking to Alpine regions in their numbers each season are contributing to a specific form of harm facilitated and propagated by the commodification of the natural environment. Without significant reorganisation, it is impossible to conceive of ski tourism as doing anything other than engaging in a protracted form of ecocide. In this sense, the tourists who engage in this form of terrorism are not simply voyeurs or consumers of crime and harm, but active participants in the destruction and degradation of a fragile and irreplaceable ecosystem.

47

Boho Zone: Middlesbrough, UK

Emma Winlow

Leeds Trinity University

Introduction

Middlesbrough is a large town in the northeast of England. It has not been a seat of government or a place of grand historical significance. Events in the town have for the most part failed to attract the interest of the global media's key gatekeepers, and the town has yet to make the steep climb to global recognition. But if we look into its quiet, unassuming nature and listen closely to the curious rhythms of its everyday life, we can move closer to an accurate understanding of the true England, an England oft discussed but barely understood by the politicians of Westminster or the opinion formers of the new mediascape, and scarcely considered by British social science's new generation of metropolitan radicals.

Middlesbrough is a relatively young town. In was, until midway through the 19th century, a rural backwater with only a tiny population. That population grew swiftly in the second half of the 19th century. The topography of the land adjoining the river Tees and its close proximity to major coal-producing sites made Middlesbrough an ideal location to build port facilities. Ancillary industries began to appear, and the town began slowly to grow.

In the first decades of the 20th century, Middlesbrough developed a reputation for the production of iron and steel. This reputation prompted huge numbers of British and Irish working-class men and women to migrate to Middlesbrough in search of work. These economic migrants contributed greatly to the town's character. For a short while, the town boomed. At its height, Dorman Long, a major producer of steel, employed over 20,000 workers and exported steel all over the world (Lloyd, 2013). Between the wars, the town also became a major producer of chemicals and petrochemicals. At its height, ICI employed tens of thousands of workers.

All of that ended as the town moved grudgingly into the second half of the 20th century. In many respects, Middlesbrough was a pioneer for British deindustrialisation. It began to shed industrial jobs sooner than its regional neighbours. The chemicals industry remained operative, but it was much reduced. The town's present character is deeply reflective of these changes. It remains a working-class town, but it has long been absent of massed working-class employment. It communicates a sense of absence and loss, and it is now more commonly associated with poverty than with industrial production.

Middlesbrough possesses some of the poorest neighbourhoods of the country, and signs of poverty, dereliction and an absence of care are everywhere. It has no major industries to speak of. As they age, many of the town's young people are faced with an ignominious decision: leave to find satisfying and remunerative work or stay and try to survive in a local economy with few worthwhile opportunities (Lloyd, 2019). Most social problems – intravenous drug use, addictions, violent crime, domestic abuse, involvement with the youth justice system, poor educational outcomes, child mortality and so on – are to be found in abundance in Middlesbrough (Telford and Lloyd, 2020).

Governments have, of course, attempted to address the gradually unfolding social crisis in Middlesbrough. These attempts have in every case been half-hearted and short-sighted, and all have failed. The unwillingness of the state to create meaningful, socially useful and sufficiently remunerated jobs in an area that so desperately needs them is not a topic I will linger upon here. However, it is certainly worth considering why successive governments came up with a diversity of ingenious but entirely ineffective strategies to reduce Middlesbrough's social problems, yet studiously ignored the importance of meaningful labour in the reconstitution of civil society. Middlesbrough has long needed real jobs, but governments have continually refused to acknowledge the state's ability to create them. Instead, governments have attempted to encourage corporations to create jobs by establishing an environment likely to create sustained high profits. Since the election of Thatcher in 1979, all governments and all three mainstream political parties have remained unerringly committed to the reductive cant of market ideology.

Walking around Middlesbrough city centre

The centre of Middlesbrough still boasts a small number of buildings that reflect the town's Victorian and Edwardian origins (Telford and Lloyd, 2020). However, it would be difficult to make the claim that the centre of the town is in any way attractive. Its main shopping thoroughfares have an undeniably drab and run-down aspect. Most big-name retailers have deserted the town. Charity shops, fast food outlets, bookmakers and pound shops are common. Many other storefronts remain vacant and boarded up. The town possesses a small number of covered market areas, but all of these areas seem rather down at heel in comparison to the high streets of nearby Newcastle or Durham. The conundrum of what to do with Britain's commercial high streets in an era of online shopping is at its most frustrating in Middlesbrough.

The town's best attempt at regeneration is the Middlesbrough Institute of Modern Art (MIMA). It is an impressive building, flanked by lawns, seating areas and water features. As a stand-alone contribution to the aesthetics of the town, it works remarkably well. However, it does not appear to attract many visitors, and nor does it employ many workers. Certainly, it has not spurred an urban renaissance. There are no signs that businesses capable of employing a large workforce will soon be encouraged to set up shop in its shadow.

The town is unusual in that some of its poorest postcodes are positioned quite centrally, close to the town's university and its most prestigious shopping streets. These areas have in recent years seen the arrival of high numbers of immigrants from around the world. Many small, terraced houses have been divided into bedsits and small flats. These neighbourhoods are now characterised by transience and a prevailing sense of absence and danger. They are no longer estates occupied by the old industrial working class and their descendants. As one might expect, a huge variety of social problems are to be found here. Antagonisms between various ethnic groups simmer constantly in the background (Lloyd et al, 2021).

As one walks from MIMA to the town's poorly served train station, boarded up retail space becomes more common. A major traffic overpass makes this edge of the town centre even less appealing. Many illicit markets, most notably in sex and drugs, are to be found nearby. On the other side of the train station are derelict buildings and disused sites of unknown province. Beyond these sites, one can see Middlesbrough's new Boho Zone.

The ghosts of Boho

The main buildings of the Boho Zone are so divorced from the surrounding environment that they look like they could have been dropped by a passing spaceship. They do not speak to the area, its inhabitants or its history. They make no attempt to either blend in with their surroundings or act as a pleasing counterpoint to the town's established and increasingly dilapidated ex-industrial aesthetic. The builds are rather odd-looking. They seem anxiously contemporary but possess no obvious character beyond that. One can imagine the architect of these buildings being encouraged to be ambitious. However, in their realisation, the buildings themselves seem cheap and ill-considered. They convey no obvious meaning beyond the rather contrived attempt to appear contemporary.

The Boho Zone was imagined as the site that would drive the town into the 21st century. The widely publicised goal of its planners was to establish Middlesbrough as a global centre for the creative and digital industries. Clearly, a huge amount of money has been poured into the development. It continues to grow, and its latest area incorporates housing units and numerous business-residential districts to cater for business start-ups and entrepreneurs keen to work from home.

Middlesbrough's Boho Zone seems to have been the brainchild of planners who paid far too much attention to the work of

Richard Florida (2004), widely acknowledged as a leading expert in economic redevelopment. Florida claimed that the best way to drive urban redevelopment in post-industrial areas is to make them a haven for the creative class. For Florida, the creative class is made up of tech workers, artists, musicians, and lesbians and gay men. These groups, he claimed, provide a high degree of economic value to an area. They are productive, innovative and aspirational. They foster an open, entrepreneurial and dynamic urban culture that attracts people and investment. As soon as a neighbourhood becomes associated with the creative class, property prices rise as it begins its transformation. Profitable investment opportunities open up. New businesses that cater for the creative class move in. In time, downwardly mobile post-industrial areas can be turned around by the new ethic of creativity, openness and innovation. Of course, as interest in the creative class advanced, competition to attract its core groups began to heat up. To be effective, any ambitious area must provide the creative class with everything its members need to be happy and successful.

That anyone with power could look at Middlesbrough's diverse problems only to conclude that what was needed was more art studios, tech spaces, tattoo parlours and coffee shops truly beggars belief. What the town needed – then as now – was real jobs: jobs that pay enough to raise a family, jobs that provide a degree of self-respect and jobs that have an obvious social function likely to garner the respect of others. Of course, given the supremacy of neoliberalism, it was impossible for governments to take this course. Instead, they ignored the reality of post-industrial Britain and desperately grabbed hold of Florida's faulty thesis on urban development. Inevitably, they failed, and post-industrial areas continued their descent.

There is no thriving multicultural, entrepreneurial, tech-savvy culture unfolding in Middlesbrough's Boho Zone. The tech companies that have been attracted to the area are small and entirely incapable of providing the forms of mass employment the town so clearly needs. Nothing of true social consequence is thriving in the Boho Zone. The area has a rather perverse post-social aspect (Winlow and Hall, 2012; 2019). There is no one around. There are no impromptu social interactions. Those lucky enough to have found work here do not spill into neighbouring pubs to make connections with like-minded others. They get in their cars and head home to the suburbs as quickly as they can. There are no microbreweries. No tattoo parlours, hairdressers' emporiums, trendy clothes shops or cupcakeries. The Boho Zone is still bordered by deeply depressing signs of post-industrial ruination. Genuine poverty and multifaceted social problems are close by. The progress trumpeted by the Boho Zones, marketeers is so small as to be insignificant.

Conclusion

Middlesbrough's Boho Zone is a dark destination because it reflects decades of economic retrenchment and the unrivalled supremacy of neoliberal ideology. It is a strangely anti-social place. In its attempt to speak of ambition and forward motion, it speaks only of alienation and indifference. It does not serve the local community. In truth, it makes no attempt to do so. Its existence is indicative of the refusal of successive neoliberal administrations to take on the real-world task of creating positive employment for the town's population.

I encourage you to visit Middlesbrough's Boho Zone. Walk to it from the train station. Think about the history of the town, and take a long, hard look at its population. As you do so, think about why the Boho Zone exists, who it benefits and why planners and bureaucrats came to the view that a tech park could drive the change that the area needs.

48

One Hyde Park: London, UK

Rowland Atkinson

University of Sheffield

Introduction

One Hyde Park is an imposing yet anonymous residential block in London's West End. Its four wings and predominantly glass façade stand opposite the Harvey Nichols department store, more or less a stone's throw from Harrods in Knightsbridge. The building comprises 86 apartments, four penthouses and sits on top of four further tiers of basement levels that include car parking, a 66 ft swimming pool, library and golf range. Developments like One Hyde Park have blossomed over the past two decades as the financialisation of the world economy and its general expansion, particularly in destabilised regions of the world, yielded a global cadre of the wealthy. If we could see through a lens capable of tracking global capital flows and massive personal gains (much of it ill-gotten or excessive), the block of One Hyde Park, and others like it, can be seen as a primary destination, for cash as much as for its highly secretive residents. Such developments are the dark lures of capital, helping to relieve wealthy clients of burdensome bags of cash, particularly where such holdings needed to be translated from criminal cash into prime real estate in order to reintegrate that money into the formal economy.

Negative destination

Why might we include a block of expensive apartments in a guide to dark tourism sites? The first answer to this question would be to say that we should reframe it. We can think of One Hyde Park as a tourist destination, but it is primarily to its owners and residents that we should look, rather than to those who might saunter round its perimeter. The owners of One's apartments are barely resident, with occupancy rates at around 10 per cent at any one time. This under-occupancy, here and in many other such blocks, has fed an imaginary of spectral presence and ghost urbanism that I have described in terms of the production of a kind of dead residential space, to feed the demands of capital – a kind of necrotecture (Atkinson, 2019). This consequence of tourist mobilities, by the rich and their capital, has been discussed by many considering the wider consequences of super-rich investment and its invitation to partial residence by elite developers, with many arguing that the city feels increasingly lifeless and damaged by the rise of many prime developments.

Around three quarters of One Hyde Park's apartments are owned through offshore finance and ownership vehicles. Thus, the general feel of the block is of a kind of dead or partial presence of capital and temporary use by bodies, temporarily sojourning in the capital before decamping to one of their several other homes or destinations in their social calendar. A view of One Hyde Park's residents as tourists fits with Bauman's idea of groups of super-mobile, choice-engaged affluent individuals against which he counterposed the insecurities, dangers and forced migration of vagabond others (Bauman, 1996). Assisted by starchitects and city planners, this place was intended as simply the most excessive and crowning achievement of design, architecture and symbolised alpha status of the wider city. Construction was also enabled by the abundant sovereign wealth of a Gulf state, whose gas reserves enabled the purchase of many prizes of London real estate holdings, and the construction of others, not least London's and Europe's tallest building, The Shard. This was an era in which the city appeared to delegate its promotion to the acts and investments of another nation as its own national accounts lay shattered after the global financial crisis of 2008. While many suffered, a new city was being born.

The second response to our question of 'why' relates to a more conventional view of crime and harm. In recent years, a series of kleptocrat tours have been conducted by investigative journalists to draw attention to a long list of properties that are connected to the tax avoidance, evasion and money laundering activities of many international, super-rich suspects and identified individuals. Playing with notions of visibility and concealment, such tours have drawn attention to a series of locations that directly or symbolically speak of a compact with circuits of dark, criminal capital, giving visibility and tangible evidence to what has otherwise appeared to be indetectable and unknowable. To visit One Hyde Park is, in this latter sense, to connect with the ambience of wealth, the allure of London as a space of entertainment, hyper-capital augmentation and to almost touch in fact the glittering social circuits of the world's super-rich as they discreetly enter and exit the building.

Ultra-prime black body

A black body in physics is an object that neither receives nor radiates light. Like such a body, One Hyde Park enables the tourist super-wealthy to be absorbed into the residential spaces they occupy while resting in transit, while also concealing the tastes and lifestyles of its occupants. One of the vital functions of such a built environment is thus to heavily restrict visibility. The building's few points of entry are guarded by special forces-trained staff to the front and, to the side, a deceptively open entry point to the car meeting point from which luxury vehicles are ingested into the building via the clever machinery of a specialist lift. This is a space that can be superficially viewed, but never entered or seen from within by more than perhaps a couple of hundred residents and their attendant staff.

Like many other prime and super-prime developments across London, now numbering in the low hundreds, One Hyde Park has become synonymous with the excesses and criminality that drive the real estate market of the city. We know that around £100 billion flows through the UK economy each year as a result of laundering, and that around £170 billion of UK real estate has been connected to offshore jurisdictions that help to permit tax avoidance and evasion. For London, the figure is £33 billion (though this figure now appears to be a huge underestimate). It is thus impossible to shake the increasingly evidenced association of London real estate to elite criminality and the wider series of harms associated with it (2021's Pandora papers, released by the International Consortium of Investigative Journalists, being perhaps the most critical). Here, the archipelago of ultra-prime developments, a kind of ultraland of excess and hyper-luxury, are marketed essentially as defensible spaces from which residents can sally forth in powerful cars and as their investments are carefully delegated to wealth managers in the City of London and to its offshore subsidiaries (Harrington, 2016).

Harm may not seem to be the immediate association of wealth for many. But if this is so, then imagination needs a little expansion. For one thing, it is clear that the excessive gains of the few rose spectacularly as many suffered in London, wracked by austerity and public cuts following the crash of 2008. London became a city that exemplified the socialisation of costs generated by failed financial institutions and the naked pursuit of public expenditure to fill the gap. On top of this social injustice, with the COVID-19 pandemic and the latest social and economic collapse of the city, the straining conditions of millions of Londoners have simply become even more evident, while also being connected more often in the public imagination to the gains and avoidance of public responsibility by the wealthy. This has meant that the hiding spaces and residential locations of the rich and their profound opulence have signalled the particular callousness of political elites overseeing yawning inequalities, particularly where it has proved wilfully neglectful of challenging flows of criminal capital that have generated thousands of luxury developments while doing so little to address profound housing need in the city.

What makes a visit to One Hyde Park and its neighbouring developments essential (such as The Knightsbridge, Claridges, The Bromptons, Park Lane Place) lies in the way that our capacity to see the relationship between global capital, spectacular development, the rich and the wider life of the ordinary city is enlightened. We begin to realise through closer observation how the social collapse of the city might barely register among those sheltering in the bunker apartments of 'One'. Their lives are carefully organised to avoid awkward questions or the need for uneasy answers, bolstered in this purpose by means of thick walls, protective staff, powerful cars and effective accountants.

Only a quarter of One Hyde Park's apartments are possessed by individuals, around 60 owned through companies which conceal the beneficial owner and help in the avoidance of tax. However, in the era of Panama, Paradise and Pandora papers, vast releases of tax and offshore ownership data, it seems that more questions will be asked, not least regarding the social and economic cost of this avoidance and evasion at a time of such profound social need. One Hyde Park is very much a part of this system. Not only do many of its residents seek anonymity and the use of offshore, tax-efficient sources of finance (the raison d'être of such facilities), but the physical infrastructure of this space is a kind of vital plug-in to the motherboard of super-affluent life. The avoidance, evasion and underlying criminality so deeply embedded in the global economy does not make sense without these physical points of relief, luxury and grounded experience.

To wander the streets around the development is not to be fully disappointed despite its hostility to outsiders. We will soon see supercars sliding across the temporarily lowered hydraulic barriers (offering the illusion of an open entrance), the glimpse of smartly dressed service staff and the occasional movement of lifts. What we are unlikely to see is the residents themselves. Better still, we might decamp to the lounge of the neighbouring Mandarin Oriental Hotel where spending double the usual cost of a coffee we are able to witness its rich social life, excited conversations and, nearby, tunnels and connecting doors to the apartment block it serves next door. We might then pass again the front of the building and examine the subtle sheen of the 15 different types of stone extracted from around the world and imagine what it might be like to be part of the social circuit of super-rich residents in apartments that are 20 times the size of the average London home. We can speculate on whether the rumours of bombproof and bulletproof glass are true and whether life at this level, including the purchase of the most expensive real estate in the world, is a happy one or whether such happiness comes at the cost of others.

Conclusion

The prime property market, usually taken as homes costing £5 million or more, has been largely immune to the storm of COVID-19 and was built during the storm of its predecessor, the global financial crisis. Political economists will not be surprised, observing not only the crisis tendencies of capitalism (even the virus being the product of a hungry and deregulated food sector) but the stability of its underlying architecture and ability to divert resource and good fortune to the rich and those linked to them in politics, commerce, finance and law. Money laundering makes up a large part of this economy and the dark side of a global economy fuelled by such finances sees vast flows emerging in tax havens, investments in property and financial instruments – all such avenues are lined with wealth managers keen to help rich clients avoid and evade tax burdens while new innovations like crypto suggest the further enabling of non-state actors circulating illicit funds. At the same time, the state, through its deregulations, scant spending on law enforcement over laundering and fraud, helps open the way to easy money for those states enabling these flows of money.

One Hyde Park has come to symbolise much of what has gone wrong in the core capital cities of the global economy. In physical terms, One Hyde Park is a statement collection of massive apartments as well as a visible sign of the accreting inequalities of the global economy and its manifold harms. This is another stop on a magical mystery city tour of what Oliver Bullough has called 'Moneyland' (2018), the spaces in which the global tax-evading elite stores and processes its cash. But the mirror half of Moneyland is the nosediving social and economic condition of the wider city and those beyond it. The taint of criminality or that of excessive wealth finds a kind of physical presence and form in these otherwise showpiece developments that are worth a little of our time to visit.

49

Amazon warehouse tours: Rugeley, UK or virtual tour

Adam Lynes

Birmingham City University

Introduction

As of 2022, the world's richest man and founder of Amazon, Jeff Bezos, is fervently working to propel himself from the already lofty heights of the exclusive and elite metropolitan clouds (Atkinson, 2014) and towards the stars. This endeavour is rather indicative of the type of character needed in order to ascend to the very top of the economic ladder – a person who sees no obstacle or barrier insurmountable in the quest to enjoy all life's pleasures and possible experiences, no matter the cost. In many ways, Bezos is the natural and inevitable result of the ever-pervasive and all-encompassing neoliberal philosophy that we exist within today.

Neoliberalism sees competition as the defining and most significant characteristic of human relations. It re-orientates individuals as consumers, whose democratic choices are best exercised by buying and selling, a process that rewards merit and punishes ineffectiveness (Monibot, 2016). It maintains that 'the market' delivers benefits that could never otherwise be achieved – especially by a state which takes a more proactive and regulatory role in its economy. Attempts to limit competition are treated as hostile to liberty. Tax and regulation should be minimised, and public services such as the prison sector or health service should be privatised. The organisation of labour and collective bargaining by trade unions are portrayed as market distortions that obstruct and hinder the development of a natural hierarchy of 'winners' and 'losers'. This, we can see, was one of the lasting legacies of Prime Minister Margaret Thatcher, who weakened the power of unions in the 1980s (Young, 1999). In one of neoliberalism's greatest trappings, inequality is reorganised and packaged as virtuous – a reward for utility and a generator of wealth.

Bezos is one of the most successful 'winners' of such a system, and the personification of the 'good life' promised to us if we adhere to the prevailing social and economic order in which consumerism is at its epicentre. To reiterate, Bezos is not an exception, but the norm when it comes to the prevailing ideology in which individuals from all echelons of society have the permission and the inclination to do what is needed in order 'to simply get things done [so that] that the competitive logic of business can be served' (Hall, 2015: 129). To demonstrate this deep-rooted belief system, Hall et al (2008) conducted interviews with individuals living within marginalised and economically abandoned locales – referred to as 'shadow-economies' – in order to determine the following:

> [They] believe wholeheartedly that the good life should be understood in terms of acquisition and conspicuous display of commodities and services that signified cultural achievement. … To be wealthy was to be happy. To be happy was to indulge, to buy, to squander, to be released from the normal restrictions of everyday life. (Hall et al, 2008: 48)

Bezos, despite his many successes, is still a part of this rigid and deaptive ideological order based on capitalist realism (Fisher, 2009), a negative ideological system in which no alternative to the current status quo can be imagined. So too, such an order casts away once positive belief systems based on community, morality, ethics and traditional commitments and responsibilities towards collective identity. Bezos' history and economic achievements are evidently indicative of these aforementioned values, with his planned space flight demonstrating the pinnacle of being 'released from the normal restrictions of everyday life' while simultaneously leaving humanity behind, including the approximately 197 million people who buy from Amazon (Dayton, 2021) and the 1.3 million workers (Soper, 2021) who have all invested money and labour into fulfilling his ultimate dream. Taking this into account, this chapter will provide an overview of the Amazon warehouse tours that, due to the COVID-19 pandemic, now take place virtually. It will also critically review the realities of working in such conditions, along with some wider discussions pertaining to the potential harms produced by one of the largest corporate giants that currently exists within the neoliberal landscape.

The Amazon virtual tour: a journey into late capitalism's 'heart of darkness'

The tour begins with a looming shot of one of Amazon's fulfilment centres, situated within a rural context and at odds with the otherwise rustic setting. This is then quickly followed by a montage of workers greeting the viewer wearing masks due to the COVID-19 pandemic. Despite this, though, they all smile as they welcome the viewer and reinforce the company ethos of unrivalled delivery times despite the current situation. After this montage, we are greeted by the first guide of the tour who explains that the fulfilment centre in Rugeley, England, is 750,000 square feet or the equivalent of ten football fields. As this information was being conveyed, the camera presented a sweeping view of the centre, filling the screen with countless individual rows lit by nearby bright lights and overshadowed only by the columns supporting the building.

When you place an order with Amazon, this is known as the first step in the 'outbound operations process', and one of hundreds of orange, rectangular robots that hold loading shelves will receive information of your order and select the correct 'pod' where your item is stowed before being picked up and moved to where the human worker is stationed. Despite this, though, the increased speed and efficiency of such technology has also resulted in increased targets for workers, who are 'allowed just a handful of seconds between each product task' (Del Rey, 2019) in order to keep up with their robotic co-workers. Let's take a closer look at what actually happens when we click on the colourful 'buy now' tab on the website or smartphone app. With the move to online shopping and apps, there is perhaps the false perception that the lack of immateriality on the side of the consumer is similar for the seller – thus creating a 'consumer-capitalist utopia' of quick and easy transactions. This is far from reality, as 'online encounters often exchange information or data with no material properties but this is frequently underpinned somewhere along the production cycle by some form of physical labour' (Scholz, 2017, cited in Lloyd, 2019: 56). One worker denotes that once you place your order, it will quickly join the 'mandated rate of 1,800 Amazon packages an hour – 30 per minute – that are sent through a chute and transported on a conveyor belt' (Sainato, 2020). These intense working conditions have even forced certain workers to urinate in bottles or sacrifice their bathroom breaks completely because fulfilment demands are increasingly too high, according to journalist James Bloodworth, who went undercover as an Amazon worker. Bloodworth's account of such conditions continues to paint a dire picture of such conditions, with workers stating that they were afraid of being disciplined for even the smallest breach from their prescribed activities designed to maximise efficiency, and potentially losing their jobs (Bloodworth, 2019). These accounts are only further compounded when we consider the quantitative data. A report from the worker rights online community *Organise* determined that 74 per cent of workers avoid using the toilet due to existing anxieties of being cautioned by their superiors that they had missed their target numbers (*Organise*, 2018: 3). So too, as more and more consumers seek to indulge in the 'good life' – now made easier than ever due to Amazon's practices – the accompanying rising targets and expectations have also significantly impacted workers' mental health, with 55 per cent of the participants reporting that they have suffered depression since working at Amazon (*Organise*, 2018: 3). So too, the increasing demands have resulted in 'backaches, knee pain, and other symptoms of constant strain [that] are common enough for Amazon to install painkiller vending machines in its warehouses' (Newton, 2020). Deaths in such conditions have also been reported, with the National Council for Occupational Safety and Health's report (2019: 12) citing six North American

Amazon worker deaths between November 2018 and April 2019. In one incident, where a man died after suffering a heart attack, workers were 'forced to go back to work [and] basically watch a man pass away and then get told to go back to work [and] act like it's fine' (Sainato, 2019).

Containers holding your order(s) are then placed on a conveyor belt and sent to the multi-pack area and this process is known as the 'flow'. The tour guide then introduces the 'flow room', which resembles a security and closed-circuit television room, with employees keeping a watchful eye in order to ensure that 'everybody's delivery is leaving on time'. The room also has engineers keeping an eye on the '16 miles' of conveyor belts in order to ensure there are no technical issues slowing down the flow of items. There were monitors displaying graphs, flow charts, conveyor belts and human workers – ensuring that every possible element is accounted for and monitored. Amazon has not been shy in the developments of monitoring staff to maximise efficiency and the flow of items. For example, it was reported that the company had been granted patents for a wristband that not only tracked employees' locations in the centre, but could also monitor their hand movements, producing a vibration to alert them when they were reaching for the wrong item. In the filing, Amazon defines it as being able to 'monitor performance of the placing of the incoming inventory item into the identified storage location by the inventory system worker' (cited in Saner, 2018). Referring back to Bloodworth (2019), it was noted that each time he picked up an item, there would be a countdown timer which would measure his productivity. Bloodworth further stated that supervisors would tell people how productive they were being, and that he was warned he was in the bottom 10 per cent. 'You were also sent admonishments through the device saying you need to get your productivity up. You're constantly tracked and rated' (cited in Saner, 2018). Such forms of invasive monitoring further infringe on the independence of the worker and continue the theme of blurring the boundaries between automated robots and supposedly autonomous humans.

The next stage is known as the 'pack' stage, in which a worker is seemingly assigned to either single or multiple packing of items. It is here where more subtle forms of technology are presented, with a simple scan of the item informing the worker of the right size box needed, along with the exact length of tape required to seal the parcel so as not to 'waste anything'. This diligent and eco-conscious approach to packing items is in stark contrast to recent reports. Here we will return to deviant leisure and the concept of *environmental harms* that consist of those ecological damages caused in the pursuit of leisure activities including, for instance, the rising levels of waste on beaches (Smith, 2016). We have to accept that, for many consumers, Amazon is a central source for the engagement of leisure practices and, as such, we need to recognise the central role of the consumer in the following discussion. While Amazon is keen to let the public know of its move to recyclable energy sources (Amazon, 2022), it was reported that the company destroys millions of stock every year at warehouses. Specifically, undercover filming from inside Amazon's Dunfermline warehouse in the UK exposed the sheer scale of the waste with 'smart TVs, laptops, drones, hairdryers, top of the range headphones, computer drives, books galore, thousands of sealed face masks – all sorted into boxes marked "destroy"' (Pallot, 2021). So too, in order to ensure that the company keeps to its delivery promises and with the advent of Amazon Prime, the environmental impact continues outside of the fulfilment centres. In September 2019, after almost a year of pressure from rank-and-file employees, Amazon finally released a report detailing the company's impact on the environment. In 2018, it emitted '44.4 million metric tons of carbon dioxide equivalents into the atmosphere – roughly equal to the annual emissions of Norway' (Reynolds, 2020). Despite the company pledging to address some of these environmental harms, Amazon Web Services still actively engages with the oil and gas industry, marketing itself as a way to 'squeeze more margin out of an industry that – in its current form – is incompatible with fixing the climate crisis' (Reynolds, 2020). This is indeed a significant departure from the 'not waste anything' attitude displayed in the virtual tour. It is vital that we, as consumers, do not take such company pledges regarding the environment at face value, and continue to critically interrogate any future 'pledges'.

Once the package is ready, it is then sent to the next stage, referred to as the 'slam' phase. 'Slam' is, according to the guide, an acronym for 'scan, label, apply, and manifest'. From what was shown on the tour, this is a mechanised process with machinery completing this process and the guide marvels at how 'this whole process [happens] without stopping the parcel, so the label is applied straight away and it continues and generates within a matter of seconds the next label'. Within this context, humans are evidently becoming more and more obsolete. One of the ways, according to Dastin (2019), that Amazon avoids the bad publicity of replacing humans with more automated machinery is focusing on the methodical erosion of the workforce rather than directly firing people:

> A key to its goal of a leaner workforce is attrition, one of the sources said. Rather than lay off workers, the person said, the world's largest online retailer will one day refrain from refilling packing roles. Those have high turnover because boxing multiple orders per minute over 10 hours is taxing work. (Dastin, 2019)

The next step is referred to as the 'ship' stage, where parcels are sent down chutes to the correct 'distribution centre', and human workers then place them into delivery vehicles with the use of pallets and carts. The realities of working as an Amazon delivery driver have been well documented (see BBC, 2016b; Carter and Kitching, 2019) with serious questions having been raised given that Amazon drivers have been arrested and charged with vehicular homicide (Lynes et al, 2021). While such a charge may appear, at first glance, as justifiable, it is important to consider how the move to a gig economy is increasing workloads while simultaneously slowly removing corporate responsibility. For instance, an undercover investigation by the BBC into conditions as an Amazon delivery driver shows that those working for one of the many agencies supplying Amazon with drivers can earn less than the minimum wage and face significant levels of stress in getting their deliveries done in time (BBC, 2016b). It also found incidents of drivers speeding to meet their deadlines and even drivers going to the toilet in their vans simply because they were pressured to get their deliveries done in the time expected (BBC, 2016b). So too, drivers routinely did 11-hour shifts and were expected to be available at least six days a week. The undercover reporter was also paid the equivalent actual pay of £2.59 per hour in his first week and £4.76 in his second (Morrell, 2016). Since 2016, there have been numerous injuries caused by workers within the courier service sector, and the general response from corporations is one of ambiguity. Specifically, Amazon stresses that such drivers are contracted via external agencies, and thus not reflective of their working practices. In essence, such companies are more than happy to generate such harmful working conditions in order to ensure delivery, but once someone is actually hurt or even killed by such conditions, it is no longer their responsibility. Such discussion pertaining to the working conditions of such jobs are omitted entirely from both Amazon's response and the mainstream media, and such issues need to be addressed in order to prevent such injuries and deaths occurring in the future.

We are now at the end of the tour, and are thanked for attending in the form of another montage of workers from around the globe and some rather jovial dancing and a wave goodbye. The general tone of the tour was one of marvel and celebration for the technical successes of such warehouses, with workers and the guides being in high spirits and working in perfect harmony with their robot counterparts. Returning to the central theme of tourism, such a virtual excursion into Amazon's warehouses serves important functions. First, this tour further removes the consumer from the realities of their purchasing actions. We already fetishistically disavow (Žižek, 2010) the various harms such practices and lifestyle causes, which is only further compounded given the legal status of many such activities and the streamlined, accelerated and immateriality of such apps (Lloyd, 2019). This tour, in many ways, is corporate public relations designed to soothe any discontents or concerns the consumer may have, and as you leave the tour, you no longer have to consider the harms faced by Amazon workers or the documented ecological devastation caused by your spending habits. Here, we must dig beneath these outward performances of happiness, and consider the importance of the 'aesthetic' being displayed to the viewer designed to obfuscate the realities of such places of work. As noted by Lloyd (2019), the significance of the aesthetic is supplemented by the use of expressive and sentimental labour within the workplace. Lloyd draws upon the work of Hochschild (2003), who describes how 'employees must draw on their personality, communicative skills and emotion to put the customer at ease and induce them into parting with their money' (p 70). Not only are the emotional forms of labour displayed in the tour designed to manage the feelings and expressions of the workforce, but also a tool in order to suppress the actualities of such conditions – further removing autonomy and freedom of expression from such people. So too, such displays of emotion allow the consumer or, in this case, digital tourist to continue to live in the blissful fetishistic disavowal of how their purchasing decisions continue to facilitate the myriad of harms previously outlined. Alongside this, the consumer's disavowal – now reinforced by such tours – further enables Bezos' sense of entitlement as we continue to give him permission and the inclination to do what is needed in order 'to simply get things done [so that] that the competitive logic of business can be served' (Hall, 2015: 129).

Conclusion

In bringing this chapter to a close, it is evident that not all is well in the land of 'corporate giants'. Behind the smiles and seemingly passionate and energetic workforce displayed in the virtual tour of one of Amazon's fulfilment centres lies a myriad of harms that are now deeply embedded in the normal status quo of late capitalism's 'gig economy' and consumer culture. In returning to Jeff Bezos' planned flight into space, it has become clear that the humans who work for his company are almost indistinguishable from the machinery that will be working to propel him to the stars. Such people, by the systems imposed on them in order to maximise efficiency, have, in many ways, been stripped of their autonomy and thus humanity, and are simply another cog in the machine designed to ensure that he can fulfil his dreams of the 'good life' in the most extreme ways possible. When Bezos finally reaches his goal and looks back at the pale blue dot we call Earth (Sagan, 1994), he will likely gaze at its beauty and reflect upon how he built such a powerful and profitable business. He will likely give little thought to the thousands of people that continually face a myriad of harms on a daily basis in order to fuel his lifestyle and next grand adventure beyond the limits most of us can only dream of. As the global capitalist system is approaching an apocalyptic zero point (Žižek, 2010), with humanity facing a number of existential threats to our very way of life, it is rather fitting that Bezos and other members of the economic elite are seeking to abandon the very dystopia that they have helped to accelerate in their own pursuit of pleasure.

50

Disney World: Orlando, Florida, USA

Anthony Lloyd

Teesside University

Introduction

Disney is one of the most successful and identifiable brands in the world (Knight, 2014). The Disney Corporation employs over 200,000 people worldwide and, as of May 2021, had reported sales of over $60 billion (Forbes, 2021). Since its earliest days of animated films, through to its global media empire today, Disney has become a corporate juggernaut (Mann and Budworth, 2018). Its resorts – situated in California, Florida, Paris, Tokyo, Hong Kong and China – represent some of the most sought-after tourist destinations in the world. According to the Themed Entertainment Association (2020), over 155 million people attended Disney theme parks worldwide in 2019. These parks constitute hotels, golf courses, theme parks, rides, parades, characters and restaurants, and represent an immersive experience that seeks to suspend reality and provide a fantasy experience built on cultural romanticism, nostalgia and consumption (Giroux and Pollock, 2010). Literally dubbed 'the most magical place on Earth', how can Disney's theme parks appear in a volume dedicated to sites of dark tourism? Strictly speaking, they do not represent 'dark tourist' destinations in the true sense of the definition but the magic of Disney rests on a set of neoliberal employment relations that may be considered dark. Here, we focus specifically upon Disney's theme parks; in the interests of full disclosure, the author has visited Disney World Florida as both a child and adult. The first section will consider the image conjured by Disney World and the second will consider the employment conditions which underpin the construction of the happiest place on Earth.

The happiest place on Earth

Disneyland Park opened in 1955 on a 160-acre site in Anaheim, California. Walt Disney World Resort is a 25,000-acre site near Orlando, Florida that opened in 1971 and now hosts six theme parks and 18 resorts (Mann and Budworth, 2018). Baudrillard (1981) famously suggested that Disneyland exists to (falsely) convince us that the rest of America is real. Disney's theme parks present an innocent, childlike, idyllic reminder of what it refers to as a 'timeless' past but Perlin (2011) perceptively notes that the Magic Kingdom's Main Street USA evokes 1950s suburban America while other zones hark back to the rugged individualism of the American frontier and the technologically inspired, space-driven future. Upon visiting the parks, it is hard not to be drawn into the 'magic', the symbolic fiction created in Disney World. Disney's film and television archive creates a rich back catalogue of characters, themes, rides and experiences that pull you in. Given the nature of this collection, how can any of this be dark? Granted, the 'magic' provides a fantasy illusion that masks the real; Disney wants guests to have fun and immerse themselves in the nostalgia, innocence and world of make-believe but they also want your dollars and the parks create a captive audience where admission, food, drinks, merchandise and photographs all come at a price. In Lacanian terms, Disney's genius lies in its understanding of lack and desire; the consuming subject is constantly in search of fulfilment and Disney provides experiences and objects designed to temporarily slake that thirst. On a deeper level, the use of nostalgia and childhood innocence provides a powerful psychological draw that allows us to forget life's pressures and worries and soak up the simulated experience of a less complicated time.

Millions of people flock to the parks every year and, crucially for this chapter, Disney is one of the most sought-after employment and internship opportunities in the world. The immersive fantasy of Disney World requires significant investment from its employees who are tasked with providing a seamless experience and avoiding any jarring interruption or encounter with 'reality'. Many will be aware of the lengths that Disney goes to in training its employees to provide the ultimate customer experience. All new starters go to 'Disney University' for training in how to 'perform' their role in ways that maximises the guests' experience. Knight (2014: 17) explains the process:

> The 'Traditions' class provides orientation, and training on how to 'create happiness' via 'emotion management'. Trainees also learn Disney Speak: park employees are 'cast members', Disney customers are 'guests', and an accident is an 'incident'. Disney Speak also emphasises the theatrical nature of the themed experience: a uniform is a 'costume', working is to be 'on stage', and a ride is an 'Adventure'. Cast Members, handpicked and groomed for the 'Disney look', are predictably alike: clean-cut and pleasant. (As one Disney park official simply stated, 'We require conformity'.) Applicants with less experience are actually preferred, as they can be trained from the start in the Disney way. For example, Cast Members are never to sit on the job, point with a single finger (they must use two or the entire hand), break character, or in any way compromise the Disney magic. The goal is to provide service-oriented entertainment via teamwork in an environment where the Guests are always right and their expectations are continually exceeded. By spoiling its customers, the company primes them to 'reflexively buy Disney products'. Despite its restrictive requirements, the company remains a sought-after employer.

Although Disney has recently loosened its policy on conformity, it uses the language of performance and guest experience to strip away identity and individuality from workers (Giroux and Pollock, 2010). This extends to the requirement that no two cast members share the same name. While the 'character' cast members dress as Ariel or Mickey Mouse and essentially perform that role, less obvious cast members must also play a part by responding to fictional names at work. The customer is placed at the forefront of Disney's business model which extends to the deliberate obscuring of labour. The parks' subterranean network of tunnels and hidden entrances mask the reality of labour behind the customer experience. When work is not overtly 'performed' in front of guests, it is hidden to maintain the fantasy experience (Giroux and Pollock, 2010). This epitomises Hochschild's (2003) 'emotional labour' and is an extreme representation of standard practice across the service sector (Lloyd, 2018). This customer-first approach and high level of employee commitment has made Disney the envy of business management and HRM departments across the world (Knight, 2014). However, the 'conditions of employment' that underpin this success engender another, darker way in which Disney is an exemplar: it utilises low-paid, insecure and temporary forms of labour to manage its operations and employs control and surveillance to discipline its workforce in ways that could be characterised as harmful.

Hi ho, hi ho, it's off to work we go ...

Prior to the COVID-19 pandemic, Disneyland employed approximately 30,000 workers while Disney World employed 74,000 workers, making it the largest single site employer in the United States. During the pandemic, Disney laid off 28,000 of its 200,000 workforce across all sites, 67 per cent of whom were part-time workers (Whitten, 2020). In Florida, Disney World generates approximately \$16 billion in revenue with \$4,709 million, 47 per cent of its operating expenditure, dedicated to labour costs (Mann and Budworth, 2018). It makes business sense to control and reduce labour costs as much as possible. To do this, Disney deploys a two-tier workforce and has a history dating back to the 1940s of fighting this workforce over pay and representation.

Employment in neoliberal labour markets has been characterised by low pay, precarious or insecure work, underemployment and a growing gap between the rich and poor (Standing, 2011; Lloyd, 2018). Disney CEO Robert Iger earned \$47 million in 2019 while a 2017 survey of 5,000 park employees at Disneyland in

California revealed that three quarters of his staff did not earn enough money to cover basic monthly expenses (Dreier et al, 2018). When a night janitor at Disneyland, Yeweinishet Mesfin, was found dead in her car in 2016, it was later revealed that she had lived in her vehicle for seven years, despite working six days a week for Disney (Walker, 2018). The employee survey revealed a set of shocking conditions:

- More than two thirds (68 per cent) of Disneyland Resort workers are food insecure.
- More than one in ten Disneyland Resort workers reported being homeless in the previous two years.
- Over half of Disneyland Resort workers worried about being evicted from their homes.
- Among Disneyland Resort employees with children who pay for child care, 80 per cent say they cannot make ends meet at the end of the month, 79 per cent are food insecure and 25 per cent say that they are unlikely to be able to pay for housing that month.

After stiff opposition and negative publicity, Disney offered its US employees a tiered pay structure that increased to $15 an hour by 2021. Of course, the COVID-19 pandemic subsequently resulted in furlough and mass lay-offs so the benefits of this pay deal are hard to measure. However, full-time hours at $15 an hour net $31,000 a year before tax. In Florida, the average wage in 2020 was approximately $61,000 (Bureau of Labor Statistics, 2021a) and in Los Angeles-Anaheim, it was approximately $62,400 (Bureau of Labor Statistics, 2021b). By all objective measures, Disney significantly underpays its employees.

Disney's two-tier employment system supplements its permanent staff, already hierarchised by job role and status (van Maanen, 1999), with an army of paid interns (Perlin, 2011). Disney 'recruits' work experience interns from universities around the world at $11 an hour. Perlin's (2011) account of these internships is revealing: students arrive to gain experience and college credits but essentially represent low-paid, temporary labour who willingly devote themselves to Disney for between four and six months. They live on-site and are charged rent, currently between $175 and $235 per week. Interns also pay a programme fee of $415 just to join the scheme (Disney Programs, 2021). Perlin (2011) notes that interns have become an increasingly sizeable portion of the workforce which leads to issues around experience and skill, particularly in terms of technical roles such as ride operators and safety, which ultimately impact on guest experience.

Disney also manages its workforce through a strict regime of control and surveillance (Bryman, 2004). This is another key feature of the harms of work under contemporary labour markets: work routines are scripted, planned and managed in ways that reduce worker autonomy and are underpinned by the belief that someone is watching and ready to reprimand for any infringement. Van Maanen (1999) noted that cast members felt supervisors were trying to catch them out rather than supporting and any evidence of infraction is severely punished (Perlin, 2011). This occurs in workplaces across the world, particularly in customer-facing roles (Lloyd, 2013; 2018) but most workplaces do not make claims to be the happiest place on Earth. There is an absence of stability, security and control that can be characterised as harmful, if we consider social harm to be the barriers and impediments to human flourishing and the idea of a 'good' life (Lloyd, 2018; Raymen, 2019). The commitment employees bring to ensuring guests experience the magic is not reciprocated by an employer who underpays, controls, monitors and exploits a precarious and insecure workforce.

Conclusion

Disney World represents an immersive consumer experience unlike any other. It is hard not to be taken in by the innocence and nostalgic fantasy created in its parks and resorts. In some respects, that is testament to the physical and emotional labour enacted by an army of low-paid and insecure cast members, many of whom look past the absence of stability, security and the potential harms of work and invest heavily in their employer as a place of dream making and magic. However, upon closer inspection, Disney's fantasy is built on precarious labour, micromanagement, control and surveillance. The fantasy is incredibly powerful as cast members are often evangelical about their role; 'insider' accounts such as Wesley Jones' (2010) *Mousecatraz* balance the negatives of the Disney College Program with glowing endorsement. The troubling reality of their exploitation is disavowed (Hall and Winlow, 2015) to the fantasy Disney creates. Consumer dreams are created through a tightly controlled work process whereby employees are scripted, shaped and monitored to ensure they do exactly as instructed, with inadequate remuneration for perfection and severe consequences for mistakes. While not strictly a 'dark tourist' site, the magic of Disney's theme parks rests upon a dark and harmful set of employment relations, even if its 'cast members' often fail to recognise that reality.

Conclusion

Adam Lynes, Craig Kelly and James Treadwell

As Jack Denham notes in Chapter 37, the sharing of online content does not immediately strike one as a form of dark tourism. The COVID-19 pandemic, however, changed the way in which we travel and consume space and place, perhaps forever. Conventional notions centred upon ideas of physical space. So too, conventional readings have concentrated upon destinations that are overtly *dark*.

This collection has aimed to challenge such a view, to recognise that as the world around us has changed, it is crucial for academic circles to recognise that the world which we move through is no longer analogue. So too, the *dark* side of tourism is no longer confined to traditional understandings of violence. Within the contemporary context, space and place transitions between the physical placement and virtual presence. The traditional, physical being is transcended. Beamed around the world through television screens, computer monitors and, most commonly, mobile phones. As such, the influence upon culture can be stark, far reaching and, in some cases, such as the suicide forest, deadly.

By utilising the deviant leisure framework that recognises the hidden, disparate and often abstract notions of harm to transform the criminological perspective of dark tourism, this book has intended to take the reader on a journey that reflects the complex nature of contemporary consumer culture and the changing world around us. In doing so, this collection has moved from the overt forms of dark tourism such as crime museums, serial killer tours and sites of execution to the increasingly opaque tourist attractions that often act as facilitators of the wider harms of consumption. Such sites include the exclusive zones of capital cities such as London, tours of Amazon warehouses and theme parks underpinned by the perpetuation of an impoverished workforce with which we end the collection. It is our perspective that the harms such sites embody are so normalised, they are too propellants of the more obvious forms of dark tourism. In an ever more glocal world, the markets of Tunis, stolen antiquities of Nepal, the corruption of beautiful coastal towns such as Scilla and the rich and powerful of One Hyde Park are intertwined with the wider culture of consumption worldwide. They do not exist within a vacuum and are not always obvious. As Mezhyhirya Residence Museum demonstrates, corruption and capital can change nations.

A reflexive approach in which these sites of global capitalism are examined within the wider spectrum of dark tourism allows a more holistic perspective to be garnered and conceptualised. So too, we can begin to observe the contours of the journey within specific threads within the collection. For example, we can trace the development of imprisonment alongside the development of consumer capitalism. From the lynchings in the United States to the asylums of Europe, we see the transition to mass incarceration. Alongside this, with the arrival of social media sites such as Instagram, we see the transition from prison museums to prison hotels and restaurants. In the simplest terms, sites of human suffering are commodified, often culminating as an orchestrated digital image posted to garner likes and attention. Such normalised forms of representation and overt consumerism disavow the harms of such sites that have often been sites of genocide and humanity's darkest hours.

The depravity of humanity is laid bare within the collection. Questions are raised as to why we take our children to sites of human suffering and extreme violence such as museums of war, disavowing the realities of such conflicts. So too, we turn off the latest serial killer documentaries to visit museums that glorify such horrific acts, often pausing at the counter and wondering if the Ted Bundy t-shirt is being purchased in poor taste. Here, we offer the utility of graze theory to understand such actions. Put simply, in our aversion to confront the real horrors of the world around us, we seek comfort in the overt acts that we can easily understand. We are comfortable drinking ourselves into oblivion on the sun-kissed beaches of Majorca or sniffing copious amounts of cocaine in Hong Kong to escape the ever-present anxiety of contemporary life. Reflecting upon the environmental damage of the drugs trade found within the malls of Kentucky is much less comfortable though. It is easy to judge those who spend their short and sparse moments of annual leave at sites of death and destruction, but not so easy to judge ourselves when confronted with the harms of the upcoming skiing holiday.

References

9/11 Memorial (2021) *Museum Admission*, available at https://www.911memorial.org/visit/visit-museum-1, accessed 29 November 2021.

Aalbers, M. and Sabat, M. (2012) Re-making a landscape of prostitution: The Amsterdam Red Light District, *City*, 16(1–2), 112–128.

Abraham, N. and Torok, M. (1972) Mourning the melancholia: Introjection versus incorporation. In N.T. Rand (ed) *The Shell and the Kernel*. London: University of Chicago Press, pp 125–138.

Abt, T. (2019) *Bleeding Out: The Devastating Consequences of Urban Violence—And a Bold New Plan for Peace in the Streets*. New York: Basic Books.

ACLU (2020) The saga of the Scottsboro boys, 27 July, available at www.aclu.org/issues/racial-justice/saga-scottsboro-boys, accessed 18 August 2021.

ACMD (2010) *Consideration of the Anabolic Steroids*. London: Home Office.

Adams, J. (2001) 'The wildest show in the south': Tourism and incarceration at Angola, *Drama Review*, 45(2), 94–108.

Adams, W.M. (2004) *Against Extinction*. London: Earthscan.

Adhikhari, D. (2021) Hunting for Nepal's stolen gods, *NIKKEI Asia*, 1 September, available at https://asia.nikkei.com/Life-Arts/Arts/Hunting-for-Nepal-s-stolen-idols, accessed 2 September 2021.

Adorno, T. (2002) *The Culture Industry*. London: SAGE.

Advocates for Human Rights (2010) *United States Universal Periodic Review Stakeholder Report*. Minneapolis: Advocates for Human Rights.

AFP (2016) Napoleon's pillaged works of art on show in Rome, *Shanghai Daily*, 17 December, available at https://web.archive.org/web/20170119180609/http://www.shanghaidaily.com/world/Napoleons-pillaged-works-of-art-on-show-in-Rome/shdaily.shtml, accessed 20 July 2021.

Agamben, G. (1995) *Homo Sacer: Sovereign Power and Bare Life*. Stanford: Stanford University Press.

Ahram Online (2020) Around 50,000 tourists visited Sharm El-Sheikh, Hurghada since 1 July: Tourism minister, *Ahram Online*, 6 August, available at https://english.ahram.org.eg/NewsContent/3/12/376059/Business/Economy/Around--,-tourists-visited-Sharm-ElSheikh,-Hurghad.aspx, accessed 6 April 2021.

Ainge Roy, E. (2016) Former Pitcairn mayor found guilty over child sex abuse images, *The Guardian*, 7 March.

Ajlouny, J. (2018) *Adventures in Leninland: An Intrepid Journalist's Quest to Understand a Place Once Called the Soviet Union*. Guntersville: Fresh Ink Group.

Al-Ansi, A., Lee, J., King, B. and Han, H. (2021) Stolen history: Community concern towards looting of cultural heritage and its tourism implications, *Tourism Management*, 87. DOI: 101.1016/j.tourman.2021.104349

Alexeyeff, K. and Taylor, J. (eds) (2016) *Touring Pacific Cultures*. Australia: ANU Press.

Allaste, A. and Lagerspetz, M. (2002) Recreational drug use in Estonia: The context of club culture, *Contemporary Drug Problems*, 29(1), 183–200.

Amazon (2022) Amazon extends position as world's largest corporate buyer of renewable energy, 20 April, available at https://www.aboutamazon.com/news/sustainability/amazon-extends-position-as-worlds-largest-corporate-buyer-of-renewable-energy, accessed 5 October 2022.

Amnesty International (2016a) Qatar: Abuse of World Cup workers exposed, available at https://www.amnesty.org/en/latest/news/2016/03/abuse-of-world-cup-workers-exposed/, accessed 1 November 2021.

Amnesty International (2016b) *This is What We Die For: Human Rights Abuses in the DRC Power the Global Trade in Cobalt*. London: Amnesty International.

Amnesty International (2022a) Qatar World Cup of shame, available at https://www.amnesty.org/en/latest/campaigns/2016/03/qatar-world-cup-of-shame/, accessed 9 June 2022.

Amnesty International (2022b) Qatar, available at https://www.amnesty.org/en/location/middle-east-and-north-africa/qatar/report-qatar/#:~:text=QATAR%202021,discrimination%20in%20law%20and%20practice, accessed 9 June 2022.

Amsterdam Guide (2018a) How to find ladyboys, shemales and transvestites in the Red Light District, *Amsterdam Guide*, available at https://guide.amsterdamescape.com/how-to-find-ladyboys-shemales-and-transvestites-in-the-red-light-district/, accessed 27 May 2021.

Amsterdam Guide (2018b) How to avoid accidently sleeping with a man in Amsterdam's Red Light District, *Amsterdam Guide*, available at https://guide.amsterdamescape.com/how-to-avoid-accidentally-sleeping-with-a-man-in-amsterdams-red-light-district/, accessed 27 May 2021.

Andersen, T.S., Scott, D.A.I., Boehme, H.M., King, S. and Mikell, T. (2020) What matters to formerly incarcerated men? Looking beyond recidivism as a means of successful reintegration, *The Prison Journal*, 100(4), 488–509.

ANSA (2016) Arte Ritrovata showcases recovered art, *ANSA*, 8 June, available at https://web.archive.org/web/20160609094448/http://www.ansa.it/english/news/lifestyle/arts/2016/06/08/arte-ritrovata-showcases-recovered-art_5b9db7df-e0a9-4f5f-b03a-d96074352c7a.html, accessed 20 July 2021.

Araújo, V. (2021) Mortes no Jacarezinho: cenário de violência marcou comunidade após operação policial, *O Globo*, available at https://oglobo.globo.com/rio/mortes-no-jacarezinho-cenario-de-violencia-marcou-comunidade-apos-operacao-policial-1-25010264, accessed 11 May 2021.

Arendt, H. (1963) *Eichmann in Jerusalem: A Report on the Banality of Evil*. New York: Viking Press.

Arford, T. (2017) Touring operational carceral facilities as a pedagogical tool: An ethical inquiry. In J. Wilson, S. Hodgkinson, J. Piché and K. Walby (eds) *The Palgrave Handbook of Prison Tourism*. London: Macmillan, pp 925–45.

Arias, E. and Rodrigues, C. (2006) The myth of personal security: Criminal gangs, dispute resolution, and identity in Rio de Janeiro's favelas, *Latin American Politics and Society*, 48(4), 53–81.

Ashforth, A. (2005) *Muthi*, medicine and witchcraft: Regulating 'African science' in post-apartheid South Africa?, *Social Dynamics*, 31(2), 211–242.

Ashworth, G.J. (1996) Holocaust tourism and Jewish culture: The lessons of Krakow-Kazimierz. In M. Robinson, N. Evans and P. Callaghan (eds) *Tourism and Cultural Change*. Newcastle: Centre for Travel and Tourism, pp 1–12.

Ashworth, G.J. and Hartmann, R. (eds) (2005) *Horror and Human Tragedy Revisited: The Management of Sites of Atrocities for Tourism*. New York: Cognizant Communication Corporation.

Ashworth, G.J. and Isaac, R.K. (2015) Have we illuminated the dark? Shifting perspectives on 'dark' tourism, *Tourism Recreation Research*, 40(3), 316–325.

Aslan, S. (2015) Prison tourism as a form of dark tourism, *Journal of International Social Research*, 8(40), 600–608.

Atkinson, C. (2013) *Reflections on Administrative Evil, Belief, and Justification in Khmer Rouge Cambodia*. London: SAGE.

Atkinson, R. (2014) *Shades of Deviance*. London: Routledge.

Atkinson, R. (2019) Necrotecture: Lifeless dwellings and London's super-rich, *International Journal of Urban and Regional Research*, 43(1), 2–13.

Atlas Obscura (nd) Museum of Confiscated Art, available at https://www.atlasobscura.com/places/museum-of-confiscated-art, accessed 20 July 2021.

Australian Government (2019) smartraveller.gov.au: Hong Kong, available at https://www.smartraveller.gov.au/destinations/asia/hong-kong, accessed 30 August 2021.

Baker, D. (2010) Exacerbated politics: The legacy of political trauma in South Korea. In M. Kim and B. Schwartz (eds) *Northeast Asia's Difficult Past*. London: Palgrave Macmillan, pp 193–203.

Bakhtin, M. (1984) *Rabelais and His World*. Bloomington: Indiana University Press.

Baldus, D., Pulaski, C. and Woodworth, G. (1983) Comparative review of death sentences: An empirical study of the Georgia experience, *Journal Criminal Law & Criminology*, 74(3), 661–753.

Baldus, D., Woodworth, G. and Pulaski, C. (1985) Monitoring and evaluating temporary death sentencing systems: Lessons from Georgia, *University of California Davis Law Review*, 18(4), 1375–1407.

Baldus, R. (2005) African wildlife: Must it be subsidized? *African Indaba*, 2, 2–8.

Bangdel, L. (1989) *Stolen Images of Nepal*. Kathmandu: Royal Nepal Academy.

Baptist, E.E. (2014) *The Half Has Never Been Told*. New York: Basic Books.

Baptist, K. (2015) Incompatible identities: Memory and experience at the National September 9/11 Memorial and Museum, *Emotion, Space and Society*, 16(5), 3–8.

Barbour, V. (1911) Privateers and pirates of the West Indies, *American Historical Review*, 16(3), 529–566.

Bartholomaeus, C. and Riggs, D. (2017) *Transgender People and Education*. London: Palgrave Macmillan.

Barnes, S.J. (2019) Understanding plastic pollution: The role of economic development and technological research, *Environmental Pollution*, 249, 812–821.

Basu, K. (2012) Slum tourism: For the poor, by the poor. In F. Frenzel, K. Koens and M. Steinbrink (eds) *Slum Tourism: Poverty, Power, and Ethics*. London: Routledge, pp 84–100.

Batavia, C., Nelson, M.P., Darimont, C.T., Paquet, P.C., Ripple, W.J. and Wallach, A.D. (2018) The elephant (head) in the room: A critical look at trophy hunting, *Conservation Letters*, 12(1), 12565.

Bates, J. (2015) *Suicide Forest (World's Scariest Places)*. USA: Ghillinnein Books.

Bathory, R. (2018) *Dark Tourism*. Darlington: Carpet Bombing Culture.

Baudrillard, J. (1981) *Simulacra and Simulation*. Ann Arbor: The University of Michigan Press.

Baudrillard, J. (2000) *The Vital Illusion*. New York: Columbia University Press.

Bauman, Z. (1989) *Modernity and the Holocaust*. New York: Cornell University Press.

Bauman, Z. (1996) Tourists and vagabonds: Heroes and victims of postmodernity. (Reihe Politikwissenschaft / Institut für Höhere Studien, Abt. Politikwissenschaft, 30). Wien: Institut für Höhere Studien (IHS), Wien. https://nbnresolving.org/urn:nbn:de:0168-ssoar-266870

Bauman, Z. (2005) *Work, Consumerism, and the New Poor*, 2nd edn. Berkshire: Open University Press.

BBC (2013) Brazil: Rio gang who raped American tourist jailed, *BBC News*, 15 August, available at https://www.bbc.co.uk/news/world-latin-america-23720497, accessed 29 October 2021.

BBC (2016a) Qatar 2020: Forced labour at World Cup, *BBC News*, available at http://www.bbc.co.uk/news/world-middle-east-35931031, accessed 1 November 2021.

BBC (2016b) Amazon agency delivery driver 'went to toilet in back of van', BBC News, 11 November, available at https://www.bbc. co.uk/ news/ av/ uk- engl and- bristol- 37947 473, accessed 5 October 2022.

BBC (2018) YouTube punishes Logan Paul over Japan suicide video, *BBC News*, 11 January, available at https://www.bbc.co.uk/news/world-asia-42644321, accessed 12 November 2021.

BBC (2019) Hong Kong protests: How badly has tourism been affected? *BBC News*, 12 August, available at https://www.bbc.com/news/world-asia-china-49276259, accessed 30 August 2021.

BBC (2020) Brazil: At least 25 killed in Rio de Janeiro shootout, *BBC News*, 6 May, available at https://www.bbc.co.uk/news/world-latin-america-57013206, accessed 14 October 2021.

Beam, C. (2007) Jobs for life: Death from overwork in Japan, *The Economist*, 19 December, available at https://www.economist.com/asia/2007/12/19/jobs-for-life, accessed 15 January 2022.

Beaumont, M. (2016) *Night Walking*. London: Verso Books.

Beck, U. (1992) *Risk Society: Towards a New Modernity*. London: SAGE.

Becker, E (1998) *When the War Was Over: Cambodia and the Khmer Rouge Revolution*. New York: Public Affairs.

Beckert, S. (2014) *Empire of Cotton: A Global History*. New York: Vintage Books.

Beckett, K. and Evans, H. (2016) The role of race in Washington State Capital sentencing 1981–2014, report commissioned by the Washington State Appellate Project, 25 August, available at https://files.deathpenaltyinfo.org/legacy/documents/WashRaceStudy2014.pdf, accessed 18 August 2021.

Bell, M.M. (2009) *An Invitation to Environmental Sociology*. Thousand Oaks: Pine Forge Press.

Bendix, R. (2002) Capitalizing on memories past, present, and future: Observations on the intertwining of tourism and narration, *Anthropological Theory*, 2(4), 469–487.

Benediktsson, M.O., Lambreta, B. and Larsen, E. (2015) Taming a 'chaotic concept': Gentrification and segmented consumption in Brooklyn, 2002–2012, *Urban Geography*, 37(4), 590–610.

Benjamin, W. (2007/1921) Critique of violence. In P. Demetz (ed) *Walter Benjamin: Reflections*. New York: Schocken Books, pp 277–301.

Bennett, T. (2005) *The Birth of the Museum: History, Theory, Politics*. London: Routledge.

Benns, W. (2015) American slavery, reinvented, *The Atlantic*, available at http://www.theatlantic.com/business/archive/2015/09/prison-labor-in-america/406177/, accessed 1 November 2021.

Benton, T. (2010) Heritage and changes of regime. In T. Benton (ed) *Understanding Heritage and Memory*. Manchester: Manchester University Press, pp 126–163.

Berg, M.T. and Huebner, B.M. (2011) Reentry and the ties that bind: An examination of social ties, employment and recidivism, *Justice Quarterly*, 28(2), 382–410.

Berman, K. (2014) The Burning Man arms race and if we should fear 'turnkey tech camps', available at https://medium.com/behavioral-economics-1/the-burning-man-arms-race-and-if-we-should-fear-turnkey-tech-camps-2a8fdfdb1eeb, accessed 5 January 2022.

Better Call Saul (2015) Uno, High Bridge Productions, 8 February.

Beynon, J. (2002) *Masculinities and Culture*. Buckingham: Open University Press.

Bigger, S. (2009) Victor Turner, liminality, and cultural performance, *Journal of Beliefs & Values*, 30(2), 209–212.

Billard, T.J. (2016) Writing in the margins: Mainstream news media representations of transgenderism, *International Journal of Communication*, 10, 4193–4218.

Biran, A., Poria, Y. and Oren, G. (2011) Sought experiences at (dark) heritage sites, *Annals of Tourism Research*, 38(3), 820–841.

Blanchette, T. and Da Silva, A. (2011) Prostitution in contemporary Rio de Janeiro. In S. Dewey and P. Kelly (eds) *Policing Pleasure: Sex Work, Policy, and the State in Global Perspective*. New York: New York University Press, pp 130–146.

Blevins, K. and Edwards, T. (2009) Wildlife crime. In J. Miller (ed) *21st Century Criminology: A Reference Handbook*. London: SAGE, pp 557–564.

Bloodworth, J. (2019) *Hired: Six Months Undercover in Low-Wage Britain*. London: Atlantic Books.

Boag, E. and Wilson, D. (2013) Does engaging with serious offenders change students' attitude and empathy toward offenders? A thematic analysis, *The Journal of Psychiatry and Psychology*, 24(6), 1–17.

Bobrova, I. (2010) The President came out of the shabby Pivnovka, *Moskovskii Komsomolets*, available at https://www.mk.ru/politics/article/2010/02/25/437164-prezident-vyishel-iz-zatrapeznoy-pivnovki-foto.html, accessed 18 October 2021.

Bolan, P. and Simone-Chateris, M. (2018) Shining a digital light on the dark: Harnessing online media to improve the dark tourism experience. In P. Stone, R. Hartmann, T. Seaton, R. Sharpley and L. White (eds) *The Palgrave Handbook of Dark Tourism Studies*. London: Palgrave, pp 727–746.

Bond, I., Child, B., de la Harpe, D., Jones, B., Barnes, J. and Anderson, H. (2004) Private land contribution to conservation in South Africa. In B. Child (ed) *Parks in Transition*. London: Routledge, pp 29–63.

Bonn, S. (2014) *Why We Love Serial Killers: The Curious Appeal of the World's Most Savage Murderers*. New York: Skyhorse Publishing.

Boorstin, D.J. (1962) *The Image: Or, What Happened to the American Dream?* New York: Atheneum.

Born Free (2019) *Trophy Hunting: Busting the Myths and Exposing the Cruelty*. Horsham: Born Free Foundation.

Botterill, D. and Jones, T. (eds) (2010) *Tourism and Crime: Key Themes*. Oxford: Goodfellow Publishers.

Boucher, A. (2019) Burning Man finally fights Instagram culture and bans high-end camp, *The Guardian*, 14 February.

Bourdieu, P. (1977) *Outline of a Theory of Practice*. Cambridge: Cambridge University Press.

Bourdieu, P. (1986) *The Forms of Capital by Pierre Bourdieu 1986*, available at https://www.marxists.org/reference/subject/philosophy/works/fr/bourdieu-forms-capital.htm, accessed 1 June 2021.

Bourdieu, P. (1993) *The Field of Cultural Production*. Cambridge: Polity.

Bowman, M. and Pezzullo, P. (2010) What's so 'dark' about 'dark tourism'? Death, tours, and performance, *Tourist Studies*, 9(3), 87–202.

Boyd, M. (2021) Inside spooky prison where Nazis slaughtered hundreds which is now a hotel, *The Mirror*, 23 June, available at https://www.mirror.co.uk/news/world-news/inside-spooky-prison-nazis-slaughtered-24366869, accessed 29 June 2021.

Bozhko, Y. (2013) The nominal value of the gold 'coin', which was presented to V. Yanukoych, is 250 thousand UAH, *Ukrainian National News*, available at https://www.unn.com.ua/ru/news/1229915-nominalnavartistzolotoyi-moneti-dlya-v-yanukovicha-stanovit-250-tis-grn, accessed 18 October 2021.

Brannagan, P.M. and Giulianotti, R. (2015) Soft power and soft disempowerment: Qatar, global sport and football's 2022 World Cup finals, *Leisure Studies*, 34(6), 703–719.

Breaking Bad (2008) Pilot, High Bridge Entertainment, 20 January.

Briggs, B. (2011) Breaking up the gangs of Glasgow from within, *Aljazeera*, 22 September, available at https://www.aljazeera.com/indepth/opinion/2011/09/201191393341539 00.html, accessed 6 July 2021.

Briggs, D. (2013) *Deviance and Risk on Holiday: An Ethnography of British Tourists in Ibiza*. Basingstoke: Palgrave Macmillan.

Briggs, D. and Ellis, A. (2017) The last night of freedom: Consumerism, deviance and the 'stag party', *Deviant Behaviour*, 38(7), 756–767.

Britannica (2021) La Paz, *Encyclopedia Britannica*, available at https://www.britannica.com/place/La-Paz-Bolivia, accessed 26 January 2022.

The British Medical Journal (1921) Pitcairn Island, *The British Medical Journal*, 5 November, 2, pp 760–761.

Brito, R. (2017) Rio rethinks favela tourism amid wave of violence, *Chicago Tribune*, available at https://www.chicagotribune.com/travel/ct-rio-favela-tourism-violence-20171121-story.html, accessed 2 November 2021.

Brooks, S. (2019) Brexit and the politics of the rural, *Sociologica Ruralis*, 60(4), 790–809.

Brown, M. (2009) *The Culture of Punishment: Prison, Society and Spectacle*. New York: New York University Press.

Brown, S. (2017) Top favela parties in Rio de Janeiro, *Culture Trip*, available at https://theculturetrip.com/south-america/brazil/articles/top-favela-parties-in-rio-de-janeiro/, accessed 14 September 2021.

Brown, S. (2018) A guide to attending a favela party in Vidigal, *Culture Trip*, available at https://theculturetrip.com/south-america/brazil/articles/a-guide-to-attending-a-favela-party-in-vidigal/, accessed 13 September 2021.

Browne, M., Crump, P., Niven, S., Teuten, E., Tonkin, A., Galloway, T. and Thompson, R. (2011) Accumulation of microplastic on shorelines worldwide: Sources and sinks, *Environmental Science & Technology*, 45(21), 9175–9179.

Bruce-Gardyne, T. (2002) Ian Rankin's Edinburgh, *The Sunday Telegraph*, 11 August.

Bryant, C.D. (2004) The quest for dead animals on the wall: The African safari as phantasmagorical experience. Annual Meeting of the American Sociological Association, San Francisco, August.

Bryant, R. and Goodman, R. (2004) Consuming narratives: The political ecology of 'alternative' consumption, *Transactions of the Institute of British Geographers*, 29, 344–366.

Bryman, A. (2004) *The Disneyization of Society*. London: SAGE.

Buck-Matthews, E. (2018) *Re-Framing Music Festivals: Exploring Space, Solidarity, Spirituality and Self with Young People*. Doctoral dissertation, Coventry University.

Bullough, O. (2018) *Moneyland: Why Thieves and Crooks Now Rule the World and How to Take it Back*. London: Profile Books.

Burch, L. (2021) *Understanding Disability and Everyday Hate*. London: Palgrave Macmillan.

Burdsey, D. (2013) 'The foreignness is still quite visible in this town': Multiculture, marginality and prejudice at the English seaside', *Patterns of Prejudice*, 47(2), 95–116.

Bureau of Labor Statistics (2021a) *County Employment and Wages in Florida: Third Quarter 2020*, available at https://www.bls.gov/regions/southeast/news-release/2021/pdf/countyemploymentandwages_florida_20210319.pdf, accessed 5 October 2022.

Bureau of Labor Statistics (2021b) *Occupational Employment and Wages in Los Angeles-Long Beach-Anaheim, May 2020*, available at https://www.bls.gov/regions/west/news-release/pdf/occupationalemploymentandwages_losangeles.pdf, accessed 5 October 2022.

Burge, R. (2017) The prison and the postcolony: Contested memory and the museumification of Sŏdaemun Hyŏngmuso, *Journal of Korean Studies*, 22(1), 33–67.

Burgess, D. (2009) Piracy in the public sphere: The Henry Every trials and the battle for meaning in the seventeenth-century print media, *Journal of British Studies*, 48(4), 887–913.

Burke, E. (1958) *A Philosophical Enquiry into the Origin of Our Ideas of the Sublime and Beautiful*, edited by J.T. Boulton. Notre Dame, IN: University of Notre Dame Press.

Campbell, R. (2013) *The $200 Million Question: How Much Does Trophy Hunting Really Contribute to African Communities. A Report for the African Lion Coalition*. Melbourne: Economists at Large.

Capuzza, J.C. and Spencer, L.G. (2018) Regressing, progressing, or transgressing on the small screen? Transgender characters on U.S. scripted television series, *Communication Studies*, 65(2), 214–230.

Caro, T.M., Pelkey, N., Borner, M., Severre, E.M., Campbell, K.I., Huish, S.A., Ole Kuwai, J., Farm, B.P. and Woodworth, B.L. (1998) The impact of tourist hunting on large mammals in Tanzania: An initial assessment, *African Journal of Ecology*, 36(4), 321–346.

Carrabine, E. (2008) *Crime, Culture and the Media*. Cambridge: Polity.

Carrabine, E. (2017) Iconic power, dark tourism, and the spectacle of the suffering. In J. Wilson, S. Hodgkinson, J. Piché and K. Walby (eds) *The Palgrave Handbook of Prison Tourism*. London: Macmillan, pp 13–36.

Carter, D. (1979) *Scottsboro: A Tragedy of the American South*. Boston: Cengage Learning.

Carter, H. and Kitching, C. (2019) Amazon driver 'delivers up to 300 parcels a day with no time for toilet breaks', *The Mirror*, 15 December, available at https://www.google.co.uk/amp/s/www.mirror.co.uk/news/uk-news/amazon-driver-delivers-up-300-21104717.amp, accessed 5 October 2022.

Census and Statistics Department (2017) *General Household Survey Quarterly Statistics Report for April to June 2017*. Hong Kong: The Government of the Hong Kong Special Administrative Region.

Chakraborti, N. (2010) Beyond 'passive apartheid'? Developing policy and research agendas on rural racism in Britain, *Journal of Ethnic and Migration Studies*, 36(3), 501–517.

Chakraborti, N. (2018) Responding to hate crime: Escalating problems, continued failings, *Criminology and Criminal Justice*, 18(4), 387–404.

Chakraborti, N. and Garland, J. (2004a) *Rural Racism*. London: Palgrave.

Chakraborti, N. and Garland, J. (2004b) England's green and pleasant land? Examining racist prejudice in a rural context, *Patterns of Prejudice*, 38(4), 383–398.

Chakraborti, N., Garland, J. and Hardy, S. (2014) *The Leicester Hate Crime Project: Findings and Conclusions*. Leicester: University of Leicester.

Chandler, D. (2000) *Voices from S-21: Terror and History in Pol Pot's Secret Prison*. Chiang Mai: Silkworm Books.

Chandler, D. (2008) Cambodia deals with its past: Collective memory, demonisation and induced amnesia, *Totalitarian Movements and Political Religions*, 9(2–3), 355–369.

Chang, S. (2005) The prodigal 'son' returns: An assessment of current 'son of Sam' laws and the reality of the online murderabilia marketplace, *Rutgers Computer & Technology Law Journal*, 31(2), 430–458.

Chardonnet, P. (1995) Faune sauvage Africaine: la ressource oubliée. Tomes 1 et 2, CEE/IGF, Luxembourg: Office for Official Publications of the European Communities, 699.

Chatterton, P. and Hollands, R. (2003) *Urban Night Spaces: Youth Cultures, Dance Spaces and Corporate Power*. London: Routledge.

Chen, K. (2009) *Enabling Creative Chaos: The Organization Behind the Burning Man Event*. Chicago: University of Chicago Press.

Cherelus, G. (2016) Sorrow, selfies compete at New York's 9/11 memorial 15 years on, available at https://www.reuters.com/article/us-usa-sept11-mood-idUSKCN11F19K, accessed 29 November 2021.

Cherrymochi (2017) Tokyo Dark. [game, steam] Square Enix, Japan.

Chesters, G. and Smith, D. (2001) The neglected art of hitch-hiking: Risk, trust and sustainability, *Sociological Research Online*, 6(3), 63–71.

Cheung, T. (2019) Hong Kong leader Carrie Lam condemns US senator Josh Hawley for 'totally irresponsible' police state comment, *South China Morning Post*, 15 October, available at https://www.scmp.com/news/hong-kong/politics/article/3033011/hong-kong-leader-carrie-lam-condemns-us-senator-josh-hawley, accessed 30 August 2021.

Child, B. (2005) *Principles, Practice and Results of CBNRM in Southern Africa*, available at https://sandcountyfoundation.org/assets/index.%20htm, accessed 22 June 2021.

Chouliaraki, L. (2006) *The Spectatorship of Suffering*. London: SAGE.

Chouliaraki, L. (2012) The theatricality of humanitarianism: A critique of celebrity advocacy, *Communication and Critical/Cultural Studies*, 9(1), 1–21.

Christiansen, A.V., Vinther, A.S. and Liokaftos, D. (2017) Outline of a typology of men's use of anabolic androgenic steroids in fitness and strength training environments, *Drugs Education Prevention & Policy*, 24(3), 295–305.

City of God (2003) Fernando Meirelles and Kátia Lund, dir. London: Buena Vista International.

Clapperton, B. (2000) Follow that detective, *Edinburgh Evening News*, 16 May.

Clarke, N. (2005) Detailing transnational lives of the middle: British working holiday makers in Australia, *Journal of Ethnic and Migration Studies*, 31(2), 307–322.

Cocaine Bear (2022) Elizabeth Banks, dir. USA: Universal Pictures.

Cohen, S. (2001) *States of Denial: Knowing about Atrocities and Suffering*. Cambridge: Polity.

Cole, T. (2000) *Selling the Holocaust: From Auschwitz to Schindler: How History is Bought, Packaged and Sold*. New York: Routledge.

Collins, M.S. (2006) Biggie envy and the gangsta sublime, *Callaloo*, 29(3), 911–938.

Colliver, B. (2020) Representation of LGBTQ communities in the Grand Theft Auto series. In C. Kelly, A. Lynes and K. Hoffin (eds) *Video Games, Crime and Next Gen Deviance*. Bingley: Emerald Publishing, pp 131–151.

Colliver, B., Coyle, A. and Silvestri, M. (2019) Gender neutral toilets: The online construction of transgender & non-binary identities. In K. Lumsden and E. Harmer (eds) *Online Othering: The Dark Side of the Web*. London: Palgrave, pp 215–239.

Coltman, D.W., O'Donoghue, P., Jorgenson, J.T., Hogg, J.T., Strobeck, C. and FestaBianchet, M. (2003) Undesirable evolutionary consequences of trophy hunting, *Nature*, 426(6967), 655–658.

Cook, I.R. (2022) Time and detective novels: Exploring the past and the night in Ian Rankin's John Rebus series, *Clues: A Journal of Detection*, 40(1), 102–13.

Cook, I.R. and Ashutosh, I. (2018) Television drama and the urban diegesis: Portraying Albuquerque in *Breaking Bad*, *Urban Geography*, 39(5), 746–762.

Coomber, R., Moyle, L. and South, N. (2016) The normalisation of drug supply: The social supply of drugs as the other side of the history of normalisation, *Drugs: Education, Prevention and Policy*, 23(3), 255–263.

Coomber, R., Pavlidis, A., Santos, G., Wilded, M., Schmidte, W. and Redshaw, C. (2014) The supply of steroids and other performance and image enhancing drugs (PIEDs) in one English city: Fakes, counterfeits, supplier trust, common beliefs and access, *Performance Enhancement & Health*, 3(3), 135–144.

Corbishly, S. (2021) Chippy where women get discount keeps name despite 'glorifying serial killer', *Metro*, 18 August, available at https://metro.co.uk/2021/08/18/customers-boycott-jack-the-chipper-chip-shop-for-glorifying-serial-killer-15108140/, accessed 27 August 2021.

Corteen, K. and Stoops, M. (2016) Sex work, hate crime and victimization. In K. Corteen, S. Morley, P. Taylor and J. Turner (eds) *A Companion to Crime, Harm and Victimisation*. Bristol: Policy Press, pp 210–213.

Cottier, C. (2020) What explains the decline of serial killers? *Discover Magazine*, available at https://www.discovermagazine.com/the-sciences/what-explains-the-decline-of-serial-killers, accessed 27 August 2021.

Courchamp, F., Angulo, E., Rivalan, P., Hall, R.J., Signoret, L., Bull, L. and Meinard, Y. (2006) Rarity value and species extinction: The anthropogenic Allee effect, *PLoS Biology*, 4(12), 2405–2410.

Craig, C., Thomson, R. and Santangeli, A. (2018) Communal farmers of Namibia appreciate vultures and the ecosystem services they provide, *Ostrich*, 89(3), 211–220.

Craig-Henderson, K. and Sloan, B. (2003) After the hate: Helping psychologists help victims of racist hate crime, *Clinical Psychology: Science and Practice*, 10(4), 481–490.

Crewe, B. (2011) Depth, weight, tightness: Revisiting the pains of imprisonment, *Punishment and Society*, 13(5), 509–529.

Crewe, B., Hulley, S. and Wright, S. (2016) Swimming with the tide: Adapting to long-term imprisonment, *Justice Quarterly*, 34(3), 1–25.

Crime scene (2018) Black dahlia: The 1947 murder of Elizabeth Short, available at http://blackdahlia.web.unc.edu/the-crime-scene/, accessed 2 July 2021.

Cumings, B. (2005) *Korea's Place in the Sun: A Modern History*. New York: W.W. Norton.

Cumings, B. (2011) *The Korean War: A History*. New York: Random House.

Curcione, N.R. (1992) Deviance as delight: Party-boat poaching in southern California, *Deviant Behavior*, 13(1), 33–57.

Dahl, K. (2018) Exploitation on the internet? The morality of watching death online, *The Guardian*, available at https://www.theguardian.com/technology/2018/oct/12/reddit-r-watch-people-die, accessed 26 July 2021.

Dalton, D. (2009) Encountering Auschwitz: A personal rumination on the possibilities and limitations of witnessing/remembering trauma in memorial space, *Law Text Culture*, 13(1), 187–225.

Dalton, D. (2015) *Dark Tourism and Crime*. London: Routledge.

Damatta, R. (1991) *Carnivals, Rogues, and Heroes: An Interpretation of the Brazilian Dilemma*. Notre Dame, IN: University of Notre Dame Press.

Darby, N. (2014) The Marshall's dance: Crime and punishment at execution dock, *Criminal Historian*, available at https://www.criminalhistorian.com/the-marshals-dance-crime-and-punishment-at-execution-dock/, accessed 11 June 2021.

The Dark Knight (2008) Christopher Nolan, dir. USA: Warner Brother Studios.

Dark Tourist (2018) Razor Films, 20 July.

Dastin, J. (2019) Amazon is replacing some fulfilment centre jobs with robots that pack orders, *Business Insider*, 13 May, available at https://www.businessinsider.com/exclusive-amazon-rolls-out-machines-that-pack-orders-and-replace-jobs-2019-5?r=US&IR=T, accessed 17 July 2021.

Dauchez, M. and Perrot, M. (2008) Pitcairn: A call at the end of the world, *New Zealand International Review*, 33(4), 21–22.

Davies, A. (2007) The Scottish Chicago: From 'hooligans' to 'gangsters' in inter-war Glasgow, *Cultural and Social History*, 4(4), 511–527.

Davies, A. (2013) *City of Gangs: Glasgow and the Rise of the British Gangster*. London: Hodder & Stoughton.

Davis, M. (1990) *City of Quartz: Excavating the Future in Los Angeles*. London: Vintage.

Davisson, Z. (2020) *Hyakumonogatari Kaidankai: Translated Japanese Ghost Stories and Tales of the Weird and the Strange*, available at https://hyakumonogatari.com/, accessed 12 November 2021.

Dayton, E. (2021) Amazon statistics you should know, *Big Commerce*, available at https://www.bigcommerce.co.uk/blog/amazon-statistics/, accessed 17 July 2021.

Death Penalty Information Center (2021) Facts about the death penalty, 1 July, available at www.deathpenaltyinfo.org/FactSheet.pdf, accessed 18 August 2021.

Debord, G. (1994) *The Society of the Spectacle*. London: Zone Books.

Decorte, T. (2001) Drug users' perceptions of 'controlled' and 'uncontrolled' use, *International Journal of Drug Policy*, 12(4), 297–320.

Delmas, C. (2018) *A Duty to Resist: When Disobedience Should be Uncivil*. New York: Oxford University Press.

Del Rey, J. (2019) How robots are transforming Amazon warehouse jobs – for better and worse, *Vox*, 11 December, available at https://www.vox.com/recode/2019/12/11/20982652/robots-amazon-warehouse-jobs-automation, accessed 17 July 2021.

Denham, J. (2016) The commodification of the criminal corpse: 'Selective memory' in posthumous representations of the criminal, *Mortality*, 21, 1–17.

Denning, A. (2014) *Skiing into Modernity*, Oakland: University of California Press.

Denton, S.A. (1985) Drew Thornton's last adventure, *The Washington Post*, 20 October, available at https://www.washingtonpost.com/archive/lifestyle/1985/10/20/drew-thorntons-last-adventure/982df601-7c8c-4955-a09c-b6d1f3b0a426/, accessed 10 October 2021.

Derrida, J. (1994) *Specters of Marx*. London: Routledge.

De Sanctis, F.M. (2013) *Money Laundering Through Art: A Criminal Justice Perspective*. Dordrecht: Springer.

De Sousa, M. (2019) Swiss tourist in Rio de Janeiro critical after gunshot, *ABC News*, available at https://abcnews.go.com/International/wireStory/swiss-tourist-rio-de-janeiro-critical-gunshot-67987258, accessed 1 December 2021.

Di Blasi, M., Cavani, P., La Grutta, S., Lo Baido, R. and Pavia, L. (2015) Growing in Mafia territories, *World Futures*, 71(5–8), 173–184.

Dickinson, I. (2021) White lions face new extinction threat as trophy hunters offered cut-price deals, *Daily Star Online*, 10 April, available at https://www.dailystar.co.uk/news/latestnews/white-lions-face-new-extinction-23891371, accessed 15 June 2021.

Digance, J. (2003) Pilgrimage at contested sites, *Annals of Tourism Research*, 30(1), 143–159.

Dimassa, C.A. and Winton, R. (2006) A plan to spread homelessness county wide, *LA Times*, available at https://www.latimes.com/archives/la-xpm-2006-mar-24-me-homeless24-story.html, accessed 5 October 2022.

Di Minin, E., Fraser, I., Slotow, R. and MacMillan, D.C. (2013) Understanding heterogeneous preference of tourists for big game species: Implications for conservation and management, *Animal Conservation*, 16(3), 249–258.

Di Minin, E., Laitila, J., Montesino-Pouzols, F., Leader-Williams, N., Slotow, R., Goodman, P.S., Conway, A.J. and Moilanen, A. (2015) Identification of policies for a sustainable legal trade in rhinoceros horn based on population projection and socioeconomic models, *Conservation Biology*, 29(2), 545–555.

Di Minin, E., Leader-Williams, N. and Bradshaw, C.J. (2016) Banning trophy hunting will exacerbate biodiversity loss, *Trends in Ecology & Evolution*, 31(2), 99–102.

Dimond, D. (2014) Foreword. In S. Bonn, *Why We Love Serial Killers: The Curious Appeal of the World's Most Savage Murderers.* New York: Skyhorse Publishing, pp 12–14.

Disney Programs (2021) *Disney Programs – Housing Fees*, available at https://sites.disney.com/lifeatdisney/housing-fees/, accessed 20 July 2021.

Ditmore, M. (2006) *Encyclopedia of Prostitution and Sex Work*, 2nd edn. London: Greenwood Press.

Dixit, K.M. (1999) Gods in exile, *Himal Southasian*, 1 October, available at https://www.himalmag.com/gods-in-exile/, accessed 16 May 2021.

Do N.Y.C. (2022) The Biggie Smalls Brooklyn tour, available at https://donyc.com/p/biggie-smalls, accessed 10 January 2022.

Dorman, T. (2021) The day it rained cocaine: Knoxville plays role in true story behind 'Cocaine Bear' movie, *Knox News*, 15 March, available at https://eu.knoxnews.com/story/news/local/2021/03/15/cocaine-bear-parachuting-smuggler-andrew-thornton-died-knoxville/4663756001/, accessed 22 July 2021.

Doss, E. (2011) Remembering 9/11: Memorials and cultural memory, *OAH Magazine of History*, 25(3), 27–30.

Dragicevich, P., Ragozin, L. and McNaughtan, H. (2016) *Lonely Planet Estonia, Latvia & Lithuania*. Melbourne: Lonely Planet Publications

Draven, J. (2020) Are favela tours ethical?, *National Geographic*, available at https://www.nationalgeographic.co.uk/travel/2018/09/are-favela-tours-ethical, accessed 15 June 2021.

Dreier, P., Flaming, D., Herrera, L., Matsuoka, M., Carlen, J. and Burns, P. (2018) *Working for the Mouse: A Survey of Disneyland Resort Employees*. Economic Roundtable Report.

Dunn, M., Mulrooney, K., Biddau, D., McKay, F. and Henshaw, R. (2020) 'Bali over the counter': Exploring the overseas use and acquisition of anabolic-androgenic steroids, *Deviant Behavior*, 43(4), 447–460.

Dunne, E., Duggan, M. and O'Mahony, J. (2012) Mental health services for homeless: Patient profile and factors associated with suicide and homicide, *Irish Medical Journal*, 105(3), 71–74.

Durkheim, E. (2002) *Suicide*. London: Routledge.

Durkheim, E. (2006) *On Suicide*. Great Britain: Penguin Books Limited.

Durnescu, I. (2011) Pains of probation: Effective practice and human rights, *International Journal of Offender Therapy and Comparative Criminology*, 55(4), 530–545.

Duru, N.J. (2004) The Central Park five, the Scottsboro boys, and the myth of the bestial black man, *Cardozo Law Review*, 25, 1315–1365.

Egyptian Tourism Authority (2017) *Sharm El Sheikh*, available at http://egypt.travel/en/regions/red-sea/sharm-el-sheikh, accessed 6 April 2021.

Eliason, S.L. (2012) Trophy poaching: A routine activities perspective, *Deviant Behavior*, 33(1), 72–87.

Elizabeth Short: The Black Dahlia (2020) *The Murder Squad*, 8 June, available at http://themurdersquad.com/episodes/elizabeth-short-the-black-dahlia/, accessed 10 November 2020.

Ellis, A. (2019) A de-civilizing reversal or system normal? Rising lethal violence in post-recession austerity United Kingdom, *British Journal of Criminology*, 59(4), 62–67.

Ellis, A., Winlow, S., Briggs, D., Silva Esquinas, A., Cordero Verdugo, R. and Ramiro Pérez Suárez, J. (2018) Liberalism, lack and living the dream: Reconsidering the attractions of alcohol-based leisure for young tourists in Magaluf, Majorca, *Extreme Anthropology*, 2(2), 22–41.

Ellis, J. (2009). What are we expected to feel? Witness, textuality and the audiovisual, *Screen*, 50(1), 67–76.

Ellis, S., Bailey, L. and McNeil, J. (2016) Transphobic victimisation and perceptions of future risk: A large-scale study of the experiences of trans people in the UK, *Psychology & Sexuality*, 7(3), 211–224.

Ellsworth, J. (2019) Street crime victimization among homeless adults: A review of the literature, *Victims & Offenders*, 41(1), 96–118.

Emsley, C. (2018) *Crime and Society in England 1750–1900*, 5th edn. Harlow: Longman.

Engle, M.B. (2014) A CN tower over Qatar: An analysis of the use of slave labor in preparation for the 2022 FIFA Men's World Cup and how the European Court of Human Rights can stop it, *Hofstra Labor & Employment Law Journal*, 32(1), Article 5.

Englebrecht, C., Mason, D.T. and Adams, M.J. (2014) The experiences of homicide victims' families with the criminal justice system: An exploratory study, *Violence and Victims*, 29(3), 407–421.

Enli, G. (2015) *Mediated Authenticity: How the Media Constructs Reality*. New York: Peter Lang.

Equal Justice Initiative (2010) U.S. Supreme Court former Justice John Paul Stevens says death penalty is corrupted by racial bias and unfair jury selection, 30 November, available at https://eji.org/news/justice-stevens-criticizes-racial-bias-in-death-penalty/, accessed 18 August 2021.

Estes, J.A., Terborgh, J., Brashares, J.S., Power, M.E., Berger, J., Bond, W.J., Carpenter, S.R., Essington, T.E., Holt, R.D., Jackson, J.B. and Marquis, R.J. (2011) Trophic downgrading of planet Earth, *Science*, 333(6040), 301–306.

Evans-Brown, M., McVeigh, J., Perkins, C. and Bellis, M. (2012) *Human Enhancement Drugs: The Emerging Challenges to Public Health*. Liverpool: Liverpool John Moores University Centre for Public Health.

Expedia (2014) *Rio de Janeiro Vacation Travel Guide* [online video], available at https://www.youtube.com/watch?v=ieWNzZPfZzk&t=70s, accessed 2 July 2021.

Fälschermuseum (2021) Fälschermuseum, available at https://www.faelschermuseum.com/, accessed 20 July 2021.

Farmaki, A. (2013) Dark tourism revisited: A supply/demand conceptualisation, *International Journal of Culture, Tourism and Hospitality Research*, 7(3), 281–91.

Fathers, D. (2020) *Bloody London*. London: Conway.

Favela Rising (2005) Matt Mochary and Jeff Zimbalist, dir. United States: THINKFilm.

Fennell, D. (2011) *Tourism and Animal Ethics*. Abingdon: Routledge

Fiddler, M. (2019) Ghosts of other stories: A synthesis of hauntology, crime and space, *Crime, Media, Culture*, 15(3), 463–477.

Fiddler, M., Kindynis, T. and Linnemann, T. (2022) *Ghost Criminology: The Afterlife of Crime and Punishment*. New York: New York University Press.

FIFA (2022) Profile of the FIFA World Cup Qatar 2022, available at https://publications.fifa.com/en/sustainability-report/sustainability-at-the-fifa-world-cup/profile-of-the-fifa-world-cup-qatar-2022/, accessed 9 June 2022.

Fink, J., Schoenfeld, B., Hackney, A., Matsumoto, M., Maekawa, T., Nakazato, K. and Horie, S. (2019) Anabolic-androgenic steroids: Procurement and administration practices of doping athletes, *The Physician and Sports Medicine*, 47(1), 10–14.

Fink, M. and Miller, Q. (2013) Trans media moments: Tumblr, 2011–2013, *Television and New Media*, 15(7), 611–626.

Finnis, J. (2011) *Natural Law & Natural Rights*, 2nd edn. Oxford: Oxford University Press.

Fischel, J. (2019) *Screw Consent: A Better Politics of Sexual Justice*. Oakland: University of California Press.

Fischer, A., Tibebe Weldesemaet, Y., Czajkowski, M., Tadie, D. and Hanley, N. (2015) Trophy hunters' willingness to pay for wildlife conservation and community benefits, *Conservation Biology*, 29(4), 1111–1121.

Fischer, S.N., Shinn, M., Shrout, P. and Tsemberis, S. (2008) Homelessness, mental illness, and criminal activity: Examining patterns over time, *American Journal of Community Psychology*, 42(3–4), 251–265.

Fisher, M. (2009) *Capitalism Realism: Is There No Alternative?* Hampshire: John Hunt Publishing.

Fiske, J. (1897) *Old Virginia and Her Neighbours*. Boston: Houghton Mifflin.

Flack, P.H. (2003) Consumptive tourism: A useful conservation tool. In D. Butchart (ed) *Vision, Business, Ecotourism and the Environment*. South Africa: Endangered Wildlife Trust, pp 155–157.

Flaskerud, J.H. (2014) Suicide culture, *Issues in Mental Health Nursing*, 35(5), 403–405.

Florida, R. (2004) *Cities and the Creative Class*. London: Routledge.

Fonseca, A.P., Seabra, C. and Silva, C. (2016) Dark tourism: Concepts, typologies and sites, *Journal of Tourism Research & Hospitality*, S2–002. doi:10.4172/2324-8807.S2-002

Forbes (2021) Walt Disney, available at https://www.forbes.com/companies/walt-disney/?sh=142809857307, accessed 19 July 2021.

Foreign, Commonwealth and Development Office (2021) *Pitcairn Financial Aid 2020 21*, available at https://devtracker.fcdo.gov.uk/projects/GB-GOV-1-300807, accessed 7 January 2022.

Fotaris, P. and Mastoras, T. (2019) Escape rooms for learning: A systematic review. In *ECGBL 2019 13th European Conference on Game-based Learning*. London: Academic Conferences and Publishing Limited, pp 235–243.

Fowler, C. (2020) *Green Unpleasant Land: Creative Responses to Rural England's Colonial Connections*. Leeds: Peepal Tree Press.

Foxlee, J. (2015) Cultural interpretation: The case of the Sorry Rock Story at ULU R U-Kata Tju t a National Park, *Tourism and Recreation Research*, 32(3), 49–56.

Freedman, T. (2004) Voices of 9/11 first responders: Patterns of collective resilience, *Clinical Social Work Journal*, 32(4), 377–393.

Freire-Medeiros, B. (2011) 'I went to the City of God': Gringos, guns and the touristic favela, *Journal of Latin American Cultural Studies*, 20(1), 21–34.

Freire-Medeiros, B. (2012) Favela tourism: Listening to local voices. In F. Frenzel, K. Koens and M. Steinbrink (eds) *Slum Tourism: Poverty, Power, and Ethics*. London: Routledge, pp 193–210.

French, B.W. (2002) Depression simmers in Japan's culture of stoicism, *New York Times*, 10 August, available at https://www.nytimes.com/2002/08/10/world/depression-simmers-in-japan-s-culture-of-stoicism.html, accessed 14 January 2022.

Frenzel, F. (2012) Beyond 'othering': The political roots of slum tourism. In F. Frenzel, K. Koens and M. Steinbrink (eds) *Slum Tourism: Poverty, Power, and Ethics*. London: Routledge, pp 49–66.

Frew, E. and White, L. (2015) Commemorative events and national identity: Commemorating death and disaster in Australia. *Event Management*, 19(4), 509–524.

From Hell (2001) Hughes brothers, dir. USA: 20th Century Fox.

Fuchs, C. (2021) *Social Media: A Critical Introduction*, 3rd edn. Los Angeles, London, New Delhi, Singapore, Washington DC and Melbourne: SAGE.

Gangoso, L., Agudo, R., Anadón, J.D., de la Riva, M., Suleyman, A.S., Porter, R. and Donázar, J.A. (2013) Reinventing mutualism between humans and wild fauna: insights from vultures as ecosystem services providers, *Conservation Letters*, 6, 172–179.

Ganji, S.K. (2016) Leveraging the World Cup: Mega sporting events, human rights risk, and worker welfare reform in Qatar, *Journal on Migration and Human Security*, 4(4), 221–259.

Garfinkel, H. (1956) Conditions of successful degradation ceremonies, *American Journal of Sociology*, 61(5), 420–424.

Garland, J. and Chakraborti, N. (2006) Recognising and responding to victims of rural racism, *International Review of Victimology*, 13(1), 49–69.

Garrett, B.L. (2010) Urban explorers: Quests for myth, mystery and meaning, *Geography Compass*, 4(10), 1448–1461.

Gattrell, V. (1994) *The Hanging Tree*. Oxford: Oxford University Press.

Gebbels, M., McIntosh, A. and Harkinson, T. (2021) Fine dining in prisons: Online TripAdvisor reviews of The Clink training restaurants, *International Journal of Hospitality Management*, 95, 1–11.

Gemie, S. and Ireland, B. (2017) *The Hippie Trail: A History*. Manchester: Manchester University Press.

Geoghegan, T. (2010) Cycling the world's most dangerous road, *BBC News*, 16 May, available at http://news.bbc.co.uk/1/hi/world/americas/8683075.stm, accessed 10 June 2022.

George, K. (2014) *The Birth of the Haunted Asylum: Public Memory and Community Storytelling*. PhD dissertation, Temple University.

George, R. (2019) Inside Biggie's Brooklyn: Murals, bodegas and neighborhood gems, *Travel Noire*, 7 March, available at https://travelnoire.com/inside-biggies-brooklyn-murals-bodegas-and-neighborhood-gems, accessed 26 April 2022.

Ghansiyal, A. (2021) What is the appeal of dark tourism?, *travel.earth*, 25 February, available at: https://travel.earth/what-is-the-appeal-of-dark-tourism/, accessed 11 December 2021.

Giddens, A. (1994) Living in post-traditional society, in U. Beck, A. Giddens and S. Lash (eds) *Reflexive Postmodernism*. Cambridge: Polity Press, pp 20–39.

Gieben, B. and Hall, S. (1992) *Formations of Modernity*. London: Polity Press.

Gilhooley, R. (2011) Inside Japan's suicide forest, *The Japan Times*, 26 June, available at https://www.japantimes.co.jp/life/2011/06/26/general/inside-japans-suicide-forest/#.WkuBJ1WnGUk, accessed 16 November 2021.

Giordano, P.C., Cernkovich, S.A. and Rudolph, J.L. (2002) Gender crime and desistance: Toward a theory of cognitive transformation, *American Journal of Sociology*, 107(4), 990–1064.

Giousmpasoglou, C., Brown, L. and Marinakou, E. (2019) Training prisoners as hospitality workers: The case of the CLINK charity. Travel & Tourism Research Association (TTRA) 2019: European Chapter Conference, Bournemouth University.

Giroux, H.A. and Pollock, G. (2010) *The Mouse That Roared*, 2nd edn. London: Rowman & Littlefield.

Giuliani, R.W. and Rose, J.B. (2001) NYC2000 results from the 2000 census: Population growth and race/Hispanic composition, summer 2001, available at https://www1.nyc.gov/assets/planning/download/pdf/planning-level/nyc-population/census2000/nyc20001.pdf, accessed 10 June 2022.

Glazebrook, P. (2019) Criminal law reform: England, *Encyclopaedia.com*, available at https://www.encyclopedia.com/law/legal-and-political-magazines/criminal-law-reform-england, accessed 10 June 2022.

Gluckman, R. (2009) Tibet's lost artifact, *Travel + Leisure*, 13 May, available at https://www.travelandleisure.com/trip-ideas/stealing-beauty, accessed 25 May 2021.

Goffman, E. (1961) *Asylums: Essays on the Social Situation of Mental Patients and Other Inmates*. Garden City: Doubleday Anchor Books.

Goodhart, D. (2017) *The Road to Somewhere: The Populist Revolt and the Future of Politics*. London: C. Hurst and Co.

Goodman, M. (2011) Star/poverty space: The making of the 'development celebrity', *Celebrity Studies*, 2, 69–85.

Gordon, A. (1997) *Ghostly Matters*. London: University of Minnesota Press.

Gössling, S. (2000) Tourism: A sustainable development option? *Environmental Conservation*, 27(3), 223–224.

Gould, M.R. (2014) Return to Alcatraz: Dark tourism and the representation of prison history. In B. Sion (ed) *Death Tourism: Disaster Sites as Recreational Landscape*. London: Seagull, pp 267–288.

The Government of the Pitcairn Islands (nd) Available at: https://www.government.pn/, accessed 18 March 2021.

Graham, A. (2020) *Serving Time: An Ethnographic Study of the Clink Restaurant, Clifford*. Unpublished PhD thesis, Cardiff University.

Graham, H. (2021) North East man recalls terrifying moment he escaped Australian backpacker murdered Ivan Milat, *Chronicle Live*, 16 March, available at https://www.chroniclelive.co.uk/news/north-east-news/north-east-man-recalls-terrifying-20168794, accessed 10 June 2022.

Graham, M., Ryan, P., Baker, J.S., Davies, B., Thomas, N., Cooper, S., Evans, P., Easmon, S., Walker, C., Cowan, D. and Kicman, A. (2009) Counterfeiting in performance- and image-enhancing drugs, *Drug Testing and Analysis*, 1(3), 135–142.

Graham-Harrison, H. (2019) How Hong Kong's local elections have become a proxy vote on the protests, *The Guardian*, 22 November 2019, available at https://www.theguardian.com/world/2019/nov/22/how-hong-kongs-local-elections-have-become-a-proxy-vote-on-the-protests, accessed 30 August 2021.

Gray, D. and Wise, A. (2019) *Jack and the Thames Torso Murders*. Stroud: Amberley.

The Guardian (2001) 16m glued to news as tragedy unfolds, *The Guardian*, 12 September, available at https://www.theguardian.com/media/2001/sep/12/overnights.september112001, accessed 29 November 2021.

Gunn, A.S. (2001) Environmental ethics and trophy hunting, *Ethics and the Environment*, 6(1), 68–95.

Gusovsky, D. (2016) Americans consume vast majority of the world's opioids, *CNBC*, 27 April, available at https://www.cnbc.com/2016/04/27/americans-consume-almost-all-of-the-global-opioid-supply.html, accessed 22 August 2021.

Guy, N.K. (2018) *Art of Burning Man* . Cologne: Taschen.

Guy-Ryan, J. (2016) Gather round for the ballad of cocaine bear, *Atlas Obscura*, 10 July, available at https://www.atlasobscura.com/articles/gather-round-for-the-ballad-of-cocaine-bear, accessed 10 June 2022.

Hall, A. and Antonopoulos, G. (2016) *Fake Meds Online: The Internet and the Transnational Market in Illicit Pharmaceuticals*. London: Palgrave Macmillan.

Hall, S. (2002) Daubing the drudges of fury: Men, violence and the piety of the 'hegemonic masculinity' thesis, *Theoretical Criminology*, 6(1), 35–61.

Hall, S. (2012) *Theorizing Crime and Deviance: A New Perspective*. London: SAGE.

Hall, S. (2014) The socioeconomic function of evil, *Sociological Review*, 62(2), 13–31.

Hall, S. (2015) What is criminology about? The study of harm, special liberty and pseudo-pacification in late-capitalism's libidinal economy. In D. Crew and R. Lippens (eds) *What is Criminology About? Philosophical Reflections*. London: Routledge, pp 122–141.

Hall, S. and Winlow, S. (2015) *Revitalising Criminological Theory: Towards a New Ultra-Realism*. Abingdon: Routledge.

Hall, S., Winlow, S. and Ancrum, C. (2008) *Criminal Identities and Consumer Culture: Crime, Exclusion and the New Culture of Narcissism*. London: Routledge.

Hall, S., Horsley, M. and Kotze, J. (2015) The maintenance of orderly disorder: Modernity, markets and the pseudo-pacification process, *Journal on European History and Law*, 1(1), 18–29.

Hamman, K., Vrahimis, S. and Blom, H. (2003) Can current trends in the game industry be reconciled with nature conservation? Available at http://www.africanindaba.com/2003/12/2003/, accessed 10 June 2022.

Han, A. (2019) Not your usual day out for a tourist in Hong Kong: Curious visitors join walking tours to see protests, *South China Morning Post*, 7 December, available at https://www.scmp.com/news/hong-kong/politics/article/3041080/not-your-usual-day-out-tourist-hong-kong-curious-visitors, accessed 30 August 2021.

Hanley Santos, G. and Coomber, R. (2017) The risk environment of anabolic–androgenic steroid users in the UK: Examining motivations, practices and accounts of use, *International Journal of Drug Policy*, 40, 35–43.

Hargrove, S. (2001) Capital punishment: 21st century lynching, *University of the District of Columbia Law Review*, 6(1), 33–49.

Harkinson, T. and Moore, C. (2019) Can training prisoners through the Clink restaurants reduce reoffending? *Hospitality Insights*, 3(2), 1–2.

Harrington, B. (2016) *Capital Without Borders: Wealth Managers and the One Percent*. London: Harvard University Press.

Harris, B. (2021) Brazil criminals turn to flash kidnapping as they take advantage of new tech, *Financial Times*, available at https://www.ft.com/content/225fd97c-ef82-4dfa-b09b-97b1671e1e00, accessed 2 December 2021.

Harris-Peyton, M. (2020) Murders. In J. Allan, J. Gulddal, S. King and A. Pepper (eds) *The Routledge Companion to Crime Fiction*. London: Routledge, pp 141–148.

Hartig, H. and Doherty, C. (2021) Two decades later, the enduring legacy of 9/11, available at https://www.pewresearch.org/politics/2021/09/02/two-decades-later-the-enduring-legacy-of-9-11/, accessed 29 November 2021.

Hartmann, R. (2005) The management of horror and human tragedy. In G.J. Ashworth and R. Hartmann (eds) *Horror and Human Tragedy Revisited: The Management of Sites of Atrocities for Tourism*. New York: Cognizant Books, pp 253–262.

Harvey, D. (2005) *A Brief History of Neoliberalism*. Oxford: Oxford University Press.

Harvey, S. (2017) *Playa Fire: Spirit and Soul at Burning Man* . New York: HarperCollins.

Hayward, K. and Hobbs, D. (2007) Beyond the binge in booze Britain: Market-led liminalization and the spectacle of binge drinking, *The British Journal of Sociology*, 58(3), 437–456.

Heaney, C. and Jonscher, S. (2019) Uluru climb closed permanently as hundreds scale sacred site on final day, *ABC News*, 25 October, available at https://www.abc.net.au/news/2019-10-25/uluru-climb-closed-permanently-by-traditional-owners/11639248, accessed 10 June 2022.

Henderson, J. (2002) Tourism and politics in the Korean Peninsula, *Journal of Tourism Studies*, 13(2), 16–27.

Henderson, P. and Kaur, R. (eds) (2004) *Rural Racism in the UK: Examples of Community-Based Responses*. London: Community Development Foundation.

Heřmanová, E. and Abrhám, J. (2015) Holocaust tourism as a part of the dark tourism, *Czech Journal of Social Sciences Business and Economics*, 1(1), 16–34.

Herrity, K., Schmidt, B. and Warr, J. (eds) (2021) *Sensory Penalities: Exploring the Senses in Spaces of Punishment and Social Control*. Bingley: Emerald.

Hess, A. and Herbig, A. (2013) Recalling the ghosts of 9/11: Convergent memorializing at the opening of the national 9/11 memorial, *International Journal of Communication*, 7(2), 2207–2230.

Heuveline, P. (1998) 'Between one and three million': Towards the demographic reconstruction of a decade of Cambodian history (1970–1979), *Population Studies*, 52(1), 49–65.

Higgins, P., Short, D. and South, N. (2013) Protecting the planet: A proposal for a law of ecocide, *Crime, Law and Social Change*, 59(3), 251–266.

Hillyard, P. and Tombs, S. (2017) Social harm and zemiology. In A. Liebling, S. Maruna and L. McAra (eds) *Oxford Handbook of Criminology*, 6th edn. Oxford: Oxford University Press, pp 284–301.

Hirsch, J. (2004) *After Image: Film, Trauma and the Holocaust.* Philadelphia: Temple University Press.

Hirschman, E.C. (1990) Secular immortality and the American ideology of affluence, *Journal of Consumer Research*, 17(1), 31–42.

Hobbs, D. (1995) *Bad Business: Professional Crime in Modern Britain.* Oxford: Oxford University Press

Hobbs, D. (1997) Professional crime: Change, continuity and the enduring myth of the underworld, *Sociology*, 31(1), 57–72.

Hobbs, D. (1998) Going down the glocal: The local context of organised crime, *The Howard Journal*, 37(4), 407–422.

Hobbs, D. (2001) The firm: Organizational logic and criminal culture on a shifting terrain, *The British Journal of Criminology*, 41(4), 549–560.

Hobbs, D. (2013) *Lush Life: Constructing Organised Crime in the UK.* Oxford: Oxford University Press.

Hobbs, J. (2000) *Collectors.* Abject Films.

Hochschild, A.R. (2003) *The Managed Heart.* London: University of California Press.

Hodgkinson, S. (2013) The concentration camp as a site of 'dark tourism', *Témoigner: Entre histoire et mémoire*, 116, 22–32.

Hodgkinson, S. (2015) Rethinking Holocaust representation: Reflections on Rex Bloomstein's *KZ*, *The Howard Journal of Criminal Justice*, 54(5), 451–468.

Hodgkinson, S. and Urquhart, D. (2016) Prison tourism: Exploring the spectacle of punishment in the UK. In G. Hooper and J.J. Lennon (eds), *Dark Tourism: Practice and Interpretation.* London: Routledge, pp 40–54.

Hohenhaus, P. (2013) Commemorating and commodifying the Rwandan genocide. In L. White and E. Frew (eds) *Dark Tourism and Place Identity: Managing and Interpreting Dark Places.* Abingdon: Routledge, pp 37–142.

Home Office (2021) *Drugs Penalties*, available at https://www.gov.uk/penalties-drug-possession-dealing, accessed 6 April 2021.

Honeycombe, G. (1982) *Murders of the Black Museum.* London: John Blake Publishing

Hood, R. and Hoyle, C. (2009) Abolishing the death penalty worldwide: The impact of a 'new dynamic', *Crime and Justice*, 38(1), 1–63.

Hood, R. and Hoyle, C. (2015) *The Death Penalty: A Worldwide Perspective*. Oxford: Oxford University Press.

Hooper, G. (2016) Introduction. In G. Hooper and J. Lennon (eds) *Dark Tourism: Practice and Interpretation*. London: Routledge, pp 1–12.

Horridge, K. (2018) What are the odds of being a serial killer's victim? Available at https://www.casino.org/blog/what-are-the-odds-of-being-a-serial-killers-victim/, accessed 27 August 2021.

Huang, S. and Lee, H, (2019) *Heritage, Memory, and Punishment: Remembering Colonial Prisons in East Asia*. London: Routledge.

Hubbard, P. (2005) 'Inappropriate and incongruous': Opposition to asylum centres in the English countryside, *Journal of Rural Studies*, 21(1), 3–17.

Huey, L. (2011) Crime behind the glass: Exploring the sublime in crime at the Vienna Kriminalmuseum, *Theoretical Criminology*, 15(4), 381–399.

Hughes, R. (2003) The abject artefacts of memory: Photographs from Cambodia's genocide, *Media, Culture & Society*, 25(1), 23–44.

Hughes, R. (2006) Memory and sovereignty in post-1979 Cambodia: Choeung Ek and local genocide memorials 1. In S. Cook (ed) *Genocide in Cambodia and Rwanda*. New York: Routledge, pp 257–281.

Hughes, R. (2008) Dutiful tourism: Encountering the Cambodian genocide, *Asia Pacific Viewpoint*, 49(3), 318–330.

Human Rights Watch (2022) FIFA: Pay for harm to Qatar's migrant workers, available at https://www.hrw.org/news/2022/05/18/fifa-pay-harm-qatars-migrant-workers, accessed 9 June 2022.

Hume, T. (2019) What the hell are Ukrainian fascists doing in the Hong Kong protests? *Vice News*, 5 November, available at https://www.vice.com/en/article/zmjjey/what-the-hell-are-ukrainian-fascists-doing-in-the-hong-kong-protests, accessed 30 August 2021.

Hunt, C. (2016) The Jim Crow effect: Denial, dignity, human rights, and radicalized mass incarceration, *Journal of Civil Rights and Economic Development*, 29(1), 15–49.

Hurley, E. (2009) Overkill: An exaggerated response to the sale of murderabilia, *Indiana Law Review*, 42(2), 411–440.

Huyssen, A. (1995) *Twilight Memories: Marking Time in a Culture of Amnesia*. New York: Routledge.

IANS (2017) Exhibition displays returned stone sculptures from Australia, *Business Standard*, 24 May, available at https://web.archive.org/web/20170525080334/http://www.business-standard.com/article/news-ians/exhibition-displays-returned-stone-sculptures-from-australia-117052401535_1.html, accessed 20 July 2021.

Ibrahim, Y. (2015) Self-representation and the disaster event: Self-imaging, morality and immortality, *Journal of Media Practice*, 16(3), 211–227.

IMDb (2014) *Tokyo Ghoul*, available at https://www.imdb.com/title/tt3741634/, accessed 15 November 2021.

IMDb (2015) *The Sea of Trees*, available at https://www.imdb.com/title/tt3450900/, accessed 13 November 2021.

IMDb (2016) *The Forest*, available at https://www.imdb.com/title/tt3387542/, accessed 13 November 2021.

Ingle, S. (2022) Trial of Sepp Blatter and Michel Platini will make for electric theatre, *The Guardian*, 5 June, available at https://www.theguardian.com/football/2022/jun/05/trial-of-sepp-blatter-and-michel-platini-will-make-for-electric-theatre, accessed 9 June 2022.

Inter-American Commission on Human Rights (2010) *United States Universal Periodic Review Stakeholder Submission Annex 8*, available at www.ohchr.org/EN/HRBodies/UPR/Pages/UPRUSStakeholdersInfoS9.aspx, accessed 18 August 2021.

Ironside, R. (2018) The allure of dark tourism: Legend tripping and ghost seeking in dark places. In D. Waskul and M. Eaton (eds) *The Supernatural in Society, Culture and History*. Philadelphia: Temple University Press, pp 95–115.

Israel, M. (1999) The victimization of backpackers, *Alternative Law Journal*, 24(5), 229–232.

Jack, M. (2020) The socio-spatial installed base: Ride-hailing applications, parking associations, and precarity in tuk tuk driving in Phnom Penh, Cambodia, *The Information Society*, 36(5), 252–265.

Jacobs, A. and Kaiser, A. (2016) Security forces of 85,000 fills Rio unsettling rights activists, *The New York Times*, available at https://www.nytimes.com/2016/08/08/world/americas/rio-olympics-crime.html, accessed 7 October 2021.

Jamel, J. (2018) *Transphobic Hate Crime*. London: Palgrave Macmillan.

James I (1597) *Daemonologie*, Edinburgh. Edited by G.B. Harrison, London: Bodley Head, 1924; reprinted New York: Barnes and Noble/Edinburgh: Edinburgh University Press, 1966.

Jarvis, B. (2007) Monsters Inc.: Serial killers and consumer culture, *Crime, Media and Culture*, 3(3), 326–344.

Jay, M. (2003) *Refractions of Violence*. London: Routledge.

Jenkins, B. (1975) International terrorism: A balance sheet, *Survival*, 17(4), 158–164.

Jenks, C. (2003) *Transgression*. London: Routledge.

Jiang, W., Stickley, A. and Ueda, M. (2021) Green space and suicide morality in Japan: An ecological study, *Social Science and Medicine*, 282, 1–10.

Johnston, T. and Mandelartz, P. (2016) *Thanatourism: Case Studies in Travel to the Dark Side*. Oxford: Goodfellow.

Jones, W. and Esola, M. (2010) *Mousecatraz*. United States: Mantra Press.

Kang, E.J., Scott, N., Lee, T.J. and Ballantyne, R. (2012) Benefits of visiting a 'dark tourism' site: The case of the Jeju April 3rd Peace Park, Korea, *Tourism Management*, 33(2), 257–265.

Kapmeier, F. and Gonçalves, P. (2018) Wasted paradise? Policies for Small Island States to manage tourism-driven growth while controlling waste generation: The case of the Maldives, *System Dynamics Review*, 34(1–2), 172–221.

Karosta Prison (2021a) Night's lodging in Karosta Prison, *Karostas Cietums*, available at http://karostascietums.lv/en/nakts-cietuma/, accessed 29 June 2021.

Karosta Prison (2021b) Excursions around Karosta Prison, *Karostas Cietums*, available at http://karostascietums.lv/en/eksursija-pa-cietumu/, accessed 30 June 2021.

Karosta Prison (2021c) Behind bars: The show, *Karostas Cietums*, available at http://karostascietums.lv/en/izrade-aiz-restem/, accessed 30 June 2021.

Kaufman-Osborn, T. (2006) Capital punishment as legal lynching? In C.J. Ogletree Jr. and A. Sarat (eds) *From Lynch Mobs to the Killing State: Race and the Death Penalty in America*. New York: New York University Press, pp 21–55.

Kaul, A. and Skinner, J. (2018) *Leisure and Death: An Anthropological Tour of Risk, Death, and Dying*. Colorado: University Press of Colorado.

Keefe, A. (2017) An ethereal forest where Japanese commit suicide, *National Geographic*, 23 February, available at https://www.nationalgeographic.com/photography/article/aokigahara-jukai-suicide-forest, accessed 12 November 2021.

Keil, C. (2005) Sightseeing in the mansions of the dead, *Social & Cultural Geography*, 6(4), 479–494.

Kelly, C., Lynes, A. and Dean-Hart, M. (2022) 'Graze culture' and serial murder: Brushing up against 'familiar monsters' in the wake of 9/11. In C. O'Callaghan and S. Fanning (eds) *Serial Killers on Screen*. London: Palgrave Macmillan.

Kelly, S. (2000) A proposal for a new Massachusetts notoriety-for-profit law: The grandson of Sam, *Western New England Law Review*, 22(1), 1–44.

Kennicott, P. (2014) The 9/11 museum doesn't just display artefacts, it ritualizes grief on a loop, *The Washington Post*, 7 June.

Kerrigan, N. (2018) *A Threatened Rural Idyll? Informal Social Control, Exclusion and the Resistance to Change in the English Countryside*. Delaware: Vernon Press.

Kettenhofen, L. (2021a) Total number of suicides committed in Japan from 2011 to 2020, available at https://www.statista.com/statistics/622065/japan-suicide-number/#statisticContainer, accessed 15 November 2021.

Kettenhofen, L. (2021b) Number of suicides committed in Japan from 2011 to 2020, by gender, available at https://www.statista.com/statistics/622691/japan-suicide-number-by-gender/, accessed 15 November 2021.

Kiernan, B. (1996) *The Pol Pot Regime: Race, Power, and Genocide in Cambodia under the Khmer Rouge, 1975–1979*. New Haven: Yale University Press.

Kiernan, B. (2008) *The Pol Pot Regime: Race, Power, and Genocide in Cambodia Under the Khmer Rouge, 1975–1979*, 3rd edn. New Haven: Yale University Press.

Killilea, A.G. and Lynch, D.D. (2013) *Confronting Death: College Students on the Community of Mortals*. Bloomington: IUniverse.

King, A. and Maruna, S. (2009) Is a conservative just a liberal who has been mugged? Exploring the origins of punitive views, *Punishment and Society*, 11(2), 47–169.

Kirkhope, D. (2006) 'Carmont' knife sentencing call, *BBC News*, 9 June, available at http://news.bbc.co.uk/1/hi/scotland/5063092.stm, accessed 29 April 2018.

Koops, T., Turner, D., Neutze, J. and Briken, P. (2017) Child sex tourism: Prevalence of and risk factors for use in a German community, *BMC Public Health*, 17(344), 1–8.

Korstanje, M.E. (2011) Detaching the elementary forms of dark tourism, *Journal of Tourism and Hospitality Research*, 22(3), 424–427.

Korstanje, M.E. and Ivanov, S. (2012) Tourism as a form of new psychological resilience: The inception of dark tourism, *Cultur: Revista de Cultura e Turismo*, 6(4), 56–71.

Kozinets, R.V. (2002) Can consumers escape the market? Emancipatory illuminations from Burning Man, *Journal of Consumer Research*, 29(1), 20–38.

Knight, C.K. (2014) *Power and Paradise in Walt Disney's World*. Orlando: University Press of Florida.

KNL999 (2019) *Private Guided Mezhyhirya Tour (Yanukovych Residence, Museum of Corruption)*, available at https://www.tripadvisor.com/AttractionProductReview-g294474-d17719907Private_guided_Mezhyhirya_tour_Yanukovych_Residence_Museum_of_corruption-Kyiv_Kiev.html, accessed 18 October 2021.

Krier, D. and Swart, W.J. (2016) Trophies of surplus enjoyment, *Critical Sociology*, 42(3), 371–392.

Krug, W. (2001) Private supply of protected land in Southern Africa: A review of markets, approaches, barriers and issues, Workshop Paper, World Bank/OECD International Workshop on Market Creation for Biodiversity Products and Services, Paris, 25–26 January.

Kuznik, L. (2018) Fifty shades of dark stories. In M. Khosrow-Pour (ed) *Encyclopaedia of Information Science and Technology*, 4th edn. Pennsylvania: IGI Global, pp 4077–4087.

Lagriffoul, A., Boudenne, J.L., Absi, R., Ballet, J.J., Berjeaud, J.M., Chevalier, S., Creppy, E.E., Gilli, E., Gadonna, J., Gaddonna-Widehem, P., Morris, C.E. and Zini, S. (2010) Bacterial-based additives for the production of artificial snow: What are the risks to human health? *Science of the Total Environment*, 408(7), 1659–1666.

Lahiri, T. and Hui, M. (2019) Hong Kong will have its only truly democratic election this weekend, *Quartz*, 22 November, available at https://qz.com/1753318/what-you-need-to-know-about-hong-kongs-district-council-elections/, accessed 30 August 2021.

Lam, J.T.M. (2020) The 2019 District Council election in Hong Kong: A localism perspective, *Asian Affairs: An American Review*, 2021, 48(2), 113–32.

Langman, L. (2003) Culture, identity and hegemony: The body in a global age, *Current Sociology*, 51(3–4), 223–247.

Large, J. (2019) Conspicuously 'doing' charity: Exploring the relationship between doing good and doing harm in tourism. In T. Raymen and O. Smith (eds) *Deviant Leisure: Criminological Perspectives on Leisure and Harm*. Cham: Palgrave Macmillan, pp 325–45.

Larkin, C. (2015) Meet our new mascot: Cocaine bear, *Kentucky for Kentucky*, 19 August, available at https://kyforky.com/blogs/journal/cocaine-bear, accessed August 2021.

Laub, J.H. and Sampson, R.J. (2003) *Shared Beginnings, Divergent Lives: Delinquent Boys to Age 70*. Cambridge, MA: Harvard University Press.

Leader-Williams, N. and Hutton, J.M. (2005) Does extractive use provide opportunities to reduce conflicts between people and wildlife? In R. Woodroffe, S.J. Thirgood and A. Rabinowitz (eds) *People and Wildlife: Conflict or Coexistence*. Cambridge: Cambridge University Press, pp 140–162.

Leader-Williams, N., Milledge, S., Adcock, K., Brooks, M., Conway, A., Knight, M., Mainka, S., Martin, E. and Teferi, T. (2005) Trophy hunting of black rhino *Diceros bicornis*: Proposals to ensure its future sustainability, *Journal of Sustainable Tourism*, 8(1), 1–11.

Leader-Williams, N., Baldus, R.D. and Smith, R.J. (2009) The influence of corruption on the conduct of recreational hunting. In B. Dickson, J. Hutton and W.A. Adams (eds) *Recreational Hunting, Conservation and Rural Livelihoods: Science and Practice*. Oxford: Blackwell Publishing, pp 296–317.

Lecker, A. (2020) *The Serial Killer Cookbook*. Berkeley: Ulysses Press.

Lee, H. (2017) Seoul's 'dark history' to see the light as tourist attraction, *The Korea Times*, 21 June, available at https://www.koreatimes.co.kr/www/nation/2017/06/281_231573.html, accessed 30 July 2021.

Lehman, S., Pereira, A. and Sibaja, M. (2013) They do not show any repentance, *National Post*, available at https://nationalpost.com/news/they-do-not-show-any-repentance-three-men-arrested-in-rio-for-gang-rape-of-tourist-are-indifferent-police-say, accessed 16 September 2021.

Lendon, B. (2019) US Sen. Ted Cruz rips Beijing 'dictatorship' during Hong Kong visit, *CNN*, 12 October, available at https://edition.cnn.com/2019/10/12/asia/ted-cruz-hong-kong-visit-intl-hnk/index.html, accessed 30 August 2021.

Lennon, J. (2010) Dark tourism and sites of crime. In D. Botterill and T. Jones (eds) *Tourism and Crime*. London: Goodfellow Publishers Limited, pp 215–229.

Lennon, J. and Foley, M. (2001) *Dark Tourism: The Attraction of Death and Disaster*. London: Cengage Learning.

Lennon, J.J. and Mitchell, M. (2007) Dark tourism: The role of sites of death in tourism. In Mitchell, M. (ed) *Remember Me: Constructing Immortality: Beliefs on Immorality, Life and Death*. Abingdon: Routledge, pp 167–179.

Leshchenko, S. (2012) Yanukovych, the luxury residence and the money trail that leads to London, available at https://www.opendemocracy.net/en/odr/yanukovych-luxury-residence-and-money-trail-that-leads-to-london/, accessed 18 October 2021.

Lewis, D. and Alpert, P. (1997) Trophy hunting and wildlife conservation in Zambia, *Conservation Biology*, 11(1), 59–68.

Lewis, D. and Jackson, J. (2005) Safari hunting and conservation on communal land in southern Africa. In R. Woodroffe, S.J. Thirgood and A. Rabinowitz (eds) *People and Wildlife: Conflict or Coexistence*. Cambridge: Cambridge University Press, pp 239–252.

Li, K. and Ives, M. (2019) Hong Kong protesters descend on airport, with plans to stay for days, *The New York Times*, 9 August, available at https://www.nytimes.com/2019/08/09/world/asia/hong-kong-airport-protest.html, accessed 20 August 2021.

Li, Z., Friedman, E. and Ren, H. (2018) *China on Strike: Narratives of Workers' Resistance*. Chicago: Haymarket Books.

Liechty, M. (2005) Building the road to Kathmandu: Notes on the history of tourism in Nepal, *HIMALAYA: The Journal of the Association for Nepal and Himalayan Studies*, 25(1&2): 19–28.

Liechty, M. (2017) *Far Out: Countercultural Seekers and the Tourist Encounter in Nepal*. Chicago: University of Chicago Press.

Liem, M. and Kunst, M. (2013) Is there a recognizable post-incarceration syndrome among released 'lifers', *International Journal of Law and Psychiatry*, 36(3–4), 1–5.

Light, D. (2017) Progress in dark tourism and thanatourism research: An uneasy relationship with heritage tourism, *Tourism Management*, 61, 275–301.

Linder, D. (2000) Without fear or favor: Judge James Edwin Horton and the trial of the 'Scottsboro Boys', available at https://famous-trials.com/scottsboroboys/2387-without-fear-or-favor-judge-horton-and-the-scottsboro-boys, accessed 10 June 2022.

Lindsey, P.A., Roulet, P.A. and Romañach, S.S. (2006) Economic and conservation significance of the trophy hunting industry in Sub-Saharan Africa, *Biological Conservation*, 134, 455–469.

Linebaugh, P. (2011) The Tyburn riot against the surgeons. In D. Hay, P. Linebaugh, J. Rule, E.P. Thompson and C. Winslow (eds) *Albion's Fatal Tree: Crime and Society in Eighteenth Century England*, revised edn. London: Verso, pp 65–119.

Linfield, S. (2010) *The Cruel Radiance*. Chicago: University of Chicago Press.

Linnemann, T. (2015) Capote's ghosts: Violence, media and the spectre of suspicion, *The British Journal of Criminology*, 55(3), 514–533.

Linnemann, T. (2016) *Meth Wars: Police, Media, Power*. New York: New York University Press.

Lloyd, A. (2013) *Labour Markets and Identity on the Post-Industrial Assembly Line*. Farnham: Ashgate.

Lloyd, A. (2018) Serving up harm: Systemic violence, transitions to adulthood and the service economy. In A. Boukli and J. Kotze (eds) *Zemiology: Reconnecting Crime and Social Harm*. Cham: Palgrave Macmillan, pp 245–265.

Lloyd, A. (2019) *The Harms of Work: An Ultra-realist Account of the Service Economy*. Bristol: Bristol University Press

Lloyd, A., Devanney, C., Wattis, L. and Bell, V. (2021) 'Just tensions left, right and centre': Assessing the social impact of international migration on deindustrialized locale, *Ethnic and Racial Studies*, 44(15), 2794–2815.

Loftin, R.W. (1988) Plastic hunting and real hunting, *Behavioral and Political Animal Studies*, 1, 317–323.

Loker-Murphy, L. (1997) Backpackers in Australia: A motivation-based segmentation study, *Journal of Travel & Tourism Marketing*, 5(4), 23–45.

A London Inheritance (2020) King Henry's stairs and execution dock, *A London Inheritance*, available at https://alondoninheritance.com/the-thames/king-henrys-stairs-execution-dock/, accessed 16 June 2021.

Lonely Planet (nd; a) Tuol Sleng Genocide Museum: Top choice museum in Phnom Penh, available at https://www.lonelyplanet.com/cambodia/phnom-penh/attractions/tuol-sleng- genocide-museum/a/poi-sig/441640/355 881, accessed 1 June 2022.

Lonely Planet (nd; b) Museum of Confiscated Art, available at https:// www.lonelyplanet.com/belarus/brest/ attractions/museum-of-confiscated-art/ a/poi-sig/1012 888/358699, accessed 20 July 2021.

Lonely Planet (2021) Maldives, available at https://www.lonelyplanet.com/maldives, accessed 25 July 2021.

Lopez, A. (2021) International tourism volume in Rio de Janeiro 2016–2019, available at https://www.statista.com/statistics/806001/number-international-tourists-rio-janeiro/, accessed 1 December 2021.

Lorenz, H. (2019) Trouble in paradise: The rise and fall of Germany's 'brothel king', *The Guardian*, 22 June, available at https://www.theguardian.com/global-development/2019/jun/22/trouble-in-paradise-rise-and-fall-of-germany-brothel-king-jurgen-rudloff, accessed 10 June 2022.

Lorenzo, P. and Ryder, N. (eds) (2020) *Corruption in the Global Era: Causes, Sources and Forms of Manifestation*. London: Routledge.

Los Angeles Times (1985) Cocaine-carrying chutist was ex-policeman, lawyer, *Los Angeles Times*, 12 September, available at https://www.latimes.com/archives/la-xpm-1985-09-12-mn-21488-story.html, accessed 1 June 2022.

Loss, J.T. (1987) Criminals selling their stories: The First Amendment requires legislative re-examination, *Cornell Law Review*, 72(6), 1331–1355.

Lowe, K. (2020) *Weekend Warriors: Cocaine Use Amongst Privileged Expatriates in Hong Kong from an Edgework Perspective*. PhD thesis, The University of Hong Kong.

Lum, A. (2019) Far-right Ukrainian activists say they were 'only in Hong Kong for protest tourism' as concerns grow they could help authorities delegitimise the movement, *South China Morning Post*, 4 December, available at https://www.scmp.com/news/hong-kong/politics/article/3040625/far-right-ukrainian-activists-say-they-were-only-hong-kong, accessed 30 August 2021.

Lutnick, A. and Cohan, D. (2009) Criminalization, legalization or decriminalization of sex work: What female sex workers say in San Francisco, USA, *Reproductive Health Matters*, 17(34), 38–46.

Lynes, A., Kelly, C. and Uppal, P.K.S. (2018) Benjamin's 'flâneur' and serial murder: An ultra-realist literary case study of Levi Bellfield, *Crime, Media, Culture*, 15(3), 523–543.

Lynes, A., Kelly, C. and Kelly, E. (2020) Thug life: Drill music as a periscope into urban violence in the consumer age, *The British Journal of Criminology*, 60(5), 1201–1219.

Lynes, A., Yardley, E. and Danos, L. (2021) *Making Sense of Homicide: A Student Textbook*. Hampshire: Waterside Press.

Lyng, S. (1990) Edgework: A social psychological analysis of voluntary risk taking, *The American Journal of Sociology*, 95(4), 851–886.

Lyng, S. (2004) *Edgework: The Sociology of Risk-Taking*. New York: Routledge.

MacCannell, D. (1973) Staged authenticity: Arrangements of social space in tourist settings, *American Journal of Sociology*, 79(3), 589–603.

MacDonald, E.E. (2020) *Ian Rankin: A Companion to Mystery Fiction*. Jefferson, NC: MacFarland and Co.

MacFarquhar, L. (2013) Last call: A Buddhist monk confronts Japan's suicide culture, *The New Yorker*, 17 June, available at https://www.newyorker.com/magazine/2013/06/24/last-call-3, accessed 14 January 2022.

Mackenzie, S. (2011) Illicit deals in cultural objects as crimes of the powerful, *Crime, Law and Social Change*, 56(2), 133–153.

Magister, C. [Wachs, B.] (2019) *The Scene that Became Cities: What Burning Man Philosophy Can Teach Us About Building Better Communities*. Berkeley: North Atlantic Books.

Magne, S. (2003) *Multi-Ethnic Devon: A Rural Handbook*. Devon: Devon and Exeter Racial Equality Council.

Magnetic Latvia (2016) Karosta Prison in Liepaja continues to surprise, available at https://www.latvia.travel/en/news/karosta-prison-liepaja-continues-surprise, accessed 25 August 2021.

Malbon, B. (1999) *Clubbing: Dancing, Ecstasy and Vitality*. London: Routledge.

Malone, E. (2015) Long-lost brothers: How nihilism provides bigger Thomas and Biggie Smalls with a soul, *Journal of Black Studies*, 46(3), 297–315.

Mann, S.L. and Budworth, M.-H. (2018) The happiest place on Earth? A case study of the Disney World employment experience. In R.J. Burke and J.C. Hughes (eds) *Handbook of Human Resource Management in the Tourism and Hospitality Industries*. Cheltenham: Elgar Online.

Manoiu, V.M., Costache, R. and Spiridon, R.M. (2015) The pleasure factor in the anthropic environment and the geography of beauty, *European Scientific Journal*, 11, 299–310.

Marcuse, H. (2005) Reshaping Dachau for visitors: 1933–2000. In G. Ashworth and R. Hartmann (eds) *Horror and Human Tragedy Revisited: The Management of Sites of Atrocities for Tourism*. New York: Cognizant Communication Corporation, pp 118–148.

Marcuse, H. (2008) *Legacies of Dachau: The Uses and Abuses of a Concentration Camp, 1933–2001*. Cambridge: Cambridge University Press.

Markham, A. (2012) 'Fabrication as ethical practice: Qualitative enquiry in ambiguous Internet contexts', *Information, Communication and Society*, 15(3), 334–353.

Marks, K. (2004) Island chief raped me when I was 11, Pitcairn trial told, *The Independent*, 30 September.

Marks, K. (2009) *Lost Paradise: From Mutiny on the Bounty to a Modern-Day Legacy of Sexual Mayhem, the Dark Secrets of Pitcairn Island Revealed*. London: Free Press.

Marks, K. (2016) Is it 'ludicrous' to ban climbers from Uluru?, *BBC News*, 11 May, available at https://www.bbc.co.uk/news/world-australia-36263849, accessed 10 June 2022.

Marshall, R. (2016) Sex workers and human rights: A critical analysis of laws regarding sex work, *William and Mary Journal of Women and the Law*, 23(1), 47–77.

Marshall, R. (2018) *Blurred Boundaries: Rankin's Rebus*. np: Out There.

Marshman, S. (2005) From the margins to the mainstream? Representations of the Holocaust in popular culture, *eSharp*, 6(1), 1–20.

Maruna, S. (2001) *Making Good: How Ex-convicts Reform and Rebuild Their Lives*. Washington, DC: American Psychological Association. https://doi.org/10.1037/10430-000

Maruna, S. and Roy, K. (2007) Amputation or reconstruction? Notes on the concept of 'knifing off' and desistance from crime, *Journal of Contemporary Criminal Justice*, 23(1), 104–124.

Maruna, S. and LeBel, T. (2015) Strengths-based restorative approaches to re-entry: The evolution of creative restitution, reintegration, and destigmatisation. In N. Ronel and D. Segev (eds) *Positive Criminology*. Abingdon: Routledge, pp 65–85.

Marx, K. and Engels, F. (nd) Manifesto of the Communist Party and its genesis. Marxists Internet Archive, available at https://www.marxists.org/admin/books/manifesto/Manifesto.pdf, accessed 1 June 2022.

Mashberg, T. (2015) The ultimate temple raider? Inside an antiquities-smuggling operation, *The New York Times*, 23 July, available at https://www.nytimes.com/2015/07/26/arts/design/the-ultimate-temple-raider-inside-an-antiquities-smuggling-operation.html, accessed 27 May 2021.

Mashberg, T. (2021) Antiquities dealer pleads guilty for role in sale of looted items, *The New York Times*, 5 October, available at https://www.nytimes.com/2021/10/05/arts/design/antiquites -dealer-looted-items-please-guilty.html, accessed 20 October 2021.

Matsubayashi, T., Sawada, Y. and Ueda, M. (2013) Does the installation of blue lights on train platforms prevent suicide? A before and after observational study from Japan, *Journal of Affective Disorders*, 147(1–3), 285–388.

Matsumoto, S. (1960) *Namo no tou [Tower of Waves]*. Not in print.

Mauro, J.C. (2012) Rethinking murderabilia: How states can restrict some depictions of crime as they restrict child pornography, *Fordham Intellectual Property, Media and Entertainment Law Journal*, 22(2), 323–358.

Mayaka, T.B. (2002) *Value Wildlife! An Ecological and Economic Assessment of Wildlife Use in Northern Cameroon*. PhD thesis, Leiden University.

Mbendana, D., Mamabolo, K., Truter, M., Kritzinger, Q. and Ndhlala, A.R. (2019) Practices at herbal (muthi) markets in Gauteng, South Africa and their impact on the health of the consumers: A case study of KwaMai-Mai and Marabastad muthi markets, *South African Journal of Botany*, 126, 30–39.

McCleskey v. Kemp, 481 US 279 (1987).

McCulloch, D. (2017) Austerity's impact on rough sleeping and violence. In V. Cooper and D. Whyte (eds) *The Violence of Austerity*. London: Pluto Press, pp 171–77.

McDaniel, K. (2018) *Virtual Dark Tourism*. London: Palgrave Macmillan.

McKean, S. (2004) Traditional use of vultures: Some perspectives. In A. Monadjem, M.D. Anderson, S.E. Piper and A.F. Boshoff (eds) *The Vultures of Southern Africa – Quo Vadis? Proceedings of a Workshop on Vulture Research and Conservation in Southern Africa*. Johannesburg: Birds of Prey Working Group, pp 214–219, available at http://sungura.co.uk/Library/VultureStudyGProceedings_final.pdf#page=217, accessed 16 August 2021.

McKean, S., Mander, M., Diederichs, N., Ntulil, L., Mavundla, K., Williams, V. and Wakelin, J. (2013) The impact of traditional use on vultures in South Africa, *Vulture News*, 65, 15–36.

McKenna, T. (2015) The suicide forest: A Marxist analysis of the high suicide rate in Japan, *Rethinking Marxism*, 27(2), 293–302.

McKie, R. (2006) Rapist relative of Bounty's mutineer enters his DIY jail, *The Guardian*, 19 November.

McLean, R., Robinson, G. and Densley, J. (2018) The rise of drug dealing in the life of the North American street gang, *Societies*, 8(3), 90.

McLynn, F. (1989) *Crime and Punishment in Eighteenth Century England*. Oxford: Oxford University Press.

McNeil, F. (2012) Four forms of 'offender' rehabilitation: Towards an interdisciplinary perspective, *Legal and Criminological Psychology*, 17(1), 18–36.

McNeill, F. (2019) Mass supervision, misrecognition and the 'Malopticon', *Punishment and Society*, 21(2), 207–230.

Mears, M. (2008) The Georgia death penalty: A need for racial justice, *John Marshall Law Journal*, 1, 71–90.

Mercer, S. (2017) Charles Manson's life and crimes: A timeline, *Sky News*, available at https://news.sky.com/story/charles-mansons-life-and-crimes-a-timeline-11135463, accessed 10 June 2022.

Mey, C. (2012) *Survivor: The Triumph of an Ordinary Man in the Khmer Rouge Genocide*. Phnom Penh: Documentation Center of Cambodia.

Mighail, R. (1999) *A Geography of Victorian Gothic Fiction: Mapping History's Nightmares*. Oxford: Oxford University Press.

Miles, W.F.S. (2002) Auschwitz: Museum interpretation and darker tourism, *Annals of Tourism Research*, 29(4), 1175–1178.

Mills, A. and Kendall, K. (eds) (2018) *Mental Health in Prisons: Critical Perspectives on Treatment and Confinement.* Cham: Springer International.

Millward, P. (2017) World Cup 2022 and Qatar's construction projects: Relational power in networks and relational responsibilities to migrant workers, *Current Sociology*, 65(5), 756–776.

Milner, J.M., Nilsen, E.B. and Andreassen, H.P. (2007) Demographic side effects of selective hunting in ungulates and carnivores, *Conservation Biology*, 21(1), 36–47.

Milner-Gulland, E.J., Bukreeva, O.M., Coulson, T., Lushchekina, A.A., Kholodova, M.V., Bekenov, A.B. and Grachev, I.A. (2003) Conservation: Reproductive collapse in saiga antelope harems, *Nature*, 422, 135.

Ministry of Tourism (2019) *Tourism Yearbook 2019*. Male: Ministry of Tourism

Minniti, C. (2018) The 'Ndrangheta in Scilla: Compromising friendships, criminal prejudices and contracts with companies in the smell of the mafia-video, *LACNews24*, 12 April, available at https://www.lacnews24.it/cronaca/scioglimento-scilla-motivazioni-sindaco-appalti-lavori-ndrangheta_47795/, accessed 13 July 2021.

Minogue, C. (2009) The engaged specific intellectual: Resisting unethical prison tourism and hubris of the objectifying modality of the universal intellectual, *Journal of Prisoners and Prisons*, 18(1–2), 129–142.

Miron, T. (2011) *Prisons, Asylums, and the Public: Institutional Visiting in the Nineteenth Century*, London: University of Toronto Press.

Monbiot, G. (2016) Neoliberalism: The ideology at the root of all our problems, *The Guardian*, 15 April, available at https://www.theguardian.com/books/2016/apr/15/neoliberalism-ideology-problem-george-monbiot, accessed 5 October 2022.

Monk, C. (1999) From underworld to underclass: Crime and British cinema in the 1990s. In S. Chibnall and R. Murphy (eds) *British Crime Cinema*. London: Routledge, pp 172–189.

Morelli, F., Kubicka, A., Tryjanowski, P. and Nelson, E. (2015) The vulture in the sky and the hominin on the land: Three million years of human–vulture interaction, *Anthrozoös*, 28(3), 449–468.

Morrell, L. (2016) Amazon comes under fire for stress placed on its delivery drivers, *eDelivery*, 11 November, available at https://edelivery.net/2016/11/amazon-comes-fire-stress-placed-delivery-drivers/, accessed 5 October 2022.

Morrison, W. (2010) A reflected gaze of humanity: Cultural criminology and images of genocide. In K.J. Hayward and M. Presdee (eds) *Framing Crime: Cultural Criminology and the Image*. Abingdon: Routledge, pp 189–207.

Mortimer, S., Powell, A. and Sandy, L. (2019) 'Typical scripts' and their silences: Exploring myths about sexual violence and LGBTQ people from the perspective of support workers, *Current Issues in Criminal Justice*, 31(3), 333–348.

Moscia, L. (2005) Rio and paying for sex, *Dodho*, available at https://www.dodho.com/rio-and-paying-for-sex-by-lorenzo-moscia/, accessed 19 September 2021.

Mostafanezhad, M. (2013a) The geography of compassion in volunteer tourism, *Tourism Geographies*, 15(2), 318–337.

Mostafanezhad, M. (2013b) 'Getting in touch with your inner Angelina': Celebrity humanitarianism and the cultural politics of gendered generosity in volunteer tourism, *Third World Quarterly*, 34(3), 485–499.

Mostafanezhad, M. (2014) Volunteer tourism and the popular humanitarian gaze, *Geoforum*, 54, 111–118.

Motmans, J., T'Sjoen, G. and Meier, P. (2015) *Geweldervaringen van transgender personen in België* [*Experiences of Violence of Transgender Persons in Belgium*]. Gent/Antwerp: University of Gent/University of Antwerp, https://biblio.ugent.be/publication/8161261

Mullany, G. (2019) U.S. issues travel warning for Hong Kong due to 'confrontational' protests, *The New York Times*, 7 August, available at https://www.nytimes.com/2019/08/07/world/asia/hong-kong-travel-warning.html, accessed 30 August 2021.

Mullen, C., Whalley, B., Schifano, F. and Baker, J. (2020) Anabolic androgenic steroid abuse in the United Kingdom: An update, *British Journal of Pharmacology*, 177(10), 2180–2198.

Mullin, M.H. (1999) Mirrors and windows: Sociocultural studies of human-animal relationships, *Annual Review of Anthropology*, 28, 201–224.

Murphy, I. (2017) Thug scarred woman for life with 'Chelsea smile' after slashing her across face with kitchen knife, *The Mirror*, 5 April, available at https://www.mirror.co.uk/news/uk-news/thug-scarred-woman-life-chelsea-10162081, accessed 29 April 2018.

museum.by (nd) Музей «Спасённые художественные ценности», available at http://values.brest.museum.by/, accessed 20 July 2021.

museum.by (2016) Музей спасенных художественных ценностей, available at http://museums.by/muzei/muzei-g-bresta-i-brestskoy-oblasti/muzey-spasennykh-khudozhestvennykh-tsennostey/, accessed 20 July 2021.

Museum Valse Kunst (2021) Museum Valse Kunst, available at https://www.museums-vledder.nl/en/museums-vledder/index.php//, accessed 20 July 2021.

Myers, N. (1981) The exhausted earth, *Foreign Policy*, 42, 141–155.

Myers, S.L. (2019) In Hong Kong protests, China angrily connects dots back to U.S., *The New York Times*, 5 September, available at https://www.nytimes.com/2019/09/05/world/asia/china-hong-kong-protests.html, accessed 30 August 2021.

Myung Ja, K., Choong-Ki, L., Petrick, J. and Young-Sik, K. (2020) The influence of perceived risk and intervention on international tourists' behavior during the Hong Kong protest: Application of an extended model of goal-directed behavior, *Journal of Hospitality and Tourism Management*, 45, 622–632.

Napper, I.E. and Thompson, R.C. (2016) Release of synthetic microplastic plastic fibres from domestic washing machines: Effects of fabric type and washing conditions, *Marine Pollution Bulletin*, 112(1–2), 39–45.

Neal, S. and Agyeman, J. (2006) *The New Countryside? Ethnicity, Nation and Exclusion in Contemporary Rural Britain.* Bristol: Policy Press.

Nelson, S.P. and Prendergast, C. (2009) Murderabilia Inc: Where the First Amendment fails academic freedom, *South Atlantic Quarterly*, 108(4), 667–688.

Newton, C. (2020) Amazon's poor treatment of workers is catching up to it during the coronavirus crisis, *The Verge*, 1 April, available at https://www.theverge.com/interface/2020/4/1/21201162/amazon-delivery-delays-coronavirus-worker-strikes, accessed 5 October 2022.

Nguyen, T. and Roberts, D.L. (2020) Exploring the Africa-Asia trade nexus for endangered wildlife used in traditional Asian medicine: Interviews with traders in South Africa and Vietnam, *Tropical Conservation Science*. doi: 10.1177/1940082920979252

NHS (2018) Anabolic steroid misuse, available at https://www.nhs.uk/conditions/anabolic-steroid-misuse/, accessed 6 April 2021.

Nishikawa, M. (2019) The reason why I started free coffee, *Earth Ride*, 12 January, available at https://note.com/earthride/n/n1dc008a8a61d, accessed 30 August 2021.

Nixon, R. (2011) *Slow Violence and the Environmentalism of the Poor*. Cambridge, MA: Harvard University Press.

Norindr, P. (1996) *Phantasmatic Indochina: French Colonial Ideology in Architecture, Film, and Literature*. Durham, NC: Duke University Press.

Norris v. Alabama, 294 US 587 (1935).

North-Best, E. (2017) The strange death, and even stranger life of 'Cocaine Cowboy' Andrew Carter Thornton II, *Muckrock*, 28 April, available at https://www.muckrock.com/news/archives/2017/apr/28/fbi-cia-cocaine/, accessed 13 June 2022.

Nshala, R. (1999) *Granting Hunting Blocks in Tanzania: The Need for Reform*. Lawyers' Environmental Action Team, Policy Briefing 5, Tanzania.

Nurse, A. (2013) *Animal Harm: Perspectives on Why People Harm and Kill Animals*. Farnham: Ashgate.

Nurse, A. (2015) *Policing Wildlife*. Basingstoke: Palgrave Macmillan.

Nurse, A. and Wyatt, T. (2020) *Wildlife Criminology*. Bristol: Bristol University Press.

Oakley, N. (2016) How common are 'naked tourism' photos? Brit arrested in Peru just one of many to join craze, *The Mirror*, 4 March, available at https://www.mirror.co.uk/news/uk-news/how-common-naked-tourism-photos-7492397, accessed 13 June 2022.

Ogada, D., Shaw, P., Beyers, R.L., Buij, R., Murn, C., Thiollay, J.M., Beale, C.M., Holdo, R.M., Pomeroy, D., Baker, N., Krüger, S.C., Botha, A., Virani, M.Z., Monadjem, A. and Sinclair, A.R.E. (2016) Another continental vulture crisis: Africa's vultures collapsing toward extinction, *Conservation Letters*, 9, 89–97.

Organise (2018) Amazon: What's it like where you work? available at https://stat ic1.squaresp ace.com/static/5a3af 3e22 aeba594ad56d 8cb/t/5ad09 8b35 62fa7b8c 90d5e1b/1523620020369/, accessed on 5 October 2022.

Packer, C., Kosmala, M., Cooley, H.S., Brink, H., Pintea, L., Garshelis, D., Purchase, G., Strauss, M., Swanson, A., Balme, G. and Hunter, L. (2009) Sport hunting, predator control and conservation of large carnivores, *PloS one*, 4(6), 1–8.

Packer, C., Brink, H., Kissui, B.M., Maliti, H., Kushnir, H. and Caro, T. (2011) Effects of trophy hunting on lion and leopard populations in Tanzania, *Conservation Biology*, 25(1), 142–153.

Padgett, D.K. and Struening, E.L. (1992) Victimization and traumatic injuries among the homeless: Associations with alcohol, drug, and mental problems, *American Journal of Orthopsychiatry*, 62(4), 525–534.

Pallot, R. (2021) Amazon destroying millions of items of unsold stock in one of its UK warehouses every year, ITV News investigation finds, *ITV News*, 22 June, available at https://www.itv.com/news/2021-06-21/amazon-destroying-millions-of-items-of-unsold-stock-in-one-of-its-uk-warehouses-every-year-itv-news-investigation-finds, accessed 5 October 2022.

Parker, H., Aldridge, J. and Measham, F. (1998) *Illegal Leisure: The Normalisation of Adolescent Recreational Drug Use*. London: Routledge.

Parsons, A.E. (2018) *From Asylum to Prison: Deinstitutionalization and the Rise of Mass Incarceration after 1945*. Chapel Hill: University of North Carolina Press.

Paterson, J., Walters, M.A., Brown, R. and Fearn, H. (2018) *The Sussex Hate Crime Project: Final Report*. Brighton: University of Sussex

Patterson, C. and Khosa, P. (2005) *Background Research Paper: A Status Quo Study on the Professional and Recreational Hunting Industry in South Africa*, available at https://www.google.com/url?sa=t&rct=j&q=&esrc=s&source=web&cd=&ved=2ahUKEwjF1LaolrPwAhWQOcAKHaz9CgQFjAAegQIAxAD&url=https%3A%2F%2Fwww.africahunting.com%2Fattachments%2Fhunting-industry-in-africa-pdf.2769%2F&usg=AOvVaw0hM9wc0YcJQR9AxPKzRgKd, accessed 13 June 2022.

Patti, T., Fobert, E., Reeves, S. and Burke da Silva, K. (2020) Spatial distribution of microplastics around an inhabited coral island in the Maldives, Indian Ocean, *Science of the Total Environment*, 748. DOI: 10.1016/j.scitotenv.2020.141263

Pattisson, P. (2013) Revealed: Qatar's World Cup 'slaves', *The Guardian*, 25 September, available at https://www.theguardian.com/world/2013/sep/25/revealed-qatars-world-cup-slaves, accessed 9 June 2022.

Pearson, J. (2015) *The Profession of Violence: The Rise and Fall of the Kray Twins*. London: William Collins.

Pedersen, C. (2017) Screening tourist encounters: Penal spectatorship and the visual cultures of Auschwitz. In J. Wilson, S. Hodgkinson, J. Piché and K. Walby (eds) *The Palgrave Handbook of Prison Tourism*. London: Palgrave Macmillan, pp 131–151.

Peel, V. and Steen, A. (2007) Victims, hooligans and cash-cows: Media representations of the international backpacker in Australia, *Tourism Management*, 28(4), 1057–1067.

Peled-Laskov, R. and Timor, U. (2018) Working behind bards: Employed prisoners' perceptions of professional training and employment in prison, *International Journal of Criminology and Sociology*, 7, 1–15.

Peñascal, M. (2020) *Yurei: The Japanese Culture of Ghosts through History*. Available at https://voyapon.com/yurei-japanese-ghosts/, accessed 12 November 2021.

Perlin, R. (2011) *Intern Nation*. London: Verso.

Perovoznaya, O. and Yakimenko, N. (2010) Yanukovych beat German, *Gazeta*, available at https://gazeta.ua/ru/articles/politics-newspaper/_anukovich-izbil-german/325366, accessed 18 October 2021.

Perrone, D. (2009) *The High Life: Club Kids, Harm and Drug Policy*. Monsey: Criminal Justice Press.

Perry, B. and Alvi, S. (2012) 'We are all vulnerable': The in terrorem effects of hate crimes, *International Review of Victimology*, 18(1), 57–71.

Peters, E.M. (1998) Prison before the prison: The ancient and medieval worlds. In N. Morris and D.J. Rothman (eds) *Oxford History of the Prison: The Practice of Punishment in Western Society*. New York: Oxford University Press, pp 3–48.

The Pew Trusts (2015) *The Pitcairn Islands Marine Reserve*, available at pitcairn_fs_final_web.pdf, accessed 9 August 2021.

Phillips, D. (2017) Brazil police shoot dead Spanish tourist in Rio de Janeiro favela, *The Guardian*, available at https://www.theguardian.com/world/2017/oct/23/brazil-police-shoot-dead-spanish-tourist-rio-de-janeiro-favela, accessed 27 October 2021.

Piché, J. and Walby, K. (2010) Problematizing carceral tours, *British Journal of Criminology*, 50, 570–581.

Picken, F. (2018) *The SAGE International Encyclopedia of Travel and Tourism: Extreme Tourism*. London: SAGE.

Pilger, J. (1979) *Year Zero: The Silent Death of Cambodia*. ITV Network and Associated Television.

Pinker, S. (2011) *The Better Angels of Our Nature: A History of Violence and Humanity*. London: Penguin Books.

Plain, G. (2018) 'Lost to the streets': Violence, space and gender in urban crime fiction. In C. Ehland and P. Fischer (eds) *Resistance and the City: Negotiating Urban Identities: Race, Class and Gender*. Leiden: Brill, pp 151–167.

Podoshen, J.S. (2017) Trajectories in holocaust tourism, *Journal of Heritage Tourism*, 12(4), 347–364.

Poon, W.C. and Kian, Y.K. (2021) Hong Kong protests and tourism: Modelling tourist trust on revisit intention, *Journal of Vacation Marketing*, 27(2), 217–234.

Postman, N. (1992) *Technopoly: The Surrender of Culture to Technology*. New York: Vintage Books.

Potter, G. (2009) Exploring retail level drug distribution: Social supply, 'real' dealers and the user/dealer interface. In T. Demetrovics, J. Fountain and L. Kraus (eds) *Old and New Policies, Theories, Research Methods and Drug Users Across Europe*. Lengerich: PABST Publications, pp 50–74.

Powell v. Alabama, 287 US 45 (1932).

Prague Daily Monitor (2017) Exhibition of art looted from Czech Jews opens in Prague, *Prague Daily Monitor*, 3 May, available at https://web.archive.org/web/20170503132903/http://www.praguemonitor.com/2017/05/03/exhibition-art-looted-czech-jews-opens-prague, accessed 20 July 2021.

Presdee, M. (2000) *Cultural Criminology and the Carnival of Crime*. London: Routledge.

Priestley, M.P. (2016) *One Autumn in Whitechapel*. London: Flower and Dean Street Ltd.

The Proceedings of the Old Bailey (2018a) The journey from Newgate to Tyburn, *Old Bailey Proceedings Online*, available at https://www.oldbaileyonline.org/static/JourneyTyburn.jsp, accessed 12 June 2021.

The Proceedings of the Old Bailey (2018b) Punishment sentences at the Old Bailey, *Old Bailey Proceedings Online*, available at https://www.oldbaileyonline.org/static/Punishment.jsp#:~:text=It%20is%20alleged%20that%20sometimes,applied%20when%20it%20was%20cold.&text=Branding%20as%20a%20punishment%20for,of%20clergy%20ended%20in%201779, accessed 27 September 2020.

Proctor, A. (nd) *The Exhibitionist*, available at https://www.theexhibitionist.org/, accessed 2 August 2021.

Prusher, I. (2015) An impossible watch heist, now on display at Jerusalem museum, *Haaretz*, 1 July, available at http://www.haaretz.com/blogs/jerusalem-vivendi/.premium-1.663902, accessed 20 July 2021.

Raine, R. (2013) A dark tourist spectrum, *International Journal of Culture, Tourism and Hospitality Research*, 7(3), 242–256.

Rajaram, P.K. and Grundy-Warr, C. (2004) The irregular migrant as homo sacer: Migration and detention in Australia, Malaysia, and Thailand, *International Migration*, 42(1), 33–64.

Rana, B. (1985) Artifact theft is big business in Nepal, *United Press International*, 2 April, available at https://www.upi.com/Archives/1985/04/02/Artifact-theft-is-big-business-in-Nepal/9693481266000/, accessed 29 May 2021.

Rankin, I. (1998) *Death is not the End*. London: Orion.

Rankin, I. (2000) *Set in Darkness*. London: Orion.

Rankin, I. (2001) *The Falls*. London: Orion.

Rankin, I. (2018) *In a House of Lies*. London: Orion.

Rashkin, E. (1992) *Family Secrets and the Psychoanalysis of Narrative*. Princeton: Princeton University Press.

Ray, L. (2011) *Violence and Society*. London: SAGE.

Raymen, T. (2017) Living in the end times through popular culture: An ultra-realist analysis of *The Walking Dead* as popular criminology, *Crime Media Culture*, 14(3), 1–19.

Raymen, T. (2019) The enigma of social harm and the barrier of liberalism: Why zemiology needs a theory of the good, *Justice, Power and Resistance*, 3(1), 134–163.

Raymen, T. and Smith, O. (2019) *Deviant Leisure: Criminological Perspectives on Leisure and Harm*. London: Palgrave Macmillan.

Reaves, W. (2011) The Scottsboro boys, 24 February, available at https://npg.si.edu/blog/scottsboro-boys, accessed 5 October 2022.

RedLightDistrictAmsterdamTours.com (2020) Window Brothels, Red Light District Amsterdam Tours, available at https://redlightdistrictamsterdamtours.com/en/windows.php, accessed 27 May 2021.

Redmon, D. (2015) *Mardi Gras: Made in China*, available at https://vimeo.com/87231218, accessed 1 June 2022.

Reiner, R. (2002) Media made criminality: The representation of crime in the mass media. In R. Reiner, M. Maguire and R. Morgan (eds) *The Oxford Handbook of Criminology*. Oxford: Oxford University Press, pp 302–337.

Remnick, N. (2017) Notorious B.I.G., Brooklyn street bard, gets official city tribute at last, *The New York Times*, 2 August, available at https://www.nytimes.com/2017/08/02/nyregion/christopher-wallace-notorious-big-tribute-brooklyn.html, accessed 1 June 2022.

Reynolds, D.P. (2018) *Postcards from Auschwitz: Holocaust Tourism and the Meaning of Remembrance*. New York: New York University Press.

Reynolds, M. (2020) Jeff Bezos wants to fix climate change: He can start with Amazon, *Wired*, 18 February, available at https://www.wired.co.uk/article/jeff-bezos-climate-change-amazon#:~:text=In%20September%202019%2C%20after%20almost,the%20annual%20emissions%20of%20Norway, accessed 5 October 2022.

Ripper Street (2012) *BBC*, 30 December.

Ripple, W.J., Newsome, T.M. and Kerley, G.I. (2016) Does trophy hunting support biodiversity? A response to Di Minin et al, *Trends in Ecology & Evolution*, 31(7), 495–496.

RNZ (2020) Former Pitcairn Island mayor faces three charges of indecent behaviour, *RNZ*, 14 October.

Roberts, C. (2018) Educating the (dark) masses: Dark tourism and sensemaking. In P.R. Stone, R. Hartmann, A.V. Seaton, R. Sharpley and L. White (eds) *The Palgrave Handbook of Dark Tourism Studies*. London: Palgrave Macmillan, pp 603–639.

Robinson, B. (2015) *They All Love Jack*. London: Fourth Estate.

Rockell, B. (2009) Challenging what they all know: Integrating the real/reel world into criminal justice pedagogy, *Journal of Criminal Justice Education*, 20(1), 75–92.

Rolando, A., Caprio, E., Rinaldi, E. and Ellena, I. (2007) The impact of high-altitude ski-runs on alpine grassland bird communities, *Journal of Applied Ecology*, 44(1), 210–219.

Ronel, N. and Segev, D. (2020) *Positive Criminology: Theory, Research, and Practice*. London: Routledge.

Ronin Dave (2021) Haunted Aokigahara Forest: Drinking and debunking with solo camper Marine Bushido Devil Dog, *YouTube*, 28 October, available at https://www.youtube.com/watch?v=sqyZWMEG1Vg, accessed 12 November 2021.

Rosenblatt, K. (2020) YouTuber Logan Paul is sued over 'suicide forest' video, *NBC News*, 31 December, available at https://www.nbcnews.com/pop-culture/pop-culture-news/youtuber-logan-paul-sued-over-suicide-forest-video-n1252610, accessed 12 November 2021.

Ross, J.I. (2012) Touring imprisonment: A descriptive statistical analysis of prison museums, *Tourism Management Perspectives*, 4, 113–118.

Rowlands, T. (2011) Investigation into death of Notorious B.I.G. heats up, *CNN*, 7 January, available at http://edition.cnn.com/2011/CRIME/01/07/california.biggie.death.probe/index.html, accessed 28 January 2022.

Rubenhold, H. (2020) *The Five*. London: Transworld Publishing/Black Swan.

Ruggeri, A. (2016) The London gallows where pirates were hanged, *BBC*, available at http://www.bbc.com/autos/story/20161216-the-london-gallows-where-pirates-were-hanged, accessed 13 June 2021.

Ruggiero, V. (2000) *Crime and Markets: Essays in Anti-criminology*. Oxford: Oxford University Press.

Sachedina, H.T. (2008) *Wildlife is Our Oil: Conservation, Livelihoods and NGOs in the Tarangire Ecosystem, Tanzania*. Doctoral dissertation, Oxford University.

Sachs, A. (2019) Is it safe to travel to Hong Kong? I went to find out, *The Washington Post*, 20 December 2019, available at https://www.washingtonpost.com/lifestyle/travel/is-it-safe-to-travel-to-hong-kong-i-went-to-find-out/2019/12/19/6cb63ed0-1d1a-11ea-8d58-5ac3600967a1_story.html, accessed 30 August 2021.

Sagan, C. (1994) *Pale Blue Dot*. New York: Random House.

Sagoe, D., Molde, H., Andreassen, C., Torsheim, T. and Pallesen, S. (2014) The global epidemiology of anabolic-androgenic steroid use: A meta-analysis and meta-regression analysis, *Annals of Epidemiology*, 24(5), 383–398.

Sainato, M. (2019) 'Go back to work': Outcry over deaths on Amazon's warehouse floor, *The Guardian*, 18 October, available at https://www.theguardian.com/technology/2019/oct/17/amazon-warehouse-worker-deaths, accessed 5 October 2022.

Sainato, M. (2020) 'I'm not a robot': Amazon workers condemn unsafe, gruelling conditions at warehouse, *The Guardian*, 5 February, available at https://www.theguardian.com/technology/2020/feb/05/amazon-workers-protest-unsafe-grueling-conditions-warehouse, accessed 5 October 2022.

Salvage Art Institute (nd) Salvage Art Institute, available at http://salvageartinstitute.org/, accessed 2 August 2021.

Sandberg, E. (2020) Crime fiction and the city. In J. Allan, J. Gulddal, S. King and A. Pepper (eds) *The Routledge Companion to Crime Fiction*. London: Routledge, pp 335–343.

Sanders, T., O'Neill, M. and Pitcher, J. (2009) *Prostitution: Sex Work, Policy and Politics*. London: SAGE.

Saner, E. (2018) Employers are monitoring computers, toilet breaks – even emotions. Is your boss watching you?, *The Guardian*, 14 May, available at https://www.theguardian.com/world/2018/may/14/is-your-boss-secretly-or-not-so-secretly-watching-you, accessed 5 October 2022.

Santora, M. (2013) Look up to Notorious B.I.G.? No way, some say. No street or avenue, either, *The New York Times*, 20 October, City Room [blog], available at https://cityroom.blogs.nytimes.com/2013/10/20/street-naming-by-marc-santora/?searchResultPosition=1, accessed 11 June 2022.

Saxena, N. (2020) Most interesting facts about Belarus, *On His Own Trip*, available at https://www.onhisowntrip.com/most-interesting-facts-about-belarus/, accessed 2 August 2021.

Scheper-Hughes, N. (1993) *Death Without Weeping: The Violence of Everyday Life in Brazil*. Oakland: University of California Press.

Schick, J. (2006) *Gods are Leaving the Country: Art Theft from Nepal*. Bangkok: Orchid Press.

Schmid, D. (2004) Murderabilia: Consuming fame, *M/C Journal: A Journal of Media and Culture*, 7(5), available at http://journal.media-culture.org.au/0411/10-schmid.php, accessed 13 June 2022.

Schmid, D. (2005) *Natural Born Celebrities: Serial Killers in American Culture*. Chicago: University of Chicago Press.

Schneider, J.C. (1988) The police on Skid Row: A historical perspective, *Criminal Justice Review*, 13(2), 15–20.

Schuster, S. (2019) She was next in line to be the president: He plays one on TV. Who will win Ukraine's election?, *Time Magazine*, available at http://time.com/longform/ukraine-presidential-election/, accessed 2 February 2022.

Scott, R. (2019) In case you missed it … Sen. Rick Scott visits Hong Kong amid unrest, *Rick Scott, Florida's U.S. Senator*, 30 September, available at https://www.rickscott.senate.gov/2019/9/case-you-missed-it-sen-rick-scott-visits-hong-kong-amid-unrest, accessed 30 August 2021.

Scott, S. and Bengtson, K.S. (2021) 'You've met with a terrible fate, haven't you?': A hauntological analysis of carceral violence in *Majora's Mask*', *Games and Culture*, 17(4), 1–20.

Scull, A. (1979) *Museums of Madness: The Social Organization of Insanity in Nineteenth-Century England*. London: Allen Lane.

Seaton, A.V. (1996) Guided by the dark: From thantopsis to thanatourism, *International Journal of Heritage Studies*, 2(4), 234–244.

Seddon, T. (2007) *Punishment and Madness: Governing Prisoners with Mental Health Problems*. Abingdon: Glasshouse.

Seedman, V. (2006) Sightseeing the abyss: The enigma of Holocaust and genocide tourism, paper presented at 'Journeys through the Holocaust' conference, University of Southampton, 11 December.

Seenan, G. (2005) Scotland has second highest murder rate in Europe, *The Guardian*, 26 September, available at https://www.theguardian.com/uk/2005/sep/26/ukcrime.scotland, accessed 29 April 2018.

Seiler, C. (2000) The commodification of rebellion: Rock culture and consumer capitalism. In M. Gottdiener (ed) *New Forms of Consumption: Consumers, Culture and Commodification*. London: Rowan & Littlefield, pp 203–227.

Selinger, E. and Outterson, K. (2010) The ethics of poverty tourism, *Environmental Philosophy*, 7(2), 93–114.

Seltzer, M. (1997) *Wound Culture: Trauma in the Pathological Public Sphere*. Cambridge, MA: MIT Press.

Seltzer, M. (1998) *Serial Killers: Life and Death in America's Wound Culture*. Abingdon: Routledge.

Seltzer, M. (2007) *True Crime: Observations on Violence and Modernity*. Abingdon: Routledge.

Serano, J. (2007) *Whipping Girl: A Transsexual Women on Sexism and the Scapegoating of Femininity*. California: Seal Press.

Serano, J. (2009) Psychology, sexualization and trans-invalidations, keynote lecture presented at the 8th Annual Philadelphia Trans-Health Conference, available at http://www.juliaserano.com/av/Serano-TransInvalidations.pdf, accessed 13 June 2022.

Sergi, A. (2020) 'Ndrangheta dynasties: A conceptual and operational framework for the cross-border policing of the Calabrian mafia, *Policing: A Journal of Policy and Practice*, 15(2), 1522–1536.

Sergi, A. and Lavorgna, A. (2016) *'Ndrangheta: The Glocal Dimensions of the Most Powerful Italian Mafia*. London: Palgrave Macmillan.

Shaahunaz, F. (2020) Maalhos unveils eco centro, first island to stop open burning, *Maldives The Edition*, 4 February, available at https://edition.mv/b_maalhos/14792, accessed 22 July 2021.

Shaany, A. (2020a) Maldives named world's leading destination at WTA, *Raajie*, 28 November, available at https://raajje.mv/91228, accessed 20 July 2021.

Shaany, A. (2020b) Maldives banning plastic bags, straws and other single-use items from June 2021, *Raajje*, available at https://raajje.mv/92939, accessed 22 July 2021.

Shackley, M. (2001) Potential futures for Robben Island: Shrine, museum or theme park?, *International Journal of Heritage Studies*, 7(4), 355–363.

Shakeela, A. and Weaver, D. (2018) 'Managed evils' of hedonistic tourism in the Maldives: Social representations and their mediation of local social exchange, *Annals of Tourism Research*, 71, 13–24.

Shammas, L.Y. (2014) The pains of freedom: Assessing the ambiguity of Scandinavian penal exceptionalism on Norway's Prison Island, *Punishment and Society*, 16(1), 104–123.

Sharpe, E.K. (2005) Delivering communitas: Wilderness adventure and the making of community, *Journal of Leisure Research*, 37(3), 255–280.

Sharpley, R. (2005) Travels to the edge of darkness: Towards a typology of dark tourism. In C. Ryan, S. Page and M. Aitken (eds) *Taking Tourism to the Limits: Issues, Concepts and Managerial Perspectives*. Oxford: Elsevier, pp 217–228.

Sharpley, R. (2009) *Darker Side of Travel: The Theory and Practice of Dark Tourism*. Bristol and Buffalo: Channel View Publications.

Shawcross, W. (2002) *Sideshow: Kissinger, Nixon, and the Destruction of Cambodia*. New York: Cooper Square Press.

Sheikh, P.A. (2019) *International Trophy Hunting*. Washington, DC: Congressional Research Service.

Sherman, E. (2016) What Brooklyn looked like before the hipster invasion, available at https://allthatsinteresting.com/brooklyn-before-hipster-invasion#7, accessed 13 June 2022.

Shin, G. (2003) Introduction. In G. Shin and K. Hwang (eds) *Contentious Kwangju: The May 18 Uprising in Korea's Past and Present*. London: Rowman & Littlefield, pp xi–3.

Shore, H. (2003) Crime, criminal networks and the survival strategies of the poor in early eighteenth century London. In S. King and A. Tomkins (eds) *The Poor in England 1700–1850: An Economy of Makeshifts*. Manchester: Manchester University Press, pp 137–166.

Shulze, R. (2014) Resisting Holocaust tourism: the new Gedenkstätte at Bergen-Belsen, Germany. In B. Sion (ed) *Death Tourism: Disaster Sites as Recreational Landscape*. London: Seagull, pp 121–138.

Silverstone, R. (2007) *Media and Morality: On the Rise of the Mediapolis*. Cambridge: Polity Press.

Sin, H.L. (2009) Volunteer tourism: 'Involve me and I will learn?', *Annals of Tourism Research*, 36(3), 480–501.

Sin, H.L., Oakes, T. and Mostafanezhad, M. (2014) Traveling for a cause: Critical examinations of volunteer tourism and social justice, *Tourist Studies*, 15(2), 119–131.

Sion, B. (2011) Conflicting sites of memory in post-genocide Cambodia, *Humanity: An International Journal of Human Rights, Humanitarianism, and Development*, 2(1), 1–21.

Sion, B. (2014) Conflicting sites of memory in post-genocide Cambodia. In B. Sion (ed) *Death Tourism: Disaster Sites as Recreational Landscape*. London: Seagull, pp 97–120.

Sjöholm, C. (2010) Murder walks in Ystad. In B.M. Knudsen and A.M. Waade (eds) *Re-investing Authenticity: Tourism, Place and Emotions*. Bristol: Channel View, pp 154–168.

Small, S. and Eichstedt, J. (2002) *Representations of Slavery: Race and Ideology in Southern Plantation Museums*. Washington, DC: Smithsonian Books.

Smallwood, K. (2017) The curious case of Pablo Eskobear: The 'cocaine bear', *Today I Found Out*, 28 August, available at http://www.todayifoundout.com/index.php/2017/08/amazing-tale-kentucky-folk-hero-pablo-eskobear-cocaine-bear/, accessed 13 June 2022.

Smith, E.C.H. (2019) *Illicit Markets in the Global City: The Cultural Property Trade in Hong Kong*. PhD thesis, University of Glasgow.

Smith, O. (2014) *Contemporary Adulthood and the Night-Time Economy*. Cham: Palgrave Macmillan.

Smith, O. (2016) *Deviant Leisure: Emerging Perspectives on Leisure, Consumerism and Crime*. British Society of Criminology, available at http://www.britsoccrim.org/wp-content/uploads/2016/04/Deviant-Leisure-Oliver-Smith.pdf, accessed 5 October 2022.

Smith, O. (2019) Luxury, tourism and harm: A deviant leisure perspective. In T. Raymen and O. Smith (eds) *Deviant Leisure: A Criminological Perspectives on Leisure and Harm*. Basingstoke: Palgrave Macmillan, pp 305–323.

Smith, O. and Raymen, T. (2018) Deviant leisure: A criminological perspective, *Theoretical Criminology*, 22(1), 63–82.

Smith, V. (1998) War and tourism: An American ethnography, *Annals of Tourism Research*, 25, 202–227.

Smithsonian Institution (2021) Welcome, available at www.si.edu, accessed 18 August 2021.

Sokolowska, P. (2019) The body as evidence: A cultural approach to America's fascination with murder, *Studies and Analyses*, 32(1).

Sollund, R. (2012) Speciesism as doxic practice versus valuing difference and plurality. In R. Ellefsen, R. Sollund and G. Larsen (eds) *Eco-global Crimes: Contemporary Problems and Future Challenges*. Farnham: Ashgate, pp 91–113.

Sollund, R. (2020) Wildlife crime: A crime of hegemonic masculinity? *Social Sciences*, 9(6), 1–16.

Soper, T. (2021) Amazon now employs nearly 1.3 million people worldwide after adding 500,000 workers in 2020, *GeekWire*, 2 February, available at https://www.geekwire.com/2021/amazon-now-employs-nearly-1-3-million-people-worldwide-adding-500000-workers-2020/, accessed 5 October 2022.

Sorte, S. (2018) Visit the Maldives before it sinks into the ocean, *InsideHook*, 16 January, available at https://www.insidehook.com/article/travel/trip-maldives-underwater, accessed 19 July 2021.

South, N. (2009) Ecocide, conflict and climate change: Challenges for criminology and the research agenda in the 21st century. In K. Kangaspunta and I. Marshall (eds) *EcoCrime and Justice*. Rome: UNICRI, pp 38–55.

Stabrowski, F. (2014) New-build gentrification and the everyday displacement of Polish immigrant tenants in Greenpoint, Brooklyn, *Antipode*, 46(3), 794–815.

Standing, G. (2011) *The Precariat*. London: Bloomsbury.

State v. Gregory, 427 P 3d 621 (Wash 2018).

Statista (2021) Number of inbound tourists in the Netherlands from 2014 to 2020, *Statista*, available at https://www.statista.com/statistics/658819/inbound-tourism- forecast-in-the-netherlands/, accessed 27 May 2021.

Stiegler, B. (2013) *Uncontrollable Societies of Disaffected Individuals: Disbelief and Discredit vol 2: Disbelief and Discredit.* Cambridge: Polity Press.

Stone, P. (2006) A dark tourism spectrum: Towards a typology of death and macabre related tourist sites, attractions and exhibitions, *Tourism*, 54(2), 145–160.

Stone, P. (2009) Dark tourism: Morality and new moral spaces. In R. Sharpley and P. Stone (eds) *The Darker Side of Travel.* Bristol: Channel View Publications, pp 56–75.

Stone, P. (2012) Dark tourism and significant other death: Towards a model of mortality mediation, *Annals of Tourism Research*, 39(3), 1565–1587.

Stone, P. (2013) Dark tourism scholarship: A critical review, *International Journal of Culture, Tourism and Hospitality Research*, 7(3), 307–318.

Stone, P. and Sharpley, R. (2008) Consuming dark tourism: A thanatological perspective, *Annals of Tourism Research*, 23(2), 574–595.

Stone, P., Hartmann, R., Seaton, T., Sharpley, R. and White, L. (2018) *The Palgrave Handbook of Dark Tourism Studies.* London: Palgrave.

Stoops, M. (2016) Sex workers and victimization. In K. Corteen, S. Morley, P. Taylor and J. Turner (eds) *A Companion to Crime, Harm and Victimisation*, Bristol: Policy Press, pp 208–210.

Strange, C. and Kempa, M. (2003) Shades of dark tourism: Alcatraz and Robben Island, *Annals of Tourism Research*, 30(2), 386–405.

Stuart, F. (2018) *Down, Out and Under Arrest: Policing and Everyday Life in Skid Row.* London: University of Chicago Press.

Tablado, Z. and D'Amico, M. (2017) Impacts of terrestrial animal tourism. In D. Blumstein, B. Geffroy, D. Samia and E. Bessa (eds) *Ecotourism's Promise and Peril.* Cham: Springer, pp 97–115.

Taylor, A. (1996) Animal rights and human needs, *Environmental Ethics*, 18(3), 249–260.

Taylor, D. (1998) *Crime, Policing and Punishment in England, 1750–1914*. Basingstoke: Palgrave Macmillan.

Taylor, D. (2010) *Hooligans, Harlots and Hangmen: Crime and Punishment in Victorian Britain*. Santa Barbara: Praeger.

Taylor, R. (2001) Participatory natural resource monitoring and management: Implications for conservation. In D. Hulme and M. Murphree (eds) *African Wildlife and Livelihoods*. London: Heinemann, pp 267–279.

Telford, L. and Lloyd, A. (2020) From 'infant Hercules' to 'ghost town': Industrial collapse and social harm in Teesside, *Critical Criminology*, 28, 595–611.

Thiel, D., Jenni-Eiermann, S., Braunisch, V., Palme, R. and Jenni, L. (2008) Ski tourism affects habitat use and evokes a physiological stress response in capercaillie Tetrao urogallus: A new methodological approach, *Journal of Applied Ecology*, 45(3), 845–853.

Tiwari, S., Shreshta, P. and Bjønness, H. (2017) Local rights in World Heritage Sites: Learning from post-earthquake rehabilitation dynamics in the Kathmandu Valley. In P. Larsen (ed) *World Heritage and Human Rights: Lessons from the Asia-Pacific and Global Arena*. London: Routledge, pp 134–152.

Thompson, E.P. (1975) *Whigs and Hunters: The Origin of the Black Act*. London: Breviary Stuff Publications.

Thompson, E. and Smith, E. (2021) Stumbling towards repatriation, *Hyperallergic*, 11 March, available at https://hyperallergic.com/628195/stumbling-towards-repatriation/, accessed 1 June 2021.

Thornbury, W. (1878) St Sepulchre's and its neighbourhood. In *Old and New London*, vol 2. London: Cassell, Petter and Galpin, pp 477–91, available at https://www.british-history.ac.uk/old-new-london/vol2/pp477-491, accessed 11 June 2021.

Tombs, S. and Whyte, D. (2015) *The Corporate Criminal: Why Corporations Must be Abolished*. London: Routledge.

Tompkins, A.B. (2014) 'There's no chasing involved': Cis/trans relationships, 'tranny chasers', and the future of a sex-positive trans politics, *Journal of Homosexuality*, 61(5), 766–780.

Treadwell, J. (2012) From the car boot to booting it up? eBay, online counterfeit crime and the transformation of the criminal marketplace, *Criminology and Criminal Justice*, 12(2), 175–191.

Treadwell, J., Ancrum, C. and Kelly, C. (2020) Taxing times: Inter-criminal victimization and drug robbery amongst the English professional criminal milieu, *Deviant Behavior*, 41(1), 57–69.

Trianni, F. (2014) How Brazil is beefing up security ahead of the World Cup, *Time*, available at https://time.com/97653/fifa-world-cup-2014-brazil-security, accessed 29 November 2021.

Tripadvisor (2022) Biggie mural, available at https://www.tripadvisor.co.uk/Attraction_Review-g60827-d13205623-Reviews-Biggie_Mural-Brooklyn_New_York.html, accessed 13 June 2022.

Trotsky, L. (1997) *Peculiarities of Russia's Development*, available at https://www.marxists.org/archive/trotsky/1930/hrr/ch01.htm, accessed 15 January 2022.

Tsai, W.S. (2010) Assimilating the queers: Representations of lesbians, gay men, bisexual, and transgender people in mainstream advertising, *Advertising & Society Review*, 11(1).

Tudor, K. (2018) Toxic sovereignty: Understanding fraud as the expression of special liberty within late-capitalism, *Journal of Extreme Anthropology*, 2(2), 1–15.

Tunbridge, J.E. and Ashworth, G.J. (1996) *Dissonant Heritage: The Management of the Past as a Resource in Conflict*. Chichester: John Wiley.

Turner, L., Whittle, S. and Combs, R. (2009) *Transphobic Hate Crime in the European Union*. London: Press for Change.

Turner, V. (2017) *Liminality and Communitas*. Oxfordshire: Routledge.

Turnock, L. (2020) Inside a steroid 'brewing' and supply operation in South-West England: An 'ethnographic narrative case study', *Performance Enhancement & Health*, 7(3–4), 1–8.

Turnock, L. (2021) *Supplying Steroids Online: The Cultural and Market Contexts of Enhancement Drug Supply on One of the World's Largest Fitness & Bodybuilding Forums*. Plymouth: Plymouth Policy Research Press.

Tyner, J. and Devadoss, C. (2014) Administrative violence, prison geographies and the photographs of Tuol Sleng Security Center, Cambodia, *Area*, 46(4), 361–368.

Tyner, J., Alvarez, G. and Colucci, A. (2012) Memory and the everyday landscape of violence in post-genocide Cambodia, *Social & Cultural Geography*, 13(8), 853–871.

Tzanelli, R. and Yar, M. (2016) *Breaking Bad*, making good: Notes on a televisual tourist industry, *Mobilities*, 11(2), 188–206.

Uggen, C. (2000) Work as a turning point in the life course of criminals: A duration model of age, employment, and recidivism, *American Sociological Review*, 65(4), 529–546.

United Nations Department of Economic and Social Affairs (2020) *World Social Report 2020: Inequality in a Rapidly Changing World*. New York: United Nations, available at https://www.un.org/development/desa/dspd/wp-content/uploads/sites/22/2020/02/World-Social-Report2020-FullReport.pdf, accessed 26 January 2022.

United Nations Human Rights Office of the High Commissioner (2009) *Witches in the 21st Century*, available at https://www.ohchr.org/en/newsevents/Pages/Witches21stCentury.aspx, accessed 11 June 2022.

United States Census Bureau (2022) QuickFacts, Brooklyn Center City, Minnesota, available at https://www.census.gov/quickfacts/brooklyncentercityminnesota, accessed 13 June 2022.

Urry, J. (1990) *The Tourist Gaze*. London: SAGE.

Urry, J. (2004) Death in Venice. In M. Sheller and J. Urry (eds) *Tourism Mobilities: Places to Play, Places in Play*. London: Routledge, pp 205–215.

van Es, N. and Reijnders, S. (2016) Chasing sleuths and unravelling the metropolis: Analyzing the tourist experience of Sherlock Holmes' London, Philip Marlowe's Los Angeles and Lisbeth Salander's Stockholm. *Annals of Tourism Research*, 57, 113–125.

van Es, N. and Reijnders, S. (2018) Making sense of capital crime cities: Getting underneath the urban façade on crime detective fiction tours, *European Journal of Cultural Studies*, 21(4), 502–520.

Van Gennep, A. (1960) *The Rites of Passage*. Chicago: University of Chicago Press.

Van Maanen, J. (1999) The smile factory: Work at Disneyland. In P.J. Frost, L.F. Moore, M.R. Louis, C.C. Lundberg and J. Martin (eds) *Reforming Organizational Culture*. London: SAGE, pp 58–76.

Van Pelt, R. (2003) Of shells and shadows: A memoir of Auschwitz, *Transactions of the Royal Historical Society*, 13, 377–392.

Veblen, T. (2007) *The Theory of the Leisure Class*. Oxford: Oxford University Press.

Veitch, S. (2021) *Obligations: New Trajectories in Law*, Abingdon and New York: Routledge.

Vella, C., Bocancea, E., Urban, T., Knodell, A., Tuttle, C. and Alcock, S. (2015) Looting and vandalism around a World Heritage Site: Documenting modern damage to archaeological heritage in Petra's hinterland, *Journal of Field Archaeology*, 40(2), 221–235.

The Velvet Rocket (2010) Visiting the Museum of Confiscated Art in Brest, Belarus, *The Velvet Rocket*, available at https://thevelvetrocket.com/2010/02/12/andrew-drury-justin-ames-and-nigel-green-visit-the-museum-of-confiscated-art-in-brest-belarus-and-justin-tries-to-make-an-absurdly-long-title/, accessed 2 August 2021.

Verhoeven, M. and van Gestel, B. (2017) Between visibility and invisibility: Sex workers and informal services in Amsterdam, *Feminist Economics*, 23(3), 110–133.

Verhoeven, M., van Gestel, B. and Kleemans, E. (2013) Legal sector, informed practices: The informal economy of legal window prostitution in the Netherlands. In D. Boels, L. Bisschop, E. Kleemans and K. van der Vijver (eds) *Illegal and Informal Economy*. Antwerp: Maklu, pp 115–130.

Verma, P. (2021) Dark tourism: Destination associated with tragedy and disaster, *Zeichen Journal*, 7(5), 52–65.

Viator (2022) *Death Road, Bolivia: Mountain Bike Tour on the World's Most Dangerous Road*, available at https://www.viator.com/tours/La-Paz/Death-Road-Mountain-Bike-Tour-on-the-Worlds-Most-Dangerous-Road/d5027-6521WMDR, accessed 26 January 2022.

Vice (2012) Suicide forest in Japan (full documentary). *YouTube*, 9 May, available at https://www.youtube.com/watch?v=4FDSdg09df8, accessed 15 November 2021.

Visher, A.C., Debus-Sherrill, D. and Yahner, J. (2011) Employment after prison: A longitudinal study of former prisoners, *Justice Quarterly*, 28(5), 698–718.

Visit Maldives (2021) Geography, available at https://visitmaldives.com/en/maldives/geography, accessed 21 July 2021.

von Essen, E. and Nurse, A. (2017) Illegal hunting special issue, *Crime, Law and Social Change*, 67(4), 377–382.

Wacquant, L. (1995a) Pugs at work: Bodily capital and bodily labour among professional boxers, *Body & Society*, 1(1), 65–93.

Wainwright, O. (2014) 9/11 memorial museum: An emotional underworld beneath Ground Zero, *The Guardian*, 13 May.

Walby, K. and Piché, J. (2011) The polysemy of punishment memorialization: Dark tourism and Ontario's penal history museums, *Punishment & Society*, 13(4), 451–472.

Walker, A. (2017) The Notorious B.I.G. mural in Bed-Stuy won't come down after all, *Curbed New York*, available at https://ny.curbed.com/2017/5/23/15678742/brooklyn-biggie-smalls-bed-stuy-mural-saved, accessed 13 June 2022.

Walker, T. (2018) The homeless Disney worker who died alone in her car became the face of a public debate, but all she wanted was privacy, *The Orange County Register*, 3 April, available at https://www.ocregister.com/2018/03/30/the-homeless-disney-worker-who-died-alone-in-her-car-became-the-face-of-a-public-debate-but-all-she-wanted-was-privacy/, accessed 22 July 2021.

Warr, J. (2021) Fire! Fire! The prison cell and the thick sensuality of trappedness. In K. Herrity, B. Schmidt and J. Warr (eds) *Sensory Penalities: Exploring the Senses in Spaces of Punishment and Social Control*. Bingley: Emerald, pp 19–35.

Watson Institute (2022) *Direct War Deaths of U.S. and Allied Forces in Afghanistan and Pakistan*, available at https://watson.brown.edu/costsofwar/costs/human/military last, accessed 29 November 2021.

Wattis, L.T. (2021) The cultural scope and criminological potential of the 'hardman story', *Crime, Media, Culture*. https://doi.org/10.1177/17416590211053795 [online first].

Wearing, S., Mostafanezhad, M., Nguyen, N., Nguyen, T. and McDonald, M. (2018) 'Poor children on Tinder' and their Barbie saviours: Towards a feminist political ecology of volunteer tourism, *Leisure Studies*, 37(5), 500–514.

Weaver, L.C. and Skyer, P. (2003) Conservancies: Integrating wildlife land-use options into the livelihood, development, and conservation strategies of Namibian communities, *Conservation and Development Interventions at the Wildlife/Livestock Interface: Implications for Wildlife, Livestock and Human Health*, 30, 89–104.

Weiser, C. (2019) You can live in Biggie Smalls' childhood home for $4,000 a month, *The Insider*, 24 June, available at https://www.insider.com/you-can-live-in-biggie-smalls-childhood-home-2019-6, accessed 11 June 2022.

Westhoff, B. (2015) Brooklyn's finest: Has the New York borough's hip-hop crown slipped? *The Guardian*, 8 July, available at https://www.theguardian.com/music/2015/jul/08/brooklyn-new-york-hip-hop-rap, accessed 13 June 2022.

White, R. (2011) *Transnational Environmental Crime: Toward an Eco-global Criminology*. Abingdon: Routledge.

Whitten, S. (2020) Disney to lay off 28,000 employees as coronavirus slams its theme park business, *CNBC*, 30 September, available at https://www.cnbc.com/2020/09/29/disney-to-lay off-28000-employees-as-coronavirus-slams-theme-park-business.html, accessed 22 July 2021.

Whyte, D. and Wiegratz, J. (eds) (2016) *Neoliberalism and the Moral Economy of Fraud*. London: Routledge.

Wicker, P. (2018) The carbon footprint of active sport tourists: An empirical analysis of skiers and boarders, *Journal of Sport & Tourism*, 22(2), 151–171.

Wilkie, D.S. and Carpenter, J. (1999) The potential role of safari hunting as a source of revenue for protected areas in the Congo Basin, *Oryx*, 33(4), 340–345.

Williams, D.J. (2009) Deviant leisure: Rethinking 'the good, the bad, and the ugly', *Leisure Sciences*, 31(2), 207–213.

Willett, R. (1996) *The Naked City: Urban Crime Fiction in the USA*. Manchester: Manchester University Press.

Williams, P. (2004) Witnessing genocide: Vigilance and remembrance at Tuol Sleng and Choeung Ek, *Holocaust and Genocide Studies*, 18(2), 234–254.

Williams, P. (2007) *Memorial Museums: The Global Rush to Commemorate Atrocities*. Oxford: Berg.

Williams, M. and Tregidga, J. (2013) *All Wales Hate Crime Research Project: Research Overview and Executive Summary*. Cardiff: Race Equality First.

Williams, V.L., and Martin John Whiting, M.J. (2016) A picture of health? Animal use and the Faraday traditional medicine market, South Africa, *Journal of Ethnopharmacology*, 179, 265–273.

Willsher, K. (2020) French ski resort moves snow with helicopter in order to stay open, *The Guardian*, 16 February, available at https://www.theguardian.com/world/2020/feb/16/french-ski-resort-moves-snow-with-helicopter-in-order-to-stay-open, accessed 1 February 2022.

Wilmot, P. and Young, M. (2011) *Family and Kinship in East London*. London: Routledge.

Wilson, A. (2014) *Ukraine Crisis: What it Means for the West*. New Haven: Yale University Press.

Wilson, C.P. (2005) 'Where's Whitey?': Black mass ethnic criminality, and the problem of the informant, *Crime, Law and Social Change*, 43, 175–198.

Wilson, D. (2017) The prison tour as a pedagogical tool: Challenges and opportunities. In J. Wilson, S. Hodgkinson, J. Piché and K. Walby (eds) *The Palgrave Handbook of Prison Tourism*. London: Palgrave Macmillan, pp 909–925.

Wilson, D., Spina, R. and Canaan, J.E. (2011) In praise of the carceral tour: Learning from the Grendon experience, *The Howard Journal*, 50(4), 34–355.

Wilson, D., Yardley, E. and Lynes, A. (2015) *Serial Killers and the Phenomenon of Serial Murder: A Student Textbook*. Hampshire: Waterside Press.

Wilson, J.Z. (2008) *Prison: Cultural Memory and Dark Tourism*. New York: Peter Lang.

Winlow, S. (2001) *Badfellas*. Oxford: Berg.

Winlow, S. and Hall, S. (2006) *Violent Night: Urban Leisure and Contemporary Culture*. Oxford: Berg.

Winlow, S. and Hall, S. (2013) *Rethinking Social Exclusion: The End of the Social?* London: SAGE.

Winlow, S. and Hall, S. (2017) Criminology and consumerism. In P. Carlan and L. Ayres França (eds) *Alternative Criminologies*. London: Routledge, pp 92–110.

Winlow, S. and Hall, S. (2019) Shock and awe: On progressive minimalism and retreatism, and the new ultra-realism, *Critical Criminology*, 27(1), 21–36.

Winlow, S., Hall, S. and Treadwell, J. (2017) *The Rise of the Right*. Bristol: Policy Press.

Wood, M. (2016) 'I just wanna see someone get knocked the fuck out': Spectating affray on Facebook fight pages, *Crime, Media, Culture*, 14(1), 23–40.

Woodroffe, R., Hedges, S. and Durant, S.M. (2014) To fence or not to fence, *Science*, 334(6179), 46–8.

Woods, O. and Shee, S.Y. (2021a) The digital void of voluntourism: Here, there and new currencies of care, *Geoforum*, 124, 46–53.

Woods, O. and Shee, S.Y. (2021b) 'Doing it for the 'gram'? The representational politics of popular humanitarianism', *Annals of Tourism Research*, 87, 1–11.

World Population Review (2021) *Suicide Rate by Country 2021*, available at https://worldpopulationreview.com/country-rankings/suicide-rate-by-country, accessed 15 November 2021.

Wright, A.C. (2020) Visitor perceptions of European Holocaust heritage: A social media analysis, *Tourism Management*, 81, 204142.

WWF (2020) *Living Planet Report 2020: Bending the Curve of Biodiversity Loss*. Gland: WWF.

Wyatt, T. (2013) *Wildlife Trafficking: A Deconstruction of the Crime, the Victims and the Offenders*. Basingstoke: Palgrave Macmillan.

Yates, D. and Mackenzie, S. (2018) Heritage, crisis, and community crime prevention in Nepal, *International Journal of Cultural Property*, 25(2), 203–221.

Young, J. (1999) *The Exclusive Society*. London: SAGE.

Young, J. (2007) *The Vertigo of Late Modernity*. London: SAGE.

Žižek, S. (2002) *Welcome to the Desert of the Real* . London: Verso.

Žižek, S. (2008) *Violence*. London: Profile Books.

Žižek, S. (2010) *Living in the End Times*. London: Verso.

Žižek, S. (2013) *The Perverts Guide to Ideology (HD)*, available at https://archive.org/details/the-perverts-guide-to-ideology-2012-hd, accessed 5 October 2022.

Žižek, S. (2014) The impasses of consumerism. In teNeus (ed) *Prix Pictet 05: Consumption*. London: teNeus, pp 4–10.

Zucman, G. (2015) *The Hidden Wealth of Nations: The Scourge of Tax Havens*. Chicago: University of Chicago Press.

Zucman Tours and Transfers (2021) *Private Guided Mezhyhirya Tour (Yanukovych Residence, Museum of Corruption)*, available at https://www.tripadvisor.com/AttractionProductReview-g294474-d17719907Private_guided_Mezhyhirya_tour_Yanukovych_Residence_Museum_of_corruption-Kyiv_Kiev.html, accessed 18 October 2021.

Index

E

N

O

P

Q

R

T

W

Y

Z

CPSIA information can be obtained
at www.ICGtesting.com
Printed in the USA
JSHW080712160223
37826JS00003B/3

9 781447 362197